CASTRUCCIO CASTRACANI

CASTRUCCIO CASTRACANI

A study on the origins and character of a fourteenth-century Italian despotism

LOUIS GREEN

CLARENDON PRESS OXFORD
1986

Oxford University Press, Walton Street, Oxford OX2 6DP

Oxford New York Toronto
Delhi Bombay Calcutta Madras Karachi
Petaling Jaya Singapore Hong Kong Tokyo
Nairobi Dar es Salaam Cape Town
Melbourne Auckland
and associated companies in
Beirut Berlin Ibadan Nicosia

Oxford is a trade mark of Oxford University Press

Published in the United States
by Oxford University Press, New York

British Library Cataloguing in Publication Data
Green, Louis
Castruccio Castracani: a study on the
origins and character of a fourteenth-
century Italian despotism.
1. Castracani, Castruccio   2. Heads of
state—Italy—Lucca—Biography
I. Title
945'.5305'0924   DG975.L82
ISBN 0-19-821992-X

Library of Congress Cataloging in Publication Data
Green, Louis.
Castruccio Castracani: a study on the origins and
character of a fourteenth-century Italian despotism.
Bibliography: p.
Includes index.
1. Castracani, Castruccio, 1281—1328.   2. Italy—
History—1268—1492.   3. Lucca (Italy)—History.
4. Condottieri—Biography.   5. Italy—Nobility—
Biography.   6. Lucca (Italy)—Biography.   I. Title.
DG536.C3G74 1986   945'.53   86-8691
ISBN 0-19-821992-X

Typeset by Joshua Associates Limited
Printed in Great Britain
at the University Press, Oxford
by David Stanford
Printer to the University

TO MY WIFE
AND TO THE MEMORY OF
GLADYS NEVADA QUILICI

Acknowledgements

I WOULD like to express my appreciation for the help I have received from many quarters during the preparation of this book and its writing. Most of all I need to thank the two directors of the Archivio di Stato in Lucca during the years I worked there. Dr Domenico Corsi and Professor Vito Tirelli, and the other archivists employed in that institution, particularly Dr Antonio Romiti, Dr Giorgio Tori, Dr Sergio Nelli, and Ivo Giannecchini. Their co-operation and guidance have been invaluable to me as have those of many others too numerous to name who have assisted me in the course of my research on Castruccio Castracani in several other repositories of sources, including the Archivio Arcivescovile and the Biblioteca Statale in Lucca, the Archivi di Stato of Florence and Pisa, the Biblioteca Nazionale in Florence, the Vatican Library and Archives in Rome, and the Archivo de la Corona de Aragon in Barcelona.

I owe another, equally considerable debt to Monash University which has generously supported my work through the grant to me of several study leaves and with the provision of facilities for typing, photocopying, and the purchase of microfilm. I have also benefited greatly from consultation with my colleagues there, particularly Dr F. W. Kent, and am under an especial obligation to Mrs Bess Brudenell who has so cheerfully and capably typed the successive drafts of this book, overcoming valiantly difficulties posed by my handwriting and obscure foreign words. I wish, furthermore, to thank the Geography department at my university for the preparation of the maps in this book.

During my period of research on this work, I have enjoyed fruitful contacts with a number of scholars. In Lucca, these have included (besides those associated with the Archives) Professors Christine Meek, T. W. Blomquist, Duane Osheim, Dr Michael Bratchel, Dr Romano Silva, Dr Giuseppe Benedetto, and Dr Mario Seghieri and, in Pisa, Professors Michele Luzzati, Ottaviano Banti, Emilio Cristiani, and Fabio Redi. I must thank Professors Gene Brucker and Nicolai Rubinstein for having read and thoughtfully commented on an earlier version of this book and Dr Daniel Waley, Keeper of the Manuscripts, the British Library, for having, in the course of his correspondence with me, offered valuable criticisms of some of the ideas expressed in this study. Needless to say, such shortcomings as this work still has are entirely to be attributed to me, notwithstanding any advice I have received from these distinguished scholars and my exchange of views with them.

I have dealt with some of the subject-matter of this book in the articles I have written over the last few years on the history of Lucca in the early fourteenth century. These are listed in the bibliography at the end of this volume. I wish to thank the Frederick May Foundation for Italian Studies, the Istituto Storico Lucchese, and the editors of *I Tatti Studies* of the Harvard University Centre for Renaissance Studies in Florence and of *War and Society* in Canberra for permission to rework, in the course of the preparation of this monograph, material which originally appeared in publications issued by them.

Contents

List of Maps   xi

Abbreviations used in footnotes   xii

Introduction   1

I   The origins of an early fourteenth-century Italian tyranny
   1. *The Italian background*   7
   2. *Lucca at the beginning of the fourteenth century*   12

II   The fall of Lucca and the rise of Castruccio Castracani
   1. *The change of regime in Lucca*   30
   2. *The battle of Montecatini and the expulsion of
      Uguccione della Faggiuola*   60

III   Lucca under Castruccio Castracani
   1. *The government of Lucca under Castruccio Castracani*   79
   2. *The emergence of Castruccio's seigneurial aspirations
      and the building of the Augusta*   104
   3. *Lucchese commerce under Castruccio Castracani*   112

IV   War and foreign policy under Castruccio Castracani to
    the battle of Altopascio (1316–1325)
   1. *The outbreak and early stages of Castruccio's war
      with Florence*   123
   2. *The rift with Pisa and the acquisition of Pistoia*   145
   3. *The Altopascio campaign*   161

V   Castruccio Castracani at the height of his power (1325–1328)
   1. *Towards a dynastic principality: Castruccio as
      landholder, patron, and family head*   183
   2. *Castruccio and the Lucchese Church*   192

Contents

3. Castruccio, protégé of Ludwig of Bavaria and
   antagonist of Charles of Calabria   201

4. The recovery of Pistoia and the death of Castruccio   227

Bibliography   260

Index   273

Maps

1. Map of Lunigiana and the eastern extremity of the Genoese Riviera 137

2. Map illustrating the campaigns of Castruccio Castracani in the valleys of the Arno and the Serchio and their tributaries 164

3. Map of the dominions of Castruccio Castracani at the time of his death 249

Abbreviations used in Footnotes

ACA	Archivo de la Corona de Aragon
ACCC	*Atti del convegno su Castruccio Castracani e il suo tempo* (Lucca, 1986)
ACL	Archivio capitolare e arcivescovile di Lucca
ASF	Archivio di Stato in Firenze
ASI	*Archivio storico italiano*
ASL	Archivio di Stato in Lucca
ASN	Archivio di Stato in Napoli
ASP	Archivio di Stato in Pisa
ASV	Archivio segreto vaticano
BNF	Biblioteca nazionale di Firenze
BSL	Biblioteca statale di Lucca
Mem. e doc.	*Memorie e documenti per servire alla storia di Lucca*
RIS	*Rerum italicarum scriptores*

Introduction

CASTRUCCIO CASTRACANI was one of a group of tyrants who made
their appearance in several of the city-states of northern and central
Italy in the early fourteenth century. These men had risen to power
partly because they provided some measure of political stability in
otherwise strife-torn communes, partly because their military leadership guaranteed the continued independence of their cities in an age
when smaller states were becoming absorbed, through conquest, into
larger ones. Their consolidation of former individual city republics
into modest regional principalities, embracing four or five previously
self-governing towns, was a development contemporary with and
parallel to the enhancement of royal influence at the expense of the
feudal nobility and the imposition of more effective centralized
control over subject fiefs which characterized the policies of late
thirteenth- and early fourteenth-century French and English kings.
Both of these forms of political change sprang from the same underlying cause—the need to extend the financial base on which depended
the resources necessary to support increasingly expensive and increasingly professional armies.

It has been customary since the nineteenth century to regard
economic factors as responsible for the so-called 'decline of feudalism' and emergence of more centralized states in the later Middle
Ages. However, if one examines the pressures which helped to bring
about the enlargement in the scale of territorial units, particularly in
Italy, in the early fourteenth century, one cannot but be struck by the
decisive role played by sheer military necessity, intensified at this time
by a rise in the costs of war.[1] This literally rendered obsolete, in Italy,

[1] On the costs of war in the fourteenth century generally, see P. Contamine, *Guerre,
état et société à la fin du moyen âge* (Paris and The Hague, 1972), 95–128, 320–33, 434–50;
J. H. Hewett, *The Organisation of War under Edward III* (Manchester, 1966), 28–74; F. Lot,
L'Art militaire et les armées au moyen âge en Europe et dans le Proche-Orient (Paris, 1946), I.
248–77, 332–469; N. B. Lewis, 'The Organisation and Recruitment of a Contract Army:
May–November 1337', *Bulletin of the Institute of Historical Research*, xxxvii (1964), 1–19, and
'The Organisation of Indentured Retinues in Fourteenth Century England', *Transac-
tions of the Royal Historical Society* (4th Ser.), xxvii (1945), 29–39; B. D. Lyon, *From Fief to
Indenture* (Cambridge, Mass., 1957), 251–69; M. M. Postan, 'The Costs of the Hundred
Years War', *Past and Present*, xxvii (1964), 35–43; A. E. Prince, 'The Payment of Army

the old communal defensive system and with it the commune as a form
of political organization—except where, as in Florence, wealth
provided the means for republican regimes to survive by depending on
hired forces. This suggests that, instead of considering the political
changes of this period as a reflection of a transition from feudalism to
capitalism, one ought more properly to distinguish between two
stages, through which both Italian and West European society passed
between the eleventh and fifteenth centuries—the first in which the
adoption of essentially local forms of defence around the nucleus of
castle or walled town made for a substantial degree of independence
on the part of noble or commune, the second in which the military
advantage enjoyed by professional troops compelled governments to
evolve institutions and acquire territories by means of which mercenary armies could be maintained.

The generation of rulers to whom Castruccio Castracani belonged,
among whom Matteo Visconti of Milan and Can Grande della Scala
of Verona were the other leading figures in Italy, were merely the
initiators of the process by which one type of politico-military
organization changed into another. As such, they were vulnerable to
failure both from the deficiencies of their resources for the tasks they
took in hand and from the subsequent annulment of their achievements through these being overtaken by forces more powerful than
their own. It is significant that the official records of the regimes of
these three Italian tyrants—who were, in their way, the pioneers of the
regional state that was to dominate the peninsula in the following
century—have all substantially been destroyed.[2] This is a testimony of

Wages in Edward III's reign', *Speculum*, xix (1944), 137–60. Most of the work done on
the organization of armies in the early fourteenth century in Italy has concerned civic
levies, for instance G. Canestrini, 'Documenti per servire alla storia della milizia
italiana dal XIII secolo al XVI raccolti negli archivi della Toscana', *ASI* (Ser. I), xv
(1851), pp. xi–cxlviii and 1–552, and S. Salvemini, *I balestrieri nel comune di Firenze*
(Bari, 1905). But there is some reference to the use of mercenaries in D. Waley's studies,
'The Army of the Florentine Republic from the Twelfth to the Fourteenth Century', in
N. Rubinstein (ed.), *Florentine Studies* (London, 1968), 70–108, '*Condotte* and *Condottieri*
in the Thirteenth Century', *Proceedings of the British Academy*, lxi (1976), 3–37, and 'Le
origine della condotta nel Duecento e le compagnie di ventura', *Rivista storica italiana*,
lxxxviii (1976), 531–8, as well as in E. Ricotti, *Storia delle compagnie di ventura in Italia*
(Turin, 1845–7), and M. Ferrer i Mallol, 'Mercenaris catalans a Ferrara 1307–1317',
Anuario de estudios medievales, ii (1965), 155–227.

   [2] For an outline of available sources on the histories of Verona and Milan under the
Scaligeri and Visconti see W. Hagemann, *Die Entstehung der Scaliger signorie in Verona
1259–1304* (Berlin, 1937), 143–65, and W. Hagemann, *Documenti sconosciuti dell'Archivio
capitolare di Verona per la storia degli Scaligeri (1259–1304)* (Verona, 1973), and *Storia di*

the precariousness of their work as innovators and also incidentally a reason—since history tends to be written from surviving sources—for the relative neglect all three have suffered and the general underestimation of their importance.[3] The aspiring creators of the first Italian regional tyrannies all operated within a narrow margin between the risks that had to be taken to achieve the minimum conditions of their continued success and the danger of the complete nullification of their efforts that these risks entailed; and none more so than Castruccio Castracani. For, while the Lombard despots who were his contemporaries had a relatively free field of action, thanks to Venetian non-interference in the affairs of the mainland and also to their occupation of the natural centres—Milan and Verona—of the areas they sought to subjugate, Castruccio had as his base Lucca, a relatively minor city in a region dominated by an ill-led but flourishing Florence which could furthermore count on the help of two formidable allies—the papacy and the kingdom of Naples. It was the almost insuperable nature of the obstacles he faced that indeed made his life what Machiavelli was later to see in it—an unflagging but finally unavailing struggle of *virtù* against *fortuna*.[4] The circumstances in which he was placed were such

---

Milano (Fondazione Treccani degli Alfieri, Milan, 1954), iv. 747–55, v. 909–14. On the sources for the history of Lucca under Castruccio Castracani, see the bibliography of this book.

[3] The classic works on the rise of the Signorie, particularly in northern Italy, were produced in the period up to the early 1950s, for instance E. Salzer, *Ueber die Anfänge der Signorie in Oberitalien* (Berlin, 1900), W. Hagemann, *Die Entstehung*, L. Simeoni, 'La formazione della signoria scaligera' *Atti dell'Accademia d'agricoltura, scienze e lettere di Verona*, ser. v, iii (1926), 117–66, and *Le signorie* (Milan, 1950), F. Cognasso, *La formazione dello stato visconteo* (Turin, 1953), F. Ercole, *Dal comune al principato* (Florence, 1929), G. Benassuti, *Storia degli Scaligeri, signori di Verona* (Verona, 1826), and H. Spangenberg, *Can Grande I della Scala* (Berlin, 1892–5). The emphasis of these studies was either juridical or politico-military, with a strong tendency either to give a narrative of events or to discuss the constitutional basis of these regimes. More recent studies such as F. Cognasso, *I Visconti* (Milan, 1966), and M. Carrara, *Gli Scaligeri* (Milan, 1966), follow the pattern set by earlier chronological accounts of the actions of successive members of these dynasties. One attempt to reopen discussion of the problem of the early Signorie has been E. Sestan's article, 'Le origine delle signorie cittadine: un problema esaurito?', *Bollettino dell'Istituto storico italiano per il medio evo*, lxxiii (1962), 41–69. On this subject, see also M. Fuiano, 'Signorie e principati', in *Nuove questioni di storia medioevale* (Milan, 1964), 325–55, which gives a good survey of the literature on the topic of seigneurial government in Italy generally, not only in the early fourteenth but right through to the fifteenth century, and J. Laurent, 'Feudalismo e signoria', *ASI* cxxxvii (1971), 155–75.

[4] See N. Machiavelli, 'La vita di Castruccio Castracani', ed. F. Gaeta, *Opere*, vii (Milan, 1962), 9, 32–3.

that the way always lay open for his inherently disadvantageous position to be overcome through superior skill—because he disposed of a political and military method more efficient than that of his opponents—yet none of his victories could be more than temporary because his resources did not permit him to alter the underlying, adverse balance of forces against him. The even matching of his strengths and weaknesses which meant that he could never fail (without seeing his work completely destroyed), but also never succeed in that his final goal lay beyond his reach, allowed his career to follow the seemingly destined curve of his fortunes from nadir to nadir through an arc of apparently irresistible advance. Elevated unexpectedly to power at the moment when he was awaiting his execution, he enjoyed twelve years of uninterrupted dominance over his own city and victory over its enemies, conspiracies against his rule and resistance to his military and political schemes meeting invariably with defeat. Then, at the point when he had apparently secured his greatest triumphs, through the acquisition of Pistoia and Pisa and the endorsement of his cause by Ludwig of Bavaria, the delicately balanced political structure he had erected was shaken by his own death, with which he had not reckoned, leaving what he had built to fall before his sons could come of age to preserve and consolidate it.

Castruccio's life follows a pattern almost like that of Faust's from the time of his deliverance from prison through the years of his charmed success to the moment when all that had been given him was suddenly reclaimed and annulled. If there are characteristic shapes that lives assume at particular periods because of the essential limits to which action is reduced by the pressure of the obstacles constraining it at that stage in historical development, then Castruccio's does conform to one such form or type. It exemplifies the predicament of someone whose existence is a series of gambles against the future, with the dice loaded his way but the chance of loss increasing at every throw.

Seen in the light of its historical background, his personal drama becomes more than a series of singular events demonstrating the conflict between character and circumstance. It illustrates and illuminates something broader than the life of a man, the emergence of a new kind of political situation and the way that its emergence is itself conditioned and, in this case, eventually blocked by its friction with the forces that hinder it.

If Castruccio's story is worth telling again, it is because it needs to be extracted from the framework in which Renaissance commentators saw it[5]—as an episode complete in itself, fulfilled in its own cycle of change—and placed in the stream of historical development as an incident of a type common to its age, born of the cross-currents of its innovations. It is less the record of a man's heroic struggle against a finally victorious fate than the account of the collision of two tendencies, both arising from the one set of circumstances: on the one hand, the gravitation towards an effective, centrally directed, militarily viable power which could extend the bounds of anachronistic, small-scale forms of political organization; on the other, the erosion of the newly assembled, larger territorial units by resistances socially and economically stronger than themselves. We are inclined to think of history as moving in straight lines towards predetermined ends, and therefore failure seems to us at first sight but an interruption of the destined course of change. But if we actually examine how innovations occur, we see that the successful adaptations to new conditions that produce them develop slowly out of the unsuccessful ones which, by falling short of or overreaching what is demanded of them, gradually define the limits of tolerance of the situations these adaptations seek to master. It is customary to draw a distinction between history and tragedy, between the record of the collective achievements of a society and the salutary examples of the failures of individual lives. But, in reality, history and tragedy are the warp and woof of the one weave. What, by its very nature, cannot attain the end it seeks, by stopping short of the line it strives to reach, indicates where this should run.

The story of Castruccio Castracani is a classic historical tragedy in its natural state. It exemplifies that limiting case of the process of trial and error—the near miss. In its personal aspect, this makes it tragedy; in its historical one, it reduces it to an eddy within the mainstream of historical progress. Yet, if we are interested in the forces that shape change, the factors that determine how and when it will occur, then the twelve-year spell of power which Castruccio enjoyed has something to teach—first as to the critical limits of the actual possibilities of its own age and then of the interweaving of effort and response, design and circumstances that is, in all times, the stuff of history.

---

[5] Ibid. and also N. Tegrimi, *Vita Castruccii Antelminelli lucensis ducis* (Lucca, 1742), and A. Manucci, *Le azioni di Castruccio Castracani* (Lucca, 1843).

I

The origins of an early
fourteenth-century Italian tyranny

1. *The Italian background*

The political situation in the Italian peninsula in the early fourteenth century had grown out of a sequence of changes over the preceding one hundred years that had brought about the rise and fall of various powers without establishing any in a securely dominant position over the country. Following the decline of the Hohenstaufen in the middle decades of the thirteenth century there had arisen a combined Angevin–papal ascendancy.[1] This, however, had been mitigated, after the revolt of the Sicilian Vespers of 1282, by the Aragonese challenge to the kingdom of Naples and the growing disparity of interests between the popes on the one hand and Charles of Anjou and his heirs on the other.[2] In the period between the early 1280s and the descent into Italy of the Emperor Henry VII in 1310–13, the city-states of the north and centre of the country enjoyed what was probably a greater measure of effective independence than at any previous time, owing to the fading out of imperial influence on Italian affairs and the increasing preoccupation of the kings of Naples with their unsuccessful efforts to regain Sicily. Only the ambitious designs of Pope Boniface VIII around the turn of the fourteenth century temporarily interrupted the relative freedom of the Italian communes from outside interference;[3] but the humiliation of the papacy by Philip IV of France and the transfer of the papal residence to Avignon soon left them once again undisturbed in their absorption with their turbulent internal

---

[1] See E. Jordan, *Les Origines de la domination angevine en Italie*, 2 vols. (Paris, 1909), C. de Frede 'Da Carlo I d'Angiò a Giovanna I 1263–1372', in *Storia di Napoli* (Naples, 1969), ii. 5–156.
[2] See S. Runciman, *The Sicilian Vespers* (Cambridge, 1958), M. Amari, *La guerra del vespro siciliano* (9th edn., Milan, 1886).
[3] See R. Davidsohn, *Storia di Firenze* (Italian translation, Florence, 1956–68), vol. iv (vol. III, pt. 2 in original German edition, Berlin, 1912), 3–354, Guido Levi, *Bonifacio VIII e le sue relazioni col comune di Firenze* (Rome, 1882), I. del Lungo, *Dino Compagni e la sua cronica*, 3 vols. (Florence, 1879–87).

politics—until the arrival in Italy of the Emperor Henry VII again forced them out of it.

The conditions which produced this situation were of shorter standing than they might have seemed in 1300 and proved to be more precarious than the tendency to regard complete autonomy as the natural attribute of the Italian city-state might make it appear. In reality, up to the middle or perhaps even the third quarter of the thirteenth century, the ruling faction in most Italian cities, and more particularly in the Tuscan ones, retained its power with the backing or moral support of either the papacy or whichever prince was for the time being identified with the imperial cause. The main exceptions to this were the maritime republics of Venice, Genoa, and Pisa which, at least at sea, were capable of defending themselves against major as well as minor enemies and so enjoyed both actually and legally a somewhat more privileged status for as long as their naval power survived. But elsewhere, even in Florence, regimes were notoriously vulnerable to the changing balance of forces in Italy as a whole; and if the period from 1268 (when the Angevin supremacy was secured) to 1310 (when Henry VII entered the country) was one in which some measure of continuity prevailed in the politics of individual Italian states, it was because there were no substantial general shifts in political equilibrium to undermine the position of existing civic governments.

The problem which arose in the aftermath of Henry VII's Italian expedition was that, while the conditions which had prevailed up to 1310 ceased to hold, neither the papacy nor the empire, which had, in an earlier period, unified and supported the factions loyal to them, both within cities and in Italy as a whole, were capable after 1313 of exercising their former influence over the politics of the peninsula. The descent of Henry VII into Italy was, in one respect, like that of Charles VIII of France nearly two centuries later. In itself, it did not achieve anything durable, yet nothing was quite the same after it as it had been before. His short-lived and fruitless efforts to resolve the differences of the Italians, while they signally failed to produce the harmony he had hoped for, did result in the breakdown of the Guelph hegemony of the previous half-century. All the forces that had been held down by the prevailing order in the states he passed through suddenly burst into renewed activity at his appearance; and in his path there mushroomed the regimes which these created.[4] When the

---

[4] See W. M. Bowsky, *Henry VII in Italy* (Lincoln, Nebraska, 1960), 78–131, David-

emperor died, abruptly and prematurely at Buonconvento in 1313, it seemed at first that these briefly established family or factional predominances would collapse now that their protector was removed. But these expectations were belied by events. Faced with the prospect of political extinction after so short a spell of power, those who had established themselves as rulers in the wake of Henry VII's progress and those, like the Pisans, whose position had been enhanced by it responded to the challenge of the occasion with energy and resourcefulness, so blocking any attempt to restore the status quo of the pre-1310 period. This gave rise to an inherently unstable state of affairs in which those who had temporarily sheltered in the shadow of the emperor's might had to find new means to preserve their position, while those who had opposed Henry VII had to endow the traditional supports of their former ascendancy with a strength sufficient to recoup what they had lost as a result of the emperor's intervention in Italian politics.

It is this situation which provides the background to the spread of regional tyrannies in Lombardy and Tuscany from 1313 onwards. The key factors in it were, on the one hand, money, and on the other, capacity to use the professional cavalry that, at this time, was proving its superiority over the citizen levies on which Italian cities had mainly depended for their defence in the past. Where they were not merchants engaged in far-flung commercial and financial operations, the leading figures of this period tended therefore to be soldiers, or at least men able to direct and enjoy the confidence of troops.[5]

It has become customary to regard the Italian tyrant of the later Middle Ages as essentially a master of intrigue, conducting his government and military campaigns from the seclusion of his palace, remote and inaccessible to all but his most trusted associates. The later Visconti and other Lombard despots of the late fourteenth and early fifteenth centuries may well have been such men. But their precursors, the founders of the states they inherited and those who tried but failed to found such states, while they certainly did not

sohn, *Storia* iv. 477–759. The emperor's visit to Milan produced a transfer of government from the Della Torre to the Visconti and the subjugations of Cremona and Brescia led to the imposition on them of new regimes.

[5] The main examples of this kind of leader were Matteo Visconti in Milan, Can Grande della Scala in Verona, Uguccione della Faggiuola in Pisa, as well as Castruccio Castracani in Lucca. See F. Cognasso, *I Visconti*, 105–43, and 'L'unificazione della Lombardia sotto Milano', in *Storia di Milano*, v. 65–99, H. Spangenberg, *Can Grande*, P. Vigo, *Uguccione della Faggiuola* (Livorno, 1879).

hesitate to resort to treachery, or to gain through bribery and negotiation what they could not acquire by force, depended for the achievement of their ends far more than their successors on open warfare in
which they participated themselves. This earlier generation of tyrants
consisted of leaders who spent their lives fighting, and who, like Castruccio Castracani and Can Grande della Scala, died relatively young,
exhausted by the strains of war.[6] In the Castel Vecchio and before the
Scaligeri tombs in Verona, one is reminded, as one would have been in
Castruccio's Augusta (or citadel) in Lucca, had it survived, of this
chivalric stage of the history of Italian despotism which preceded its
courtly one. It was brief, transient, and evidence of it was soon overlaid by what followed or replaced it; but in its time it exalted an ideal
atypical both of the age of the communes before it and of that of the
principalities after it. Essentially, this was that of the citizen turned
soldier, not yet become prince, who combined the outward qualities of
a north European knight with the inner finesse of an Italian faction
head, for whom military success outside the walls of his city could
never completely overcome the need to preserve his power within it
through fear, favour, and ties of family and personal influence.

In Lombardy, the transition from commune to regional Signoria
was fairly quickly accomplished.[7] In Tuscany, the movement towards
the establishment of regional tyrannies was slower in coming. The
Visconti and Della Scala who had taken advantage of the creation of a
power vacuum in Lombardy to enlarge the states under their control
were able to expand their territories so quickly because they already
had a secure base in their own cities.[8] The trend which their conquests
reflected was the eclipse of smaller political units by larger ones which
had, on a minor scale, been reflected even in Tuscany by the neutral-
ization of Pistoia between 1306 and 1309 through the concerted efforts

---

[6] Castruccio Castracani died in 1328 at the age of 47, a month after the conclusion of
the siege of Pistoia, Can Grande the following year, when he was only 39, a mere four
days after the end of the investment of Treviso. The deaths of both were probably due to
infections contracted during the preceding campaigns. Other prominent leaders who
succumbed to illness about the same time were Galeazzo Visconti who died in August
1328 shortly after taking part in the siege of Pistoia and Charles of Calabria who expired
three months later.

[7] See Cognasso, 'L'unificazione' 65 seq., *I Visconti*, 115–23, Carrara, *Gli Scaligeri*, 72–
98.

[8] The Visconti had been in power in Milan from 1277 to 1302 (see G. Franceschini,
'La vita sociale e politica nel Duecento' in *Storia di Milano*, iv. 331–92, Salzer, *Ueber die
Anfänge*, 119, Cognasso, *I Visconti*, 68–90. In Verona, the Della Scala ascendancy went
back to 1262 when Mastino della Scala was elected captain of the people. (See Salzer,
op. cit., 120–4, Carrara, *Gli Scaligeri*, 39–74, Simeoni, 'La formazione', 117–55.)

of the Black Guelph strongholds of Florence and Lucca.[9] Since the leading states of Lombardy were in effect tyrannies by 1313, it was only to be expected that the growth in the size of states which was to characterize Italian history in the century or so after this date was, in this part of the country, to be to the profit of despotic governments. But in Tuscany both the leading Guelph and the leading Ghibelline city were still communes. Florence and Pisa alike had proud traditions of civic liberty and, though both had admitted foreign lords to exercise military command in times of emergency (Pisa, Guido da Montefeltro in 1289 and Florence, Robert of Naples in 1313),[10] neither had conceded any lasting political power to the temporary protector of its republican regime.

Such an independence the Florentines, with their greater resources and their more favourable position, were able to preserve; but not the Pisans. The death of Henry VII left Pisa exposed to an attack from a Guelph coalition made up of all the other city-states of Tuscany with the exception of Arezzo. It could defend itself only by securing the services of part of the dead emperor's German cavalry and placing it under the command of Uguccione della Faggiuola, who, though appointed merely to lead the city's armed forces, was soon able to make himself virtually a tyrant. It was he, in fact, by his use of military power both to secure his position within a city and to expand its terri-tories into a small regional state, who anticipated the methods Castruccio Castracani was to employ shortly afterwards in Lucca. And it was he, also, who, by his exploitation of family rivalries in Lucca, provided Castruccio with the opportunity for gaining control of his city, like Uguccione, initially in the guise of its military protector.

While in Tuscany, as in Lombardy, it was the situation created by the death of Henry VII which opened the way for the establishment of regional tyrannies, the base on which these were to be erected in Pisa and Lucca was a far more precarious one by reason of the recent usurpation of communal authority on which they rested. Another factor which was to differentiate the Tuscan from the Lombard posi-tion was the unique role of Florence in the region of which it was the pre-eminent centre. Whereas in northern Italy city-states already effectively under family predominances, such as Milan and Verona,

[9] On the capture of Pistoia and its subsequent position, see Davidsohn, *Storia*, iv. 439–42, 515–18, G. Villani, *Cronica*, ed. F. G. Dragomanni (Florence, 1844–5), viii. 8, 111.
[10] Bowsky, *Henry VII*, 193, 260, Vigo, *Uguccione*, 4–5.

had a natural advantage in terms of population and wealth, in Tuscany
it was Florence which was the logical focus for any expanded territorial state, not merely by virtue of its size and resources but also
because of the strength it derived from its alliances with the papacy
and the kingdom of Naples. The tendency of the Florentine government, however, to preserve its influence over the city-states which
surrounded it by the traditional method of supporting or installing in
them Guelph regimes depending on its favour, rather than upon their
acquisition,[11] meant that it did not at this stage aim at the establishment of direct control over Tuscany. This left its rivals within the
region, first Pisa and then Lucca, with the relatively hopeless task of
maintaining their position against Florence through efforts at territorial expansion that would go some way towards reducing their
political and military inferiority. In these circumstances, it was to be
expected that the fairly smooth transition from communes to regional
principalities which occurred in Lombardy in the fourteenth century
would either not take place in Tuscany, or would do so in the face of a
far more formidable resistance.

Nevertheless, in Tuscany as in Lombardy, the essential conditions
which helped to produce this tendency were clearly present and were,
so to speak, activated by the extraordinary political circumstances
which issued from the death of Henry VII. The possibilities opened
up by the extensive use of mercenary cavalry, the exploitation of civic
discord for the establishments of tyrannical regimes or the acquisition
of subject cities, and the need for increased military and political
power to preserve a city's independence—all these were as much
factors in the Tuscan as in the Lombard situation and created opportunities for territorial expansion though with much less prospect of the
establishment of durable regional states.

2. *Lucca at the beginning of the fourteenth century*

Lucca stands in the centre of a plain formed by the broadening of the
valley of the Serchio. Ringed by hills that divide it from the coastal
region known as Versilia in the west, from the valley of the Arno in the
south, and from Pistoia and its territory to the east, it is in Tuscany but
not entirely of it. Its geographical separation from the area watered by
the Arno and its tributaries and its proximity to Liguria have always
set it slightly apart from the other Tuscan cities.

---

[11] This policy had been adopted towards Siena after 1269 and towards Pistoia after
1306.

Yet, while it is thus confined within its natural boundaries, it was not, at least in the Middle Ages, therefore isolated. Passing through it, one of the principal trade-routes of the period, the so-called Via Francigena,[12] linked it with Rome to the south and Lombardy, and beyond it France, in the north-west. This road, running north from Siena, passed through the Val d'Elsa, crossed the Arno at Fucecchio, and then swung north-west through the marshes of Altopascio to reach Lucca, through Porcari in the east. Thence it went over the Serchio at Ponte San Pietro, immediately north of the city, to follow one of its minor tributaries to a pass between the hills, beyond which lay Versilia, Lunigiana, the Genoese Riviera, and the Apennine crossing through Pontremoli into the Po valley. Lucca was strategically placed on what was, after the malarial swamps led the old Roman coast road of the Via Aurelia to fall into disuse, the most direct and convenient means of communication by land between Rome and north-western Europe.

This circumstance was to be important in bringing about the early prominence of Lucca as a trading and manufacturing centre.[13] Another was the proximity of Pisa, the rise of which as a significant maritime power in the eleventh century made it the natural early focus of commercial and cultural initiative in Tuscany. Until the emergence of Florence as the leading city of the region in the thirteenth century, Lucca found itself in an enviable situation, on the one hand protected by its strong defensive position, while on the other within easy reach of Pisa, Genoa, and Siena and, beyond them, the Mediterranean world, north-western Europe, Rome, and the south of Italy.

The favourable location of the town was reflected in its early development as a leading Tuscan commune and, from the twelfth century, as a major silk manufacturing centre.[14] The growth of its population and

---

[12] This would appear to have been established as early as the Lombard period. See *Cambridge Economic History*, ii. 279. For the route followed by this road, see *Cambridge Medieval History*, v. 227, and R. Stopani, *La via francigena in Toscana* (Florence, 1984).

[13] On the early growth of Lucchese trade and manufacture, see G. Tommasi, *Sommario della storia di Lucca* (Florence, 1847), 153–4, E. Lazzareschi, *L'arte della seta in Lucca* (Pescia, 1930), T. Bini, *I lucchesi a Venezia* (Lucca, 1853–6), S. Bongi, *Della mercatura dei Lucchesi nei secoli XIII e XIV* (Lucca, 1858), G. Livi, 'I mercanti di seta lucchesi in Bologna nei secoli XIII e XIV' (*ASI* Ser. IV), vii. (1881), 29–55, T. Blomquist, 'Trade and Commerce in Thirteenth Century Lucca' (unpublished thesis, University of Minnesota, 1966), C. Meek, 'The Trade and Industry of Lucca in the Fourteenth Century', *Historical Studies* (Dublin, 1965), 39–42.

[14] E. Lazzareschi, *L'arte della seta*, G. Livi, 'I mercanti', C. Meek, 'Trade and Industry', 41–2.

wealth prompted its citizens to expand its territory—first north up the Serchio Valley into Garfagnana, then west into Versilia, the coastal plain beyond the Apuan Alps.[15] This extension of Lucchese control over lands previously subject to the old 'feudal' nobility inevitably brought the city into conflict not merely with dispossessed families, such as that of the lords of Corvara and Vallecchia[16] (which could easily be overcome by their expulsion from their strongholds or their absorption into the urban aristocracy), but more seriously with Pisa, which was simultaneously seeking to enlarge its zone of influence to its north. The clash between the expansionist tendencies of the two cities in the twelfth and thirteenth centuries set the pattern not only for relations between them, but also for Tusco-Ligurian politics generally. In its opposition to Pisa, Lucca found itself in a natural alliance with that republic's other enemies, Genoa[17] and Florence,[18] the one Pisa's rival for dominance of the western Mediterranean, the other in competition with her for control of the lower Arno valley. In the short term, the encirclement of Pisa by hostile powers, of which Lucca was one, was to enhance Lucchese military and political prestige and permit a considerable extension of her territories which came to hem in the Pisan *contado* on the north and east.[19] In the long run, however, the weakening of Pisa, particularly after the disastrous naval rout at the hands of the

---

[15] The best account of Lucchese territorial expansion in the twelfth and thirteenth centuries is still Tommasi, *Sommario*, 29–117. His main source for this period was Ptolemy of Lucca's *Annals* (the best modern edition is Tholomeus von Lucca, *Die Annalen*, ed. B. Schmeidler in *Monumenta Germaniae historica scriptores* (NS), viii (Berlin, 1930), supplemented by Genoese and Pisan chronicles.

[16] The lords of Corvara and Vallecchia were the overlords of most of Versilia. They were driven out of their castles in 1254 (Tommasi, *Sommario*, 85–7), and these nobles then retired to Pisa where they had their jurisdiction briefly restored to them in 1315 by Uguccione della Faggiuola (*Mem. e doc.*, vol. iii, pt. 3, pp. xliv–xlv). Other families, dispossessed in the twelfth and thirteenth centuries, however, such as the Soffredinghi, became first Lucchese vassals (Tholomeus von Lucca, *Die Annalen*, henceforth referred to as Ptolemy, *Annals*, 97) and then citizens.

[17] The Lucchese collaboration with Genoa against Pisa dated back to 1166 (Tommasi, *Sommario*, 38) and lasted till 1188 (ibid., 58).

[18] The Florentine alliance, which became the keystone of Lucchese foreign policy in the thirteenth century, was established only in 1197 (ibid. 59 and 69).

[19] By the beginning of the fourteenth century, Lucca had gained control of a very extensive territory, the limits of which can be determined from the list of subject communes given in the Statute of 1308. (*Mem. e doc.*, vol. iii, pt. 3, 36–64). It stretched from Pontremoli in the Magra valley in the north to include the former Malaspina lands in Lunigiana, Versilia down to Viareggio, the valley of the Serchio from Garfagnana down to Ripafratta, the Val di Lima and the Val di Nievole, the western half of the Pistoian *contado*, and a thin strip of the central Val d'Arno.

Genoese at Meloria in 1284,[20] was to create difficulties for Lucca as well,
leaving it dangerously dependent on its allies and shifting the
commercial and cultural centre of gravity of the Tuscan region away
from its previously pre-eminent western fringe inland towards
Florence and Siena.

In the late thirteenth century, when Lucca could benefit from the
onset of Pisa's decline without yet feeling her independence compromised by effective Florentine dominance over Tuscany, the old
political alignment clearly served her well. As a Tuscan champion of
the Guelph cause, second only to Florence, as a city of merchants and
craftsmen, engaged in textile manufacture and far-flung trading and
banking activities, Lucca could exploit increasing Florentine power as
a means of enhancing its own position. The problem, however, that
this created for the city was that, though Pisa and Lucca were and had
traditionally been implacable enemies, each in fact needed the other
to form a state viable in the changing conditions of the early fourteenth
century. As the maritime base of Pisa's former prosperity declined
with the loss of the naval war against Genoa, her general weakness
rendered her vulnerable to land-based attack. Unable like Venice or
Genoa to retreat beyond her lagoons or the Ligurian Alps, she needed
a secure hinterland. Lucca, on the other hand, lacking an efficient port
of her own and increasingly at a disadvantage as a trading power as
Florence outstripped her in population and wealth,[21] could only do
without some special understanding with Pisa by relying on Florence
to a degree that risked eventually reducing her to a mere satellite.

In these circumstances, two courses of action were open to Lucca.
One was an acceptance and furtherance of the traditional Florentine
alliance. The other was experiment with new political alignments that
could counterbalance the growing Florentine preponderance in

[20] For its immediate effects, see G. Benvenuti, *Storia della repubblica di Pisa* (Pisa,
1968), 249–50, R. Roncioni, *Istorie pisane*, 4 vols. (Florence, 1844–5), 615–24, P. Tronci,
Annali Pisani (Lucca 1829), Anno 1284. E. Cristiani, *Nobiltà e popolo nel comune di Pisa*
(Naples 1962), 19–22, while playing down the impact of this particular defeat, sees it as
the culminating event in a gradual process of decline. See also G. Rossi-Sabatini,
L'espansione di Pisa nel mediterraneo fino alla Meloria (Florence, 1935), 112.
[21] Lucca's thirteenth-century walls enclosed an area of 75 hectares, slightly less than
the late twelfth-century walls of Florence (80 hectares) and about two-thirds of the area
within those begun in 1150 in Pisa. Florence's fourteenth-century walls contained 630
hectares; some of this was land that was not built on, but, even allowing for this, the size
of the walled area greatly exceeded that of Pisa or Lucca at the same period (D. Herlihy,
Pisa in the Early Renaissance (New Haven, 1958), 37 and 41–2; K. J. Beloch, *Bevölkerungsgeschichte Italiens* (Berlin, 1939), ii. 165; J. C. Russell, *Medieval Regions and their cities*
(Newton Abbot, 1972), 42–5).

Tuscany, while at the same time creating a secure base, through alliance or expansion, for a power sufficiently strong to survive on its own resources. The exigencies of Lucchese politics in the first quarter of the fourteenth century were to lead to the identification of these alternative policies with one or other of the contending civic factions. This, however, does not mean that the kind of choice which lay before the city's government was purely a matter of support for a Guelph or Ghibelline party loyalty: the issue went beyond this to a definition of the sort of state Lucca was to become. Yet the fact that the prevailing regime in Lucca in the thirteenth century had been Guelph led those forces in Lucchese society which were dissatisfied with its policies eventually to seek support from its Ghibelline enemies. While the two broad directions in which Lucca could move were set by the general political situation in Tuscany, the immediate reasons for the change in Lucchese government and foreign policy between 1314 and 1328 are to be found in internal developments in Lucca itself.

The dilemma confronting the commune in its external relations had its counterpart in the internal problems it experienced in the period up to 1314. Lucca had, like Florence in the late thirteenth century, been borne, under the Guelph ascendancy, towards a form of government in which greater participation in politics of the 'popular' forces in the city, while it did not eliminate the power of all or even most great families, did have the effect of alienating some from their support of the regime. This made for potential instability and rendered the commune far more vulnerable to external threats than its apparent political strength suggested. What had in fact happened was that the alliance with Florence against Pisa and, latterly, Pistoia had modified the balance of forces within the city to the advantage of some groups but against the interests of others, so generating both a latent opposition within and an exile community outside, eager to exploit any opportunity of undermining the constitution, particularly in its most recent elaboration, the Statute of 1308.

To understand the situation in Lucca at this stage, it is necessary to outline briefly developments in Lucca in the course of the thirteenth century and to indicate how the government of the city had come to work as a result of these. From the very beginning of this period, there appears to have been conflict between the leading families, on the one hand, who provided mounted troops for the city's army, and the craftsmen and lesser merchants who fought on foot. According to Ptolemy of Lucca, discord between '*milites* and *pedites* erupted in

1203',[22] while in 1257 it was the 'popolo grasso' and 'popolo magro', that is, the rich and poor, who came to blows.[23] It is not clear to what extent *milites* and *pedites* of the one conflict corresponded with the 'fat' and 'thin' of the other, but what is evident from the form of the Lucchese constitution as it emerged at this time is that the military organization which distinguished between knights and infantry and which, roughly speaking, thus divided the more affluent from the poorer families in terms of the branch of the civic militia in which they fought, had its place in the political institutions of the town. In the course of the thirteenth century,[24] there had grown up side by side, with the formal government of the commune, a network of offices based on the *popolo* and the *Società delle Armi*. Sovereign authority, when it did not rest with the *Parlamento* or assembly of the citizens, was vested in two representative councils. The first, the *Consiglio del Comune*, represented citizens from the five wards of the city, chosen by indirect election from those over the age of eighteen with property worth £25 or more.[25] The second council, that of the *Popolo*, included the captains of the guilds and the priors of the *Società delle Armi*.[26] This in effect controlled the military organization of the infantry with its seventeen *gonfaloni* grouped in the fourteen *società* that, according to the Statute of 1308, excluded the *potenti* or *casastici* from their ranks.[27] The first council elected the *podestà*, a foreigner who remained formal head of the Lucchese state, the *anziani* who served a term as its executive government, and most of the civic officials. The second, though its functions are less well known because the statute defining its powers has been lost, was clearly intended to be the champion of the popular interest and the guardian of its armed might, through the *Società delle Armi* and the *gonfaloniere* of justice who was chosen from among its priors.[28]

[22] Ptolemy of Lucca, *Annals*, 93.   [23] Ibid., 139.

[24] See the documents published in Tommasi, *Sommario*, *Documenti*, 7–12. These prove the existence from 1203 of priors of the *Società di concordia de'pedoni* which Tommasi considers to be the forerunner of the *Società delle Armi* mentioned in the Statute of 1308. The establishment of these 'società' may, however, go back to 1198; according to Ptolemy (p. 90), 'societates' were then first formed in the city of Lucca, perhaps because of the hostilities taking place against the feudal lords of Versilia and the Pisans.

[25] S. Bongi and L. del Prete (eds), 'Il statuto del comune di Lucca del 1308', bk. II, ch. 11, *Mem. e doc.*, vol. iii, pt. 3, p. 63.

[26] Ibid., bk. I, ch. 31, p. 26.

[27] Ibid., bk. III, chs. 165, 170, pp. 239 and 241–4. The seventeen *gonfaloni*, twelve of them each constituting a *società*, the other five divided between the two *società* of *Tre cappelle* and *Leone sbarrato*, are listed in Tommasi, *Sommario*, 143.

[28] See Tommasi, *Sommario*, 143, 148.

Although the uneven survival of sources from this period makes it difficult to trace the origins of this dual constitution and its exact method of operation, it would seem that its development was intimately connected with the emergence of the *Società di Concordia de' Pedoni* (later to become the *Società delle Armi*)[29] at the beginning of the thirteenth century and the institutionalization of their effective political powers, together with those of the guilds. The conflict between the magnates and the rest of the citizenry which, in Florence, reached its climax in the last quarter of the Duecento,[30] manifested itself earlier in Lucca and therefore led to the survival there of institutions which in fact had a close similarity with those of Florence at the time of the *Primo Popolo* in 1250.[31] In both cities, the guilds almost certainly formed the backbone of the 'popular' movement, but in Lucca the system of politically representing the 'popolo' through its military organization persisted, while in Florence guild membership became with time the crucial qualification for the exercise of the most important political rights.[32] It is significant that the term 'priors' which in Florence came, after 1280, to designate the effective successors of the earlier *anziani*, though now chosen from or by the guilds or guild members, in Lucca continued to indicate the leaders of the city's infantry companies.

It is not clear how the first clashes between the *pedites* and *milites* of 1203 eventuated in the political settlement formulated by the Statute

[29] See n. 27 above.

[30] There is a vast literature on the question of the *magnati* and *popolani* in Florence at this period. G. Salvemini, *Magnati e popolani a Firenze dal 1280 al 1295* (Florence, 1899), and N. Ottokar, *Il comune di Firenze alla fine del Dugento* (Florence, 1926) present contrasting interpretations of its significance. See also P. Villari, *I primi due secoli della storia di Firenze* (Florence, 1893) and R. Davidsohn, *Storia*, iii. For recent surveys of the question see G. Pampaloni, 'I magnati a Firenze alla fine del Dugento', *ASI*, cxxix (1971), 387–423, and S. Raveggi, M. Tarassi, D. Medici, and P. Parenti, *Ghibellini, guelfi e popolo grasso* (Florence, 1978), 262–9.

[31] Davidsohn, *Storia*, ii. 509–17. In Florence in 1250 as in Lucca, under the Statute of 1308 (and presumably considerably earlier), the *anziani*, under the formal headship of the *podestà*, administered the government of the commune, while the captain was in charge of the companies or *gonfaloni* (at first twenty in number in Florence and then nineteen) into which the *popolo* was divided for military purposes. This set of institutions, according to Davidsohn of Bolognese origin (R. Davidsohn, *Forschungen zur Geschichte von Florenz* (Berlin, 1892–1908), iv. 102), had, in all likelihood, been adopted in Lucca in 1261, judging from a surviving extract from the otherwise lost statute of that year (Tommasi, *Sommario, Documenti*, 15–16).

[32] F. Bonaini, ed., 'Ordinamenti di Giustizia', *ASI* (Ser. II), pt. 1 (1855), 38–41. See also J. M. Najemy, *Corporatism and Consensus in Florentine Electoral Politics 1280–1400* (Chapel Hill, 1982), 18–48.

of 1308; but the most likely construction to be put upon such evidence as is available is that conflict between those who fought on foot and those who fought on horseback had, by 1203, led to the creation of the *Società di Concordia de'Pedoni*, which by 1261 had come to be integrated (perhaps as a result of the resolution in favour of the *popolani magri* of their rift with the *popolani grassi* in 1257) within a constitution modelled either on that of Bologna in 1232[33] or on that of Florence in 1250. The success of this in curbing the influence of the aristocracy, combined with the absence in Lucca of a Ghibelline restoration such as that of 1260–7 in Florence, probably explains the persistence into the first decade of the fourteenth century of the set of institutions so defined. It is not clear whether the Lucchese statute of 1261 already included the anti-magnate provisions of that of 1308; but it seems likely that, at least in detail, this aspect of the Lucchese constitution underwent modifications between 1261 and 1308, reflecting the tendency apparent in the Florentine Ordinances of Justice of 1293 to list the families excluded from the *popolo*. Despite these, however, the form of government set out in the Statute of 1308 is closer in spirit to the constitution of Florence in 1250 than to that of 1293, in that it does not make guild membership a qualification for the exercise of the most important civic rights and excludes the *potenti* or *casastici*, as the Lucchese equivalents of the Florentine magnates are called, only from the *Società delle Armi* and the Council of the *Popolo*.

As against this, perhaps because its provisions against the Lucchese *casastici* were less severe than those against the Florentine magnates, the social group in effect defined as aristocratic by the Statute of 1308 appears to have been considerably more extensive than that represented by the magnate families in Florence. In addition to all knights, their sons and grandsons, and all members of old noble, landed families (*proceres et cattani*), the Statute lists over 120 families of *potenti* and *casastici*[34] while the Florentine Ordinances of Justice specify only about 140 names, half of which are those of members of the rural nobility.[35] When it is taken into account that Florence in 1293

[33] Davidsohn, *Storia*, ii, pt. 1, 514. See G. Salvemini, *Magnati*, 318–30, for a comparison between Florentine and Bolognese institutions in the thirteenth century. It is worth noting that the term *Società delle Armi*, used in Lucca to denote citizen infantry companies, was of Bolognese origin, but that otherwise the form of government in Lucca in 1308 corresponded more closely with that in Florence between 1250 and 1260 than with that in Bologna in the late thirteenth century.

[34] Bongi and Del Prete, 'Il statuto', bk. III, ch. 170, pp. 241–5.

[35] G. Salvemini, *Magnati*, 34.

was substantially more populous than Lucca in 1308,[36] and that the revision of the Ordinances of 1295 in effect reduced the number of those designated as magnates by allowing branches of magnate families to revert to being *popolani* if there had not been at least two knights in that lineage over the previous twenty years[37] (a condition which did not apply in Lucca where all branches of clans named as *casastici* were considered as such unless explicitly excepted), it becomes clear that the group subject to the disqualifications specified by the Statute of 1308 in Lucca was wider than that of the Florentine magnates, including not merely what one might loosely term the old nobility but also a substantial section of the city's merchant patriciate.

An examination of the names in Rubric 170 of Book III of the Statute of 1308 which lists the *casastici* reveals only four which could definitely be described as belonging to the rural aristocracy,[38] but the remaining 118 or so are clearly those of urban families, including most of those comprising the upper echelons of the merchant community. The proportion of leading traders and bankers described as *casastici* was high. The families most prominent as merchants in the subsqent Castruccian period, such as the Guinigi, Sbarra, Rapondi, and Forteguerra fall within this category. So, probably, do most of the leading Lucchese merchants of the thirteenth century, though in all likelihood

---

[36] In the 1330s, Lucca's population has been estimated, on the basis of its revenues, by S. Bongi (*Bandi lucchesi del secolo decimoquarto* (Bologna, 1863), 319–20) at $\frac{11}{30}$ of that of Florence at the same time. If the usually accepted figure of 90,000–100,000 inhabitants is allowed for Florence, this would have given Lucca at that time over 30,000 people. My own calculations, from ASL Proventi, no. 1 (see Chapter IV, n. 29 below), suggest that the ratio between the revenues of Lucca and Florence in the 1330s was more like 2:7, which would make the population of Lucca in the second half of that decade about 26,000. Other indications point, however, to a rather lower number of citizens than these totals would imply. In 1331, King John of Bohemia required all Lucchese adult males to swear an oath of loyalty to him. The list of these contained in ASL Capitoli, no. 52 have been calculated by Beloch (*Bevölkerungsgeschichte Italiens*, ii. 166) to contain 4,746 names. On the basis of this he estimated the population to have been about 15,000 in that year: Russell (*Medieval Regions*, 45), however, using a higher multiplier, reached the figure of 23,800. In the light of the evidence, it would appear that the population of Lucca in the early fourteenth century was somewhere between 15,000 and 25,000. Beloch, *Bevölkerungsgeschichte Italiens*, loc. cit., and Meek (*Lucca 1369–1400: Politics and Society in an Early Renaissance City-State* (Oxford, 1978), 24) opt for the lower figure. The relationship between Lucchese and Florentine taxation revenues in the 1330s suggests, however, that it was somewhat higher within this range.

[37] Davidsohn, *Storia*, ii, pt. 2 (German edn.), iii (Italian edn.), 74.

[38] The Gallicioni, Caccianimici, and Upezzini, all of which were from Pescia, and the nobles of Anchiano and Rocca. The blanket exclusion of 'proceres et cattani' from the *popolo* doubtless accounts for the small number of rural noble families listed in this chapter of the statute.

not the majority of those engaged in foreign trade.[39] Notwithstanding this, it is clear that the Lucchese *casastici* were a considerably more extensive group than the Florentine magnates and one far more representative of the trading interests of the city.

With a population that was probably a quarter or less of Florence's, Lucca had one and a half times as many urban families described as *casastici* as there were Florentine magnates who did not belong to the rural nobility. This suggests that this group was five or six times as large proportionately as its Florentine equivalent, even without counting the members of the old feudal nobility whom the Statute of 1308 excluded from the *popolo* without naming them individually, or allowing for the inclusion in some of the Lucchese clans specified in that document of several, separate lineages. Whereas, in Florence, the magnates constituted no more than a section of what Ottokar has called 'il ceto dirigente', omitting the *popolani grassi* and not reaching down into the social layer of the *mezzani*, in Lucca, their counterparts would have included the great majority of the rich merchants, some of the middling ones, and all the big powerful *consorterie* such as the Obizi, Interminelli, and Quartigiani, together, of course, with the descendants of the old feudal nobility.

Given that this was the case, it is difficult to understand how a regime excluding so influential a sector of the city's society from the *popolo* ever managed to become established and maintain itself. In part, the relatively limited nature of the disqualifications imposed on the *casastici* in Lucca compared with those inflicted on the Florentine magnates make comprehensible, if not entirely explicable, the size of the group they affected. Whereas the Florentine Ordinances of Justice of 1293 had denied magnates the right of election to the priorate and most other major offices of the Florentine state,[40] the Lucchese

[39] I have used T. W. Blomquist's unpublished thesis 'Trade and Commerce in Thirteenth Century Lucca' (University of Minnesota, 1966), especially pp. 45–8 and 62, and R. Kaeuper's *Bankers to the Crown: The Ricciardi of Lucca and Edward I* (Princeton, 1973), 56–9 as a means of identifying the leading figures in Lucchese trade at this period. Of the families from which these came, the Ricciardi, Poggio, Guidiccioni, Malisardi, Gherarducci, Sesmondi (a branch of the Quartigiani), Guinigi, Cardellini, Forteguerra, Melanesi, Mordecastelli, Bettori, Onesti, Corbolani, and Martini were to be described as *casastici* in 1308, whilst the Roscimpeli, Talgardi, Battosi, Tignosini, Paganelli, Bonanni, and Moriconi were to be among the *popolani*. This ratio of roughly 2 to 1 in favour of *casastici* is, however, reversed in the much longer list provided by Blomquist (on pp. 150–8 of his thesis) of Lucchese merchants trading in the Champagne fairs in 1284: of these only 66 out of 218 appear to have belonged to houses later designated as *casastici*.
[40] Salvemini, *Magnati*, 232–3.

Statute of 1308 implied no diminution of political rights for the *casa-stici*, apart from their inability to belong to the *Società delle Armi* and the *popolo*. Nor were the Lucchese *grandi*, like the Florentine ones, compelled to pay a surety as an earnest of good behaviour, liable to mutilation for wounding a *popolano*, and to immediate execution and the demolition of their houses for killing one.[41] They were, however, discriminated against in the law courts and denied the special privileges of members of the *Società delle Armi*, including the right to bear arms.[42] The Statute of 1308 laid down a range of penalties for them if they attacked or assaulted a *popolano* but these took the more traditional form of fines or banishment,[43] rather than the Draconic, summary justice meted out in the same circumstances to Florentine magnates. The harshest of the provisions against them were those which stipulated that while accusations against *popolani* could be made only with the consent of their priors,[44] and *casastici* could not give evidence against them,[45] *casastici* could be condemned on the testimony of any eyewitness or the accusation of any two citizens of good repute and had no legal redress against unsubstantiated charges since *popolani* could not be convicted of making unproven accusations against *casastici*.[46]

In effect, the Statute of 1308 gave the *Società delle Armi* and the *popolani* who belonged to them a privileged position, ensuring that by recourse neither to arms nor to the law could the Lucchese *grandi* prevail against them and so leaving the leading families of the city subject to the organized might of the artisans and lesser merchants. In judging the provisions of the Statute against the *casastici*, one has, of course, to take into account the natural advantages of the *consorterie* or family groupings that composed this group: complete legal equality with the *popolani* would have enabled them, in fact, to make full use of their military power, their family connections, and their ability to intimidate ordinary citizens and perhaps even the courts. In the light of the situation existing in virtually all the Italian communes of this period, the Lucchese measures against the *casastici* should be seen essentially as a means of rectifying what would otherwise have been a preponderance of armed force and social influence on the part of the

[41] Bonaini, 'Ordinamenti', 50–1.
[42] Bongi and Del Prete, 'Il statuto'.
[43] Ibid., bk. III, ch. 162.
[44] Ibid., bk. III, ch. 162.
[45] Ibid., bk. III, ch. 169.
[46] Ibid., bk. III, ch. 168.

greater families. What is nevertheless remarkable about the form that this repression of the *grandi* took in Lucca is the number of prominent citizens subject to it. Elsewhere, as in Florence, action against a small group of magnates had been made possible by a coalition of many of the richer merchants with the *mezzani* and the artisans. In Lucca, however, the movement against the *casastici* appears to have been more genuinely a popular one, at least to judge by its results, and to have involved the expulsion from the 'people' of most of the *haute bourgeoisie* of the city.

This raises a question to which it is difficult to give an answer with any degree of certainty, in view of the paucity of surviving sources, but which is nevertheless important for its bearing on the subsequent history of Lucca. When and how did the Lucchese constitution acquire its anti-magnate provisions and what circumstances enabled these to be as comprehensive in their proscriptions as they were? The relative mildness of the measures against the *casastici* would have made them to some extent tolerable to the richest and best-connected families in the town, but they can hardly have been welcome. What special conditions made it possible for these to have been imposed against the resistance, if not the active opposition, of so large a section of the city's élite?

The only evidence we have which points towards an answer to these questions is that which links the enactment of the Statute of 1308 and the earlier one of 1261 to the aftermath of periods of war and civic conflict. In the mid-1250s, Lucca had been engaged in military operations with the support of the Florentines against the lords of Corvara and Vallecchia and their Pisan allies. In 1256 peace had been made on terms which gave the Lucchese effective control over Versilia, as a result of the destruction of the strongholds of these nobles, the resettlement of their inhabitants in the Lucchese town of Pietrasanta, and the granting to the Lucchese of the port of Motrone and the town and citadel of Massa in Lunigiana by the Florentines who had just received them from the Pisans.[47] It was in the following year that conflict had erupted in Lucca between what Ptolemy calls the 'popolo magro' and the 'popolo grasso'.[48] It would seem a reasonable inference from this conjunction of events that it was the organization of the Lucchese citizenry into a military force for the purposes of war which enabled the majority, enrolled in its infantry companies, to challenge

[47] Ptolemy of Lucca, *Annals*, 137–8.
[48] Ibid., 149.

the power of the *grandi* and the *popolani grassi* once peace was concluded. Similarly, the maintenance of a Lucchese army at the siege of Pistoia between 1302 and 1306 was probably not unconnected with the subsequent ability of the *Società delle Armi* that made up the mass of it to secure or confirm their privileged position within the commune through the Statute of 1308. Two other factors which might also have enhanced the ability of the *popolani* to isolate the *casastici* and neutralize their otherwise stronger position were feuds among the great families—for example that which issued in the exile of the Interminelli and their associates at the prompting of the Obizi in 1301—and Florentine backing for those regimes most fervent in their support of the Guelph cause. In the 1250s, the Florentine alliance was the key to the Lucchese victories in Versilia and against Pisa; on the other hand, it was the military organization of the *popolani*, so similar in structure to that of the Florentine *primo popolo* then in power, which made of Lucca an effective and ideologically reliable collaborator in the Guelph League. Equally, at the time of the siege of Pistoia, Lucchese territorial expansion to the east was closely linked with the continued co-operation with the Florentine Black Guelphs who, in turn, would have seen the *Società delle Armi* as the best buttress in Lucca against a possible Ghibelline or White reaction.

In fact, it was, in all likelihood, the continued success of the alliance with Florence which underpinned the pre-1314 regime in Lucca and made it possible for it to restrict the privileges of those who might, in other circumstances, have been the natural leaders of the city's society. This was all the more the case after 1310 when the commune adopted an even more aggressively populist stance under the influence of demagogues such as Bonturo Dati, Picchio Caciaiuolo, and Cecco dell'Erro who, according to the chronicler Giovanni Sercambi,[49] seized control of Lucca, removing the *gabella del vino* from Arrigo Bernarducci and ousting him and many *popolani grassi* from their group.

The narrowing of the social base of the regime which resulted from this undoubtedly contributed to its vulnerability to the crisis it encountered, in the face of military defeat, in 1314. However, the

---

[49] G. Sercambi, *Le croniche*, ed. S. Bongi (Lucca, 1892), pt. I, c.113 (vol. i, p. 57), basing himself on an earlier source, probably the chronicle contained in BNF MS Palat. 571 (c. 17ʳ). In this particular manuscript, this episode is placed under the rubric for 1312, there being no entries for 1310 or 1311. But in another version of this chronicle in the possession of Signor Franco Calabrese of Lucca it is, as in Sercambi's work, attributed to the year 1310.

effects of this were also compounded by the factionalism which had bedevilled Lucca in the late thirteenth century and the repercussions of which were to have such a decisive impact on the events of that year. For it was the part played then by the exiled Lucchese Whites which was to be critical in the overthrow of the previous prevailing Guelph order. The feud which had led to their banishment was almost certainly of long duration but had come to a head in 1301,[50] when Obizo degli Obizi, leader of the Obizi and Bernarducci faction, had been murdered by Bacciomeo Ciapparoni and Bonuccio Interminelli who belonged to another group of families which had, over the previous few years, come to be regarded as supporters of the so-called White party. This incident almost certainly had causes deeper than those suggested by Giovanni Sercambi, who saw only Pisan intrigues at the root of the assassination and its political consequences.[51] The fact that Ranuccio Mordecastelli was executed for his alleged complicity in the crime and that interfactional conflict erupted in its wake which led to the exile of the entire White party suggests rather that it must have been the product of more than a private vendetta and had arisen rather from an already well-established hostility between the Obizi and their associates on the one hand and the Interminelli, Mordecastelli, and their allies on the other.

There is confirmation of the long-standing nature of the feud which

[50] There is some disagreement in the sources as to this date. Ptolemy of Lucca's *Annals* (Schmeidler edn., 236) gives it as 1300, Giovanni Villani in his *Cronica* (viii. 46) as 1301 as does G. Sercambi (*Chroniche*, pt. I c. 105 (vol. i, p. 50)). While G. Tommasi, (*Sommario*, 120) accepts the date 1300, R. Davidsohn (*Storia*, iii. 207) comes down, in my opinion rightly, for the year 1301. The only documentary evidence of the date of the banishment of members of the White faction gives it as 4 September 1301 (Davidsohn, *Storia*, iii. 207–8). The date of Castruccio's father's will, made in Ancona and mentioned in Castruccio's own testament (E. Lazzareschi, 'Documenti della signoria di Castruccio Castracani . . .', in *Atti della R. Accademia Lucchese* (NS), iii (1934), 398), was 29 September 1301; and this, together with the assertion by N. Tegrimi (*Vita*, 8) that Gerio died within seven months of going into exile, places the exile in the early months of 1301. Given that the date of Obizo degli Obizi's murder was 1 January, this makes 1301 a more plausible year for it than 1300, since all chroniclers agree that the White faction was driven from Lucca shortly after that murder. Ptolemy' dating can, furthermore, be questioned on the grounds that in his entry for 1300 he also places the banishment of the Whites from Pistoia, which in fact occurred in 1301. (Davidsohn, *Storia*, iii. 203, Ptolemy, *Annals*, 127).
[51] According to Sercambi, the Pisans resolved to weaken Lucca by causing divisions within the city and so induced Bacciomeo Ciapparoni and Bonuccio Interminelli to kill Obizo degli Obizi with whom they were at odds over a legal dispute. Subsequently, according to the same account, they spread rumours to the effect that the murder had been inspired by the leaders of the White faction and thus secured its exile. (Sercambi, *Croniche*, pt. I, c.105 (vol. i, pp. 49–50).)

provoked this assassination in an entry in Ptolemy's *Annals* from which we learn that in 1280 'war' had erupted between the Obizi and the Mordecastelli.[52] It may also be relevant to that clash and to the later events of 1301 that in 1279, a year before the Obizi and Mordecastelli had fallen out, Ciapparone dei Ciapparoni had been executed by drowning 'on account of his misdeeds'.[53] If the rift between the Obizi and Mordecastelli in 1280 had been provoked by the death, shortly before, of Ciapparone dei Ciapparoni, then the beheading in 1301 of Ranuccio Mordecastelli for the murder by one of the Ciapparoni of an Obizi becomes explicable: the crime committed on New Year's Day of that year would have been seen as an act of revenge, not merely on the part of the two individuals who carried it out, but on that of the families who had formerly taken up arms against the Obizi in retaliation for the execution of one of their faction. Unfortunately there is insufficient evidence to test this possibility. What is clear, however, is that the group of families which later came to be aligned with the White Guelphs in Pistoia and Florence[54] did form a cohesive, mutually protective group in opposition to the Obizi and also incidentally to the popular regime whose favour the Obizi enjoyed.[55] It is interesting that members of the Interminelli, Mordecastelli, and Ciapparoni families, some of them closely linked with the assassination of Obizo degli Obizi in 1301, figure prominently among a group of Lucchese patricians whom the priors of the *Società delle Armi* in 1294 deprived of what were in effect feudal rights over the village of Sommocolonia near Barga. Arbitrating in a dispute between the *sindaco* of Sommocolonia and an association of Lucchese citizens who collectively owned property and enjoyed jurisdiction over his village, the priors (one of whom was the Picchio Caciaiuolo who was to be among the leaders of the popular movement of 1310) declared 'that it was not consistent with the honour or interests of Lucca that any particular or private person should hold jurisdiction or a village or fortified place within Lucchese territory, but rather that it was fitting and proper that this jurisdiction should be restored to the commune of Lucca'.[56]

[52] Ptolemy of Lucca, *Annals*, 191. The date is open to question because the same entry contains a reference to the expulsion of the Della Torre from Milan which occurred in 1277.   [53] Ibid., 180.

[54] Ptolemy of Lucca mentions in his entry for 1289 that the feud between the Whites and Blacks of Pistoia spread to Lucca and Florence.

[55] Sercambi in his chronicle speaks of Obizo degli Obizi as 'molto amato del popolo' (G. Sercambi, *Croniche*, pt. I, c.105 (vol. i, p. 49).)

[56] ASL Diplomatico Biblioteca F. M. Florentini, 10/12/1294. (Also noted in BSL MS 1294.25).

Among those thus deprived of their former rights over Sommocolonia were three members of the Interminelli clan[57] (including Coluccio Castracani, Castruccio's uncle), Bacciomeo Ciapparoni, one of the two assassins of Obizo degli Obizi in 1301, and three of the Mordecastelli[58] of whom one, Nello, was the son of Ranuccio Mordecastelli who was to be executed for complicity in that crime. Three other families represented in the list of the former landlords of Sommocolonia, the Poggio, the Martini, the Avvocati, also occur together with the Interminelli, Mordecastelli, and Ciapparoni among the members of the White faction in Pisa in 1310,[59] though only two individuals, Davino Interminelli and Giovanni Parghia degli Interminelli, formed part both of the exiled White community in 1310 and the group claiming jurisdiction over Sommocolonia in 1294.

The correspondences between the families involved in this legal dispute in 1294 and those in exile some sixteen years later do not in themselves necessarily indicate a continuity between the group enjoying collective proprietary rights over Sommocolonia and the White faction expelled from Lucca in 1301. Several of the partners in the Sommocolonia venture were not exiled with the Whites; however, it is significant that none of them belonged to the Obizi faction banished in 1314 and all, in fact, came from families which later supported the Castruccian regime in its early stages.[60] Furthermore, the list of men involved in the 1294 dispute is interesting in itself in that it links figures closely associated with the assassination of 1301 with a group whose interests brought them in conflict with communal policy as

[57] Giovanni and Coluccio Parghia degli Interminelli, Davino Interminelli, Coluccio Castracani.

[58] Puccio, Nello, and Marcovaldo Mordecastelli.

[59] ASL Archivio notarile no. 29, 30/6/1311 (Pisan style), also published in G. Sforza, 'Castruccio Castracani ... e gli altri lucchesi di parte bianca in esilio 1300–1314', *Atti dell'Accademia di Scienze di Torino* (Ser. II, vol. xlii (1891), 96 seq.

[60] The Lucchese families listed among the co-owners of Sommocolonia were the Interminelli (including its Parghia and Castracani branches), Mordecastelli, Sartori, Della Rocca, the Simonetti and Cristofani branches of the Quartigiani, the Poggio, Martini, Talgardi, Ciapparoni, Morla, Avvocati, Salamoni, Spinabelli, and Cassuola. Members of the Del Bosco, Brancasecca, Pettinati, Peri, Talliamelo, Maracchi, and Tadolini were further represented by agents or *procuratori* in these legal proceedings. With the exception of the Talgardi, Ciapparoni, Pettinati, and Maracchi all these families were among the *casastici* or *proceres* of the Statute of 1308, the Morla as part of the Allucinghi, the Del Bosco as part of the Del Fondo, and the Spinabelli as part of the Del Gelso. Families in this group which were in the front rank of the supporters of the post-1314 regime were the Interminelli, Quartigiani, Poggio, Mordecastelli, and Avvocati.

early as 1294 and who were to remain involved with each other socially, politically, and perhaps financially well after 1314.

Despite the fragmentary nature of the surviving sources of this period, the evidence which they provide does permit the outlines of a picture to be drawn. Between about 1280 and 1314 Lucchese society was divided in two ways, in the first place along broadly class lines between the wealthier merchant and aristocratic families on the one hand and the artisans and smaller traders on the other, and secondly between factional groupings that in effect constituted social and economic as well as political alliances. In the course of this period, there was a narrowing of the power base of the regime dominant in the city. To begin with, the *popolo*, already strongly organized in its infantry companies and guilds, was able to exploit the feuds that had arisen among rival patrician factions, allying itself with the Obizi–Bernarducci party against its Mordecastelli, Interminelli, and Ciapparoni enemies, and pursuing an anti-aristocratic policy by making common cause with the Obizi against their rivals. This phase in the history of the commune culminated in the assassination of Obizo degli Obizi in 1301 and in the ensuing exile of the Lucchese Whites. The fundamental features of it appear to have been the harassment and political isolation of a closely linked group of powerful families by those who, for different reasons, saw them as the principal threat to their particular interests and the gradual driving of some of the members of those families to the point of desperation where, either through motives of revenge, or in an ill-conceived attempt to restore their position through violence, they precipitated their own banishment and that of their relatives and supporters. Following the expulsion of the Whites in 1301, the Pistoian war created opportunities for the popular party first to consolidate its position through the Statute of 1308 and then, in 1310, to set up a government in which leadership passed from the Obizi and Bernarducci to the upstart merchant Bonturo Dati and the artisans Picchio Caciaiuolo and Cecco dell'Erro.

The alienation of the Interminelli–Mordecastelli faction and its allies who were forced thereby into alignment with the Pistoian Whites, the degradation of the leading members of the Lucchese merchant class through their designation as *casastici*, and finally the relegation of the Obizi and their associates to a subordinate role within the governing party represented the successive stages of a contraction of the political base of the Guelph regime.

That this exclusion of such formidable interests from power was successful was due in part to the effectiveness of the popular military and political organization and in part to the bonds that linked the state of Lucca to the Florentine alliance. Whatever the government of the commune had been, the exigencies of Tuscan politics and the common Guelph tradition of the two cities would have favoured Florentine support for the ruling faction in Lucca and opposition to its enemies. In the event, this committed the Florentines to the endorsement of a regime that, by 1310, had gone in its popular tendency beyond even the anti-magnate Florentine government of 1293–5. Equally, the extent to which the forces dominant in Lucca in the first decade of the fourteenth century needed the backing of Florence as the strongest power in Tuscany left them with little option as to foreign policy. If they were to hold off the challenge of an aristo-cratic reaction which, in the circumstances, could be expected to count on Pisan assistance, they would have to counterbalance that threat with the assurance of Florentine aid. Thus, the situation that had developed by 1310 placed Lucca externally firmly in the Guelph camp, while internally it left the survival of the government dependent on the persistence of a balance of forces in Tuscany that would enable the prevailing regime to hold at bay any attempt by exiles outside or dissidents within it to break its precarious hold on power. Ultimately, it was the military situation which held the key to the future: if this changed, all the internal pressures working against the ruling party would be released and, as a result, the form both of the city's govern-ment and of its foreign policy would be called into question.

II

The fall of Lucca and the rise of Castruccio Castracani

1. *The change of regime in Lucca*

On 24 August 1313, the Emperor Henry VII died at Buonconvento near Siena on his way from Pisa to Rome. His death brought to an end a three-year conflict with the Guelph communes of Italy, the papacy and the Angevin monarchy in Naples. It signalled, or appeared to signal, a return to the status quo of Guelph predominance in Italy and Florentine ascendancy in Tuscany which had been temporarily suspended by the presence of the emperor's army in the peninsula.

Since 1310, Lucca like Florence had maintained its posture of defiance towards Henry VII. In 1312, when the emperor was in Pisa, some of his troops had skirmished on the borders of Lucchese territory and taken a few villages claimed by the Pisans.[1] Early in the following year, after Henry VII had returned from Rome and besieged Florence, elements of the imperial army defeated a Lucchese force at Vicopisano and took Pietrasanta,[2] while the Malaspina, in alliance with the emperor, captured the town of Sarzana further north.[3] Despite these reverses, the Lucchese had held firm to the Florentine alliance.[4] The Lucchese Whites, on the other hand, in exile since 1301, had seen in Henry VII's Italian expedition their great hope of return to their native city. Meeting in Pisa on 30 June 1310, the members of the Lucchese exile community had sworn fealty to Henry VII and authorized emissaries to meet and negotiate with his ambassadors.[5] On 17 October of the same year, they had despatched representatives direct to the emperor to offer him their services.[6] By 1313, the presence of the

---

[1] Davidsohn, *Storia*, iv (iii, pt. 2, German edn.), 643.
[2] Ibid., iv. 719–22.   [3] Ibid., iv. 723.
[4] According to Davidsohn (ibid., iv. 720) negotiations between Lucca and the emperor took place in 1313; but when they came to nothing, the resumption of hostilities against the Lucchese ensured the continuance of Lucchese loyalty to Florence.
[5] ASL, Archivio notarile no. 29, 30/6/1311 (Pisan style).
[6] Ibid., 17/10/1311 (Pisan style).

imperial army in Pisa and the capture of Pietrasanta and Sarzana would have encouraged them in their confidence that Henry VII was to be their saviour. But these hopes were now, a few months later, dashed by his death.

Pisa, the city in which most of them had taken refuge since 1301, was itself clearly threatened by the new turn of events. Ranged against it were not merely the Guelph communes of Tuscany, Florence, Lucca, Pistoia, and Siena, but also the papacy and King Robert of Naples. In their desperate predicament, the Pisans turned to Uguccione della Faggiuola, Henry VII's vicar in Genoa, who for many years had been a leading Tuscan Ghibelline political figure and military commander. Born about 1250 near Massa Trabaria at his ancestral castle which gave him his surname, Uguccione had been captain-general of the troops of Cesena, Forlì, Faenza, and Imola, and *podestà* of Gubbio and Arezzo,[7] before Henry of Luxemburg's journey into Italy took him away from his preoccupation with politics in Arezzo, Montefeltro, and in the Romagna and brought him to Genoa. Though consistently Ghibelline in his sympathies, he had been the father-in-law of the most famous of the Florentine Black Guelphs, the haughty magnate Corso Donati, and, according to Davidsohn, had not been averse, when it suited his interests, to coming to terms with Pope Boniface VIII.[8] Wily and ruthless, expert in war, Uguccione came of the turbulent lesser nobility of the Apennine borderlands between Tuscany and the Marches and had been involved as soldier of fortune and administrator in a career of political intrigue which, however, had not, until he reached his sixties, provided him with the opportunity of establishing himself as a ruler in his own right. Called to Pisa shortly after the death of the emperor, he was proclaimed *podestà* and captain of the people and of war on 20 September 1313.[9] Initially, he was no more than a servant of the commune; but he was soon able to exploit his control over its troops to make himself effectively into a tyrant.

The key to his power and to Pisa's survival as an independent state after the emperor's death was the detachment of cavalry from Henry VII's former army which passed into the service of the city. Not all the

---

[7] For details of Uguccione della Faggiuola's life before 1313, see Vigo, *Uguccione*, 4–5, 96–7.

[8] Davidsohn, *Storia*, iv, 763–4.

[9] Ibid., iv. 763, on the authority of ASP Comune A85 c.52ᵛ. According to Sardo, he entered the city on 12 September (*Cronaca di Pisa*, ed. O. Banti (Rome, 1963), 60), though the anonymous chronicle, using the same source, gives the date 22 September ('Cronica di Pisa', *RIS* xv, col. 987).

imperial soldiers were prepared to go into the pay of a mere Italian commune: according to the chronicler Raniero Sardo, only ten of the emperor's constables took up the Pisan offer of employment as mercenaries.[10] But, in terms of the kinds of forces available to Tuscan states in the early fourteenth century, the ten companies of professional, heavily-armed knights who came, under these foreign *condottieri*, to form the nucleus of the Pisan cavalry, were a military formation of some significance. Contemporary writers differed as to its exact size—Giovanni Villani estimated this at 'about a thousand horse',[11] Giovanni di Lemmo da Comugnori at 800,[12] an anonymous Siense chronicler at 600,[13] while slightly later accounts, based on earlier sources, give it as 1,500,[14] 1,100,[15] and 800.[16] Davidsohn accepts the figure of 800;[17] however, the most detailed description of the engagement of these mercenaries is that copied by Sardo and an anonymous Pisan chronicler from what might have been an archival source and this (depending on which of the two transcribed it right) gave the figure of 1,500 or 1,100.[18]

The force which came under Uguccione's command can safely be assumed, taking all the evidence into account, to have consisted of about a thousand foreign knights, mainly German but including some Flemings and English,[19] together of course with the Pisan and Lucchese Ghibelline cavalry and infantry. When the Pisans first enlisted their contingent of Henry VII's former troops, the emperor's marshal, Count Henry of Flanders, had offered his services as their commander; but these had been rejected,[20] so that Uguccione enjoyed

[10] Sardo, *Cronaca*, 58–9.
[11] G. Villani, *Cronica*, ix. 54.
[12] Giovanni di Lemmo da Comugnori, 'Diario', in *Cronache dei secoli XIII e XIV* in *Documenti di storia italiana* (henceforth referred to as Giovanni di Lemmo, 'Diario'), vi (Florence, 1876), 190.
[13] 'Cronaca senese dei fatti riguardanti la città ed il suo territorio di autore anonimo', ed. A. Lisini and F. Iacometti, in *RIS* (n. edn.), xv, pt. 6, 98.
[14] Sardo, *Cronaca*, 59.
[15] 'Cronica di Pisa', in *RIS*, xv, col. 987.
[16] Sercambi, *Croniche*, pt. I, c.115 (vol. i, p. 59).
[17] Davidsohn, *Storia*, iv, 762.
[18] The text in Sardo, *Cronaca*, and the 'Cronica di Pisa' cited in n. 15 above correspond closely except that Sardo has 'mille cinque cento' where the anonymous chronicler has 'mille cento' and that Sardo omits two of the names of the ten *caporali*. The source used by both gave the date when the troops were taken into the pay of Pisa as 11 September. In view of the estimates of the other contemporary writers, the figure 1,100 would seem to be the more likely to be correct.
[19] G. Villani, *Cronica*, ix. 54.
[20] 'Cronica di Pisa', in *RIS*, xv, col. 987.

complete and direct control over them, by virtue of his authority not only as *podestà* but also as captain of war. It was his position both as titular political head of the state and as its military leader which he was able to put to good use to secure his dominance over the city.

In his early months in Pisa, Uguccione's path to power was obstructed by two main obstacles. The first was the threat posed by the Tuscan Guelphs, particularly by Lucca. The second was the prospect of a peace with Robert of Naples which would have enabled the Pisans to dispense with the services both of their new *podestà* and captain and of the mercenaries under his command. Uguccione's way of dealing with these potential hindrances to the establishment of his dominance over the city was characteristically bold, prompt, and ruthless.

In meeting the danger presented by the resurgent power of the Tuscan Guelphs, he was aided by the intransigence and over-confidence of the Lucchese. When Pisan ambassadors went to Lucca in September 1313 in an attempt to make peace, their terms were scornfully rejected by the brash Bonturo Dati and his fellow nego-tiators. The Pisans had asked for the return to them of the villages of Avane, Buti, and Asciano which lay on their side of the Monti Pisani, a range of hills which formed the natural boundary between the *contadi* of the two cities. But the Lucchese, having held these against even Henry VII's army, were in no mood to yield them, particularly at a time when the tide of events appeared to be turning in their favour. Indeed, they took a certain pride in their possession of Asciano which overlooked Pisa. In 1288, when they had first captured it, the Lucchese had erected mirrors, as a gesture of contempt for their enemies who, even in their own city, would be able to see the light shining off them.[21] It was to this incident that Bonturo Dati now referred as, adding insult to injury, he brought the negotiations to a close by saying that the Lucchese wanted to keep Asciano so that the women of Pisa could see themselves reflected there.

It was rash for the Lucchese so to provoke the Pisans when, follow-ing the emperor's death, they had discharged some of their mer-cenaries[22] at the very time that the Pisans had taken into their pay a thousand or so of Henry VII's former troops—all the more since Bonturo Dati's words served to unite the peace and war parties in Pisa

---

[21] G. Villani, *Cronica*, vii. 122.
[22] Sardo, *Cronaca*, 60, 'Cronica di Pisa', *RIS*, xv, col. 987.

in a common resolve to avenge the offence done to their city. Banduccio Buonconte, who was the moving spirit behind the peace initiative
and had been a member of the delegation to Lucca, now offered to
lend a thousand florins to the commune to help finance the expedition
against Lucca, a gesture in which he was joined by other Pisan
merchants.[23]

Uguccione, finding events playing into his hands, lost no time in
organizing an attack on the Lucchese *contado*. Taking his army over
the Monti Pisani on 19 September, he surprised and captured the
Lucchese frontier post of Santa Maria del Giudice. He was, however,
compelled to withdraw from it a fortnight later when the Lucchese
called in contingents of troops from their allies. It was not until the 18
November that his campaign against Lucca began in earnest with
another surprise attack, this time spearheaded by his foreign knights.
Burning and ravaging everything in their path, the mercenaries
destroyed Santa Maria del Giudice, Massa Pisana, and Gattaiola and
laid waste the valleys of Compito, Vorno, and Massa Macinaia. The
Guelph army issued forth from Lucca to block their way but was easily
scattered by a cavalry charge. It withdrew in such disorder back into
the town that the *borgo* outside the Porta San Pietro was abandoned to
the advancing enemy who took it and promptly burnt it.[24]

According to one Sienese chronicler, whose account makes it clear
that he participated in the rout as one of the Guelph troops, the
German knights were disguised in Pisan surcoats and thus at first
indistinguishable from the mounted citizen levies of the city for which
they were fighting. This eyewitness of the battle records the terror
inspired by the ruthlessness of the foreign professional soldiers. 'They
burnt many houses and slaughtered many people, and it was no use
saying "I give myself up" because they did not understand our
language.'[25] He also notes the remarkable discipline of their cavalry,
who rode in serried ranks and communicated so effectively through
signs that their formations moved as one man.[26] If another chronicler,

---

[23] 'Cronica di Pisa', *RIS*, xv, col. 987.
[24] The best chronicle account of these events is in Sardo, *Cronaca*, 60–2. Tommasi,
Sommario, 131–2, and Davidsohn, *Storia*, iv. 765, provide good modern syntheses of the
chronicle and other evidence. Other sources for the above narrative are 'Cronica di
Pisa', *RIS*, xv, col. 988, A Mussato, 'De gestis italicorum', *RIS*, x, cols. 593–5, 'Storie
pistoresi', *RIS*, (n. edn.), xi, pt. 5, 58–9, Giovanni di Lemmo, *Diario*, 190, BNF MS
Palat. 571, c.18ʳ., and 'Cronaca senese attribuita ad Agnolo di Tura', *RIS* (n. ed.), xv, pt.
6, 337–9.
[25] 'Cronaca senese dei fatti . . .', *RIS* (n. edn.), xv, pt. 6, 98.
[26] Ibid.

the Pisan Raniero Sardo, is to be believed, this degree of co-ordination had been achieved by Uguccione through the imposition of the Draconic penalty of having a foot chopped off any soldier who fell out of line![27] On reaching the Porta San Pietro, the Pisans and Teutonic knights camped by the meadow below the town walls where they set up two high poles to which they attached large round mirrors. On these they hung placards addressed to Bonturo Dati, inviting him to look at himself in the mirrors which the women of Pisa had sent him.[28] The unfortunate Bonturo meanwhile fled to the Dominican convent of San Romano to hide both from the mockery of the Pisans and from the wrath of his fellow-citizens.[29] Henceforth disgraced, he was soon afterwards compelled to leave Lucca for Florence.[30]

The shock of the Pisan attack was most devastating in its psychological consequences. While it had laid waste an area of the Lucchese *contado* and while Uguccione did manage to follow it up by the systematic conquest of a few disputed frontier villages,[31] its immediate military effects were negligible. Lucca was secure behind its walls and Florentine reinforcements soon once again ensured the withdrawal of the Pisan troops from Lucchese territory. In the long term, however, its impact was considerable. First, it altered the diplomatic balance between Pisa and Lucca, enabling the former to obtain peace terms virtually as a victor and not as a state under threat of attack from an overwhelmingly more powerful coalition. This in turn changed the situation in Pisa itself by discrediting those prepared to come to terms with the Guelphs on any conditions that might be offered and endorsing the hard line of those, such as Uguccione, who believed in improving the bargaining position of the commune through aggressive military action. Secondly, the success of the lightning attack on Lucca had clearly demonstrated the inability of the citizen levies to stand up against a body of well-drilled professional troops, and thus ushered in a period dominated militarily by highly paid foreign knights and politically by those who could afford to engage them.

In the immediate aftermath of his dramatic coup against Lucca that had disposed, for the time being, of the Guelph threat to Pisa, Uguccione found himself confronted with the second danger to his growing

---

[27] Sardo, *Cronaca*, 60. The same information is contained also in 'Cronaca senese' (Tura), *RIS*, xv, pt. 6, 337.
[28] 'Cronica di Pisa', *RIS*, xv, col. 988. [29] Ibid.
[30] Davidsohn, *Storia*, iv. 766–7. [31] Sardo, *Cronaca*, 63–4.

ascendancy over the city—the prospect of a premature peace that would make possible a reduction of the number of his troops and render him no longer indispensable as the commune's defender against its many foes. While the campaign against Lucca had been in progress, negotiations with King Robert of Naples had begun at the instance of the *anziani*, or executive council of Pisa, at this time under the influence of Banduccio Buonconte.[32] By the end of February, agreement had been reached on terms which in effect restored the status quo before the opening of hostilities and committed the Pisans to helping King Robert in his war against Frederick of Sicily by supplying him with five galleys, while at the same time placing an embargo on trade and the dispatch of war materials to Sicily.[33] In practice, the projected treaty implied that the Pisans would buy peace with Naples, and by extension with its Tuscan allies, at the price of sacrificing the gains made in the preceding war and entering the Guelph coalition as supporters of King Robert in any future expeditions against Ghibelline Sicily.

While Uguccione certainly knew of the Pisan negotiations in Naples, it is not clear how well he was informed of the concessions made in the course of them to secure the proposed peace.[34] His reaction after the announcement of its terms suggests that they came as a surprise to him; but this may have been because it was only then that he realized that one of its implications would be the reduction by about half in the number of mercenaries in Pisan service.[35] Whatever the truth as to the extent of his knowledge of the proposed terms of the treaty, there is no doubt that, once its provisions were published in Pisa, he condemned it and exploited public disappointment with it to undermine the position of Banduccio Buonconte and his son Pietro,

[32] The authority to negotiate had been issued on 26 November 1313 (F. dal Borgo, *Raccolta di scelti diplomi pisani* (Pisa, 1765), 228–9), with Uguccione's knowledge. Raniero Sardo asserts (*Cronaca*, 65) that the treaty had been concluded in Naples on 27 February 1314 without the knowledge of Uguccione or the Pisans; which, if it is not simply incorrect, suggests that the terms arrived at were kept secret from him until that date.

[33] F. dal Borgo, *Raccolta*, 221–8. Original in ASP Comune A29 cc. 1–8. In detail, the terms stipulated (i) that taxes and duties on foreign merchants be not raised; (ii) that King Robert of Naples's exiles and enemies be not allowed to remain in Pisan territory; (iii) that the grain trade with Sicily be stopped; (iv) that arms and galleys should not be supplied to Sicily; (v) that five galleys, equipped at Pisan expense, be put at the disposal of King Robert or his heirs whenever a fleet of ten or more galleys was assembled against Sicily; (vi) that all prisoners of war should be released and reprisals suspended; (vii) that peace should be made with the other Tuscan communes.

[34] See n. 32 above.

[35] According to Mussato 'De gestis italicorum', col. 600, from 700 to 300.

who had been its principal sponsors. Accusing them of having betrayed the city through a secret understanding with the Guelphs, he arrested them and used his foreign mercenaries to seize control of the streets and overawe the Pisan population into acquiescence in his action. He then, on 24 March 1314,[36] had Banduccio and Pietro Buonconte beheaded. Two days later,[37] assembling a general council of the commune in the cathedral, he obtained from it the extension of his authority as captain of war for another ten years and the compilation of new lists from which the *anziani* were to be drawn, to ensure the future adherence of the city's governors to Ghibellinism.[38]

Having effectively seized power in Pisa, Uguccione immediately turned his attention to achieving better peace terms with Lucca than those which would have flowed from the projected treaty with King Robert. Calling a conference with the Lucchese at the border village of Ripafratta, he succeeded in wringing concessions from them which the Pisan negotiations had not been able to obtain in Naples. Asciano and Viareggio were to be restored immediately to Pisa, Buti and Bientina to be handed back later when marriages had been arranged between Pisan and Lucchese families to seal the peace, the castle of Ceretello was to be demolished, and both cities were to readmit their exiles, to whom any property which had been confiscated from them was to be returned. Why the Lucchese were prepared to accept this agreement, concluded on 25 April,[39] a mere two months after the Treaty of Naples had offered them more favourable terms, is unclear. Probably, the main reason for the conciliatory posture of their delegation was a fear of the repetition of the events of the previous November. According to Giovanni Villani,[40] and the anonymous author of the 'Storie pistoresi',[41] divisions in Lucca contributed to the commune's willingness to come to terms with Pisa: since the eclipse of the influence of Bonturo Dati, the Guelph patrician families of the Obizi and Bernarducci had re-established their dominance; but there was conflict between them, with the Bernarducci, as the weaker group,

---

[36] Sardo, *Cronaca*, 66; but one anonymous San Miniatese chronicler (in G. D. Mansi, *Stephani Baluzii tutelensis miscellanea* (Lucca, 1761–4), i. 463) gives the date 20 March 1314.
[37] Sardo, *Cronaca*, 67, and 'Cronaca senese' (Tura), *RIS* (n. edn.), xv, pt. 6, 341.
[38] The foregoing account is based substantially on Sardo, *Cronaca*, 67, BNF MS Palat. 571, c. 18ᵛ, Giovanni di Lemmo, 'Diario', 190. A. Mussato, 'De gestis', col. 600, 'Chronicon sanminiatese', in Mansi, *Miscellanea*, i. 463.
[39] Giovanni di Lemmo, 'Diario', 190, Mussato, 'De gestis italicorum', col. 602.
[40] G. Villani, *Cronica*, ix. 58.
[41] 'Storie pistoresi', in *RIS* (n. edn.), xi, pt. 5, 59–60.

favouring a return of the banished Whites in the hope that it might swing the political balance in their favour.

Whatever the motives for its acceptance by the Lucchese, the peace of April 1314 was to prove a turning-point in the histories of both Lucca and Pisa, though not so much because of the minor territorial changes it brought about as because of the consequences of the re-admission of the White exiles into Lucca. The faction expelled in 1301 which now returned to its native city was no mere miscellaneous group of individuals but a closely knit bloc of families which had preserved its corporate identity through its years of absence from Lucca. At the centre of it was the Interminelli (or Antelminelli)[42] family to which Castruccio Castracani belonged.[43] If one adds to the main stem of this clan those who belonged to its subordinate branches, the Savarigi, Parghia, Gonella, Bovi, Castracani, and Mezzolombardi, one finds that thirty-seven of the Lucchese White community in Pisa in 1310 belonged to it.[44] The next largest group among the exiles was that of the Mordecastelli, with fourteen members. Several other prominent families were represented in smaller numbers, notably the Poggio, Del Fondo (in its Del Bosco branch), Avvocati, Martini, Carincioni, Rapondi, Onesti, Rapa, Ghiotti, Benettoni, and Barca, not to mention the Ciapparoni,[45] who, though not a major Lucchese house, had played a significant role in the past as allies of the Interminelli and Mordecastelli.

[42] Antelminelli, the name later adopted by the family, appears originally to have been the Latinization of the Lucchese Interminelli which is the form used in the vernacular chroniclers up to and including Sercambi, for instance, the authors of BNF MS Palat. 571 (at c. 19ʳ.), of the 'Storie pistoresi' (at *RIS* (n. edn.), xi, pt. 5, 70), of the 'Cronaca senese dei fatti' (at *RIS*, xv, pt. 6, 101), Giovanni Villani (ix. 60), and Giovanni Sercambi, *Croniche*, pt. i, c.117, (vol. i, p. 61).

[43] It has recently been suggested by Mario Seghieri in 'Fra Castracani e Antelminelli: note di genealogia e di consortato', *Rivista di archeologia, storia, costume, del Istituto Storico Lucchese*, ix (1981), 3. 3–8, that the Castracani did not originally form part of the Inter-minelli family since the earliest archival reference to a coupling of the name Castracani with the designation 'de Antelminellis' dates from 1285 and since earlier allusions to members of the Castracani lineage did not include this further title. This is, however, an argument only from the absence of evidence which overlooks the tendency in Lucchese records of this period to refer to members of the junior branches of clans by their own surname rather than that of the clan and only occasionally to give the full expanded form of the name. All contemporary sources (for instance, Villani, ix. 88, BNF MS Palat. 571, c. 19ʳ) associate Castruccio with the Interminelli and none disputes the link between that *casata* and the Castracani.

[44] ASL Archivio notarile, no. 29, 30/6/1311 and 17/10/31 (Pisan style), published by Sforza, 'Castruccio . . . in esilio', 96–100, 101–2.

[45] Ibid. Other families among these exiles, but not especially active in Lucca after 1314, were the Accettanti, Bacarella, Barsellotti, Campanari, and Giordani.

All in all, taking into account that not all Lucchese exiles would have been in a position to attend the meetings of the White faction in the church of San Sisto in Pisa in 1310 or to have taken the trouble to get others to represent them there, those entitled to return to Lucca by the peace of 1314 constituted quite an extensive and formidable addition to the city's patriciate.[46] Interestingly enough, the man who was to become their spokesman and leader, Castruccio Castracani, had taken only a very minor part in their activities in Pisa. At the time of their 20 June 1310 meetings, he had been absent from that city, and had made Coluccio Savarigi his agent. Though back in Pisa by 22 August of that year,[47] he did not figure among the councillors of the party who held office in late October.[48] He was also not a prominent member of the Interminelli family, coming as he did from one of its less distinguished branches, the Castracani. It was all the more surprising therefore that he should emerge in the early months of 1314 as the principal negotiator on behalf of the Lucchese Whites in their dealings with Uguccione della Faggiuola and as the acknowledged head of the readmitted exiles.

The only explanations that can be given for his sudden rise to prominence are in terms of his military experience and skill and of the trust which Uguccione appeared at this stage to have placed in him. He issues from obscurity at this point in time as a supporter among the returned Lucchese Whites of Uguccione's political schemes and as the man who could most persuasively enlist Pisan help for their faction. His background as a soldier of fortune may well have suggested him to Uguccione as a suitable instrument for the realization of that intriguer's designs, while his relatively humble position in the hierarchy of the Lucchese White faction would presumably have made him both easier to handle and more willing than cautious merchants or hoary family heads to acquiesce in the kinds of methods Uguccione had in mind.

---

[46] Excluding those from smaller towns in the Lucchese *contado*, there were altogether over 120 men, either present or represented by others, in the three meetings recorded by Ser Orlando Ciapparoni. The fact that there were some names in the later more selective lists of councillors which were not included in the first, full one of members on 30 June 1310 suggests that not even this was comprehensive of all of the Lucchese White exile community. Ferreto Vicentino, in his 'Historia rerum in Italia gestarum' in *Opere* (ed. C. Cipolla) (Rome, 1914), ii. 193, gives a total of almost 200 men for the exiled faction.

[47] ASL Archivio notarile no. 29, 22/8/1311 (Pisan style).

[48] Ibid., 15 and 17/10/1311 (Pisan style).

Castruccio was a man very much formed by the instabilities of his age. Despite his later wholehearted dedication to war and government, he came of a mercantile family. His grandfather Castracane Ruggieri had been a trader and banker whose career had displayed in the field of commerce something of the same acquisitive and aggressive energy and skill in making the most of circumstances that Castruccio was to reveal as a military commander and a tyrant. It is possible to trace the progress of his business ventures in some of the earliest surviving Lucchese notarial registers, those of Ser Ciabatto[49] and later of Bartolomeo Tegrimo and Fulcerio Fulcieri.[50] Blomquist has given a detailed account of his financial operations between the 1250s and 1280s on the basis of these sources.[51] What emerges clearly from them is that Castracane, taking up the profession of *campsor* or money-changer in 1252, had by the 1270s and 1280s expanded his activities into those of an international merchant, banker, and investor in land and mining ventures. The origins of his branch of the family, known as the Castracani of San Martino to distinguish them from the Castracani of San Cristoforo,[52] can be followed back only to the beginnings of the thirteenth century,[53] that is, to about fifty years before he himself became active in business, so the line to which he was to bring wealth if not, as yet, fame, would appear to be a relatively new one, perhaps only recently issued from the main stem of the Interminelli lineage. His financial success, however, though surpassing that of his relatives, was not entirely unmatched by the efforts of his closer kinsmen: both his cousin Savarigio and his brother Lutterio were, like him, money-changers and merchants, the former of whom at least left a substantial fortune.[54]

---

[49] ACL LL 24–7, 30–3, and 36.

[50] ASL Archivio notarile no. 15.

[51] T. W. Blomquist, 'The Castracani Family of Thirteenth Century Lucca', *Speculum*, xlvi (1971), 459–76.

[52] F. P. Luiso, who dealt with the Castracani of S. Cristoforo in his article 'Mercanti lucchesi dell'epoca di Dante II: gli antenati di Castruccio Castracani', *Bollettino storico lucchese*, x (1938), concluded that there was no relationship between the two Castracani families (p. 71).

[53] There are references to the first Castracane in 1202, 1218, and 1228 (Blomquist, 'Castracani Family', 459), while his son Ruggiero is mentioned in Ser Ciabatto's notarial register from 1251 up to his death in 1258 (ACL LL 26, c.103^r, c.104^v., LL 27, c.110^r., LL 31, c.9^r., c.21^r.).

[54] Blomquist, 'Castracani Family', 460–1 and 463–6. On p. 460 there is a genealogical table of the Castracani of S. Martino, while F. P. Luiso, 'Mercanti', 88, gives one for the Castracani of S. Cristoforo.

Starting in partnership with his brother Lutterio and with Guido and later Genovese Perfettucci, Castracane built up extensive holdings of capital and property.[55] By the 1280s when his sons Gerio, Coluccio, and Neo had become associated in his business dealings, he was trading in the Champagne fairs,[56] acquiring rights to iron-mines in Versilia and Lunigiana,[57] and presumably continuing with his transactions in houses and land in Lucca and its *contado*.[58] When his grandson Castruccio was born to his eldest son Gerio, on 29 March 1281,[59] the family of which Castracane was head was therefore entering the period of its greatest prosperity and social eminence. A minor but rising branch of the Interminelli—in other words of one of the two most important kinship groupings in the city—it appeared to offer the new-born eventual heir to the Castracani wealth remarkable prospects as a merchant and citizen of Lucca. That these expectations were not realized was due to the political situation in the city. After 1292, the year in which Castruccio's grandfather probably died,[60] the antagonism between the Obizi faction, on the one hand, and the Interminelli and their allies, on the other, sharpened and, as the previous chapter

[55] Blomquist, pp. 467–70. See also in particular ACL LL 30, c.107ʳ., LL 32, c.36ʳ. and c.159ʳ. and ʳ., LL 32, c.42ʳ., LL 36 c.37ʳ., for the partnership agreements between Castracane and his associates which reveal the increases in the capital which the partners and, in particular, Castracane had at their disposal. (His share rose from between £400 and £700 between 1256 and 1259 to £2,000 in 1271.)

[56] In 1284 (Blomquist, 'Castracani Family', 471). See also T. Blomquist, 'Trade and Commerce'.

[57] Sforza, 'Castruccio . . . in esilio', 53. Castracane on 16 June 1287 purchased a vein of iron ore in the commune of Farnocchia in Versilia (ASL Ufficio sulle differenze dei confini no. 541, Filza F3) from a group of representatives of that commune; in January 1288 he bought rights over iron deposits in the commune of Antona near Massa in Lunigiana (ASL Diplomatico Tarpea, 2/1/1288, and ASL Capitoli no. 1 c.164ʳ.) and in the same year he acquired control over a wood in the mineral-bearing area of Stazzema in the Apuan Alps (ASL Diplomatico Tarpea, 26/3/1298).

[58] The registers of Ser Ciabatto which record Castracane's property dealings run out in 1271. Those of the Fulcieri brothers (ASL Archivio notarile no. 15) contain mainly contracts relating to foreign trade, loans, etc.

[59] The date is that given by Castruccio's first biographer Nicolao Tegrimi, *Vita*, 15. There is no documentary confirmation of it, but the presumption that Tegrimi had access to a source now lost (perhaps Castruccio's original tomb-inscription in the church of San Francesco in Lucca) and the consistency of the date with the other known facts of Castruccio's life have led it to be generally accepted.

[60] Castracane's death occurred between 1 July 1292 and 12 August 1294. By the latter date he was definitely dead (ASL Diplomatico S. Romano, 12/8/1294), while on the former, in amending his will, he described himself as sound of mind but infirm of body from which we can assume he was probably then in his final illness (ASL Diplomatico Fregionaia 1/7/1292).

has indicated, became caught up in the wider Tuscan Black–White feud.

In the interval between Castracane's death and the expulsion of his family, together with their kinsmen and partisans, from Lucca in 1301, his sons Gerio and Coluccio (Castruccio's father and uncle) continued to carry on his business. Two traces of their commercial activities remain in contracts drawn up in 1294[61] and 1296,[62] the latter of which is the first known document to mention Castruccio, described as 'filio emancipato dicti Gerii', in the record of a transaction involving the repayment of £1,000 *tournois* by the Castracani partners—who now included the young Castruccio—to the Ricciardi company.

Whatever wealth remained to the family in 1301 as a result of Castracane's financial gains appears, however, to have been lost with the banishment of his heirs and the confiscation of their property in that year. Fleeing to Ancona, probably about February 1301, Gerio and his son found themselves in the unenviable plight fourteenth-century Italy reserved for exiles. Gerio's death in either late September or early October[63] made Castruccio's position all the more hopeless. His predicament led him to travel to England, thereby opening a period of his life about which little is known for certain and in which it is difficult to disentangle fact from legend. According to Nicolao Tegrimi, his first biographer, who wrote at the end of the fifteenth century and who obviously had access to information since lost, but who did not hesitate to embroider it for fitting dramatic effect, Castruccio went to London to stay with his kinsman Alderigo Antelminelli, a wealthy merchant at King Edward I's court. Here, he learnt English with remarkable speed and became an intimate of the royal circle, excelling in ball games. It was while engaged in one of these that the incident occurred which forced him suddenly to flee the country. Defending himself against a member of the royal family who had struck him in the course of an argument over the game, he killed this aristocrat and was consequently compelled to escape punishment for his offence by making for the nearest ship which took him to

---

[61] ASL Diplomatico S. Romano, 12/8/1294.

[62] ASL Archivio notarile no. 17, c.94ʳ. and ʳ., cited by Blomquist, 'Castracani Family', 474.

[63] Castruccio's testament (Lazzareschi, 'Documenti', 398) refers to his father's will as having been drawn up at Ancona on 29 September 1301. Tegrimi (*Vita*, 8) says that Gerio died seven months after leaving Lucca. If we assume that Gerio's will was drawn up on his deathbed and accept Tegrimi's statement, the date of Gerio's departure from Lucca would have been late in February.

Flanders. Finding the English and French at war there, he joined the latter and thus became a mercenary soldier.[64] This improbable story, calculated to arouse the scepticism of any critical historian,[65] has nevertheless found partial confirmation in subsequent research. Mancini[66] discovered in the Calendar of Patent Rolls[67] a reference to a pardon given to Castruccio by Edward II on 12 December 1325 at the request of his Lucchese physician, Master Pancini of Controne, for the murder of one Ciato Ronzini and 'of the abjuration of the realm he [Castruccio] made on that account'. It is clear from this not only that Castruccio had been to England as Tegrimi had suggested, but also that he had had to leave in haste after killing a man. The only details of Tegrimi's account that were obviously distorted in an effort to romanticize the story were those relating to the identity of Castruccio's victim and to the circumstances of his crime. The Ciato Ronzini whom he dispatched was a fellow Lucchese merchant[68] and not an English noble.[69] And the occasion of Ciato's death was more likely a sordid brawl than the quarrel among courtiers Tegrimi described. Alice Beardwood remarks, in her work on *Alien Merchants in England*, that, among the Italians resident in London in the fourteenth century, 'murders were not infrequent', though 'very rarely was the accused punished . . .. In most cases he had fled and could not be found. In many cases he was pardoned because the deed was done in self-defence'. She adds that 'it seems to be a fact that there were few of the outstanding merchants of this period who were not connected in one way or another with acts of violence'.[69] This being so, the most plausible construction that can be put upon the evidence as to Castruccio's murder of Ciato Ronzini is that, in common with many other Italians in England at the time, he resorted to force to defend himself or to avenge an injury, knowing that he would be able to evade arrest through flight. Having killed Ronzini, however, he was henceforth excluded from England and from the mercantile career which he had presumably intended to pursue there.

[64] Tegrimi, *Vita*, 8–12.

[65] It was in fact rejected by Sforza, 'Castruccio . . . in esilio', 61–2.

[66] A. Mancini, 'Castruccio in Inghilterra', *Atti della R. Accademia Lucchese* (NS), iii (1934), 147–59.

[67] Calendar of Patent Rolls, Edward II.5, 200. The full text of the document is published in Mancini, 'Castruccio', 150–1.

[68] The Ronzini (or Roncini) were a fairly prominent Lucchese family of the Borgo San Frediano.

[69] A. Beardwood, *Alien Merchants in England 1350–1377* (Cambridge, Mass., 1931), 79.

Arriving in Flanders, he turned instead to soldiering with implications for his future the full significance of which was only to emerge years later. The one question which remains to be examined concerning his stay in England is what it was that attracted him there in the first place. Tegrimi's Alderigo Antelminelli is a mythical character, his name taken from a Lucchese merchant active in Flanders and France later in the fourteenth century.[70] But does his identity mask that of some actual friend or relative of Castruccio whose presence in London would explain why he went so far afield after the death of his father, instead of simply rejoining his kinsmen and political allies in the White exile community in Pisa? Reference to the names of the Lucchese merchants known to have been in England towards the end of the thirteenth century[71] reveals none immediately related to Castruccio, but does indicate that the Poggio, the family into which Castruccio's uncle Coluccio, or Nicolo, had married[72] was well represented among the members of the Lucchese Ricciardi company in England. Indeed, there is some reason to believe that the Arrigo di Poggio who was prominent as a Ricciardi partner and banker to Edward I was in fact Castruccio's uncle's father-in-law.[73] One is therefore tempted to see in him the original of Tegrimi's Alderigo Antelminelli, for he had had close relations with the royal court as a financier, particularly in the late 1290s.[74] However, by the time Castruccio came to England in late 1301 or 1302, Arrigo di Poggio would have been in disgrace, together with the Ricciardi company, the English operations of which had in

---

[70] E. Lazzareschi, ed., *Libro della comunità dei mercanti lucchesi in Bruges* (Milan, 1947), pp. xxv, 74–8, 87, 92, 105, 108, 111, 124, and 136.

[71] I have used the following sources to establish a list of Lucchese merchants in England, c.1300: W. E. Rhodes, 'The Italian Bankers in England and their loans to Edward I and Edward II', in T. F. Tout and J. Tait, *Historical Essays* (Manchester, 1907), 142–4, E. Re, 'La compagnia dei Ricciardi in Inghilterra e il suo fallimento alla fine del secolo XIII', *Archivio della società romana di storia patria*, xxxvi (1913), 96, R. W. Kaeuper, *Bankers to the Crown: The Ricciardi of Lucca and Edward I* (Princeton, 1973), 56–8, M. Prestwich, 'Italian Merchants in late thirteenth and early fourteenth century England', *The Dawn of Modern Banking* (New Haven, 1979), 77–104.

[72] ASL Archivio notarile no. 67, c.209ʳ. shows that Nicolo Castracani was married to Franceschina, daughter of the late Arrigo and sister of Dino and Vanni di Poggio.

[73] The Arrigo di Poggio who was a representative of the Ricciardi company in England was the son of Tegrimo (ASL Archivio notarile no. 17, c.94ᵛ.). That Arrigo di Tegrimo had a son Vanni can be established from ASL Archivio notarile no. 89, Register 7, 1/3/1315, which is partial confirmation that the Arrigo who was Nicolo Castracani's father-in-law was also the Ricciardi partner.

[74] Kaeuper, *Bankers*, 93–4.

effect collapsed by 1294.[75] In fact, he might no longer have been in the country: we know that in 1300 he was on a mission to Rome together with two other members of the Ricciardi *societas*.[76] But his brother Orlandino did undoubtedly remain in London throughout the first decade of the fourteenth century,[77] so that it is possible Castruccio might have stayed with him while in England—though since he was by then virtually a bankrupt, he can no longer have played the kind of role assigned to Alderigo Antelminelli in Tegrimi's story.

The next stage of that rather fabulous account of Castruccio's early life also receives some confirmation in historical sources. We know from a Flemish chronicle[78] that by April 1303 Castruccio was in command of a detachment of Italian mercenaries employed by the French in the defence of Thérouanne in Artois against Philip IV's Flemish rebels. Under the leadership of Alberto Scotti of Piacenza and Musciatto Francesi, he took part in the day-long battle for the town and in the blocking of the enemy's advance through the destruction of the bridge over the Lys.[79]

Not long after this, he must have returned to Italy, for on 29 January 1304 he was in Pisa together with his uncle Coluccio.[80] Between this time and 22 August 1313,[81] there is no record of him in this city, and we can conclude from this and other evidence that he was absent for a considerable part of this period from it.[82] That he spent a substantial portion of these years in service as a mercenary in northern Italy is clear from two sources. In the first place, his will later stated that he had fought in many parts of Tuscany and Lombardy and particularly in Brescia, Soncino, Vicenza, in Capodistria, and elsewhere.[83] Then there is a letter written in 1325 by Marino Sanudo the elder to Ingramo, the archbishop of Capua and chancellor of the king of Naples. This speaks of Castruccio having been a mercenary in Verona sixteen years earlier, that is, 1309, with two horses, one of which he had

---

[75] Ibid., 209–27.   [76] Ibid., 240–1.   [77] Ibid., 246.

[78] 'Anciennes Chroniques de Flandres', in *Recueil des historiens des Gaules et de la France*, (ed. De Wailly and De Lisle), xxii, (Paris, 1865), 391. But see M. Luzzati's remarks in 'Castruccio nelle fonti cronachistiche documentarie oltramontane', *ACCC*, 79–97, which raise the possibility of subsequent re-editing of this chronicle to include references in it to Castruccio.

[79] G. Villani, *Cronica*, viii. 76.

[80] ASL Archivio notarile no. 29, 29/1/1304 (Pisan style).

[81] Ibid., at date 22/8/1314 (Pisan style).

[82] We know from ASL Archivio notarile no. 29, 30/6/1312 (Pisan style), that he was definitely absent on 30 June 1311, being represented then by Coluccio Savarigi.

[83] Lazzareschi, 'Documenti', 398.

bought, one of which had been given to him, and of going then into
Venetian service for half a year as constable or commander of twenty-
six knights whom he had hired with a loan of 300 florins from the
commune. About to be discharged six months later, he appealed to the
podestà of Capodistria where he was stationed and had his period of
service extended, being allowed, as a special favour when he eventually left, to have his place taken by his uncle.[84]

The references in Castruccio's will to hostilities at Vicenza and
Brescia almost certainly refer to campaigns in 1311,[85] in other words to
the period after he had resigned his command to his uncle Coluccio
and at the time of Henry VII's earliest Italian wars. Can Grande della
Scala, in whose service Castruccio had been in 1309, seized Vicenza
from Padua in April 1311,[86] and we can presume that Castruccio
fought in his army on that occasion. The allusion to Brescia must refer
to fighting at the time of Henry VII's siege of that city between May
and September 1311,[87] while that to Soncino may relate to hostilities
around that town in June of the same year[88] or may simply be an indication that Castruccio was garrisoned there after Henry VII deprived
Cremona of control over its *contado* (within which Soncino lay) in
May. There seems little doubt that Castruccio must have returned to
service with the Veronese forces in 1311 and accompanied these to the
siege of Brescia.[89] It is also possible that he knew Giovanni da Castiglione, another Lucchese exile, whom Henry VII made Proctor-
General of the Fisc in Lombardy and the March, and who was in
Cremona at this period collecting fines and taxes and confiscating
rebel goods.[90] If so, this could also perhaps explain is presence in
Soncino.

On Castruccio's life between 1304 and 1309 there is little or no reliable information. There is a suggestion by Raniero Granchi, in his

[84] S. Bongars, *Gesta dei per Francos* (Hanover, 1611), ii. 292.

[85] F. Winkler, *Castruccio Castracani: Herzog von Lucca* (Berlin, 1897), 14.

[86] Carrara, *Gli Scaligeri*, 66, C. Cipolla, *La storia politica di Verona* (Verona, 1900–54),
155.   [87] Bowsky, *Henry VII*, 117–25.

[88] L. Cavitelli, *Cremonenses annales* (Cremona, 1588), 106.

[89] That he was with the imperial army at Brescia is further suggested by the fact that
he named his second son Vallerano after Walram, Henry VII's brother killed during the
siege of that town (his first, Arrigo, was called after the emperor himself, the third,
Giovanni, after the emperor's son John, and the fourth, Guarnerio, after Werner von
Homburg, who was appointed captain-general in Lombardy by Henry VII in 1312, and
whom Castruccio almost certainly got to know at this period). (See Winkler, *Castruccio*,
9–10, I del Lungo, *I Bianchi e i Neri* (Second edn., Milan, 1921), 455.)

[90] Bowsky, *Henry VII*, 113.

poem *De proeliis Tusciae*,[91] that he was among the defenders of Pistoia at the time of its siege between May 1305 and April 1306. According to Davidsohn, he was among the Ghibellines who flocked to Cardinal Napoleone Orsini in Imola in 1306 and was already in Verona and Bergamo, presumably as a mercenary, in 1307.[92] The evidence for both these claims is, however, indirect and, to some extent, conjectural. The first rests on a statement by the Aragonese ambassador to Avignon in 1323 in which Castruccio is described as a former 'domicellus' and intimate of Napoleone Orsini.[93] Davidsohn feels this must refer to 1306 since it was only in that year that the cardinal's anti-Florentine political stance would have made it possible for Castruccio to serve him. This may well be so, but the evidence as it stands does not necessarily endorse this conclusion. The second claim derives from a notarial act of 1317 which acknowledges the deposit of 1,500 florins made by Castruccio in Verona and Bergamo at a date which Davidsohn gives as 1307.[94] This year does not appear, however, in this document as published by Mosiici[95] and may be the result of a misreading of the text or scribal error. What this source does establish is that Castruccio was paid 150 florins interest in Milan at a time when he was about to rejoin the Emperor Henry VII in Pisa, in other words in 1312, or 1313, a fact which suggests that the deposit was made in 1311 or 1312.[96]

The available evidence therefore provides no secure basis for determining Castruccio's movements between 1304 and 1309, though it hints at the possibility that he may have fought at Pistoia in 1305–6 and been in service thereafter with Cardinal Napoleone Orsini, and it confirms a financial windfall for him, most probably in 1311 or 1312. What can be said with near certainty, however, is that he was a mercenary in Verona for some time up to 1309, that he then went into

---

[91] *RIS*, xi. col. 344. At the time when Castruccio was besieging Pistoia in 1328, Granchi has him say that he himself had spent a year besieged in the town.

[92] Davidsohn, *Storia*, iv. 455, 823.

[93] H. Finke, *Acta aragonensia* (Berlin and Leipzig, 1908–22), ii. 607.

[94] Davidsohn, *Forschungen*, ii. 280.

[95] L. Mosiici, 'Ricerche sulla cancelleria di Castruccio Castracani', *Annali della scuola speciale per archivisti e bibliotecari dell'università di Roma* vii (1967), 32–3.

[96] The document specified that the sum of 150 florins was 10 per cent annual interest payment (ibid., 33) and no earlier interest payment was recorded. It is also unlikely, in view of Castruccio's need to borrow 300 florins from the commune of Venice in 1309, that he had deposited 1,500 florins with a banker in Verona and Bergamo two years earlier. If he had done so, why did he not withdraw some of his own capital to pay for his troops, rather than request an advance from his new employers?

Venetian service during the war of Ferrara when the Venetians engaged more troops for their military campaign against the papacy, and that he returned into employment with the Scaligeri after Henry VII's arrival in Italy. This in turn brought him into the imperial army at the siege of Brescia and, as a result, into contact with the other Ghibelline and White Guelph exiles who had flocked to it. It may well have been here, or later when the emperor moved on to Genoa and Pisa, that he first came to know Uguccione della Faggiuola, then Henry VII's imperial vicar in Genoa.[97] The critical link between the two men was probably forged at this period: the trust which Uguccione was to place in Castruccio was in all likelihood a product of his faith in the latter's impeccable Ghibelline credentials and his confidence in the Lucchese exile's proven military capacity exhibited as a soldier with the imperial army.

Whatever qualities Castruccio had, however, there is still something surprising in his choice, whether by Uguccione or the Lucchese Whites, as the head of their faction. At the time when the new peace terms between Pisa and Lucca were about to allow the exiles to return to their city, Castruccio could claim in his favour only his bonds of kinship with the powerful Interminelli family and his experience as a mercenary. Otherwise his early life had been without distinction. By now in his thirties, he had, since being banished and orphaned in 1301, led an existence that was precarious, violent, and (at least till about 1309) impoverished. An outlaw in England, a soldier of fortune in Flanders and Verona, he had been forced to borrow and beg to hold the modest position of a captain of twenty-six horse in the service of Venice. His marriage, contrary to Tegrimi's assertion,[98] repeated by later biographers,[99] that his wife came of the noble house of the lords of Corvara and Vallecchia, was a relatively humble one.[100]

---

[97] W. Doenniges, *Acta Henrici VII imperatoris romanorum et monumenta quaedam alia medii aevi*, 2 vols. (Berlin, 1839), i. 102, 103, 113–16.

[98] Tegrimi, *Vita*, 60.

[99] For instance, by Aldo Manucci, *Le azioni*, 29–30, who also attributes to Castruccio a spurious genealogy (pp. 5–10) and makes his mother Puccia a member of the same family as his wife (p. 12): Puccia was in fact Castruccio's mother's name as his will testifies (Lazzareschi, 'Documenti, 398), but this source gives no indication of her family.

[100] The origin of the legend that the Streghi, Castruccio's wife's family, were lords of Corvara and Vallecchia, is doubtless connected with the fact that, during Castruccio's period in power, his brothers-in-law Perotto, Ghirarduccio, and Giuffredo bought rights over parts of the lake of Porta Beltrame which had earlier been under the feudal jurisdiction of the lords of Corvara and Vallecchia. Some of these purchases were made

The Streghi, to whom his wife Pina belonged, were an undistinguished and seemingly fairly new Lucchese family. The earliest record I have been able to discover of them refers to Pina's grandfather Corbolano, the son of Jacopo Streghi, and is dated 12 June 1273.[101] The fact that this document appoints Corbolano guardian over the daughters of Pagano Corbolani, together with the evidence of his first name, may indicate that the Streghi had been a minor branch of the Corbolani which had broken off into a separate surname family only in the quite recent past. In the early years of the fourteenth century, there appear to have been only two Streghi families in Lucca, one descended from Corbolano, the other from Overardo Streghi—in itself a sign that the name then went back only a few generations. The Overardo branch, living in Borgo San Frediano, was represented by a Ghirardo or Gadduccio, the son of the late Overardo, who occurs in notarial records in 1300,[102] and 1311[103] and was dead by 1317 when his daughter Duccia and son Giovanni sold part of his estate to the other branch of the Streghi,[104] a circumstance that further indicates the close relationship between the two sides of the family. Corbolano's surviving descendants at this time were his sons Jacopo, Bindocco, and Ghirardo and Jacopo's four children—Pina who married Castruccio and her three brothers, Ghirardo (called Ghirarduccio to distinguish him from his

directly from the descendants of these nobles, together with lands in the Pietrasanta district, once subject to those lords. (ASL Diplomatico Corte dei Mercanti, 11/2/1322, 4/3/1322, 5/6/1322, 11/6/1322, 18/7/1322, 11/1/1323, Spedale 13/6/1322, and 6/9/1323.) It is clear from the deeds of sale involving the Streghi and the descendants of the lords of Corvara and Vallecchia that the two families were completely unrelated. See also ASL Diplomatico Archivio dei Notari 30/9/1295 and A. N. Cianelli, 'Dissertazioni sopra la storia lucchese', *Mem. e doc.*, iii, pt. 1, p. 196, the latter of which contains a petition of 1314 from the lords of Corvara and Vallecchia asking for the restoration of their rights over the lake of Porta Beltrame, the iron-mines at Farnocchia, and various villages, of which they had been deprived by the commune of Lucca. The purchases of land in and around Pietrasanta by the Streghi go back, in fact, even before the return of the White exiles to Lucca. (ASL Archivio notarile no. 29, 2/6/1314 and 7/6/1314 (Pisan style).) By the time of Castruccio's death, Perotto Streghi was so well established in Pietrasanta that, even with the Castracani out of favour, he was able to get from Ludwig of Bavaria endorsement of his title to the lake of Porta Beltrame (ASL Diplomatico Spedale, 4/4/1329) while in 1331 he was confirmed as *signore* of the town by a general parliament of its citizens (ASL Diplomatico Spedale, 22/2/1331). Tegrimi's assumption that the Streghi had been lords of Corvara and Vallecchia is therefore understandable: in a sense they succeeded to part of the possessions and dignities of these former feudal nobles.

[101]   ASL Diplomatico Archivio di Stato, 12/6/1273.
[102]   ASL Archivio notarile no. 52.
[103]   Ibid., no. 61, c. 254ᵛ.   [104]   Ibid., no. 64, c. 10ᵛ.

uncle), Perotto, and Giuffredo. This latter part of the family does not appear to be mentioned in any of the sources until February 1311 when Jacopo appeared in Pisa.[105] He had not earlier figured as a member of the Lucchese exile community, not even in the relatively comprehensive list of 30 June of the previous year,[106] so we can assume that he had only fairly recently arrived in the city, his sons and brothers following him after a short pause, for their names occur shortly after in notarial records in Pisa.[107] Since, by this time, Castruccio must have been married to his daughter Pina,[108] Jacopo's move to join the Lucchese Whites in their main centre may well have been influenced by his desire to identify himself with the political cause of his socially better-connected son-in-law, now that the Emperor Henry VII's presence on Italian soil had raised hopes of the restoration of Ghibelline exiles to their former positions. Castruccio, of course, was not then in Pisa, and by the time we know for certain that he was back there, Jacopo had died.[109] That the connection between Castruccio and the Streghi was, at this period, already a close one is nevertheless attested by the fact that, on his return to Pisa, he stayed in the house of his brother-in-law Ghirarduccio.[110]

But whatever material support he might at this stage have derived

---

[105] ASL Archivio notarile no. 29, 16/2/1311 (Pisan style).

[106] Ibid., 30/6/1311 (Pisan style). Nor is he mentioned in the less extensive list of exiles of 17 October 1310 (ibid., 17/10/1311 (Pisan style)), nor in the listing of the Lucchese and Pistoian Whites by the commune of Pisa on 31 July 1310 (Sforza, 'Castruccio . . . in esilio', 98–100, ASP Provvisioni degli Anziani, 4, c. 20ᵛ.–22ʳ.).

[107] Ghirardo is recorded in Ser Orlando Ciapparoni's notarial registers as present in Pisa from 5 January 1312, Perotto from 27 January 1312, Giuffredo and Ghirardo the elder (Jacopo's brother) from 7 June 1313, and Bindocco, Jacopo's other brother, from 22 April 1313. (ASL Archivio notarile no. 29, 5/1/1312, 27/1/1312, 22/4/1314, 7/6/1314 (Pisan style).) On the other hand, Ghirardo (or Gadduccio) was still in Lucca on 25 September 1311 (ASL Archivio notarile no. 61, c. 254ʳ.), so that his arrival in Pisa must have occurred between that date and the beginning of the following year.

[108] See Winkler, *Castruccio*, 10. The marriage dates of his two elder daughters (1325 and 1326) (see Lazzareschi, 'Documenti', 400) suggest that they were born well before 1311. Since it is unlikely that circumstances would have permitted Castruccio to marry between 1301 and 1304 and since he was almost certainly too young to have married before being exiled in 1301, his marriage probably took place between 1304 and 1309, in the period of his life about which we have no reliable information. Most likely it occurred in Pisa while Castruccio was still there in 1304 or a little later.

[109] Jacopo Streghi died between 15 April and 28 August 1312 (ASL Archivio notarile no. 29, 15/4/1313 and 28/8/1313 (Pisan style). The first mention of Castruccio in Pisa since 1304 is on 22 August 1313, at least a year after his father-in-law's death, ibid., 22/8/1314 (Pisan style).

[110] Or at least had his notarial act witnessed there: ASL Archivio notarile, no. 29, 22/8/1314 (Pisan style).

from his wife's family, it is clear that it can hardly have enhanced his standing with the major figures among the Lucchese Whites: the Streghi had not been banished in 1301, did not belong to the patrician sector of Lucchese society from which the leading exiles came, and had only joined their faction belatedly,[111] in what must have seemed an opportunist gesture aimed at exploiting their relationship to Castruccio when the political tide was beginning to turn in favour of the Ghibellines. Married, then, into a family more modest than his own, with little in his past to recommend him, with few resources but his military skill, Castruccio must have seemed at this time, as Marino Sanudo was to describe him in his letter of 1325, an ant risen from the dust destined, with that other upstart, Galeazzo Visconti of Milan, to throw Lombardy and Tuscany into confusion.[112] But from this point onward, his fortunes changed dramatically, thanks partly to the use Uguccione della Faggiuola sought to make of him, partly to a combination of force of personality and what one can only describe as sheer luck.

Returned to Lucca, he became the spokesman of the repatriated exiles, particularly in the negotiations with Uguccione which became necessary once it was evident that the Lucchese authorities were not prepared to honour the pledge they had made, in the terms of the peace, to restore to the members of the readmitted faction the property, offices, and benefits of which they had been deprived in 1301. When the dissatisfied Lucchese Whites objected to their treatment, Uguccione remonstrated with the Lucchese ambassadors that their commune had failed to carry out its side of the agreement. These, however, replied that they had understood its terms differently, as not entailing the compensation of the returned exiles for their previous losses, nor their installation as part of the ruling regime.[113] Dispute also arose over the handing over of Buti and Bientina to the Pisans,[114] which should have followed the reconciliation between the formerly opposed Lucchese factions. Having obtained no satisfaction from his representations to the Lucchese government, Uguccione now turned to the exiles themselves. Meeting them in the church of San Jacopo

---

[111] Jacopo Streghi appears on the list of exiles only on 7 and 15 October 1311: ibid., 7/10/1312 and 15/10/1312 (Pisan style).
[112] Bongars, *Gesta*, ii. 292.
[113] BNF MS Palat. 571, c. 18ᵛ., Sardo, *Cronaca*, 67, Mussato, 'De gestis italicorum', col. 603, Giovanni di Lemmo, 'Diario', 190–1.
[114] Mussato, 'De gestis italicorum', col. 603.

del Poggio, he listened to their complaints and then conferred secretly with two of the Interminelli, Castruccio Castracani and Giovanni Parghia,[115] with whom he hatched the plot that was to bring about the betrayal, capture, and sack of Lucca.

Whilst Castruccio and the Interminelli were undoubtedly the prime movers in this conspiracy, however, the chroniclers agree that those who adhered to it were not merely the members of the White faction. A powerful group of families which had remained in Lucca between 1301 and 1314 was both privy to it and supported it actively. Villani associates the Quartigiani and Onesti with it, as well as the formerly banished Poggio and Interminelli.[116] Ser Giovanni di Lemmo and the anonymous author of the 'Storie pistoresi'[117] add the name of the Bernarducci, previously allies of the dominant Obizi family, but now estranged from it. Whether their motive was jealousy of the Obizi or disenchantment with the Guelph regime which had discriminated against them through the Statute of 1308 (still in force at this time, despite the disgrace of Bonturo Dati and the decline in the influence of the artisan 'demagogues'), there were clearly many sections of the Lucchese patriciate prepared to invite Pisan intervention in order to overthrow the existing government. They doubtless failed to realize the full implications of the plot they allowed themselves to be involved in: the sack of Lucca and the establishment of Uguccione's tyranny can hardly have been among their aims. Yet their role in the events of June 1314 is evidence of the strength of the undercurrent of opposition to the prevailing political order on the part of the greater families of the city whose power it restricted. Once an opportunity for change offered itself in the form of external intervention which could counter-balance the effects of Florentine support for the status quo, a group of previously Guelph houses or *casate*[118] did not hesitate to seize it, even if it meant alliance with Ghibellines and former exiles.

The plan of the conspirators involved an advance of the Pisan army to the walls of Lucca under the cover of darkness, followed by a rising in the city of their supporters, signalled to those outside by the display of a sheet from the top of the Torre del Veglio.[119] The Pisans had been

---

[115] Ferreto Vicentino, 'Historia', ii. 194. Sardo, *Cronaca*, BNF MS Palat. 571 (c. 18ᵛ.), and 'Cronica di Pisa', *RIS*, xv, col. 990.

[116] G. Villani, *Cronica*, ix. 60.

[117] Giovanni di Lemmo, 'Diario', 191, 'Storie pistoresi', 60.

[118] Sercambi, *Croniche*, pt. I, c.116 (vol. i, p. 61), states that there were twenty-two houses, that is, clans or extended families, prepared to yield Lucca to Uguccione.

[119] Ibid., Sardo, *Cronaca*, 69, says 'uno manto', a cloak.

worked up for the attack by a display of popular indignation at the
refusal of the Lucchese to observe the terms of the recently concluded
peace: crowds shouting, 'To Lucca, to Lucca', had surged through the
streets after the unsuccessful meeting with the Lucchese ambassadors,[120] their mercenaries had been sent to Pontetetto on the
Lucchese *contado* to intimidate the enemy, and finally the Pisan citizen
levies were marshalled and led, in haste, on to Lucchese territory on
the evening of 13 June 1314.[121] In the meantime, in Lucca itself,
Castruccio seized the tower of the Tre Cappelle at sunset on the
thirteenth and, during the night, fortified the houses of the Onesti, the
Faitinelli, and the campanile of San Frediano.[122] His followers then
rode through the streets to the war-cry of 'Death to the traitors' and
'Long live the people'.[123] Roused by the noise, the Obizi and their
partisans gathered together their forces and mounted an assault on the
Onesti houses and the San Frediano quarter which the Ghibellines
had made their stronghold. In the ensuing scuffle, Nantino Salamoncelli, one of their supporters, was killed. They were beginning, nevertheless, to gain the upper hand, having recaptured the campanile of
San Frediano, when Uguccione and his troops arrived at the city
gates.[124] Setting fire to the posterns of San Frediano and of San Giorgio, the Pisans scaled the town walls, meeting with no resistance. Once
the Obizi realized that Uguccione's men had entered Lucca, they
withdrew hurriedly, not merely from the quarter in which they had
been fighting, but from the city itself.[125] They took with them the vicar
of the king of Naples, Gherardo da San Lupidio (Guelph Lucca, like
Florence, had earlier accepted the sovereignty of King Robert of
Naples as a form of protection against its Ghibelline enemies),[126] and
the leading members of the Tassignano, Porcari, and Salamoncelli
families.[127] These patricians of the Obizi faction then retired to Fucecchio where they met the contingent of Florentine troops which had
been dispatched in a belated attempt to save Lucca from the Pisans.

---

[120] Sardo, *Cronaca*, 68, and Mussato, 'De gestis italicorum', col. 603.
[121] Mussato, 'De gestis italicorum', col. 604, Sardo, *Cronaca*, 69.
[122] 'Storie pistoresi', 61.
[123] Sardo, *Cronaca*, 69.
[124] 'Storie pistoresi', 61, Mussato, 'De gestis italicorum', col. 604.
[125] Sardo, *Cronaca*, 69, Mussato, 'De gestis italicorum', col. 604.
[126] The Lucchese had made Robert of Naples their protector and received his vicar
after the Pisan incursions on their *contado* at the end of the previous year. See 'Storie
pistoresi', 59.
[127] Giovanni di Lemmo, 'Diario', 191.

Here, and in the neighbouring Val d'Arno towns of Santa Maria a Monte, Santa Croce, and Castelfranco, they established their line of defence.[128]

The city they had left was consequently abandoned to its captors who, for the next two days,[129] mercilessly sacked it. 'Then Uguccione's men', a chronicler wrote, 'began to rob the city, to take men and women prisoner and make them ransom themselves, and corrupted girls, generally sleeping with all those that they captured, and it happened that one lady let herself die of grief, rather than ever eat or drink again, on account of the great sorrow that she felt at having been carnally known against her will. The Pistoian Whites and Ghibellines who were there were those who robbed most and were worse in killing men and in holding prisoners to ransom than any other group . . .'[130] In addition to the robbing, killing, raping, and extortion of money, there was the burning of the houses of the members of the expelled faction, the Obizi, the Chiavari, Rafagnelli, and Porcari.[131] The German mercenaries in Pisan pay appear to have been the most systematic in their plunder of the city, sparing only the property of the Whites and Ghibellines. They even looted the shop leased by Castruccio's uncle Coluccio and Santo Castracani, on the grounds that it contained merchandise belonging to its owners, the Guelph Uberti. When Castruccio was called to the scene, they punctiliously pointed out that they had not touched Coluccio's house, but agreed to leave the shop alone also, if they were paid 100 florins.[132] Considering that only the recently introduced White exiles and the families who had joined them in the plot against the city would have been regarded as non-Guelph, virtually the whole of the wealth of Lucca was prey to the depredations of the Germans, the Pisans, the Tuscan Ghibellines, and Castruccio and his associates.

The immense amount of booty taken from the city in the sack was augmented by the plunder of the bulk of the papal treasure that happened at this time to be housed in the sacristy of the Augustinian church of San Frediano. After Clement V had moved his residence from Rome to Avignon, Cardinal Gentile da Montefiore had been

---

[128] G. Villani, *Cronica*, ix. 60, 'Storie pistoresi', 62, Giovanni di Lemmo, 'Diario', 191.
[129] According to the 'Storie pistoresi', 60; G. Villani, *Cronica*, ix. 60, says eight days.
[130] 'Storie pistoresi', 60.
[131] BNF MS Palat. 571, c. 19ʳ.
[132] The whole bizarre episode is recounted in full in Santo Castracani's will, published by F. P. Luiso, 'Mercanti', 92–4.

charged with the task of bringing the papal treasure to the south of France from Perugia where it had been since the death of Benedict XI. He did not, however, set out with it until 1312, when Henry VII's presence in northern Italy forced him to interrupt his journey in Lucca. Here he died on 27 October of that year, leaving the greater part of the treasure at San Frediano and the remainder at the Dominican house of San Romano.[133] According to the anonymous author of the 'Storie pistoresi', it was worth more than a million florins.[134]

In the course of the sack of the city, the sacristy of San Frediano was plundered and the treasure it contained stolen. We know from chroniclers' accounts and from the text of a subsequent papal bull of excommunication directed at Castruccio that this act of robbery was commited by him, some German mercenaries, and certain Lucchese,[135] doubtless aided and abetted by Uguccione and the Pisans who also received their share of the loot.[136] The extent to which members of leading Lucchese families were implicated in their plunder is evident from later notarial records. In late 1322 and early 1323, when Castruccio's regime had become unpopular with many of its previous aristocratic supporters, some of those responsible for pillaging the papal treasure in San Frediano in 1314 sought to make their peace with the papacy. As a result, we have a number of remarkable notarial acts in the register of Ser Federigo del fu Ser Bianchi of Marlia[137] which constitute confessions of complicity in the thefts from San Frediano and which offer compensation to obtain pardon for the

---

[133] K. Wenck, 'Ueber päpstliche Schatzverzeichnisse des 13. und 14. Jahrhunderts und ein Verzeichnis der päpstlichen Bibliothek vom Jahre 1311', *Mitteilungen des Instituts für oesterreichische Geschichtsforschung*, vi (1885), 273–4, L. Caforio, 'Il sacco di Lucca e il furto di S. Frediano e di S. Romano', *La biblioteca delle scuole italiane*, xvii (1905), 201–2; G. Villani, *Cronica*, ix. 22.

[134] 'Storie pistoresi', 60.

[135] Sardo, *Cronaca*, 69, BNF MS Palat. 571, c. 19ʳ. G. Villani, on the other hand, attributes the theft to Uguccione, his German mercenary bands, and the Pisans (ix. 60). The first of the papal bulls referring to the theft of the treasure, that of 31 March 1317 (see S. Riezler, *Vatikanische Akten zur deutschen Geschichte in der Zeit Ludwigs des Baiern* (Innsbruck, 1891), 19–20, E. Baluze (S. Baluzio), *Vitae Paparum Avenionensium* (Paris, 1693), vol. ii, cols. 305–8, and ASV Registro Vaticano, no. 63 fo. 352ᵛ.), makes no mention of Castruccio but does allude to the later appropriation of the treasure in San Romano by Francesco della Faggiuola. The papal letter, 'Angit nos', of 30 April 1325 (ASV Reg. Vat. no. 114, ff. 188ᵛ.–189ʳ.) does however accuse Castruccio and his accomplices of seizing and carrying away the papal treasure in San Frediano.

[136] G. Villani, *Cronica*, ix. 60.

[137] ASL Archivio notarile no. 95, cc. 63ᵛ.–80ʳ. See also BSL MS 920 vol. iii 1324, no. 46, for evidence of the participation of Frediano di Barone, goldsmith of Borgo San Frediano, in this theft.

offences committed. The list of those acknowledging their crimes and proposing to make amends for them consists of members of some of the most prominent families in the Borgo San Frediano and the adjoining *contrada* of San Giovanni in Capo di Borgo, including Andreuccio, Vanni, and Coluccio Martini, Lippo Toringhelli, Mottino Squarcialupi, Vanni Maurini, and Franceschino and Ciandorino Pantassa. On their own admission (which must surely have underestimated the full value of what they took) their combined haul amounted to gold and silver and other goods which were later sold for over 3,000 florins. We do not know how many other leading citizens of these *contrade* which lay in the immediate vicinity of the church of San Frediano participated in the plunder; but it is likely that many more took advantage of the confusion preceding the entry of the Pisan troops into the city to help themselves to what they could grab of the papal treasure. Indeed, the fact that it was the quarter of San Frediano that the rebels and would-be Lucchese traitors made their stronghold on the night of 13 June may well not be unconnected with the presence in its principal church of several hundred thousand florins' worth of gold and silver. The prospect of all that wealth temptingly within their midst might well have persuaded some waverers of the potential financial advantages of joining in the conspiracy.

While there can be little doubt about the immediate impact of the sack of Lucca upon the city's industry and prosperity, its long-term effects are more difficult to estimate. Traditionally, scholars have taken the year 1314 as marking a turning-point in the history of the town, bringing to an end the age of its commercial expansion and signalling the onset of its decline. In particular, it has been assumed that those who were sent into exile at that time took with them the secrets of silk manufacture and so brought about the transplanting of that industry from Lucca to Florence, Venice, and Bologna.[138] But such claims are, in reality, impossible to substantiate (or for that matter to refute conclusively) because of the paucity of evidence on the level of either silk production or general business activity in the thirteenth century relative to that prevailing in the fourteenth. The sources recording commercial transactions are as ample, if indeed not more extensive, in the period 1316 to 1328 as they are for the years before 1314. While many Guelphs undoubtedly went into exile when Uguccione took Lucca, the Whites who had been expelled in 1301 also

---

[138] See, for instance, T. Bini, *I lucchesi*, 158.

returned at this time. It is difficult to find reliable evidence on the relative sizes of these two groups. Tegrimi[139] claimed that as many as 300 families left Lucca after the sack of 1314; but this figure finds no confirmation in contemporary sources. Most probably, it derives from a misreading of a Venetian chronicle which speaks of the arrival of 300 Lucchese silkworkers (not families) in Venice between 1310 and 1340.[140] The evidence there is suggests that individual members of a fairly large number of families did leave Lucca, but many of them before 1314 and some in the course of the following twenty or thirty years.[141] Equally, the sack of that year cannot be blamed for the passing of the secrets of silk manufacture to other centres since evidence of the migration of Lucchese silk workers goes back to 1272.[142] At the same time, it is clear that a number of artisans working in that industry did leave Lucca in 1314 and that their flight to such cities as Florence, Bologna, and Venice did give a fillip to the emerging silk industries there. The communes of Florence and Bologna made special provision to encourage exiled silk weavers to settle in their towns within a short period after the fall of Lucca in 1314,[143] explicitly referring in the relevant decrees to the expulsion of these artisans following the change of regime there. That a number did so is evident from Florentine documentary sources[144] and from later appeals by the commune

[139] Tegrimi, *Vita*, 32.

[140] G. B. Gallicholi, *Delle memorie venete antiche* (Venice, 1795), ii. 274, on the authority of an earlier chronicle.

[141] A manuscript biography of Castruccio Castracani written in the sixteenth century and attributed to Agostino Ricchi (ASL Manoscritti Orsucci 36, c. 15ᵛ.) named thirty-one families which allegedly fled between 1310 and 1320, but of these at least thirteen were present in Lucca in the Castruccian period. His list was almost certainly derived from a register which had once belonged to Nicolo Marcello who was doge of Venice in 1473–4 and which indicated those Lucchese families which were trading in that city in 1320 (see BSL MS 1556, p. 177, and ASL Manoscritti 10, ii. p. 508). Confused with this was another list of Lucchese merchants who contributed money for the chapel of the Volto Santo in Venice (see ASL MS Orsucci 36, cc. 15ᵛ.–16ᵛ., BSL MS 1556, pp. 177–84). Bernardino Baroni, the eighteenth-century genealogist (BSL MS 925 Quaderno 44, no. 13 and Quaderno 55, no. 46), conflated these lists and others of Lucchese families resident in Venice at various dates between 1310 and 1340 to produce three sets of 31, 18, and 148 names of families supposedly driven into exile by Uguccione della Faggiuola and Castruccio Castracani. These, however, include a large number of houses which can be shown to have resided in Lucca under these rulers.

[142] See S. Bongi, *Della mercatura*, 41, G. Livi, 'I mercanti', 30–3. On Lucchese silk merchants in Venice before 1314, see also Bini, *I lucchesi*, i. 167.

[143] See the decrees in favour of Lucchese silk workers of 9–12 August 1314 in Florence and of 25 April 1315 in Bologna published in Livi, *I mercanti*, 54–5 and 50–1.

[144] See Davidsohn, *Forschungen*, iii. 215, 217, for references to Lucchese silk weavers in Florence in 1319.

of Lucca in 1342 to departed silk workers to return home.[145] Just how many, however, of those who had gone by that date left in 1314 and how many earlier or later is difficult to determine. Of those who did come back between 1343 and 1347 in response to the amnesty from penalties for carrying on silk manufacture elsewhere,[146] the majority were of families whose names occur in notarial registers in the Castruccian period. This makes it likely that most of them had gone away in the troubled years after 1328 and had not escaped from the city in 1314.

From all contemporary evidence it seems clear that there is little basis for believing in a mass exodus of Lucchese families in 1314. The view that this occurred is the product of a much later historical legend. Equally, the belief that the decline of the economy of Lucca began in this year would appear to be the result of telescoping the temporary arrest of commercial activity which did follow the sack of the city with the far more serious recession in trade and agriculture of the years after 1328. Such indications as the sources furnish point rather to a revival of economic prosperity under the Castruccian regime in which silk manufacture, in particular, played an important part,[147] though, in our present state of knowledge, it is impossible to say whether this represented an advance on the pre-1314 period or merely on the immediate aftermath of the fall of the city.

Whatever the long-term results of the sack, there is no doubt that its immediate consequences, coupled with the effective subjugation of the town to the hated Pisans and Uguccione, made the situation in Lucca difficult for both victors and vanquished. The city was drawn into the war against Florence and, while Uguccione directed the military operations this entailed, placed under the administration of his son Francesco. Border villages which had been taken from the Pisans over the previous half-century or so were now returned to them: Asciano, Quosa, Castiglione di Val di Serchio, Cotone, Aquilata, Ponte al Serchio, Avane, Nozzano, and Passerino had their fortifications demolished while Ripafratta, Viareggio, Rotaio, and Sarzana became Pisan strongholds guarding against the possibility of a resumed expansion of the Lucchese territory.[148] Motrone the small

[145] Livi, 'I mercanti', 46, 53.

[146] See lists of the families who returned to Lucca in these years in Livi, 'I mercanti', 46–7.

[147] See my article, 'Lucchese commerce under Castruccio Castracani', *ACCC*, 217–64.   [148] G. Villani, *Cronica*, ix. 68, Sardo, *Cronaca*, 70.

Lucchese port on the Versilian coast, held out till August, when it too passed into Pisan hands.[149] In the meantime, Uguccione pressed the advantage he had gained through the capture of Lucca further with incursions into the *contado* of Pistoia, into the Val d'Arno, and towards Volterra.[150] The Florentines, following the fall of Lucca, had seized the small towns in the east and south of the Lucchese state that were still held by the Guelphs.[151] On these Uguccione now mounted a systematic attack, taking Cigoli and Montecalvoli in May 1315 and then moving on with as many as 6,000 Lucchese citizen troops,[152] to concentrate his attention on Montecatini, the hill village that dominated the Val di Nievole and to which he had laid siege for some time.[153]

Meanwhile, in Lucca itself, Francesco della Faggiuola took over from his father Uguccione the offices of captain and *podestà* to which the latter had been appointed after the capture of Lucca.[154] At the time of the change in regime, all former communal statutes, including that of 1308, had been annulled[155] and new *anziani* or aldermen chosen.[156] Secure in his control of the government, Francesco proceeded with his expropriation of Guelph property by seizing the remainder of the papal treasure left in Lucca by Cardinal Gentile. Most of it had been taken from San Frediano on the night of the fall of the city. About a third of it, however, remained in the Dominican convent of San Romano. On 2 December 1314, Francesco della Faggiuola's vicar forced his way in there and appropriated it,[157] doubtless to help pay for

---

[149] Sardo, *Cronaca*, 70. See also BNF MS Palat. 571, c. 19ʳ.

[150] G. Villani, *Cronica*, ix. 68. See also Davidsohn, *Storia*, iv. 786–7, 793–5, for a detailed account of the minor hostilities between Uguccione and the Florentines at this period.

[151] G. Villani, *Cronica*, ix. 71. The towns were Fucecchio, Santa Maria a Monte, Montecalvoli, Santa Croce, Castelfranco, and Montopoli in the Val d'Arno and Montecatini and Monsummano in the Val di Nievole. Serravalle, however, fell into the hands of the Whites and Ghibellines at the time of the fall of Lucca and was given by them to Uguccione.

[152] BNF MS Palat. 571, c. 19ʳ.

[153] Davidsohn, *Storia*, iv. 793–5, Mussato, 'De gestis italicorum', cols. 630–3, G. Villani, *Cronica*, ix. 68, 70.

[154] Cianelli, 'Dissertazioni', i. 243–4.

[155] Bongi and Del Prete, 'Il statuto', p. xliii.

[156] Cianelli, 'Dissertazioni', 243.

[157] See ASL Diplomatico Biblioteca Miscellanea, 2 December 1314, published in G. D. Mansi, *Miscellanea*, vol. i, 617–18, for a description of the seizure of the treasure. ASV Reg. Vat. 63, fo. 352ᵛ., published by E. Baluze, *Vitae*, vol. ii, cols. 305–8, and S. Riezler, *Vatikanische Akten*, 19–20, for the papal condemnation for the theft, and L. Caforio, 'Il sacco', 202, for a discussion of it.

the military campaign then being waged by Uguccione against the Florentines.

2. The battle of Montecatini and the expulsion of Uguccione della Faggiuola

In the months that followed the capture of Lucca in which he had played such a vital part, Castruccio did not remain idle; but it is interesting that his energies at this time were directed less to supporting Uguccione's attempts to recover control of the eastern and southern frontiers of the former Lucchese state than to establishing his own position at the opposite end of it, in the bishopric of Luni. Equally remarkable is the fact that, as Giovanni Sforza has shown,[158] this arch-Ghibelline owed the right to exercise administrative power which he obtained here (the first territorial jurisdiction he enjoyed in his life) not to any of his partisans but to the exiled Guelph bishop of Luni, Gherardino Malaspina, who saw in him a means by which to retain some degree of influence over his see in which, for political reasons, he had otherwise lost real authority. Gherardino, chosen as bishop in a disputed election after the death of his predecessor in 1307 and confirmed by Pope Clement V in 1312 had, on account of his Guelph sympathies, been deprived of his possessions by the Emperor Henry VII in 1313 and had since lived in exile at Fucecchio.[159] It was here, in a town still under Florentine control, that, on 4 July 1314, he received Castruccio's agent, Ghibellino Mariano, and, though him, conceded to Castruccio the title of viscount of the episcopate of Luni, which gave the latter jurisdiction over its lands in the absence of the bishop.[160] This appointment was followed up, on 5 December of the same year, by the election on the part of the commune of Sarzana, which lay within the bishopric, of Castruccio as its vicar-general for the period of two years, or until the emperor (or his vicar) resumed his authority over the town.[161] In effect these grants made Castruccio the virtual ruler of a small territory in the extreme north-west of the state of Lucca, in the area where it adjoined Liguria. The jurisdiction which he enjoyed was, of course, conditional and temporary; but Castruccio

[158] G. Sforza, 'Castruccio Castracani degli Antelminelli in Lunigiana', *Atti e memorie delle deputazioni di storia patria per le provincie modenesi e parmensi* (Ser. III), vi, pt. 2 (1891), 315–17.

[159] Ibid., 305–12. See also G. Volpe, *Toscana medievale* (Florence, 1964), 523–4.

[160] Text of deed in ASL Atti di Castruccio, no. 1, cc. 8ᵛ.–95 published in Lazzareschi, 'Documenti', 291–2.

[161] ASL Atti di Castruccio, no. 1, cc. 9ʳ.–10ʳ. in Lazzareschi, 'Documenti', 292–4.

was not the man to allow that to prevent him from consolidating his hold on it. On 5 and 6 August 1315, he managed, through the good offices of Werner von Homburg, his one-time companion in arms at the siege of Brescia and now an intimate of the new emperor-elect, to obtain from Frederick III his appointment as imperial vicar over all the places in his possession.[162] This confirmed his authority, giving it a legitimate basis. The tactic which he employed in this case was to serve him as a model later when, as tyrant of Lucca, he aspired to find a firmer foundation for his government than popular election or the violent seizure of power.

At this stage, however, Castruccio probably saw himself, and was certainly seen by others, not as a would-be despot of Lucca but as a war-lord whose Ghibelline connections and military and political capacities made of him an ideal protector for a vulnerable territory or town. The documents granting him his rights as administrator over the bishopric of Luni and over Sarzana make it clear that he was regarded in the one case as 'a noble, powerful and vigorous man' and, in the other, as one distinguished by 'power and virtue' as well as by his actions performed for 'the exaltation of the Empire and its supporters'.[163] Doubtless Castruccio saw the gains he had achieved as a foothold for further advance, but as yet his ambition seems to have been limited to acquiring a territorial base of his own while remaining subject to Uguccione as a citizen of Lucca. Uguccione for his part, as later events were to show, could not have viewed with favour the assumption by a leading Lucchese patrician of such independent power; but for the time being he was too preoccupied with the war against Florence to risk a confrontation with one of his most prominent supporters. By the summer of 1315, hostilities in the Val di Nievole were reaching a critical stage and he needed all the forces he could muster against an increasingly formidable enemy.

The Florentines had reacted in a way characteristic of them to the fall of Lucca and Uguccione's subsequent campaign against the line of fortified places to the east and south of that city. As when they were faced with attack by the Emperor Henry VII, they called for help from the kingdom of Naples and from their other Guelph allies, providing money for the raising of mercenary cavalry that was to be commanded in the field by a member of the Angevin ruling family or one of his

---

[162] Ibid., 294–6.
[163] Ibid., 291, 293.

generals. In this case, King Robert of Naples chose not to come himself to the aid of Florence, but sent first one of his brothers, Peter of
Eboli, nicknamed 'Tempesta', and then another, Philip of Taranto,
accompanied by the latter's son Charles. Peter of Eboli had reached
Florence with 300 knights as early as 18 August 1314; but his lack of
success in containing Uguccione's advance led to the dispatch from
Naples in June of the following year of an additional force of 500
cavalry and 300 infantry under the command of Philip of Taranto who,
however, having been held up by a bout of quartan fever in Siena, did
not enter Florence until 6 August. His arrival was almost immediately
followed by a renewed assault upon the Val di Nievole by Uguccione
who, anticipating the increase in the size of the Florentine forces, was
determined to press his attack on Montecatini before that stronghold
could be relieved.[164]

The armies of both sides had by this time grown considerably as the
result of the calling in of contingents from allies. The Ghibelline
forces consisted of Uguccione's German cavalry, other mercenaries,
Tuscan and Italian exiles, Pisan and Lucchese knights, detachments
of horse sent by the Ubertini and Pazzi of Val d'Arno, the bishop of
Arezzo, Matteo Visconti of Milan, Can Grande della Scala of Verona,
and other north Italian tyrants—together with a considerable body of
mainly Pisan and Lucchese infantry. Albertino Mussato estimated
that it contained 2,750 cavalry and 20,000 infantry,[165] Giovanni Villani
2,500 cavalry and a very large number of infantry,[166] Ferreto Vicentino
no more than 3,000 knights and over 70,000 infantry,[167] and Cortusio
about 3,000 knights and 20,000 infantry.[168] There is sufficient correspondence between these figures, with the exception of Ferreto's
clearly inflated one of 70,000, to suggest that Uguccione had under his
command somewhere between 2,500 and 3,000 knights and about
20,000 foot soldiers.

The Guelph army was, by general agreement of the chroniclers,
substantially larger. By the time Philip of Taranto and his son Charles
reached Florence, the original nucleus of the Florentine civic militia

[164] Davidsohn, *Storia*, iv. 785–6, 795–8. The date of the arrival in Florence of Philip of
Taranto and his son is that given by Giovanni di Lemmo, 'Diario', 196, which is generally accepted, not 11 July as in G. Villani, *Cronica*, ix. 70. Uguccione left Pisa on 10
August (ASP Comune A214, c. 23ᵛ.).
[165] Mussato, 'De gestis italicorum', col. 634.
[166] G. Villani, *Cronica*, ix. 71.
[167] Ferreto Vicentino, 'Historia', 200.
[168] G. Cortusio, 'Historia de novitatibus Paduae et Lombardiae', *RIS*, xii, col. 793.

had been augmented by the knights who had accompanied Peter of
Eboli and Philip of Taranto from Naples, by the Sienese contingent
that had joined the latter in the closing stages of his journey, by
various mercenaries, and by detachments from Bologna, Perugia,
Viterbo, Orvieto, Città di Castello, Gubbio, Pistoia, Prato, the Val
d'Elsa, and the Romagna. Altogether, the mounted troops were
reckoned by Mussato to number 4,200 after the arrival of Peter of
Eboli and between 3,500 and 3,700 on the eve of the battle of Montecatini,[169] when Villani put them at 3,200 and Cortusio at 4,000.
Mussato and Cortusio agreed on the figure of 30,000 as representing
the size of the Guelph infantry, once again merely described as 'very
large' by Villani.[170] Accepting Mussato's figures as a mean in both
cases and most likely to be accurate, we can assume that the Guelphs
had nearly a thousand more knights by the late summer of 1315 than
Uguccione and about 10,000 more infantry, but that the Ghibellines
probably had a slight advantage in mercenary cavalry.

The intensification of the attack on Montecatini and the plight of its
two thousand defenders,[171] by now very short of food and reduced to
eating 'asses, dogs and cats',[172] almost certainly led Philip of Taranto
to move his army without delay to a position where it might dislodge
the besieging forces or at least enable the beleagured town to be
resupplied. Still suffering from sickness, he left Florence soon after his
arrival and advanced with his troops down the Arno valley to Fucecchio from where he moved north towards Montecatini, setting up
camp near Montevettolini on 16 August.[173] The two armies now
confronted each other across the tiny stream of Nievole and the
marshes which lay on either side of it. For the next thirteen days leading up to the decisive battle of the twenty-ninth, their commanders
played out an opening game of move and counter-move, manœuvring
their forces into position for the final engagement.

The area in which the clash between them was to be resolved
formed a natural amphitheatre ringed on three sides by hills, with the
swamps north of the Arno valley closing it off to the south. Like
Castruccio's victory at Altopascio a decade later, the battle which was

[169] Mussato, 'De gestis italicorum', cols. 624–5. James II of Aragon's Genoese correspondents, Bernabò Doria and Christiano Spinola, claimed Philip of Taranto had 3,700
and 4,000–5,000 knights respectively (Finke, *Acta*, iii, 292–3).
[170] Mussato, 'De gestis italicorum', col. 625. Cortusio, 'Historia', *RIS*, xii, col. 793, G.
Villani, *Cronica*, ix. 71.   [171] Vigo, *Uguccione*, 170.
[172] 'Storie pistoresi', 65.   [173] Giovanni di Lemmo, 'Diario', 197.

to be fought in it would be dominated by the interplay of two positional strategies, each suggested by the nature of the terrain.

On the face of it, the situation in which the opposing armies were
placed in the fortnight preceding the battle of Montecatini seemed
more favourable to the Florentines. Uguccione was in the predicament of having, against superior odds, both to maintain the siege he
was engaged in and to keep open his lines of communication and
supply with Lucca. This left him vulnerable to attack along a relatively
long front, all of which he could not hope to defend. Philip of Taranto
realized this weakness in the position of the Ghibellines. After moving
his camp foward to the foot of Monsummano on 19 August so that only
the Nievole separated him from the besieging force of Pisans and
Lucchese, he sent a troop of cavalry under one of his captains, Carroccio, across that stream the next day to probe their defences. In the
ensuing skirmish, several Pisans were killed and a German knight,
Wilhelm von Löwenberg, captured. Cautioned by this attack, Uguccione brought his army forward three days later to block Philip of
Taranto's advance. Undeterred by this, however, the Guelphs also
edged in closer to the Nievole, so narrowing the distance between the
two bodies of troops.

At the same time, Uguccione was clearly becoming nervous about
the possibility of a Guelph thrust to his rear, aimed at cutting his
supply route, for on the twenty-fifth he redeployed part of his forces at
Buggiano in Piano on the road to Lucca. His fears proved well
founded. Early on the following morning, while the main body of
Philip of Taranto's army advanced to within a bowshot of the Pisan
lines, a small detachment of two hundred knights and some infantry
executed a rapid flanking movement by way of Fucecchio which took
them well beyond Buggiano in Uguccione's rear to the village of
Vivinaia, situated on the hill slopes in the next valley in the direction
of Lucca. Knowing beforehand that its inhabitants were ready to rise
against Uguccione, this small party could move quickly, first taking
Vivinaia with the support of its people and then seizing the neighbouring hamlet of San Martino in Colle where it overwhelmed and killed
the defending garrison of sixty Ghibellines who were guarding the
road to Lucca. This route they cut the next day, capturing a supply
train of forty wagons on its way to the Pisan and Lucchese camp below
Montecatini.[174]

[174] Ibid.

This in effect interrupted the flow of food to the Ghibelline army which was consequently placed in a very serious position. Up until this time, Uguccione had been playing a waiting game: if the chronicler Cortusio is to be believed,[175] he was attempting to postpone a major engagement until more troops had reached him from Can Grande della Scala of Verona and other north Italian tyrants. The daring manœuvre executed by Philip of Taranto's cavalry now denied him the chance to hold his enemy at bay until the arrival of reinforcements enabled his army to match that of the Florentines. He was faced with a choice between withdrawal and clinging on to the siege with rapidly dwindling supplies. In fact, the strategy of his opponent had, up to this stage, worked brilliantly against him. By keeping up a constant pressure on the Pisans and Lucchese entrenched around Montecatini, Philip of Taranto had drawn forward and then held down the main body of the Ghibelline forces, so attenuating their lines of defence against the kind of lightning strike in their rear which had now succeeded with such devastating effect.

Having, however, up to this point, waged an impeccable campaign, the Guelph commander failed to exploit with sufficient speed the advantage he had gained. Instead of immediately moving his troops forward to block Uguccione's retreat, he was induced by the plight of the besieged garrison of Montecatini to dispatch, on the night of 28 August, a relief force of a hundred knights under Simone da Villa to bring provisions into the town. Only when this detachment had successfully crossed and recrossed the enemy lines did he strike camp on the following morning and lead his army towards Buggiano with the intention of placing himself between Uguccione's main force and Lucca.[176] But by then it was too late. 'That fox, that is Uguccione', as one chronicler described him,[177] had begun to withdraw the previous night, burning the 'battifolli' or palisades protecting the besieger's camp around Montecatini as he left.[178] It was undoubtedly this that had accounted for Simone da Villa's ability to reprovision that stronghold without resistance. And it was this too that explained why, as Philip of Taranto's men approached the western end of the valley, Uguccione's forces were already firmly in control of the pass leading towards Vivinaia and in strong defensive positions.

[175] Cortusio, 'Historia', *RIS*, xii, col. 793.
[176] Ibid., Giovanni di Lemmo, 'Diario', 197, and 'Storie pistoresi', 65.
[177] 'Chronicon estense', *RIS* (n. edn.), xv, pt. 3, p. 85.
[178] G. Villani, *Cronica*, ix. 71.

But the Guelphs, unfortunately for themselves, did not at first appreciate the true position. Seeing the Pisans withdrawing, they began a rather disorganized pursuit of what they considered to be a fleeing enemy.[179] Philip of Taranto was now operating with the main body of his army, drawn from the civic militias of Florence and her allies, and not, as earlier in the campaign, with small groups of professional cavalry. This made it more difficult for him to keep a tight rein on his troops than for Uguccione, a larger proportion of whose men were mercenaries and who had had his forces under his command for long enough for him to have firm control over them. Indeed, a council of war of his captains had, on the previous evening, resolved on severe penalties for any soldier who fell out of line:[180] this would ensure that, in the coming battle, as in the campaign against Lucca in the spring of the previous year, troop formations would be maintained and that ranks would not break either under the impact of a single attack or because of a deceptive, early promise of victory.

As the vast, ill-ordered Florentine host approached a branch of the Nievole called the Bona that lay across its path, it became clear that the enemy had by no means yet been defeated. Beyond the stream, the Ghibelline forces were drawn up: in the first cohort of cavalry were the Italians under the command of Francesco della Faggiuola, Uguccione's son, in the second were the German and French mercenaries, and behind them were the Pisans, Lucchese, and Tuscan exiles, both mounted and on foot.[181] As the van of the Guelph army was advancing across the bridge that spanned the rivulet before them, Uguccione's cavalry moved forward to the attack.[182] Leading the first charge, Francesco della Faggiuola broke through the front rank of Guelphs, scattering the troops from Siena and Colle di Val d'Elsa; but when his knights reached the main body of the Florentine forces under Peter of Eboli, they were held and the assult repulsed. Francesco himself and his second-in-command, Giovanni Giacotti Malaspina, were killed, and the imperial standard which the latter had been carrying was overthrown.[183]

Whatever advantage Uguccione had in the battle seemed at this point to have been thrown away. But it was a tribute to him as a

[179] Ibid.
[180] Cortusio, 'Historia', col. 794.
[181] Ibid.
[182] 'Chronicon estense', 85.
[183] G. Villani, *Cronica*, ix. 71, Cortusio, 'Historia', col. 796.

commander and to the discipline of his men that, despite this initial reverse, he was able to continue to exploit the weaknesses of the Florentines and keep his own army under firm control. When Peter of Eboli's knights, having broken the charge against them, advanced in their turn, protecting their flanks with lancers, Uguccione called up four thousand Pisan archers who rained down a hail of arrows on the Florentine cavalry and their horses, compelling them to retreat.[184] As they withdrew, the second line of Uguccione's army made up of the main body of his mercenaries, mostly Germans, attacked, penetrating through the now broken formation of Peter of Eboli's knights to the Florentine rear which consisted of troops who were in marching rather than fighting order. With their arms in many cases packed away,[185] even the archers' crossbows being carried on the backs of pack-animals,[186] they were in no position to offer effective resistance to the furious German onslaught that broke in upon them once the protective screen of their own cavalry, that had so far shielded them from the battle, was suddenly pierced. It was by now late in the afternoon and the attacking Ghibellines, coming in from the west, had the sun behind them.[187] The Guelph infantry therefore had difficulty in seeing the enemy knights until these were right in the midst of their ranks. The result was confusion, panic, and flight. As one chronicler put it, '. . . whoever had a good horse, availed himself of it to avoid . . . remaining a prisoner.'[188] What made things even worse for the disintegrating Florentine army was the terrain through which it sought to escape. This was criss-crossed with watercourses and bounded by marshes into which heavily armoured riders sank with their richly caparisoned horses. Those who were not captured or killed by the pursuing cavalry drowned in the streams and swamps that barred their passage away from the Ghibelline-controlled roads. Philip of Taranto, the Guelph commander, who, still sick with fever, had directed the battle from his litter in the rear, managed to escape. But both his son Charles and his brother Peter 'Tempesta' of Eboli died in the fray. Charles was probably killed in the early stages of the battle: the troops which he had led had been those on the right of the Guelph front line[189] through which Francesco della Faggiuola's first charge had

[184] Cortusio, 'Historia', col. 795.
[185] G. Villani, *Cronica*, ix. 71.
[186] Cortusio, 'Historia', col. 795.
[187] 'Cronaca senese dei fatti . . .', *RIS* (n. edn.), xv, pt. 6, p. 107.
[188] Ibid.
[189] Mussato, 'De gestis italicorum', col. 641.

broken before being stopped by the second line of the Florentine cavalry. Tradition, indeed, was to link his death with that of Uguccione's son, their two bodies allegedly being later found close to each other on the battlefield.[190] Peter of Eboli's corpse was never recovered and it was assumed he perished, drowned, in the marshes during the flight.[191]

In addition to the loss of two out of three of the Neapolitan princes commanding it, the Guelph army suffered enormous casualties. The Catalan mercenary Carroccio, who had captained the left wing of its front rank, lost his life, as did his countryman, Brasco of Aragon, and Charles, count of Battifolle,[192] together with Florentine nobles, such as Rodolfo della Tosa, and Lucchese exiles, such as Lucio degli Obizi.[193] According to Villani, 114 Florentine knights either died or were taken prisoner, but this is probably an underestimate since Nicolo Doria, in a letter to King James II of Aragon, reckoned the dead among the Florentine nobles alone at 140.[194] The total who lost their lives on both sides was said by Villani to have been 2,000,[195] while the combined number of dead and captured is given by Sardo as 2,206 cavalry and 800 infantry and by Cortusio as 3,000 cavalry and 15,000 infantry.[196] Other chroniclers such as Ferreto Vicentino, put the figure for those killed much higher than Villani, in his case at 10,000.[197] Since the number captured, or at least held in prison in Pisa after the battle, was between 1,300 and 1,500,[198] a consensus of the chronicles, with the exception of Villani and Mussato,[199] would seem to suggest that the

---

[190] See Davidsohn, *Storia*, iv, 801, 'Chronicon estense', 85.

[191] G. Villani, *Cronica*, ix, 72; Sardo, *Cronaca*, 72; 'Chronicon estense', 85.

[192] Ibid., Mussato, 'De gestis italicorum', col. 641.

[193] Cortusio, 'Historia', col. 795.

[194] G. Villani, *Cronica*, ix. 72, Finke, *Acta*, ii. 555. Davidsohn, *Storia*, iv. 802, quotes a list of 157 names of casualties among Florentine knights which he claims is incomplete.

[195] Villani, *Cronica*, ix. 72.

[196] Sardo, *Cronaca*, 72, Cortusio, 'Historia', col. 795.

[197] Ferreto Vicentino, 'Historia', 206. Nicolo Doria, in a letter from Genoa on 1/9/ 1315 (Finke, *Acta*, ii. 552), says 30,000 died or were captured in the battle. One Pisan source reported in Florentine archival documents gave the figures of 10,000 dead and 7,000 prisoners (Davidsohn, *Storia*, iv. 802) while another (ASP Commune A214, c. 23ᵛ.) estimated those killed as more than 10,000. See Vigo, *Uguccione*, 79, for a discussion of the various chronicle estimates.

[198] G. Villani, *Cronica*, ix. 72, says 1,500, Nicolo Doria (Finke, *Acta*, ii. 555) 1,342, and Pisan archival sources (ASP Comune A214, c. 23ᵛ.) 1,300.

[199] Mussato, 'De gestis italicorum', col. 644, gives the number of knights killed on the Guelph side as 400 and on the Ghibelline side as 250, while he estimates infantry losses at 600 for the Guelphs and 120 for the Ghibellines. These figures seem far too low for the Guelph infantry: perhaps 6,000 was meant.

total number of dead approached 10,000, though in considering this figure some allowance needs to be made for the tendency to exaggeration in the sources of this period.

Uguccione's victory was, in fact, politically and psychologically an even more complete triumph than it had been militarily. Following it, he was able to take the fortresses of Montecatini and Monsummano and assert his power over most of the former Lucchese territory that had remained in Guelph hands since June of the previous year. Florence could no longer challenge his position as ruler of Lucca, and was in effect compelled to tolerate a Ghibelline enclave in the northwest of Tuscany.

In the long term, however, the significance of Montecatini was to reside less in these temporary advantages gained by Uguccione than in the watershed it represented in the history of war in central Italy. When one compares Montecatini, and the campaign leading up to it, with the two preceding major military encounters in Tuscany, at Montaperti in 1260 and Campaldino in 1289, it becomes clear that it belonged militarily to a new era. At Montaperti and at Campaldino, victory had depended on the impact of a single charge: in the former case, it was the 800 German knights sent by King Manfred to support the outnumbered Sienese who had swung the fate of the battle in the favour of the Ghibellines by breaking and putting to flight the unwieldy Guelph army;[200] in the latter, it had been Corso Donati's unorthodox cavalry attack on the enemy's flank, in defiance of strict orders, that had scattered the Aretine forces.[201] In both instances, the troops taking part in the fighting were predominantly citizen levies;[202]

---

[200] G. Villani, *Cronica*, vi. 79, Davidsohn, *Storia*, ii. 689.

[201] G. Villani, *Cronica*, vii. 131, D. Compagni, 'Cronica' *RIS* (n. edn.), ix, pt. 2, pp. 25–31; H. L. Oerter, 'Campaldino, 1289', *Speculum*, xliii (1968), 447–9.

[202] At Montaperti, the Sienese had 800 German mercenaries to 3,200 civic knights (see Davidsohn, *Forschungen*, iv. 151, quoting Guido Bonatti, *Liber astronomiae*) and an unspecified number of Florentine exile cavalry. The Florentines had a small detachment of German knights under Kroff von Fuglingen, amounting to 500 at the beginning of the campaign, according to Villani (vi. 79), in a total force of 3,000 knights (or 5,300 if we accept Guido Bonatti's figure). The civic infantry contingents would, of course, have been much larger: 12,300 on the Sienese and 17,000 on the Florentine side according to Bonatti's conservative estimates, more according to other sources (Davidsohn, loc. cit.). At Campaldino, again according to Villani (viii. 131), there were 400 mercenaries out of 1,600 cavalry in the Florentine army and probably hardly any foreign ones among the 800 Aretine knights whom that chronicler merely describes as 'being the flower of the Ghibellines of Tuscany, the Marches, the duchy [of Spoleto] and Romagna'. The figures for the infantry on the two sides are given in the same source as 10,000 for the Florentines and 7,000 for the Aretines.

and the result was determined by a panic reaction to a first unexpected assault. At the time of the battle of Montecatini, Tuscan armies still retained their soft core of civic infantry; but between these and the enemy forces were interposed a protective double shell of cavalry, the first line including Italian knights, but the second made up of foreign mercenaries. Essentially, what happened in the critical stages of that engagement was that Francesco della Faggiuola's initial charge, though it failed in its object of fully penetrating the Guelph ranks, had broken the enemy's first line of defence; this, given the elimination in the process of his own body of knights, had effectively meant an exchange of attacking pieces, leaving the second layer of each army's cavalry confronting the other; when Peter of Eboli's trops had, in turn, been repulsed through the use of archers, the vulnerable infantry in the Florentine rear had therefore been exposed to the full force of the subsequent German mercenary assault and had crumpled under the shock. This last phase of the battle encompassed in a vestigial form one of those thirteenth-century routs in which a single charge had dispersed a whole army. But, at Montecatini, before this point could be reached, another battle had had to be fought out between bodies of professional cavalry, in which one side eliminated the offensive capacity of the other.

Apart from the testimony of one chronicler[203] that (together with Spinetta Malaspina) he distinguished himself in the fighting at Montecatini, as the commander of forty knights and a thousand infantry from Sarzana, we know nothing of the part played by Castruccio Castracani in this battle. It is not clear whether he participated in, and survived, the initial charge led by Francesco della Faggiuola, or whether he remained in the rear with the Lucchese and Pisan levies to be involved only in the pursuit of the fleeing Guelphs. That he would probably not have taken part in the crucial second attack that won the day for the Ghibellines is suggested by the fact that this, by common agreement of the chroniclers and according to Uguccione della Faggiuola's own account of the battle,[204] was carried out by German mercenaries whom, at this time, Castruccio was not commanding. Whatever his role in the victory, however, there can be no doubt that his presence on the field of Montecatini would have taught him much about the direction in which warfare was evolving at this period in

---

[203] 'Cronica di Pisa', *RIS*, xv, col. 996.

[204] P. Vigo, 'La battaglia di Montecatini descritta da Uguccione della Faggiuola', *Rivista storica italiana*, vi (1889), 38.

Italy. What we know about his subsequent generalship makes it evident that he took the lessons he had learnt to heart, for his later campaigns show signs of having been thought out in terms of the sorts of military problems and solutions here exemplified. His exploitation of a terrain of hills, marshes, and streams, characteristic of much of his strategy, must surely have owed something to the recollections of this battle, as must his use of mercenary cavalry as shock troops, attacking downhill from strong defensive positions, and his ability virtually to destroy an enemy army, once it was defeated, by swiftly cutting off its lines of retreat.

But however much Castruccio's education as a soldier benefited from Montecatini, the outcome of the battle itself was, though he could not have realized it, fraught with danger for him. Uguccione was now firmly enough established as a tyrant no longer to need his former henchmen. Having hoisted himself into power, in Pisa because of the predicament of the city after Henry VII's death, in Lucca as champion of the exiled Whites, he had, by virtue of his victory, dispensed with the threat of deposition by the Guelphs, while retaining under his own direct control a sufficient force of mercenaries to quell any opposition from among his own supporters. Castruccio was, besides, a thorn in Uguccione's side as a man with an independent following in Lucca through his membership of the Interminelli clan and his prominent position in the White faction, as well as a would-be war-lord carving out for himself his own fief in Lunigiana. It therefore only needed a pretext for Uguccione to move against him.

In the period following the battle of Montecatini, Castruccio continued with his service in the Ghibelline Army. According to one chronicler,[205] he was wounded by an arrow in the expedition which Uguccione led against Fucecchio in January 1316. In the meantime, the rebellions which had broken out in the Lucchese *contado* on the eve of Montecatini, at Vivinaia and in the 'Sei Miglie' in the immediate vicinity of Lucca, were put down,[206] and the dead Francesco della Faggiuola replaced as *podestà* of the city by his brother Nieri. It was this son of Uguccione's who, at the beginning of April 1316, was to be the instrument of the plot against Castruccio that all but cost him his life but which, at the same time, by an ironic quirk of fortune, resulted in his elevation to the position of captain of the city.

[205] BNF MS Palat. 571, c. 20ʳ., Sardo, *Cronaca*, 7–23, 'Cronica di Pisa', *RIS*, xv, col. 996, 'Cronaca senese' (Tura), *RIS* (n. edn.), xv, pt. 6, p. 357.
[206] BNF MS Palat. 571, c. 20ʳ.

The sources disagree as to the exact circumstances that preceded and precipitated the dramatic events between April Fool's Day and Easter Sunday of that year. The most probable reading of the evidence is that Castruccio put to death thirty men at Massa in Lunigiana,[207] a town which adjoined the territory where he had jurisdiction, perhaps in an attempt to quell a rebellion or coerce a defiant community into submission.

But, whatever justification he may have had, there is no doubt that to Uguccione and to Nieri as his lieutenant in Lucca his action could only have appeared as an usurpation of power properly belonging to the constituted government they represented. It is likely, too, that they saw the technical illegality of what Castruccio had done as providing a convenient opportunity of either eliminating him or of putting pressure on him to relinquish the lands he was administering on behalf of the bishop of Luni and the commune of Sarzana. Whatever their motives, they moved swiftly against him, taking advantage of his complete trust in them to trap him into captivity before he had a chance to mobilize his supporters against them. Nieri della Faggiuola simply allowed Castruccio to come to dinner on his return to Lucca and, when he arrived, unarmed, as a guest, had him seized and clapped in irons. Having got Castruccio in his power by this deception of 1 April 1316, Nieri did not then, however, have him immediately put to death, but kept him in prison for the next ten days.[208] According to Giovanni di Lemmo da Comugnori,[209] the reason for this delay was that Castruccio was given three days[210] to consign the lands he held from the bishop of Luni to Uguccione if he wanted to save his life. His deadline appears, however, to have been extended, for he was still alive on Easter Saturday, 10 April, when a rebellion broke out in Pisa against Uguccione's rule there. Nieri and Gaddo della Gherardesca, counts of Donoratico, and members of one of the great aristocratic houses of the city, led a rising against the absent tyrant's officials and

---

[207] Ibid., Sardo, *Cronaca*, 73, 'Cronica di Pisa', *RIS*, xv, col. 996. Ferreto Vicentino, 'Historia', 211, gives the number of men killed as 36, 'Storie pistoresi', 68, as 22, the latter source also transposing the whole incident from Massa to Camaiore.

[208] The dates are provided in the documents in ASL Atti di Castruccio no. 1, cc. 4ᵛ.– 5ʳ., published in Lazzareschi, 'Documenti', 296–7.

[209] Giovanni di Lemmo, 'Diario', 200. See also 'Chronicon sanminiatese', in G. D. Mansi, *Miscellanea*, i. 466.

[210] Ibid. Giovanni di Lemmo says he was given until the following Monday, which was in fact 4 April, to hand over the lands he administered in the diocese of Luni. However, later in the same passage, this writer implies that the Saturday the revolt against Uguccione broke out in Pisa was Castruccio's deadline, and not the previous Monday.

troops—Uguccione being away in Lucca at the time—and when these had been won over, killed, captured, or driven out, had themselves proclaimed respectively *podestà* and captain of the commune.[211]

This Pisan revolt delivered Castruccio from an apparently impending death. On hearing what had happened in the neighbouring town, Uguccione immediately left Lucca in an effort to retrieve the situation. Nieri, remaining in charge there, could not risk beheading someone as prominent and influential in Lucchese society as his prisoner until his father returned with an armed force sufficient to crush the insurrection which such an execution might provoke. So Castruccio was spared and, as it turned out, was to be strangely favoured by the succeeding turn of events.

For, by the time Uguccione reached the village of San Giuliano, on the slopes of the Monti Pisani overlooking Pisa from a distance of about three miles,[212] he learnt that its gates were held by the rebels and the city lost to him. Returning to Lucca where he did not arrive until after nightfall, he found that town, too, restive and rebellious.[213] The next morning, that of Easter Sunday, Castruccio's supporters were out in strength, demanding his release and calling for the death of Uguccione.[214] The latter, frightened, first freed Castruccio and then, to save his own life and that of his son, relinquished his authority on condition that he, his family, and retinue be permitted to leave the city. These terms were accepted and, together with Nieri and with his associates, friends, and those who wished to go with him,[215] he promptly departed, making his way northward, to seek refuge and hospitality

[211] 'Cronica di Pisa', *RIS*, xv. cols. 996–7. Giovanni di Lemmo, 'Diario', 201, Mansi, *Miscellanea*, i. 467, ASL Atti di Castruccio, no. 1, cc. 4^v.–5^r., published in Lazzareschi, 'Documenti', 296.

[212] He was three miles away from Pisa according to Giovanni di Lemmo, 'Diario', 201, and Mansi, *Miscellanea*, i. 467, and two miles according to the 'Storie pistoresi' (p. 69), when he realized the city was firmly in the hands of the rebels. Sardo, *Cronaca*, 74, the anonymous Pisan chronicle *RIS*, xv, col. 997, BNF MS Palat. 571, c. 20^r., and G. Villani (ix. 78) state that it was at Monte a San Giuliano that he realized that all was lost. Villani and the author of the 'Storie pistoresi', however, have Uguccione travelling at this point from Pisa to Lucca to bring troops there so as to enable Castruccio to be executed and not, as the other chroniclers do, returning to Pisa after hearing the news of the revolt.

[213] ASL Atti di Castruccio, no. 1, c. 5^r. in Lazzareschi, 'Documenti', 296. The revolt in Pisa had occurred at noon on the tenth; Uguccione had news of it while finishing his midday meal; but by the time he and his troops had ridden to San Giuliano and back, night had fallen. ('Cronica di Pisa', *RIS*, xv, cols. 996–7.)

[214] Giovanni di Lemmo, 'Diario', 201.

[215] ASL Atti di Castruccio, no. 1, c. 5^r., BNF MS Palat. 571, c. 20^r.

first with Marquis Spinetta Malaspina in Lunigiana and later with Can Grande della Scala in Verona.[216] The wheel had indeed turned full circle. Within a week (on 17 April) Castruccio had, in association with Pagano Cristofani, been elected commander of the commune's troops[217] and by 12 June was alone endorsed (for a six months' term) as captain-general of Lucca and defender of the imperial faction in it.[218] Although this, of course, gave him control only over the military functions of the civic government, the groundwork for his later political power had none the less been laid. From being a man under threat of execution, he had suddenly become the dominant figure in the city.

The events by which this extraordinary transition was effected occurred in such rapid and surprising succession that it is at first difficult to explain them. In particular, there is the problem of whether the Pisan revolt which saved Castruccio and set him on the road to power was a fortunate accident or an occurrence that he himself had a hand in. The anonymous author of the 'Storie pistoresi' credited him with conspiring with the Pisans against Uguccione even before his arrest;[219] but the account in that chronicle of the whole episode of his imprisonment is otherwise so unreliable that this provides only the weakest grounds for believing in his complicity in the plot that led to the Pisan rebellion. The circumstantial evidence, though not conclusive, is more persuasive. Although, when Castruccio was first seized by Nieri della Faggiuola, it was generally believed in Lucca that he had been beheaded 'rather out of fear and suspicion of his magnificence than from any other cause',[220] the impression that he was dead can hardly have persisted for the full ten days of his captivity, particularly if negotiations were going on between him and Uguccione concerning the cession of his rights in Lunigiana—negotiations which would at some point have had to be communicated to others if their object was to be achieved. We know from Villani that the freeing of Castruccio and the expulsion of the Della Faggiuola was effected by such leading

---

[216] G. Villani, *Cronica*, ix. 78, Giovanni di Lemmo, 'Diario', 201. On Uguccione's later life, in the course of which he became *podestà* of Vicenza for Can Grande up to his death in 1318, see Vigo, *Uguccione*, 88–9.

[217] The title conferred on the two men was, in fact, 'gubernatores guerre et conductores gentis intus et extra civitatem'. The Atti di Castruccio (no. 1, c. 11ᵛ.) survive only in a sixteenth-century copy which gives the name of Castruccio's fellow commander as Pagano Cristofori (Lazzareschi, 'Documenti', 297); that his name was in fact Cristofani is evident from ASL Archivio notarile no. 65, c. 121ᵛ.

[218] Atti di Castruccio no. 1, cc. 16ᵛ.–18ᵛ, in Lazzareschi, 'Documenti', 298–9.

[219] 'Storie pistoresi', 68.

[220] ASL Atti di Castruccio no. 1, c. 4ᵛ., in Lazzareschi, 'Documenti', 296.

Lucchese families as the Quartigiani, Poggio, and Onesti.[221] It seems likely that, when the heads of these urban dynasties, together with the Interminelli, discovered that Castruccio was still alive, though under threat of execution, they would have made approaches to other patrician houses, not merely in Lucca but in Pisa also. The fear which Uguccione's move against a man as prominent as Castruccio would have aroused among the leading Ghibelline aristocrats in both cities would have been enough to create the resolve to overthrow the tyrant, while Uguccione's absence from Pisa would have provided the occasion for a coup against him.

This speculative reconstruction of the background to the events of Easter 1316 would also make it easier to explain their other puzzling feature, namely the ease with which, after losing one of the towns he held, Uguccione was prised out of his dominant position in the other. While one reason for this would have been the defection to the rebels of eight hundred of his mercenaries who had remained in Pisa,[222] another could have been the prior knowledge the ringleaders of the plot against him in Lucca had of the Pisan revolt which would have enabled them to organize on Easter Saturday the resistance to him which proved so effective the following morning.

Uguccione's overthrow in fact demonstrated the precariousness of the power of a tyrant who relied on military strength alone without real political support in either of the cities he had come to control. With troops who were, after all, mercenaries whose loyalty went to whoever paid them, such a ruler could not afford any lapse in the continuity of his authority. The fact that he could not count on the allegiance of a faction, but instead had to face the potential opposition of those he had offended by usurping the power they felt to be their due, made him peculiarly vulnerable to the kind of insurrection which overthrew him on 10–11 April.

While Castruccio probably owed his elevation to the captaincy of Lucca, in the wake of Uguccione's expulsion, to his military experience, his position at this stage was quite different from that of the tyrant whom he had displaced. By virtue of his membership of one of the leading families—indeed the most distinguished Ghibelline house in the town—he was essentially a representative of the social group of *casastici*, those discriminated against by the Statute of 1308

---

[221] G. Villani, *Cronica*, ix. 78.
[222] 'Cronica di Pisa', *RIS*, xv, col. 996.

and therefore favourable to the change of regime in 1314, but also apprehensive of the increasing arbitrariness of the rule of the Della Faggiuola, as Uguccione's successes in the field laid the foundations of a power based on armed might. When he was first elected commander of the city's troops, Castruccio was flanked in that office by Pagano Cristofani of the Quartigiani clan which, before changing sides in 1314, had been the largest Guelph family grouping in Lucca,[223] as the Interminelli had, up to its exile in 1301, been the most extensive one in the White faction. Together, they therefore had behind them the two major *consorterie* of the town.

Nor should one assume that, at least to begin with, Castruccio was regarded as the dominant member of this pair. The evidence, in fact, indicates rather that the partnership between him and Pagano Cristofani represented an alliance of his military skill and family connections with the social influence of the Quartigiani who, as the middle force in Lucchese politics, had probably played as vital a role in the overthrow of Uguccione as they had in the Ghibelline take-over of 1314. That Castruccio's liberation and subsequent appointment to joint command of the city's troops depended on an understanding with the Quartigiani is strongly suggested by an intriguing entry in the Lucchese notarial archive. While it was not until 17 April that he and Pagano were formally elected as 'governors of war and captains of the troops both within and without the city', as early as the eleventh, in other words, on the day that Castruccio was released from prison, the register of Ser Rabbito Toringhelli records the betrothal of his daughter Dialta (here called Dialtuccia) to Pagano's brother Antonio. The extraordinary nature of this contract is evident not only from the circumstances in which it was drawn up and from the personalities involved, but also because it appears in isolation as the only act noted by Ser Rabbito between 7 and 16 April, and because it was in fact set down on Easter Sunday when no notary would normally have been working! It appears from it that, no sooner was Castruccio free, than he was taken to the house of Sandeo Boccadivacca where, in the presence of witnesses, he promised his daughter in marriage to Antonio. No dowry was specified, but arbiters were chosen to determine it. Then the engaged couple were without delay whisked away to the steps of the cathedral of San Martino where they solemnly de-

---

[223] This was then the largest *consorteria* in Lucca after that of the Interminelli. According to Villani (x. 25), it included at the time of its banishment in 1327 more than a hundred adult males.

clared their consent to the match by Antonio's placing of a gold ring
on the finger of Dialta's right hand.[224]

The exceptional timing of the settlement of the contract, its obvious
haste, and the fact that it envisaged an alliance between the families of
the two men who were to be given control of the city's armed forces six
days later are strong grounds for supposing that it sealed no mere
private agreement but a political bargain. The marriage proposed
never eventuated-Dialta was destined to become the wife of Filippo
Tedici as the result of one of Castruccio's other political ploys aimed
at gaining Pistoia in 1325. In 1316, she would almost certainly not even
have been of marriageable age,[225] and in any case there would have
been no reason to rush her engagement through in this way had other
considerations not dictated the formal ratification of the family alliance it represented. In all likelihood, the terms of the wider agreement
of which it was a part had, earlier, while Castruccio was still a
prisoner, been settled between his partisans and the Quartigiani and
their following; consequent on it had come the freeing of Castruccio
and the expulsion of Uguccione; now, the critical link in the structure
of the new regime had to be secured without delay with a marriage
contract linking the families of the two men who were to head it in
anticipated ties of blood relationship.

According to Raniero Granchi and Giovanni Villani,[226] the compact
arrived at provided for an alternation of power between Castruccio
and Pagano. There is some confirmation of this in the appointment of
Castruccio alone in that office for only six months from 13 June 1316.[227]
Well before his term elapsed, however, he had so consolidated himself
in his position, by securing the loyalty of the city's troops to himself
alone and building up political support in the town, that he managed
to obtain, on 2 November, his re-election as captain-general for a full
year, from the conclusion of his original term as commander of the
communal army. At this point, Pagano Cristofani appears to either

[224] ASL Archivio notarile no. 65, c. 121ᵛ. This document was discussed by V. Tirelli
at the conference on Castruccio Castracani in Lucca in 1981.
[225] See n. 108 above.
[226] G. Villani, *Cronica*, ix. 73, R. Granchi, 'De proeliis Tusciae, poema', *RIS*, xi, cols.
301–2. Villani says they decided each to have power over city and *contado* in alternate
years and to change about at the end of each year. However, the fact that Castruccio was
originally appointed captain-general of Lucca for a six months' term on 12 June 1316
suggests that Granchi was right in his account of the original agreement between the
two men.
[227] ASL Atti di Castruccio no. 1, cc. 16ᵛ.–18ʳ., in Lazzareschi, 'Documenti', 289–9,
304–6.

have left Lucca in disgust at the breach of the undertaking made with him, or to have been driven out.[228] This left Castruccio in sole charge of the city's armed forces, though not as yet, at least in any formal sense, the head of its government.

By the end of 1316, he had therefore emerged unquestionably as the most powerful man in Lucca. But it would be a misinterpretation of his position between April and June of that year to assume that he achieved that degree of pre-eminence the moment he emerged from captivity. Initially, he had had to build upon the support of the Lucchese aristocracy which saw him more as an instrument than as a master. It was only when he had the reins of power—and more particularly military control—firmly in his hands that he was in a position to raise himself from mere commander of the city's toops, by the grace of its leading families, to an effective ruler already well on the way to establishing his tyranny. Even then, however, he still needed the co-operation of these elements in Lucchese society which had first given him authority and, in the internal administration of the town, he continued to some extent to work through them, allowing those whom he favoured to govern nominally as *anziani* and other civic officials while he retained the influence over them and the armed might to overawe or crush them if they threatened his power.

[228] Granchi says he withdrew voluntarily, Villani claims that Castruccio found a pretext to expel him from Lucca and its *contado*.

III

Lucca under Castruccio Castracani

1. *The government of Lucca under Castruccio Castracani*

Uguccione della Faggiuola had ruled Lucca by virtue of his own title as captain-general of the city, bestowed on him on 13 July 1314, following his capture of the town, and through his sons Francesco and Nieri who held the office of *podestà*. He retained the *anziani* or aldermen who had traditionally exercised executive authority in the commune, but reserved the right to appoint them himself.[1] Under him, their role in government appears to have been a subordinate one; however, the survival of the institution they represented, together with the continuation under his rule of the other civic councils and offices, meant that, after his expulsion, the transition to the new regime could be easily effected according to the appropriate constitutional forms. The appointment of Castruccio Castracani and Pagano Cristofani to joint command of the city's troops, though made through a properly conducted election, cannot in itself be regarded as part of a general reconstruction of the machinery of state. It was more a stop-gap measure, prompted by the need to have someone to lead the city's armed forces at a time when Uguccione was no longer available, but when hostilities were continuing against the Florentines around the village of Vinci. (It was, indeed, here that Castruccio's uncle Nicolo won a victory on his behalf on 25 April, a mere eight days after his nephew had taken over control of the Lucchese army.[2]) But by 4 June—a little more than a week before Castruccio's election for a six-month term as sole captain of Lucca—sufficient time had elapsed since Uguccione's departure for details of new constitutional forms to be worked out; and these were proclaimed on that date in a new

---

[1] Cianelli, 'Dissertazioni', 243–4, Vigo, *Uguccione*, 42–5.
[2] According to ASL Atti di Castruccio no. 1, c. 5ᵛ., Castruccio himself was so ill at the time that he could not ride; hence he delegated to his uncle Nicolo his command over the foreign mercenaries and Italian exiles in Lucchese pay; these attacked the Florentine forces and defeated them on 25 April. (See also Giovanni di Lemmo, 'Diario', 201, 'Storie pistoresi', 73, G. Villani, *Cronica*, ix. 73, and Finke, *Acta*, ii. 565.)

statute, replacing that of 1308 which had been annulled on 4 September 1314.[3] Unfortunately, the full text of this has been lost and only fairly brief extracts survive, the main one dealing with the mode of election of a new general council.[4] This was to be chosen annually by the *anziani* and by ten others whom they had selected, two from each of the five wards of the city ('the four gates and the Borgo'), and was to be made up of fifty members from each ward who had to be over twenty years of age, have an *estimo* of at least £25, and be Ghibellines, as well as inhabitants and natives of Lucca or its suburbs.[5] It is not clear from the fragment of the statute which has come down to us whether the *anziani* themselves were to be elected by this council or appointed, as under Uguccione, by the *podestà* or captain.[6] In the choice of these two officials, however, the council evidently had a part, though the records of the procedure followed in the various elections of Castruccio as captain-general of the commune suggest that the *anziani* and the *savi*, whom they had co-opted to vote with them in such cases, chose the new incumbent of the office whose appointment was then ratified by a wider *parlamento*, or assembly consisting of the general council and other 'invited' citizens.[7]

[3] ASL Curia dei Ribelli e dei Banditi no. 1, c. 2ʳ.

[4] Published in Bongi and Del Prete, 'Il Statuto', pp. xlix–li.

[5] It was further stipulated that the quorum for this assembly was to be 150, except during the harvest and in the months of September and October when it could be 100. Motions before it needed, however, a three-quarters majority to be passed. Elections to choose the general council had to be conducted by 1 December and it was to hold office from the beginning of each year. Brothers, sons, and fathers of those already chosen for the council were disqualified for election to it.

[6] Alternatively, it is possible that the *anziani* were elected according to the procedure for election of the captain or the voting of taxes or resolutions in which the *anziani*, joined by the *savi* they had co-opted, selected their successors, their choice being then put before the general council augmented by the *invitati* for ratification, rejection, or amendment.

[7] The election of Castruccio Castracani and Pagano Cristofani as 'governors of war and commanders of troops', which took place on 17 April, 1316, before the enactment of the new statute, had been carried out by the *anziani* and *savi* without further ratification. In the 12 June appointment of Castruccio alone as 'captain-general and defender of the imperial party', the *anziani* and ten *savi* had first met to choose him; then the general council had been assembled, together with many other invited members, and had unanimously endorsed his election. The same basic procedure was followed on 4 November 1316, 7 July 1317, and 26–27 April 1320, when Castruccio was made captain and, on the last date, captain and *signore* of the city, for periods of one year, ten years, and life respectively. Initially, *savi* were selected by the *anziani* to vote with them (ten in June 1316, twenty in 1317, and forty-one in 1320), then the matter was resolved by the *anziani* and *savi* sitting together and finally put to the *parlamento* consisting of the general council and the *invitati*. (ASL Atti di Castruccio no. 1, cc. 16ᵛ.–18ʳ., 17ᵛ.–18ʳ., 19ᵛ.–20ᵛ., 21ʳ.–24ʳ., in Lazzareschi, 'Documenti', 298–9, 304–10, 317–24.)

In this form of government there was a closed circle of appointment of officials by those whom they had directly or indirectly chosen. At the time when the new statute was first enacted, it is likely that the Ghibelline aristocracy saw it as a means by which its own power could be perpetuated. The election of Castruccio Castracani as captain-general within just over a week of its proclamation indicates, however, that already by this stage there was a despotic element more or less built into the structure of the constitutional system. Control of the military forces was to be vested, for a six month period, in one of the two men who had up to this point held it on a more temporary basis. Executive authority was, however, to remain with the *anziani* and the *podestà*, while the general council was to share with the *anziani* the right to approve taxes.[8] This meant that, even if the captain and *podestà* had extensive power, they needed the collaboration of a group of other leading citizens to put what they wanted into effect.

Had the statute operated as those who had designed it probably intended it to, it would have laid the basis for a mixed regime, strong and dictatorial against its enemies both within and outside the city,[9] but allowing the participation in government in a real sense of the favoured minority of its prominent partisans. As it turned out, Castruccio's military power, increasingly independent as time went on because of his hold over his mercenary troops, was to make nonsense of any constitutional limitations to his authority. Consequently it was easy for him to have extended the originally circumscribed commission he had received. As has already been mentioned, on 4 November 1316, more than a month before his term as captain had elapsed, it was reconfirmed for another year from 14 December. Well before that period had run out, on 7 July 1317, he secured his reappointment for no less than ten years from the following 13 December. And, on 26–27 April 1320, he was elected not merely captain but also 'dominus generalis' of Lucca for life.[10]

This last elevation of him to political power in a formal sense was backed by the endorsement of imperial authority in a way that made him to some degree independent of the support of those who had

---

[8] Bongi and Del Prete, 'Il statuto', p. xlix.

[9] The reasons given for Castruccio's election as captain-general on 12 June 1316 include dissensions among citizens and the fear of riots, suggesting that there was opposition at this time in Lucca to the Ghibelline regime that could be met only by the creation of a single, strong military authority.

[10] References as in n. 7 above.

conferred his position on him. On 4 April 1320, just before his election as *signore* and captain of the city for life, Frederick III bestowed on him the title of vicar-general of Lucca and its territories.[11] This, together with his subsequent act of homage on the first of the following month,[12] meant that Castruccio was technically a vassal of the Empire. His appointment as 'dominus generalis', which occurred between the announcement that he had been made vicar-general and his formal oath of fealty, could therefore be seen as no more than a ratification by the apposite communal councils of a dignity he already enjoyed by virtue of an imperial grant. Legally, he owed his position to a delegation of authority from above as well as to a concession of sovereignty from below.[13]

Any juridical position, however, must ultimately be grounded in a political reality; in Castruccio's case it depended on a combination of military force and the collaboration, willing or reluctant, of many patricians. As time went on, his political authority came increasingly to rest on his military power, partly because of the prestige acquired through his victories in the war with Florence after 1320 and partly because his alienation of his own former aristocratic supporters after his suppression of the Poggio in 1321 forced him to employ the mercenaries within the Augusta or citadel to cow his subjects into submission. Before that, while his soldierly reputation made him indispensable as a barrier against the Guelphs, his control of government depended primarily on his ability to act through the men who were chosen as *anziani, savi*, and members of the general council.

Up to 1320, Castruccio in any case needed the co-operation of civic bodies and officials to have his authority enhanced and extended. These years provided a breathing space of virtual external peace in which the absence of severe pressures from outside made it possible to consolidate his position and reconstruct the Lucchese state. It is worth noting that Castruccio, who was later to become notorious as

[11] ASL Capitoli, no. 4, c. 47ᵛ., in Lazzareschi, 'Documenti', 314–15.

[12] Ibid., c. 47ᵛ.–48ʳ. and pp. 316–17 and 325. On 9 April, Frederick III received ambassadors from Castruccio with the offer of homage and, on the following day, imperial envoys were dispatched formally to accept his act of fealty. This was sworn to them on 1 May.

[13] See T. E. Mommsen, 'Castruccio Castracani and the Empire', *Medieval and Renaissance Studies* (Ithaca, NY, 1959), 23. Mommsen also makes the point on p. 22 that Castruccio's choice of Frederick of Austria as the ruler from whom he sought his vicariate over Lunigiana on 5 August 1315 already placed him in opposition to the more rigid Ghibellines such as Uguccione della Faggiuola who at this time supported Frederick's rival, Ludwig of Bavaria.

the warlike enemy of Florence, began his political career as captain-
general of Lucca at the very time when overtures of peace were being
made to bring to an end the long-drawn-out conflict between the
Guelph and Ghibelline powers. More significantly still, he himself
appears, like the counts of Donoratico in Pisa, to have been identified
with a more conciliatory diplomatic stance by virtue of his role in the
overthrow of Uguccione della Faggiuola whose intransigence had
been the main obstacle to a reconciliation with the Guelphs. It is
interesting that when the groundwork for a *rapprochement* between the
kingdom of Naples and the emperor-elect Frederick III, was laid by a
marriage alliance between Frederick's sister Catherine and Robert of
Naples's son Charles of Calabria, Castruccio was personally informed
of the proposed match. As imperial vicar for Lunigiana, he was urged,
in a letter from his patron Frederick III, written on 30 June 1316, less
than three weeks from his election as captain-general of Lucca, to use
his best offices to facilitate the restoration of peace and concord in
Italy which, it was hoped, the union between the leading Guelph and
Ghibelline royal houses would effect.[14] Negotiations to that end
proved, as it happened, rather slow: although the Pisans concluded a
truce with Naples as early as 12 August 1316,[15] it was not until 3 February of the following year that Lucca sent any ambassador[16] to a peace
conference which took till 12 May to bring hostilities in Tuscany to an
end with a general treaty between Florence and its allies on the one
hand and Pisa and Lucca on the other.[17] However, in the period leading up to the signing of that accord, the expectation that it would be

[14] Lazzareschi, 'Documenti', 299–300, J. Ficker, *Urkunden zur Geschichte des Römerzuges Kaiser Ludwig des Baiern und der italienischen Verhaeltnisse seiner Zeit* (Innsbruck,
1865), 5.
[15] The appointment of a Pisan delegation to go to Naples was made on 29 May 1316
(1317 Pisan style) (F. dal Borgo, *Raccolta*, 238–9). Davidsohn, *Storia*, iv. 832, gives details
of the treaty of 12 August of that year based on archival evidence in Neapolitan sources
(now presumably lost).
[16] F. dal Borgo, *Raccolta*, 323–4.
[17] The full text in F. dal Borgo, *Raccolta*, 322–61. Another version is in ASP Comune A29. As far as Lucca was concerned (ibid., 338–41 and cc. 16ʳ.–18ʳ.), the treaty
stipulated the lifting from the Guelph exiles (represented at the negotiations by Luto
degli Obizi and Dino Salamoncelli) of all penalties imposed on them and the restoration to them of their former property. With the exception of adult males declared
'suspect' by the commune, they were to have the right to return to the city and have
liberty of movement in its territories. Those towns or villages which the Guelphs had
continued to hold since the fall of Lucca and which Uguccione della Faggiuola had not
retaken from them (namely, the Val d'Arno communes of Fucecchio, Castelfranco,
Santa Croce, Montefalcone, Cappiano, and Santa Maria a Monte) were to remain in
their hands.

reached led fighting between the two sides to lapse. This meant that, while Castruccio, as newly appointed commander of the Lucchese forces, was at this stage fairly busily engaged in minor operations aimed at recovering for Lucca control of lost territories in Lunigiana and in Garfagnana,[18] he was not committed to a major war against Florence. The military action at Vinci which his uncle Nicolo had won at the end of April had in effect concluded a campaign which the new regime in Lucca had inherited from Uguccione della Faggiuola, but had no real interest in continuing.

Although the emergency which that last phase of fighting had created was partly responsible for Castruccio's choice in April 1316 as joint 'governor of war' and although fear of internal dissension played its part in his confirmation as captain-general in June of that year,[19] once external peace was clearly in prospect and the government had consolidated its hold on the city, the need for a military protector would have ceased to be the overwhelming consideration it had been earlier. Undoubtedly Castruccio's control of the mercenaries in Lucchese service went on being of decisive political advantage to him, but, given the nature of the constitution introduced by the Statute of 1316, whatever benefit he derived from this could only have been translated into real power through the agency of those selected for the various communal offices. These men were of key importance both in the running of Castruccio's government and in the passing of the decrees that prolonged and gave legal title to his rule. Unfortunately, we do not possess the names of all of them since the registers recording the lists of elected officials at this period have been lost. However, it is possible to reconstruct from other sources[20] the composition of

[18] Sforza, 'Castruccio ... in Lunigiana', 327–9. Whereas, before 1314, Lucca had received tribute from eleven communes in Lunigiana, by April 1316 only Montignoso remained subject to the commune, though Sarzana and the lands of the bishopric of Luni were, of course, temporarily still under Castruccio's administration by virtue of his vicarial powers over them. On 1 July 1316 (ibid., 461–6 and ASL Capitoli no. 8, pp. 52–3 or cc. 166ᵛ–167ᵛ.), however, the bishop and marquises of Massa conceded jurisdiction over Massa to the commune of Lucca, following a campaign by Castruccio which had culminated in an attack on the citadel of Massa and its Corsican garrison on 24 June (BNF MS Palat. 571, c. 20ʳ.). At the same time, a Lucchese expedition, mounted to recover Coreglia in Garfagnana, which had been captured earlier by the Guelph Count Nerone of Frignano, succeeded in retaking and pacifying the town (ibid.).

[19] See n. 9 above.

[20] The *anziani* for 1322 are listed in ASL Curia dei Ribelli e dei Banditi no. 1, c. 10ʳ., those for 1320 in BSL MS 1889 c. 109ᵛ. and, in another version, in BSL MS 1009 *ad annum*. This latter source also contains all but one of the names of the *anziani* for both terms of 1316 while eight of those for the first half of that year are also given in ASL

the two groups of *anziani* for 1316, one group in 1320, and one in 1322, and we can also establish the identity of six of the ten *savi* in office in mid-1316 and the twenty and forty-one *savi* selected on 7 July 1317 and 26 April 1320 respectively.[21] We therefore can determine, with the exception of the *anziani* of July 1317 and the *savi* of November 1316 (if these were different from those of June–July of that year), the member-ship of the boards which initiated the decision to extend Castruccio's captaincy of Lucca on four occasions between 1316 and 1320. We also incidentally have a sample of those filling the principal executive posi-tions in the communal government from 1316 to 1320 or 1322, that is, in the early 'constitutional' phase of Castruccio's regime.

A study of these names shows a very high concentration of men from the leading merchant families among those holding office as *anziani* and *savi* over these years.[22] Also, while there are no names common to the four lists of *anziani*, suggesting that the members of this body tended to be drawn in rotation from a general pool of the chief partisans of the regime, there are considerable overlaps between the three groups of *savi* and between these and the *anziani*. Evidently, the *savi* were politically experienced citizens co-opted to act with the main executive council of the commune on special occasions, with the result that the same figures recur among them. If one examines the lists in more detail, one cannot but be further impressed by the repeti-tion in them not merely of the same names but also of members of the same families. Of the 106 places (39 of *anziani*, 67 of *savi*) in the surviv-ing records of these two offices between 1316 and 1322, 72 were filled from the 25 families whose names occur in these lists twice or more

Capitoli no.8, p. 52 or c. 166ᵛ. S. Dalli's *Cronica di Lucca* (ASL MS 10, ii. 460, 489–90), written in the late sixteenth century, gives the lists of *anziani* for 1320 and of *savi* for 1317 and 1320.

[21] The six *savi* on 1 July 1316 are given in ASL Capitoli no. 8, p. 32 or c. 166ᵛ. The *savi* involved in extending Castruccio's term on 7 July 1317 and 26 April 1320 were elected especially for this purpose and are listed in Atti di Castruccio no. 1, cc. 19ᵛ. and 21ʳ. Because this is a sixteenth-century copy of a lost fourteenth-century original, the spelling of the names is somewhat erratic owing to misreading or misguided emenda-tion by the copyist. ('Schiatta' is rendered as 'Stiacte' and 'Perotto dello Strego' as 'Petrus dello Strego', for instance.)

[22] None of the *anziani* or *savi* can be definitely identified as an artisan, and the number of men who do not belong to prominent patrician or merchant families is small in the lists of both *anziani* and *savi*. Among the *anziani*, there are only Puccinello Lommori (1320), Nicolo Ciampa, and Nuccio Berlescia (1322)—three out of thirty-nine—and among the *savi*, Ser Perfetto Nicolai and Ser Bonagiunta Rolenzi (1320), two out of fifty-four, both of whom were notaries and thus, even if not of leading families, members of the professional classes by reason of their occupation.

over this period—or, if we extend the clan branches into clans and count the latter as families—then 77 positions were occupied by 19 families. The Interminelli, including its related lineages, the Castracani, Savarigi, Saggina, and Bovi, held 10 positions, the Poggio 5, the Quartigiani with their Simonetti and Diversi branches 4, as did the Rapondi, Streghi, and Boccansocchi, while the Del Fondo with their Accettanti and Giordani branches, the Mordecastelli, Martini, Spada, Dardagnini, Sbarra, Boccadivacca, Mingogi, Galganetti, and Casciani each account for 3 officers in these lists. The sample we have is too small for the differences in these numbers to be particularly significant in themselves, but the names thrown up by selecting the families most frequently represented in it are nevertheless interesting in that they do give an impression of where the regime they sustained received its support.

One can distinguish among this group of *anziani* and *savi*, in the first place, a group consisting of the returned exiles of the White faction and their relatives. This includes those of the Interminelli clan (who occupied 10 places), of the Poggio family (5), of the Mordescastelli (3), Castruccio's brothers-in-law, the Streghi (4), the Rapondi (4), the Del Fondo (3), the Dal Portico (2), and the Ciapparoni, Avvocati, and Lieti with one place each—in all holding 37 positions or just over one-third of the total.[23] Then, there are among these office-holders the members of houses which did not go into exile in 1301 but were designated *casastici* by the Statute of 1308. There were the Bettori, Boccansocchi, Burlamacchi, Guinigi, Onesti, Mangialmacchi, Mercati, Pantassa, Rossiglioni, Sartori, Sbarra, Spoletini, Tadolini, and Upezzini families, the Schiatta and Disfaciati branches of the Bernardini, and the Boccadivacca of the Lanfredi, together with the various ramifications of the Quartigiani clan—between them accounting for thirty-four places or nearly another third of the whole number. If one eliminates from the remainder one person who is listed without a surname and five from obscure families,[24] this leaves a further twenty-nine places occupied by a more miscellaneous group. Four men, each of whom held office more than once—Ser Betto

[23] I have taken the families represented in the lists of the White faction in Pisa between 1310 and 1313, as recorded by Ser Orlando Ciapparoni in ASL Archivio notarile no. 29, as constituting the exile community for the purpose of this analysis.

[24] See n. 22 above. The man without a surname was Coluccio di Messer Mondino who, being the son of a knight, was an aristocrat and may have belonged to the Sesmondi branch of the Quartigiani, among whom there was a Messer Mondino.

Dardagnini, Puccino Galganetti, Guelfo Casciani, and Coluccio Mingogi—and their close relatives fill fifteen, or more than half of these. The rest are distributed between fairly prominent families such as the Passamonti, Del Veglio, Talgardi, and Moriconi and a few minor figures, such as Giovanni Boccella, a kinsman of Castruccio's notary, Ser Nicolao Boccella.

Of the 106 positions of the *anziani* or *savi*, 37 or 32.1 per cent of them were held by those belonging or related to the former White exile community, 34 or 32.1 per cent by ex-Guelph *casastici*, and a further 20 or 18.9 per cent by members of other leading families actively associated with the regime. The rest were taken up by individuals, probably singled out because of their particular loyalty to Castruccio or to the ruling faction. The inference to be drawn from the evidence this provides would seem to be that it was the banishment of the Whites in 1301 and the later discrimination of the Luccese commune against the chief families of the town in 1308 that, between them, created the conditions which made an extensive section of the city's patriciate amenable to collaboration with the Castruccian despotism in its early stages. Another conclusion which emerges is that, until about 1320 in any case, side by side with the growth in the personal power of the captain-general of Lucca due to his military authority, there was a persistence, in the actual running of the government, of a substantial degree of aristocratic influence that went beyond that of the White or Ghibelline faction. While that party can be said to have occupied a larger number of positions among the *anziani* and *savi* than any other group, it was still in a minority; the base on which the regime rested was wider than its principal element and included also a solid aristocratic bloc formerly aligned with the Guelphs but now estranged from them because of their identification, in the years immediately prior to 1314, with the 'popular' cause. The rise of Castruccio to a position of undisputed supremacy has to be seen against the background of the alliance, formed in 1314 and confirmed two years later, of two restricted but socially elevated segments of Lucchese society which wanted government to remain exclusively in the hands of a select minority and was prepared to tolerate a military protector to ensure the survival of their narrowly based rule. As it turned out, Castruccio used them rather than they him; but he could hardly have got where he did without their crucial, if misguided, early support. In this sense, their role at this period was vital. They were valuable to him not merely on the political level but as part of the very fabric of his administration. In the fourteenth century, Italian city-states employed not only professional civil servants but also elected citizen officials to act as vicars in subject communes and as judges, treasurers, and other functionaries both in the capital and in its territories. Tyrannies were no different from republics in this respect and Castruccio's government made extensive use of the practice of cementing the links between the regime and its leading partisans by rewarding these with important and lucrative official positions. The best evidence we have of the degree of its dependence on substantial sections of the Lucchese merchant class belongs, interestingly enough, to the closing stages of Castruccio's rule. We are fortunate in possessing a full picture of the civic administration in the last six months of 1327 (less than a year before his death) together with the names of some officials from the previous half year.[25] We can also gather some information from the legal records of the personnel serving in one of the key Lucchese courts. From these sources, it emerges clearly that, despite the exclusion from the city before this time of some of the leading Lucchese family groupings such as the Avvocati, Quartigiani, and Poggio (with the exception of its Porco branch) as a result of their disgrace and subsequent exile of some of their members, the Castruccian regime continued to rely heavily on the merchant patriciate in staffing its legal and civil service and doubtless kept the loyalty of key citizens both from that sector of society and from professional groups, such as that of the notaries, with the aid of the money it could disburse through stipends paid to those elected to administrative positions.

The list of civic officials for the last half of 1327 indicates that, even at a time when Castruccio was at the height of his power and had the means to crush all political opposition by force, he chose to distribute the control of much of the machinery of his state at the local level largely among a group of citizens, the composition of which bears a close resemblance to that of the *anziani* and *savi* who had played a critical role in endorsing and extending his authority in the early years of his rule. Even more remarkably, it shows that the participation of members of leading Lucchese families was more pronounced among the holders of important than of minor positions in his administration. If we divide the offices mentioned in the records for the latter half of 1327 into three classes, the first consisting of vicars of provinces and

---

[25] ASL Libri di Corredo, no. 4, cc. 2–56.

podestà of subject communes, the second of *camarlenghi* (treasurers), *gabellieri* (tax-collectors), *castellani* (commanders of fortresses), and other middle-rank financial and administrative positions, and the third of judges and notaries, we find that the proportion both of citizens of Lucca and of members of families represented in the *anziani* and *savi* between 1316 and 1322 is largest in the first group and smallest in the third. With the notable exception of vice-vicars of the city of Lucca and the province of Luni and the vicar of Pontremoli who were foreigners,[26] and a local vicar in Castiglione and Camporgiano,[27] all the vicars or captains of provinces were Lucchese. Of the *podestà* of subject communes, all but one or two[28] came from metropolitan families. Of a total of fifty-four men who are recorded as occupying positions of vicars, *podestà*, or captains at this time, only six at the most were non-Lucchese. Furthermore, thirty-one officials or more than half the whole number belonged to fourteen families represented among the *anziani* or *savi* in the surviving lists for the years 1316–22, or counting the various branches of the Interminelli clan (in this case the Savarigi, Castracani, Bovi, Mugia, and Mezzolombardi, as well as the main Interminelli line) as one family, thirty belonged to eleven houses.[29]

If we examine the second group of officials, which includes all those occupying the next rung of the administrative hierarchy, with the exception of judges and notaries, we rediscover the pattern evident in the list of vicars, captains, and *podestà*, but in a considerably diluted form. The majority of these office-bearers was still Lucchese, but to a less marked extent—44 out of 64, or just over two-thirds, as against eight-ninths for their superiors. And of these 44, those who belonged to families represented among the *anziani* and *savi* of 1316–22

---

[26] Matteo da Assisi was vice vicar-general of Lucca, Ser Tano di Ceppatello held the same position in Lunigiana, and the Florentine exile Ciupo de'Scolari was vicar in Pontremoli.

[27] Lemmo da Castiglione, elected on 3 June 1327 to replace the previous vicar, Burnetto Malisardi.

[28] Ser Martino da Avellano, *podestà* of Massarosa, Fibialla, Gualdo, and Bisceto, and the *podestà* of Falcinello in the province of Luni, Corraduccio di Messer Chello Cirindi, who may have been Lucchese, although I have found no other reference to his family.

[29] The families represented among both the *anziani* and *savi* of 1316–22 and the vicars and *podestà* of 1327 were the Interminelli (six officials: the Mezzolombardi, Bovi, Castracani, and Mugia junior branches of that *consorteria*, one each and the Savarigi, two), the Onesti and Martini, four each, the Mordescastelli, Boccadivacca, Del Veglio, and Porco (di Poggio), two each, and the Dal Portico, Schiatta, Ciapparoni, and Guinigi one each.

numbered 19,[30] or about two-fifths of those who were citizens of the capital, as against five-eighths among the vicars and *podestà*.

With the judges and notaries, who were in the main appointed for their professional competence rather than for political motives, the proportion both of Lucchese and of members of leading families was even smaller. Just over half were either foreigners or men from the *contado* and, of the Lucchese, only fourteen out of fifty-two bore the same names as the *anziani* and *savi* of 1316–22.[31] Moreover, those who did belong to families closely associated with the regime tended to be concentrated in certain special offices. For instance, Ser Spalla Rapondi and Ser Bartolomeo Sbarra were custodians of the registers of exiles, while Ser Tedaldino Lazzari Gay was one of the two custodians of the records of the commune. These were evidently positions of particular responsibility which had to be filled by men whom the government could trust and were therefore rather different in character from the routine posts normally entrusted to notaries. Excluding such exceptional appointments, however, it would seem in general that the legal service of the Lucchese state was less used for the purposes of patronage than were either the provincial administration or the bureaucracy associated with tax collecting. As in the chancellery,[32] headed by a series of lawyers, some of foreign, some of

---

[30] Including one Mezzolombardi, reckoned for the purpose of this analysis an Interminelli, otherwise eighteen. The families from which they came were the Martini, three officials, the Schiatta and Bettori, two each, the Bovi, Saggina, and Mezzolombardi branches of the Interminelli, one each, and the Talgardi, Del Maestro, Moriconi, Guinigi, Boccansocchi, Ciampa, Streghi, Dal Portico, and Accettanti, one each.

[31] Two Boccansocchi, two Sartori, two Mercati, and one each from the Serughi, Dardagnini, Rapondi, Sbarra, Boccella, Casciani, Bettori, and Martini families.

[32] Mosiici, 'Ricerche', 25–7, gives the names of Giovanni di Nuccio da Viterbo, Ser Giovanni Cassiani, Ser Baldo Bellasta da Pistoia, and Ser Giovanni del fu Guido di Raniero as chancellors under Castruccio. The evidence of Lucchese archival sources allows a number of other 'chancellors' to be identified but also indicates that the office they occupied was not necessarily under Castruccio one held continuously by one person for a fixed period. What appears to have happened was that each of a number of government notaries could assume that position on particular occasions to record an act of the chancellery. Thus Ser Giovanni di Nuccio da Viterbo is recorded as 'chancellor' on 28 May, 1 July, 29 October, 10 November 1316, 9 July 1317, 31 December 1318, 15 and 26 November 1319, 4 January, 23 March 1320, 29 December 1322, 2 March 1323 (ASL Archivio notarile, no. 65, 28/5/1316, no. 93, 10/11/1316, 26/11/1319, 4/1/1320, 23/3/1320, Proventi no. 13, pt. 1, cc. 1–47, Capitoli no. 1, cc. 14ᵛ.–15ᵛ., Diplomatico Serviti, 29/10/1316, Opera di S. Croce, 9/7/1317), but within the period covered by these dates this title is also accorded to Ser Genovese Bonifazi (ASL Diplomatico Spedale, 16/8/1316), Ser Alluminato Jacobi (ASL Diplomatico Archivio di Stato, 1/2/1317, S. Giustina, 28/2/1317, S. Nicolao, 14/5/1317), Ser Ubaldo Bellasta (Mosiici, 'Ricerche', 39, Sforza, 'Castruccio . . . in Lunigiana', 508), Ser Pietro di Bonaccorso da Camaiore (ASL

Lucchese origin, the government relied, as for that matter did those of republican communes, on men who made a profession of serving as notaries or judges in cities of which they were not natives or on less distinguished local notaries who sought service with the state to make up for the deficiencies of their private practices.

The records of the Lucchese commercial court, the Curia di San Cristoforo,[33] from which it is possible to establish the personnel employed by it during the whole of the Castruccian period, indicate, however, that the judges and lay consuls of at least this metropolitan tribunal were overwhelmingly drawn from the members of the city's politically influential families and only to a very minor extent from the ranks of foreign or provincial legal men. Of twenty-six serving in these capacities, only two or three were foreigners,[34] while seventeen belonged to families represented among the *anziani* and *savi* of 1316–22.[35] And of the remaining six, four bore names of families closely linked with the regime,[36] and the other two came from substantial

Diplomatico S. Nicolao, 10/12/1321), Ser Nicolao Bugarone (ibid., 28/7/1322), and Ser Lapo di Ciandoro da Prato (ASL Proventi no. 13, pt. 1, c. 14ʳ.). Ser Ubaldo Bellasta is similarly recorded as 'chancellor' on dates between 6 February 1321 and 6 May 1327 (reference above and ASL Archivio notarile no. 75, 20/2/1326, 1/1/1326 and no. 76, 6/5/1327) over a period in which Ser Nicolao di Ser Lapo da Pistoia also exercised this office (ASL Proventi no. 13, pt. ii, cc. 1 and 46). In 1328 Ser Lorenzo di Raniero Buonvisi and Ser Giovanni di Guido di Raniero were both described as 'chancellors' (ASL Diplomatico, 9/11/1328 and Lazzareschi, 'Documenti', 406). Ser Giovanni Cassiani, whom Mosiici claims was a 'chancellor', appears, however, in the only reference I have found to him, with the designation of 'notary of the . . . lord's chancellery' (Lazzareschi, 'Documenti', 372) though it is possible that, like other notaries in the Lucchese chancellery, he, too, assumed, at times, the title of 'chancellor'.

[33] ASL Curia di S. Cristoforo nos. 25–7, 30, 33–6, 38–40, 43, 46, 49–50, 52, 55, 58, 61, 64, 67 *ad annum*.

[34] Bommese da Barga, judge on two occasions in 1321 and 1326, Nicolao di Gualfredotto da Pistoia (1323), and possibly Bendino Malliveris (1326) who may well, however, have been Lucchese.

[35] Marco Cristofani dei Quartigiani (judge in 1316, 1322, and 1324), Davino Interminelli (1316) and Davino di Giovanni Savarigi (1319), Tommasello di Barca Bovi (1318) and Nuccio Bovi (1328), and Corradino di Barca Mugia, all of the Interminelli clan, Lambruccio and Matteo di Nicolao di Poggio (1316 and 1320), Totto di Dino Mordecastelli (1316), Parente di Francesco degli Onesti (1319), Giovanni and Nicolao Boccansocchi (1318 and 1325), Fiore, Cavalca, and Giovanni Sbarra (1323, 1324, and 1327), Nicolao degli Avvocati (1316), and Landuccio Sartori (1325).

[36] Guido Pollani (1316), who came from a family designated *casastici* in 1308 and whose relative Vanni was a consul of the Curia Nuova di Giustizia in 1325 (BSL MS 1009 *ad annum*); Nicolao Gigli (1317 and 1320), who had been consul of the Curia dei Treguani in 1315 and 1317, was consul of the Curia dei Foretani in 1320 (ibid.), and was to be a judge in Pietrasanta in 1327 (ASL Libri di Corredo no. 4); Tegrimo Tegrimi (1328) from the family of Castruccio's later biographer, generally considered to be a

Lucchese houses.[37] The notaries assisting the court were, on the other hand, divided roughly equally between members of leading Lucchese families and men of relatively obscure origins,[38] the former group in turn consisting half of relatives of the *anziani* and *savi* of 1316–22 and half of others from the merchant and patrician classes.[39] Overall, the proportion both of the socially elevated and of favoured partisans of the regime was higher than among the corresponding levels of the provincial or financial administrations, though even so about half of the notaries appointed were outsiders.

Notwithstanding the fragmentary nature of the surviving records, an analysis of the sample of available information which has just been examined does permit certain conclusions to be drawn about the character of Castruccio's government of Lucca and its social base. It is clear that there was a group of families, drawn partly from the returned exiles of the White faction, partly from those proscribed as *casastici* in 1308, and partly from new men of substantial means for whom loyalty to the regime was an avenue for advancement, that was prepared to be the instrument of Castruccio's rise to power in return for its acceptance as a political and administrative élite from which appointments to civic councils and offices were made. Despite the increasingly tyrannical tendency of Castruccio's rule in the course of the 1320s and the exile or execution of some of the aristocrats who had originally supported him, it would still be true to say that, at the end of his regime as in its beginning, he governed through a body of men whose co-operation he secured by virtue of the privileged position in which he placed them. The legislative power was still technically exercised by them and, while key officials such as the *podestà*, vicar-general, and the vice-vicars of Lucca and Luni were out of their number,[40] they held the majority of the higher administrative posts in

supporter of the Interminelli regime (for instance in BSL MS 1886, c. 110ʳ.); Betto Scortica (1327) whose nephew Ghinuccio was a consul of the Corte dei Mercanti.

[37] Andreuccio di Cecio de'Fiandrada (1317) and Landuccio Bandini (1322).

[38] There were fourteen notaries from great families including the Cristofani and Simonetti branches of the Quartigiani, the Dal Portico, Bettori, Serughi, Lanfredi, Passavanti, Armanni, Gentile, Paruta, and Bandini to twelve from lesser families.

[39] The Dal Portico (2 notaries), Cristofani (2 notaries), Simonetti, Bettori, and Serughi belonged to families represented among the *anziani* and *savi* of 1316–22.

[40] Ugolino da Celle, doctor of laws, was appointed vicar-general of Lucca on 4 July 1317 (ASL Atti di Castruccio no. 1, c. 6ᵛ. published in Mosiici, 'Ricerche', 31) and appears to have held that office till 1324 (ibid., 15). The *podestà* of Lucca normally changed every six months and full records of those who held that office have not

the *contado*, supervised the collection of taxes,[41] and sat as judges in the courts.[42]

The structure of government, with its blend on the one hand of professionals from outside and, on the other, of leading citizens favoured by the regime made it possible for a considerable sharing of political responsibility to be combined with an effective retention of power by Castruccio. The men who held titular office always had creatures or employees of the tyrant either immediately below or above them in the administrative hierarchy so that his authority could only be threatened as a result of a general revolt against him of the great patrician houses and not through any subversion of the governing process itself. The circumstance explains both Castruccio's continued tolerance of extensive participation by the Ghibelline aristocracy in the formal conduct of his government and the harshness with which he reacted to any hint of insubordination or conspiracy from the major families which he judged capable of overthrowing him.

The three instances in his period in office of the crushing of opposition by a section of the Lucchese nobility are his suppression of the Avvocati, Poggio, and Quartigiani in the decade between 1317 and 1327. In the first of these, the imprisonment or execution of the Avvocati in 1317, however, Castruccio was acting more as an agent of the commune faced with a revolt by a prominent noble family than as an aspiring tyrant eliminating a threat to his power. In that year, the Avvocati rebelled and held their stronghold of Cul di Pozzo against Lucca; Castruccio, with the civic levies, besieged the place, captured it, and imprisoned its defenders, with the exception of Bernocco and Nicolao degli Avvocati who were killed.[43] The resulting proscription

survived; but Baroni's reconstruction of the lists of Lucchese officials before 1400 (BSL MS 1009) enables most to be identified.

[41] The general collector of gabelles for the last six months of 1327 was Coluccio Savini and the major official for them for the same period Jacopo da San Gimignano, neither of whom were members of leading Lucchese families; but the *camarlenghi* on the whole were, for instance, Coluccio Bettori, Ser Veltrino di Ciandoro Veltri, Pietro del Maestro, Nicolao Cenami, Vanni Maurini, Betto Ronzini, Francesco Buiamonti, Ciomeo Falabrina, Ser Chellino Pontadori, Datone Moriconi, Opizo Orbicciani, and Bonaccorso Luppicini.

[42] The Curia di S. Cristoforo is the only one for which we have full lists of judges, together with the names of some lay consuls (see n. 33 above); but the records of the other courts allow some of the judges and notaries serving in them to be identified and these indicate substantial similarity between the personnel of all Lucchese law courts. See ASL Curia Nuova di Giustizia e dell'Esecutore no. 1, Curia dei Treguani no. 1, and BSL MS 1009.

[43] BNF MS Palat. 571, cc. 20ᵛ.–21ʳ. See also ASP Comune A48, cc. 74ᵛ., 81ʳ. and ᵛ.,

of those of the family involved in the revolt did not, however, in any way affect his relations with the rest of the city's patriciate: at this time, he was still no more than a captain-general of Lucca whose term of office was about to be extended for ten years (perhaps because his prompt defence of the commune's authority had effectively demonstrated his usefulness to it).

But Castruccio's next move in 1321 against a leading family—the Poggio—was rather different in character. In this case, he had to confront a direct challenge to his recently acquired position as lord of the city, and over-reacted to it. While away campaigning in Garfagnana, he received news that Stefano di Poggio had killed one of his officials in Lucca, Lando da Cachiano. He immediately returned in haste to the capital, fearing a plot to overthrow him. According to the anonymous Lucchese chronicler who has left a detailed account of this episode,[44] had the Poggio wished, they could have prevented him from re-entering the city, but they chose not to do so, being prepared to allow their kinsman to be punished for the crime he had committed, rather than defy the authority of the state. Once in Lucca, however, Castruccio, apprehensive lest the Poggio *consorteria* resist his actions against one of their number, resolved—at least according to the testimony of our chronicler informant—to seize the heads of that family. Using a stratagem that had been employed against him by Uguccione and Nieri della Faggiuola five years earlier, he invited Colao Porco di Poggio and the other leading men of the house to come to see him. They, thinking they were being summoned merely to discuss what was to be done about their kinsman's crime, went unarmed and without suspicion, only to be arrested on their arrival at Castruccio's residence. Two of the family, Stefano di Arrigo and Bernarduco di Poggio, the former of whom was the man responsible for the murder of the civic official which had set in motion this whole train of events, were executed. The Poggio tower and loggia were demolished and—if the chronicle account is to be trusted—some of the family were exiled.

95ᵛ. On 25 January 1318 the Avvocati made representations to Pisa, complaining of Castruccio's actions against them. After Lucchese ambassadors had, on 3 February, explained that the dispute between the commune and the Avvocati had arisen because of a conflict over claims to certain castles and because of the efforts of the *podestà* of Lucca to bring to justice some of the family who had committed murders, the commune of Pisa sent emissaries to Lucca to try to settle the differences between the Avvocati and Castruccio. See also ASL Curia dei Rettori no. 2, p. 67, in which the date of the expropriation of the property of the Avvocati is given as April 1318.

[44] BNF MS Palat. 571, c. 22ʳ.

There were also confiscations of property. We know from an independent source,[45] a plea by one Lemmo di Puccino di Guglielmo di
Poggio to Ludwig of Bavaria's vicar in Lucca in 1329, Count Friedrich
von Oettingen, for the restitution of a house seized by Castruccio, that
'seven years and more' after the return of the Poggio from banishment
in 1314 (in other words in the year following the spring of 1321), the
lord of Lucca, 'among other innumerable injuries which he had
committed against God and justice, unprovoked by any cause or
blame . . . rather to return evil for good to his closest and most faithful
friends' had confiscated Lemmo's property, presumably as part of a
general penalty imposed on the Poggio for the crime of their kinsman
Stefano. This petition provides confirmation of the anonymous
chronicler's testimony as to the proscription of the Poggio at this time.
But the archival evidence we have makes it clear that his statement
that, following the condemnation of two of their number, 'all the good
Poggio men were sent into exile in Lombardy' has, at least, to be quali-
fied. It can be shown that two members of the family, one of them a son
of Colao Porco, held office under Castruccio in 1327 and several
others, including Lemmo (or Lemmuccio) di Puccino di Poggio, who
was later to make his complaint to the imperial vicar, continued to live
in the city.[46] It is likely that the chronicler's assertion has some basis
and that those most closely associated with the two executed members
of the family were banished, but the sources available do not permit us
to say how many.

Notwithstanding the relatively limited nature of Castruccio's
actions against the Poggio, the impact that his treatment of them had
on his position in Lucca was certainly greater than that of his earlier
condemnation of the Avvocati and his later much more severe
repression of the Quartigiani. The reasons for this were that, in
striking against the Poggio, he had turned against his formerly closest
associates and that he had done so in circumstances which, in the eyes
of contemporaries, did not merit the punishment of more than an

---

[45] ASL Curia dei Rettori no. 1, pp. 213–14, copy in ASL Opera di S. Croce no. 7,
pp. 149–50.
[46] BNF MS Palat. 571, c. 22ʳ., ASL Libri di Corredo no. 4, Archivio notarile no. 45,
Reg. i, 2/3/1324, 19/3/1324, Reg. ii, 14/11/1323, no. 46, 30/5/1325, no. 47, 6–7/5/1326,
9/9/1326, 15/11/1326, no. 48, 13/6/1327, 3/10/1327, 12/11/1327, no. 72, 16/2/1322, 28/6/
1322, 10/11/1322, no. 73, 8/4/1323, 18/4/1323, 19/4/1323, no. 74, 11/3/1325, 30/5/1325,
no. 75, 27/11/1326, 20/2/1326, 4/4/1326, 19/4/1326, 9/5/1326, no. 76, 21/3/1327, no. 96,
13/3/1325, 27/1/1328, Diplomatico Sbarra, 20/4/1323, Podestà di Lucca no. 1, c. 109ʳ.
and ˇ.

individual. In both the anonymous chronicler's account and Lemmo di Poggio's letter one senses the shock produced by what was felt to be a disproportionate penalty in that it was imposed not only on the wrongdoer but also on those who had no part in his crime. The implications of what Castruccio had done for his relations with the Ghibelline aristocrats who were his strongest supporters can be gauged from the fact that the Poggio had been, after the Interminelli and Mordescastelli, the largest and most powerful family in the Lucchese White exile community in Pisa between 1301 and 1314, that Nicolo Castracani, Castruccio's uncle, had married into it (and possibly that, as a result, Castruccio himself had been helped by them when banished and orphaned), and that, until this time, it had occupied a privileged place among the governing élite of the town.[47]

The conspiracy of the Quartigiani in 1327,[48] nipped in the bud before it could take effect and resulting in their exile, doubtless indicates the presence of the latent opposition on the part of the great patrician houses to the increasingly powerful and arbitrary Lucchese tyrant. This family had, of course, played a critical part in the events of both 1314 and 1316 which had, between them, laid the foundations of the Castruccian despotism; but it had done so without previous commitment to the Ghibelline cause and in the expectation of political rewards which had only partly eventuated. Members of the various branches of the Quartigiani clan had held high office.[49] However, the

---

[47] There were seven Poggio either present or represented by proxies at the meetings of the White faction in Pisa in 1310–11 (ASL Archivio notarile no. 29, 30/6 and 7/10/1311); Nicolo Castracani was married to Franceschina del fu Arrigo di Poggio (ASL Archivio notarile no. 67, c. 209ʳ.); while the positions held by members of the family included those of *anziani* (1316, 1320), *savi* (1316, 1317, 1320), consuls of the Curia dei Treguani (1315 and 1317), Curia dei Foretani (1319), Curia di S. Cristoforo (1316), Nuova Corte di Giustizia (1316) (BSL MS 1009, ASL Capitoli no. 8, c. 166ᵛ. and Atti di Castruccio no. 1, cc. 19ʳ. and 21ʳ.). It is not clear whether the Stefano di Arrigo di Poggio responsible for the death of Lando da Cachiano was a brother of the Franceschina di Arrigo married to Castruccio's uncle, but if he was, then the relationship of the executed members of the Poggio family to the tyrant of Lucca would have been even closer. For the possibility that Castruccio might have been helped by Orlandino di Poggio while in England, see p. 45 above.

[48] G. Villani, *Cronica*, x. 25, BNF MS Palat. 571, c. 24ᵛ.

[49] Guerruccio Quartigiani and Coluccio Diversi had been *anziani* in 1316 and 1322 respectively and Labro Simonetti an *anziano* in 1316, a *savio* in 1320, and vicar of Pietrasanta in 1318 (BSL MS 1009 *ad an*., ASL Curia dei Ribelli no. 1, c. 10ᵛ., and Atti di Castruccio no. 1, c. 21ʳ.). Marco di Lando Cristofani was a judge of the Curia del Podestà in 1316 and of the Curia di S. Cristoforo in 1316 and 1324 and a consul of the Curia dei Treguani in 1318, of the Curia di S. Cristoforo in 1322, and of the Nuova Corte di Giustizia in 1323, while Ugolino Cristofani was consul of the Curia dei Treguani in

prospect of a condominium over Lucca in partnership with the Interminelli which events at the time of the expulsion of Uguccione della Faggiuola had seemed to promise had never been realized, thanks to the displacement of Pagano Cristofani as joint commander of the commune's armed forces and the subsequent elevation of Castruccio to a position of political as well as military dominance. There were therefore particular reasons why the Quartigiani should have acted as the spearhead of resistance to the establishment of a tyranny under the Castracani. Yet it is significant that they made no move in the aftermath of the condemnation of the Poggio and that, when they did plot against Castruccio, it was at the prompting of a foreign power, Florence under the lordship of Charles of Calabria, which they doubtless hoped might enable them not only to overthrow a hated despot but also to insure their position in the event of a Lucchese defeat.

As it happened, the Quartigiani once again miscalculated in 1327, as they had in 1314 and 1316. Won over to the conspiracy against Castruccio, according to Giovanni Villani, by 'slights received from his tyrannical lordship and by much money expended on them by the duke of Calabria and the commune of Florence',[50] they agreed, at a pre-arranged signal, to raise the papal banner in Lucca and open the gates of the city to the Guelph troops which were to approach its walls from Fucecchio and the other Val d'Arno towns, after Castruccio had been drawn away to defend Pistoia by a diversionary Florentine attack upon it. Long before this plan—all too reminiscent of that more successfully put into effect with the aid of the Quartigiani thirteen years earlier to the benefit of the Ghibellines—could come into operation, Castruccio got wind of it. If Villani is right in his assertion that the papal emblems which were to be hoisted up as a sign of revolt had already been smuggled into the town in preparation for the uprising, the discovery of the plot was hardly surprising! On 12 June, two days before the thirteenth anniversary of the betrayal of Lucca to the Pisans in 1314, Castruccio made sure that history did not repeat itself to his cost, by seizing the Quartigiani, executing twenty-two of them,[51] and driving more than a hundred of the remainder into exile.

1317. Upezzino and Nicolo Sesmondi were consuls of the Curia dei Treguani (1317) and of the Nuova Corte di Giustizia (1322) respectively (BSL MS 1009 *ad an*.).

[50] G. Villani, *Cronica*, x. 25.

[51] BSL MS Palat. 571, c. 24ᵛ. G. Villani, *Cronica*, x. 25 says that he arrested twenty-two of the family, had Guerruccio Quartigiani and his three sons hanged, and buried the remainder head downward in the ground, exiling the whole of the rest of the house.

His punishment of what had been the largest and most powerful
family grouping in Lucca after the Interminelli was therefore more
severe than that meted out earlier to the Avvocati and the Poggio. It is
unlikely, however, that it would have produced the same sense of
dismay that Castruccio's actions against the Poggio had evoked. The
Quartigiani, after all, had attempted to betray their city to an enemy in
time of war; and any Italian state of this period, whether a tyranny or a
republic, would have savagely put to death anyone guilty of such a
crime. Castruccio himself could hardly have expected any other fate in
the event of a miscarriage of his plan to admit the Pisans to Lucca in
1314.

There is a temptation to see, in the crushing of these three families
by the Lucchese tyrant, an application of the Machiavellian precept
that a prince should consolidate his state by destroying those who
have given him power and are therefore capable of taking it from him.
In fact, however, such a reading of the evidence underestimates the
extent to which the suppression of these aristocratic conspiracies falls
into the pattern of the history of late thirteenth and early fourteenth-
century Italian communes with its conflicts between the aspirations of
magnate dynasties and the efforts of the state, whether republican or
autocratic, to keep these under control. The Avvocati family, for
instance, claimed what was in effect feudal jurisdiction over certain
sections of the Lucchese *contado* which the pre-1314 regime had over-
ridden, which Uguccione della Faggiuola had probably allowed it to
exercise (as King John of Bohemia was to do later),[52] but which
Castruccio, in line with traditional communal policy, had denied. The
Quartigiani *casata*, for its part, had made every effort since 1314 to
bring about changes of government to enhance its own position, while
the Poggio *consorteria* typified the tendency of aristocratic houses
returned from exile to take liberties with the civic administration on
the assumption that the restoration of their privileges gave them
powers greater than those of ordinary citizens. The clash between
Castruccio Castracani and his former supporters has, in other words,
to be seen in terms of the transformation which occurred under his
rule from a purely factional to a despotic regime. The men who
brought him to power had been aristocrats expelled or discriminated
against because their pretensions clashed with the populist temper of

[52] See ASL Curia dei Rettori no. 2, pp. 67–82, Diplomatico Spedale 3/8/1332, and
also V. Tirelli, 'Sulla crisi istituzionale del comune di Lucca (1308–1312)', *Studi per
Enrico Fiumi* (Pisa, 1979), 317–60.

Lucca in the first decade of the Trecento. Once in office, however, he found himself compelled to identify less with their interests than with those of the state which had come under his control. While continuing to favour them in many ways, he had, of necessity, to restrain their tendency to violence, conspiracy, or lawlessness.

Notwithstanding his falling-out with particular patrician dynasties, he remained dependent on the support of the Lucchese aristocracy and merchant class. Except for the families which were banished because of the complicity of their members in crimes against the state, he counted on the collaboration (increasingly reluctant, as time went on, if the chroniclers are to be believed[53]) of the bloc of his original partisans. And, whether willingly or not, they went on working for him and so played a key role in sustaining his tyranny.

The question of how representative of the Lucchese social élite was the group of leading citizens who thus participated in the administration of Lucca under his rule is difficult to determine. An examination of the city's notarial archive for this period, involving a comparison of those known to have held office under Castruccio with those noted in contracts in surviving registers,[54] suggests that perhaps half the leading families in the city took some part in the running of its government at this time and that the section of that half most strongly committed to the regime held an overwhelming majority (of more than two-thirds) of the offices the dominant party distributed among its followers.[55]

[53] For evidence of this see 'Storie pistoresi', 73–4, G. Villani, *Cronica*, x. 25, and BNF MS Palat. 571, c. 24ʳ.

[54] The registers surveyed were ASL Archivio Notarile no. 19, Reg. iv, Ser Alluminato Jacobi, no. 22, Reg. ii, Ser Bartolomeo Paganelli, no. 27, Reg. ii, Ser Giovanni Spiafami, no. 31, Ser Bindo da Coreglia, no. 40, Reg. ii, Ser Giovanni Beraldi, nos. 44–9, Ser Finocchio Martini, nos. 65–77, Ser Rabbito Toringhelli, no. 89, Reg. v, Ser Nicolao Moccindenti, no. 92, Reg. ii, Ser Veltro Marchesi, no. 93, Regs. i and ii, Ser Nicolao Notte, no. 94, Reg. i, Ser Nicolao Boccella, nos. 95–6, Ser Federigo di Ser Bianchi da Marlia, no. 98, Reg. i, Ser Opizzone di Ser Bindo da Coreglia, no. 99, Reg. i, Ser Lucchese Ciandocchi da Fibialla.

[55] Of the families dubbed *casastici* in 1308 also occurring in the notarial registers cited above, forty-one included at least one member whose name is on the surviving lists of officials and councillors, while sixty-two did not. Of eighty-seven families which appear to have been the biggest in the city on the basis of the information furnished by these registers, fifty-eight included men who held office, according to extant records, though fifteen of them only once. Thirty-five of these larger houses also occur among the sixty-five families two or more members of which were officials or councillors under Castruccio (of these sixteen, or nearly half, were ex-*casastici*). Taking these 'larger families' together with other ex-*casastici* present in Lucca between 1316 and 1328 as a combined group of one hundred and forty-four houses, we find that forty-five of these provided rather more than two-thirds of office-bearers at this time, twenty-three had a single

The picture that emerges from this admittedly very tentative
analysis of the fragmentary data available to us is therefore one of an
aristocratic society still to some extent divided on factional lines, with
an in-group collaborating, albeit with growing reluctance, with a more
and more evident tyranny, and an out-group remaining aloof from, or
kept out of active participation in government. Closer examination of
the structure of the in-group reveals it to be made up of the three
elements already mentioned: the old White or Ghibelline houses, the
converted ex-Guelph *casastici*, and a miscellaneous collection of other,
sometimes quite minor families, who, for one reason or other, became
protégés of the regime. The former members of the White exile community appear to have been the strongest and most consistent supporters of the government. Of the families represented in it, only two, the
Carincioni and Manni, appear both to have been present in Lucca
under Castruccio and not to have had any of their members elected as
officials or councillors. The others, notably the Interminelli and its
various branches, the Mordecastelli, the Poggio and Avvocati until
their condemnation, the Accettanti, Giordani, Rapa, and Bosco
branches of the Del Fondo, the Martini, Ciapparoni, Rapondi,
Onesti, and Barca, formed the nucleus of the ruling group. The exiling
of two of these families—the Avvocati and Poggio—between 1317 and
1321 would clearly have weakened both its strength and its cohesion.
The ex-Guelph *casastici* who constituted the next most important
element in it were a more disparate collection of great houses, headed
by the Quartigiani with its Cristofani, Diversi, Sesmondi, Simonetti,
and Ceci branches, and including the leading merchant dynasties of
the Guinigi and Sbarra, and also the Sartori (or Sartoy), Salamoni,
Boccansocchi, Dal Portico, the related Lanfredi and Boccadivacca
and Buiamonti and Rossi families, the Malisardi, Mercati, Bettori,
Peri, Pantassa, Pollani, Spoletini, Beccafava, Burlamacchi, Callianelli, Cenami, Falabrina, Gherarducci, Mangialmacchi, Marrachi,
Panichi, Pinelli, Tadolini, and Villanova. The defection of the Quartigiani in 1327 seriously reduced the effective size of this bloc which,
however, even earlier had not made up more than about a third of the
non-White *casastici* houses. Its role in the period when Castruccio had
been laying the foundations of his power had undoubtedly been
crucial in enlarging his originally restricted political base, but its

member among those known to have been councillors or officials, and seventy-six
appear not to have been represented in political or administrative positions.

importance probably declined thereafter. The third group of his supporters who had belonged neither to families banished in 1301 nor to those declared *potenti* in 1308, though socially less influential than the other two, probably included more individuals who made a significant contribution to the maintenance of the regime. In it were some prominent houses, the Cagnoli, Dardagnini, Galganetti, Passamonti, Perfettucci, Schiatta, Talgardi, Bandini, Bianchi, Borgognoni, Jacobi, Pontadori, Saulli and Terizendi; but it was through a few distinguished members of these and other smaller families that this group made itself invaluable to Castruccio's government. Among these men were Puccino Galganetti, *anziano* in 1316 and *savio* in 1317 and 1320, Mingo and Triumpho Spada, the former *savio* in 1317 and 1320, the latter *anziano* in 1316, Coluccio Mingogi, *savio* in 1316 and 1320, and his son Puccinello, *anziano* in 1322, Guelfo Casciani, *anziano* in 1316 and *savio* in 1317 and 1320, Ser Betto Dardagnini, *savio* in 1316, 1317, and 1320, Pietro del Maestro, *anziano* in 1320 and *provisor gabelle* in 1327, Coluccio Serughi, *savio* in 1317, and his nephew Ser Ghirardo, notary to the Court of San Cristoforo in 1322 and to the vicariate of Val di Nievole in 1327, and Ser Nicolao and Passamonte Passamonti, *savi* in 1317 and 1320 respectively. These were obviously henchmen of the regime, among whom one might include Castruccio's brothers-in-law Perotto and Ghirarduccio Streghi who, although late recruits to the White faction in the closing stages of its Pisan exile, in fact more properly belong with this handful of devoted servants of the regime which (if one includes the Streghi among them) held no fewer than 23 of the 106 positions of *anziani* and *savi* whose occupants we can identify between 1316 and 1322.

The 'in-group' which helped Castruccio establish and maintain his power is relatively easy to analyse into its main components. The composition of the sector of the Lucchese upper and middle class which remained outside it is, however, more difficult to determine. The indications we have of it are, of necessity, negative. Some large aristocratic families are not represented in the known lists of office-bearers, such as the Obizi, Bernarducci, and Salamoncelli, were mere remnants of houses the majority of whose members were in exile. Others appear, from the evidence of notarial records, to have been very small during the Castruccian period, even if earlier they had been sufficiently formidable to earn the title of *casastici* or *potenti*. Nevertheless, there were at least fifty sizeable families present in Lucca between 1316 and 1328 which appear not to have been involved in

active participation in government under Castruccio. From the existing evidence, it would seem, however, that they were not a cohesive
group,[56] but were rather a miscellaneous set of families who had
neither come over to the victorious Ghibellines in 1314, nor been
exiled by them, nor included individuals who particularly sought to
serve or ingratiate themselves with the new masters of the town. One
can conclude, then, at least on the basis of indications furnished by the
surviving sources, that the restriction of the ruling group during the
Castruccian period to about half of the city's leading families did not
imply the division of the city into two clear-cut factions, each with its
own social substructure. Participation in government in Lucca
between 1316 and 1328 was fairly narrow; but it did not for that reason
fail to reflect the interests of the bulk of the aristocracy, some of the
unrepresented members of which had connections with, and therefore
lines of communication to, those who did hold office.[57]

While there has been a tendency to regard the Castruccian era as an
interruption in the political history of Lucca which is seen as
progressing from the communal period ending in 1314 to the aristo-

---

[56] Some of the families not represented in the lists of officials, such as the Toringhelli
and Forteguerra, had strong links with known strong supporters of the regime (see ASL
Archivio notarile no. 48, 13/5/1327, 10/9/1327, no. 68, 17/7/1319, no. 69, 1/2/1320, no.
72, 28/6/1322, no. 73, 22/1/1323, no. 77, 11/5/1328). Others, however, such as the
Bambacari, Faitinelli, Broccoli, Porta, and Bernardini, do not appear to be so
connected and were probably sympathizers of the former regime who had been able to
escape the penalty of exile. Others again, such as the Dombellinghi, Taddiccioni,
Cassuola, Appicalcani, Del Gelso, Moccindenti, Spiafami, Squarcialupi, Notte, and
Scandaleone, would seem to have had no particularly evident political loyalties or
bonds of kinship to link them to the ruling group in Lucca either under Castruccio or
before 1314.

[57] Apart from families such as the Overardi (connected with the Mordescastelli (ASL
Archivio notarile no. 45, Reg. ii, 14/2/1323) and the Malpigli (married into Raponi and
Cristofani, ibid., nos. 77, 9/2/1328 and 45, Reg. i, 3/1/1324)—which perhaps fall into the
same category as the Toringhelli and Forteguerra, of houses which are more closely
associated with the ruling faction than with those outside it—there is a number of
families with connections that cut across the apparent political divisions in Lucchese
society at this time, for instance, the Castagnacci which had been business associates of
both the Guinigi and Benettoni (ibid., no. 64, 31/12/1313 and 12/2/1314) and were inter-
married with the Ranieri and Falconi (ibid., no. 48, Reg. ii, 27/1/1323 and no. 67, 24/10/
1315); and the Guidiccioni who were related to the Onesti and Gualfredi and acted for a
member of the Schiatta family (ibid., nos. 66, 69, 71, 25/3/1317, 24/1/1320, 27/6/1321,
27/7/1321). Other examples of such houses are the Testa—related to the Appicalcani
and Onesti, Baratella, Mangialmacchi, Orselli, and Bettori (ASL Archivio notarile nos.
68, 71, 73, 77, 24/9/1319, 6/6/1321, 14/5/1323, 2/4/1328, 26/5/1328), and the Morla
branch of the Allucinghi with its links with the Galganetti, Cannavecchia, and Da Fondora (ibid., nos. 31, 17/4/1318, 6/7/1318, 30/9/1318, 7/11/1318, 15/11/1318, 5/12/1318,
44, Reg. ii, 8/3/1320).

cratic republic set up in 1430, after an interlude in which civic liberty was suppressed in turn by Castruccio, the Pisans, and the Guinigi, one could perhaps more accurately see the city in the years between 1314 and 1328 as witnessing a reaction against the 'popular' movement of the previous half-century and laying the foundations of the oligarchic state that eventually emerged more than a hundred years later. Many of the characteristics of the subsequent government by an élite were already present under Castruccio. However, politically the situation was vastly different between 1316 and 1328 from what it was to be after 1430. In the former period, the aristocracy was being used to buttress the authority of a tyrant and lacked the power it later enjoyed. Also, although the divisions between those appointed to offices and those excluded from them do not appear, at least on the basis of the meagre evidence we possess, to indicate any sharp rift in Lucchese upper-class society at this time, the size and influence of the group not involved in active participation in government certainly made for a restriction of the political base of the Castruccian regime. The significance of the apparent withdrawal of many important families from the service of the state lies not so much in their real or potential opposition to it as in the constitution by them of a bloc of uncommitted citizens which grew with every defection from the dominant faction. It was Castruccio's failure to become leader of more than a section of the city's aristocracy that rendered him vulnerable to losing the support of the majority of the Lucchese patriciate when he broke with some of his former followers. The condemnation of the Avvocati, Poggio, and Quartigiani undoubtedly weakened his political position. At the same time, it also represented part of a process by which the great families which, by their traditional tendency to violence, had helped to bring him to power were eliminated because of the threat they represented to the regime he was trying to establish. As in most Italian city-states of the period, there was a repression of the more turbulent elements of the old aristocracy to the advantage of a mercantile élite, prepared to serve the prevailing government in order to maintain and extend its influence over it, thereby profiting from the decline of the feuding patrician dynasties of the Duecento. In Lucca, those who underpinned the Castruccian tyranny were increasingly, as time went on, men of rising merchant families whose role in the administration of Castruccio's state became more prominent as some of its former supporters fell out with it and so ceased to exercise their previous power.

2. *The emergence of Castruccio's seigneurial aspirations and the building of the Augusta*

If a modification of the character of the ruling élite was one of the effects of the crushing of the Avvocati and Poggio and later of the Quartigiani, another was the gradual change of the Castracani Signoria from a factional to a princely regime and a broadening of its area of operation from the restricted field of civic politics to diplomatic and military activity involving the whole west Tuscan region. While one reason for the more aggressive foreign policy adopted by Castruccio from about 1322 onwards was his realization that his state had to expand if it were not to be overcome by its enemies, another was the recognition that the best means of securing his hold over Lucca was to extend his authority beyond it and, in the process, obtain imperial endorsement of his position which would free him from his original dependence on the favour of his subjects.

Whereas, up to 1322, Castruccio's relations with neighbouring cities had been governed by his support of the Ghibelline cause in northern Italy as a whole, in April and May of that year the first signs appear of designs against Pisa and Pistoia, the long-term end of which was not to advance the interests of his faction but to exploit the situation in these communes to his own long-term advantage. In each case Castruccio sought to intervene in civic dissensions by applying military pressure which, he hoped, would secure the installation of a regime he could later supplant. In April, he exploited divisions in Pistoia by initiating the intrigues with the Tedici family there which were to lead three years later to the annexation of that town by Lucca.[58] In Pisa, in May 1322, a similar opportunity for intervention seemed to present itself: following the death of Gaddo delle Gherardesca two years earlier, discord had arisen between some of the great families who had supported him, notably the Lanfranchi and Gualandi, and Nieri della Gherardesca, his successor as captain of the city's troops, though not yet as lord of the town. Nieri had offended these patricians by choosing Lippo da Caprona as his principal adviser and confidant: the Lanfranchi reacted by killing Lippo's son Guido, so unleashing violent street battles in which Corbino de' Lanfranchi, the instigator of Guido's death, was captured and beheaded.[59] The resulting turmoil

[58] See p. 160 below.

[59] The best account of these events is in a contemporary Aragonese dispatch published in Finke, *Acta*, ii. 579–80. See also G. Villani, *Cronica*, ix. 153.

also brought out the forces of the 'popular' party, the exiled leader of which, Coscietto del Colle, was encouraged to return, only to be betrayed and executed. In the midst of the confusion provoked by this three-way conflict, Castruccio suddenly appeared with his troops at San Giuliano on the fringes of Pisan territory,[60] evidently with the intention of exploiting the situation to his own advantage, though whether he was at this stage supporting Coscietto, as Meliconi suggests,[61] or the Lanfranchi, with whom he was subsequently to conspire against Nieri delle Gherardesca, is not clear. Whatever his motives, his plan failed, for the fear of a Lucchese military attack enabled Nieri to unite his partisans, pacify the city, and have himself proclaimed *signore* on 13 June. The result was a straining of relations between Lucca and Pisa which was followed by a complete rift between the two cities when Castruccio's complicity in the Lanfranchi plot was revealed to Nieri della Gherardesca in October 1323.[62] While the alliance with Pisa which had been the corner-stone of Lucchese foreign policy since 1314 did not formally end until then, it was in fact the events of May and June 1322 which were responsible for reversing the previous trend of close association between the two west Tuscan communes.

It is probably not entirely coincidental that it was in the early days of June 1322, when it became clear that his designs on Pisa had not borne fruit and when, consequently, his situation, both externally and internally, had become far more vulnerable, that he resolved on the construction of his 'Augusta' or citadel. Giovanni Villani, reporting on the building of this 'marvellous castle', as he called it, remarked that

[60] G. Villani, *Cronica*, ix. 153, Granchi, 'De proeliis', *RIS*, xi, cols. 313–14 or *RIS* (n. edn.), xi, pt. 2, pp. 94–100, and 'Storie pistoresi', 69–70 (the last work, however, misdates the episode of Coscietto's return and death).

[61] Footnote in C. Meliconi's edition of 'De proeliis Tusciae', cited in previous footnote *RIS* (n. edn.), xi, pt. 2, p. 95.

[62] Finke, *Acta*, iii. 420, G. Villani, *Cronica*, ix. 230. Villani dates the Lanfranchi conspiracy 24 October 1323. Finke gives the date 22 December 1322 for a letter in which Ginevra, countess of Donoratico, informs her father, Bernabò Doria of Genoa, of the Lanfranchi plot. Unfortunately, the date is not contained in the text of the letter, so that it seems likely that Finke, confused by reference in it to Lippo da Caprona, may have mistakenly attributed it to 1322 instead of 1323. (Lippo da Caprona was, in fact, involved in the events of both May–June 1322 and those of October 1323 and Finke, by telescoping his role in one of these disturbances with that in the other, could have supposed that the Countess of Donoratico's words referred to the earlier rather than the later outbreak of civil violence.) If, as seems almost certain, Finke did misdate this letter then Villani's testimony as to when the Lanfranchi plot occurred has to be accepted.

Castruccio, frightened by the death of Federigo of Montefeltro (who had been killed by his subjects the preceding April) and the recent disturbances in Pisa against Count Nieri and 'fearing lest the people of Lucca might rise in fury', decreed the enclosure, by means of a very strong wall containing twenty-nine large towers, of almost a fifth of the city, from which 'he expelled the inhabitants and where he went to live with his household and troops'.[63] According to another chronicler, the task was undertaken with a sense of extreme urgency for, after the foundation stone had been laid on 7 June, work proceeded on the enterprise 'day and night in haste, even on feast days'![64] From both of these contemporary or near-contemporary accounts, it is evident that the building of the Augusta was inspired by a fear of insurrection at a time when Castruccio, after his harsh treatment of the Poggio the previous year, could no longer count on his former followers in the city, and when the open hostility of Florence and the veiled antagonism of Pisa made external support for moves against him in Lucca a strong possibility. The speed with which the project was completed would seem to indicate, further, the extent of his feelings of insecurity at this period and his determination to put himself, his household, and soldiers out of reach of the anger or resentment of his fellow-citizens as quickly as he could.

Notwithstanding later historians' tendency to take the chroniclers' description of the Augusta as a castle at its face value in the modern meaning of the term,[65] the fortified enclosure to which Castruccio gave this name was in fact an inner city rather than a *rocca* or free-standing citadel; that is to say it was a walled-in section of the town within which certain changes were made to meet the need of the troops and officials who came to occupy it, but which otherwise retained most of its former buildings. As a document preserved in the Lucchese state archives, detailing purchase or compensation payments to those whose houses and towers were demolished during its

    [63] G. Villani, *Cronica*, ix. 154.

    [64] BNF, MS Palat. 571, c. 22^r. The anonymous Lucchese author of this places the building of the Augusta in 1323, but the omission of a section on the year 1322 and the inclusion of his entry describing the construction of that citadel between those reporting the defeat of Ramon de Cardona by the Milanese (6 July 1322) and the expulsion of Galeazzo Visconti from Milan (8 November 1322) indicates that the year heading is wrong and should read 1322.

    [65] In fact, as J. Plesner points out in the first chapter of his *L'Émigration de la campagne à la ville libre de Florence au XIIIe siècle* (Copenhagen, 1934), 1–33, the term 'castello', as distinct from 'rocca', was employed for a fortified village in medieval Italy, not a castle in the English meaning of the word. (See also ibid., 94.)

construction, indicates,[66] the area cleared to make way for the Augusta consisted of a swathe cut through Lucca along the line of that structure's walls (and just beyond them) and two limited spaces opened out within it for the Cortile del Signore and for two official buildings, called the Casa Treustrix and the Palazzo della Terzenaia.[67] The only additional buildings which, at least according to this source, were destroyed in the course of its erection were several towers, one of which was in the Augusta, some of which lay along its periphery, and the rest of which were outside it, in some cases a considerable distance away.

Before it came into being, Castruccio had lived in the house of the descendants of Percivalle dal Portico which lay within the area it was to occupy.[68] In constructing it, therefore, he did no more than put a wall around the quarter of the town in which he resided, which he then filled with his soldiers and administrators and within which he acquired and altered the disposition of existing buildings to accommodate them. Other structures enclosed, so to speak incidentally, in the Augusta, such as the Dominican convent of San Romano, were left undisturbed.

An analysis of the records of payments for buildings taken over or destroyed in the course of its construction reveals that the space cleared began in the *contrada* of Santa Maria Filicorbi around the 'Magione' or temple of St John of Jerusalem, extended eastwards into the *contrada* of Sant' Alessandro Maggiore (taking in one house in the *contrada* of San Sensio to the north), and then entered the *contrada* of San Pietro in Cortina in the *brachio* or branch of the Callianelli. From here, it swung south, turning within the *contrada* of Santa Maria in

[66] ASL Fortificazioni no. 1.

[67] Ibid., cc. 94ʳ. and ᵛ, and 99ʳ.–101ᵛ. for 'Casa Treustrix' and cc. 79ᵛ.–82ᵛ. for 'Palatium Tersanarie'. A further building 'palatium pontis Lucane Comunis' is mentioned in ASL Fortificazioni no. 1, c. 77ᵛ.; but this may not have been within the Augusta but outside it.

[68] ASL Archivio notarile no. 44 Reg. i, loose sheet dated 10/7/1318 at 2/10/1317 in register. See also ASL Diplomatico Serviti, 29/10/1316, where a meeting of the *anziani* is recorded as taking place in the same house which apparently served not merely as Castruccio's residence but as the centre of his administration as captain. The location of the house is given in the full description of it on ASL Fortificazioni no. 1, cc. 92ʳ.–95ʳ. which records the deed of his purchase of the place on 1/7/1324 (published in A. Romiti, 'Il palazzo signorile ed il palazzo comunale di Lucca nel XIV secolo: problemi strutturali e funzionali', in I. B. Barsali, *Il palazzo pubblico di Lucca* (Lucca, 1980), 43–7). There is also another description of this building in ASL Archivio Guinigi 130 bis, c. 39ʳ.

Palazzo to cut through the edge of the *contrada* of Santa Reparata and approach the city wall west of the *contrada* of San Dalmazio.[69]

Since Matraia published his *Lucca nel milleduecento* in 1843, it has generally been considered that the limits of the Augusta were the thirteenth-century city walls to the south and east and the line of the present Vie Vittorio Emanuele and Vittorio Veneto to the north and west.[70] The evidence of compensation payments for buildings destroyed in the course of its erection suggests, however, as I have argued elsewhere,[71] that it lay a little to the east of this position, extending in this direction to cover what are now the Piazza Napoleone and part of the Piazza del Giglio. There are, in addition, other indications which show that the church of San Pietro in Cortina, which used to stand in the area covered by the former square, was within the circuit of the Augusta.[72] Also, the account given by the chronicler Giovanni Sercambi of its demolition in 1370 supports the view that its eastern wall lay some distance beyond the street now known as the Via Vittorio Veneto.[73] The western boundary of this fortified enclosure is more difficult to define because there is no record of indemnities paid for houses or other structures pulled down to make way for it. While at first this would make it seem that it corresponded with the city wall, there are difficulties about accepting this view: firstly, the absence of any reference to buildings razed between that wall and the vicinity of the Piazza della Magione and secondly, the problem of the location of the Castello Cesareo constructed by the Emperor Charles IV one year before the Augusta was demolished. This lay at the western extremity of the city and must have been outside the Augusta. Part at least of it

[69] For details of the houses demolished in each of these *contrade*, see L. Green 'Il problema dell'Augusta e della villa di Castruccio Castracani a Massa Pisana', *ACCC*, 358–62.

[70] G. Matraia, *Lucca nel milleduecento* (Lucca, 1843), 13 and map at end of volume. Modern guides, such as I. B. Barsali, *Guida di Lucca* 2nd edn. (Lucca, 1970), 22, 88, have accepted this definition of its position.

[71] See my article, 'Il problema', 362–3.

[72] See ASL Capitoli no. 52, pp. 276–7, 283, 286–91, 295, 298, 300, and especially p. 284 and ASL Fortificazioni no. 1, c. 143ʳ. The church of San Pietro in Cortina was pulled down early in the nineteenth century to open up space for the Piazza Napoleone.

[73] Sercambi, *Croniche*, pt. i, c. 216 (vol. i, p. 189), states that the workmen who pulled down the Augusta in 1370 demolished it up to the postern of San Martino. This lay some way east of the Porta San Pietro which we know from another passage in the same work (ibid., pt. i, c. 206, (vol. i, p. 180)) led into the Augusta. There is disagreement as to the exact location of the Porta San Pietro, but only as to whether it lay on the line of the eastern or western boundary of the Piazza Napoleone. Whichever of these positions it occupied, the area of the Augusta must have covered this square.

extended to one of the gates of that citadel so it must have occupied at least some of the space which the latter would have to have covered if it had gone to the town wall.[74] For this reason, it is most likely that the western side of the Augusta followed the line of the former Roman wall and that its western gate, the Porta del Cavallo or San Romano, opened on to the Prato del Marchese that lay in the south-western corner of the city. The absence of compensation payments for struc-tures levelled in this area could then be accounted for by the existence of unbuilt-on land on the edge of the Prato or along the former town wall, parts of which might well still have been standing in 1322.

The swathe cut through the houses of Lucca to accommodate the Augusta would have run along and just north of the present Via Vittorio Emanuele and then south from the Piazza XX Settembre through the Corte Paoli and Piazza del Giglio.[75] It would have allowed not only for the walls of that fortified enclosure but for a space beyond to make it more easily defensible in the event of an attack on it from the direction of the town. The reduction in the height of the towers lying some distance from its perimeter would also, in all likelihood, have been carried out to prevent it from being dominated, in such an eventuality, by any other structure in the city. The records we have show, in fact, that five towers, lying beyond the zone cleared of houses in the *contrade* already mentioned (which formed a kind of arc around the Augusta), were brought down to roof level. They were the Malagallia–Manciorini tower in San Martino,[76] the Morla tower in Santa Giulia,[77] the Ruggeroni tower in San Gregorio,[78] the Fiandrada

---

[74] Ibid., pt. I, c. 200 I (vol. i, p. 172). See also the account given by Sercambi of the location of Paolo Guinigi's citadel, built in 1401 on the site of Charles IV's former Castello Cesareo which had been destroyed at the same time as the Augusta in 1370 (ibid., pt. II, c. 215 (vol. iii, pp. 36–7)) and my discussion of this question in 'Il problema', 368–71.

[75] It is worth noting that, in the seventeenth-century manuscript history of Lucca by Francesco Bendinelli (BSL MS 2588, ii, c. 90ʳ.), the boundaries of the Augusta were defined as going from the Gigli palace (the present Cassa di Risparmio di Lucca) to the walls of the city near the convent of San Girolamo, then along the city wall up to the tower of San Paolino (near the present *baluardo* of the same name) and then north towards the hospital of the Misericordia, turning near the nunnery of San Domenico (near the present Via San Domenico). Bendinelli claims that, in his day, traces could still be seen of former walls of the Augusta, near the convents of San Girolamo and San Domenico and beside the church of Santa Maria della Rotonda.

[76] ASL Fortificazioni no. 1, c. 57ᵛ.

[77] Ibid., cc. 63ʳ. and ᵛ., 79ʳ. and ᵛ.

[78] Ibid., cc. 64ᵛ. and 65ʳ.

tower in the Lischia district,[79] and the Pinelli tower, the location of
which is given as 'opposite the church of San Salvatore in Mustiolo'.[80]

Compared with the fairly large number of buildings demolished or
cut down in height along the walls of the Augusta or beyond them, the
records inform us of only a few properties acquired within its limits;
and the deeds relating to these refer to sales made directly to Castruccio rather than to compensation for demolition paid by the commune.
Also, apart from the Montemagno tower,[81] the houses or pieces of land
purchased within the Augusta were situated, as has already been
mentioned, in two areas, that immediately around Castruccio's
palazzo and that in the vicinity of the Casa della Terzenaia. The first
group of acquisitions consisted of a continuous bloc of buildings
around the Cortile del Signore. It included the Dal Portico palace in
which the lord of Lucca lived, the house next door, formerly owned by
the same family, with the portico from which it had derived its name,
the 'casalino' or cottage on the other side of Castruccio's residence
which was converted into the Casa Treustrix, and a group of houses
surrounding the large court 'del Signore' which had been opened out
behind the Dal Portico *palazzi*.[82] With the exception of the 'casalino'
next door to his palace, all the houses recorded as being bought by
him were evidently still standing in their original state at the dates of
purchase between 10 May 1324 and 25 June 1326, which provides some
positive evidence (together with the negative indication of the almost
complete absence of compensation payments for the demolition of
structures within the Augusta) of the retention within this 'citadel' of
most of the buildings originally in the area it covered.

The other set of properties acquired by Castruccio in the Augusta
was in the *contrada* of Arestano around the hospital of St. Nicholas of
Arestano which gave the district its name and the new building called
the Casa or Palazzo della Terzenaia. The exact location of this
complex is more difficult to establish than that around the Cortile del
Signore, but it probably lay south-west of San Romano near the site of

---

[79] Ibid., c. 73ʳ.
[80] Ibid., c. 82ʳ. and ᵛ.
[81] Ibid., cc. 58ʳ. and ᵛ. and 71ʳ.
[82] The Dal Portico palace in which Castruccio lived was on a corner bounded on the
north and east by streets; to the west it was adjoined by the 'casalino' which became the
Casa Treustrix and to the south by the house 'del Portico' and the Cortile del Signore.
(ASL Fortificazioni, no. 1, cc. 92ʳ., 99ʳ.–101ᵛ.). Six other houses all adjoined the Cortile
del Signore (ibid., cc. 87ʳ–89ʳ., 90ʳ–91ᵛ., 104ʳ–111ʳ.), probably along its south-eastern and
southern sides.

the then monastery of San Ponziano, the lands of which appear later to have passed to the former Dominican convent.[83] Here, between 1324 and 1327, Castruccio bought four houses, two 'casalini', and some land, some in the immediate vicinity of the Casa della Terzenaia[84] and others elsewhere in the Arestano district.[85]

On the basis of the available evidence, it would therefore appear that the modifications effected in the interior of the Augusta were fairly minor and that it was only the necessity of clearing space for its northern and eastern walls and for an area of open ground beyond them which led to substantial demolition of existing buildings.

Despite, however, the limited nature of the changes effected in the process of the erection of Castruccio's new inner city or citadel, there is no doubt of the significance of its construction. It marks a turning-point in the history of his rule, dividing the first half of his period in power, when he governed very much as the head of his faction, from the second in which military considerations came to dominate his actions and he sought to make himself the hereditary lord of an extended territorial principality. The Augusta, though not the reason for the transition from the one phase to the other, was its symbol. The man who shared it with his officials and troops was no longer a citizen, but a general and would-be prince whose horizons extended beyond Lucca from which its walls now protected him.

It expressed the tendency which his government had been taking ever since his election as lord of Lucca two years earlier and which was to be confirmed, near the end of his life, by his elevation to the title of duke by Ludwig of Bavaria. As far as the city itself was concerned, however, it signified more the withdrawal of its ruler from the kind of contact with its day-to-day activities that had marked the early years of the regime than any sharp change in the character of the urban community. Lucca continued to be an essentially trading and silk-manufacturing town despite the new directions followed by its tyrant's

---

[83] See ibid., cc. 79ᵛ.–80ʳ., where two 'casalini' belonging to the hospital of St. Nicholas of Arestano are described as adjoining the Palazzo della Terzenaia and the city wall 'ex parte anguli qui respicit versus monasterium S. Ponziani'. Matraia, *Lucca*, 86, gives a reference to a parchment roll of San Romano (which unfortunately he fails to date) recording the cession by the monks of San Ponziano of some of their land to the friars of San Romano for the building of their church and Barsali, *Guida*, 144, records the existence of the monastery of San Ponziano 'in Placule' in the south-western corner of early medieval Lucca.

[84] ASL Fortificazioni, no. 1, cc. 79ᵛ.–82ʳ, 102ʳ.–103ᵛ., 114ʳ.–115ᵛ.

[85] Ibid., cc. 96ʳ.–98ʳ. and 111ᵛ.–112ᵛ.

policies. Indeed, there are some grounds for believing that it was precisely in the years when Castruccio's government, in its external aspect, was becoming more militaristic and expansionary, that the city's economy, subject to a temporary recession since the sack of 1314, began to revive. The growth of the political power of Lucca, after it had freed itself from the Pisan yoke in the form of Uguccione's despotism in 1316, seems to have gone hand in hand with its commercial resurgence.

3. *Lucchese commerce under Castruccio Castracani*

Evidence of economic activity at this period is, of course, not sufficiently complete for any accurate estimate of its extent to be made. But the city's notarial archive does provide a rough gauge of the volume of business contracts at this time and of the nature of the trading transactions in which Lucchese merchants were engaged. We are fortunate in the almost complete survival of the registers of Ser Rabbito Toringhelli, not merely in the period of Castruccio's predominance over Lucca,[86] but also during the preceding sixteen years – particularly since he appears to have been the most important of the Lucchese notaries concerned with commercial dealings. (Certainly, his clients included the town's leading banking and trading families, such as the Guinigi, Sbarra, Forteguerra, and Rapondi.) From his record of contracts, we can get an impression both of the fluctuations of Lucchese business activity under Castruccio and of the level of capital investment in partnerships and in raw silk purchases, which approximately indicate the amount of money available for commerce and manufacture.

The general picture which emerges from them is of economic revival in the 1320s. Up until about 1320, the main Lucchese trading company was that of the Guinigi, which appears in the early years of the Trecento to have taken the place of the Ricciardi, the dominant banking and commercial house in the city in the late thirteenth century that had gone bankrupt in the 1290s.[87] In 1321, the Guinigi

---

[86] In the Castruccian period, there are gaps for the last seven months of 1323 (ASL Archivio notarile no. 73) and between 9 May and 27 December 1324 (ibid., no. 74). Otherwise the record of notarial acts is complete except for some water damage in the opening pages of no. 71, the content of which, however, overlaps with that of no. 70.

[87] On the Ricciardi operations in England see the references quoted above in Chapter II, n. 71 and, on their Lucchese connections, T. W. Blomquist, 'Lineage, land and business in the thirteenth century: The Guidiccioni Family of Lucca', *Actum Luce*, ix (1980), 7–19 and xi (1982), 7–34, 'Commercial Association in Medieval Lucca', *Business History Review*, xlv (1971), 175. In Lucca, the Ricciardi company, though effectively bankrupt, carried on with the winding up of its affairs at least until 1296 (see ASL

partnership broke up, leaving the field open for other smaller companies which had begun to form in the immediately preceding period and which operated on short-term partnership agreements, sometimes taking in merchants formerly involved in the Guinigi system. Over the next few years, an increasingly intense rhythm of business activity seems to be indicated by Ser Rabbito Toringhelli's record of contracts, particularly notable in 1325–7, but maintaining itself to some degree right up to the end of the Castruccian era.

The Guinigi, who are recorded as a family company as early as 1284[88] and were active as merchants in the first decade of the fourteenth century,[89] had undoubtedly the most prominent business partnership in the early stages of Castruccio's period in power. Its main members at this time were Ruberto del fu Panfollia, Nicolao del fu Filippo, Giovanni del fu Bonifazio, and Nicolozo, his son, all of whom were Guinigi, and Guarniero Guarnieri, Benetto Barca, and Pietro del Maestro who were not.[90] Later, two other Guinigi, Pero del fu Filippo and Fassino, the son of Ruberto del fu Panfollia, joined the firm as did Nicolao di Oderigo Pettinati, one of its former 'factors'.[91] Shortly afterwards, in May 1318, another Guinigi partnership appeared, made up of Francesco and Lazzaro del fu Bartolomeo, Dino del fu Lazzaro, and his nephew Lazzaruccio del fu Opizo, associated briefly with another important Lucchese merchant, Ciucco del fu Guido Rapondi.[92]

These two Guinigi companies are recorded in the Lucchese notarial archive as involved in wide-ranging commercial activities between 1318 and 1321.[93] The larger of them was wound up in the latter year when its assets can be conservatively estimated to have been of the order of £12,000 in Lucchese *buona moneta* or about 4,000 florins.[94] Though this was a substantial sum, it represented a capital

Archivio notarile no. 17, Reg. i, c. 94^r.) and still owed money twenty years later (ibid., no. 89, Reg. v, 30/12/1316).

[88] Blomquist, 'Trade and Commerce', 153–4. The Guinigi company operating in 1284 consisted of four of the partners of 1300, together with Conte, Filippo, and Puccio del fu Albertino Guinigi, and Filippo and Ubaldo del fu Uguccione Brancoli.

[89] ASL Archivio notarile no. 42, 7/10/1308, no. 52, cc. 20^r., 26^r., no. 61, cc. 69^v., 118^r., 212^r.–213^r.

[90] Ibid., no. 65, c. 205^v., no. 66, c. 102^v.–103^r. 181^v.

[91] Ibid., no. 67, cc. 13^v.–14^r., 67^v., 129^v., 149^v.–150^r., no. 68, cc. 10^v., 13^r., no. 71, c. 43^v.

[92] Ibid., no. 67, c. 87^r., no. 68, c. 5^v.

[93] For details of these see my article, 'Lucchese commerce under Castruccio Castracani', in *ACCC*, 220–9.

[94] Ibid., 229.

investment far inferior to that of the bigger Florentine merchant companies of the same period[95] and one lower than that of comparable Lucchese business partnerships of the 1320s. For, while no single dominant firm replaced the 'societas dicta Guinigiorum' after its break-up in 1321, there was a proliferation of smaller enterprises from about that time onwards[96] which led to an increase in the total volume of money outlayed in the silk trade, then the principal industry of Lucca. Between 1322 and 1327, this economic revival gathered momentum and there emerged, as leading participants in it, the Sbarra, Rapondi, and Forteguerra family companies which took their place with revived Guinigi partnerships as the principal commercial concerns in the city. The Sbarra firm in particular, under the management of Jacopo di Puccetto Sbarra, played a prominent part in the importation of raw silk and its resale to Lucchese cloth manufacturers. On the basis of surviving records alone, one can calculate that, in the two years betwen February 1325 and February 1327, it disposed of 6,665 florins worth of silk in Lucca.[97] As Leon Mirot has shown,[98] it was also engaged around this time in financial transactions in France, making loans to members of the French aristocracy and even to the king of France who, in 1328, intervened in favour of Puccino Sbarra when the latter was imprisoned by papal officials in Avignon.[99]

The Rapondi brothers, Ciucco and Giovanni, together with their partners, Landino Gigante and Giovanni Orselli, were likewise involved in the importation and resale of silk, notably in 1322 when

[95] According to A. Sapori ('Storia interna della compagnia mercantile dei Peruzzi', *Studi di storia economica*, ii. 667–8 (Florence, 1955)), the total sum invested in the Peruzzi company by seventeen partners in 1312 amounted to 116,000 pounds Florentine and, in 1324, by sixteen partners, to 59,000 pounds, equal (on conversion rates of 25/- and 29/- to the florin respectively) to over 90,000 florins in one year and 40,000 florins in the other. The Frescobaldi, though, like the Ricciardi, in a state of virtual collapse in the early fourteenth century, managed to recover 14,000 florins in 1313, together with various assets in the form of property, from the bankruptcy to which their financial operations in England had brought them (ibid., 917). The company of Alberto del Giudice, a much more modest concern than the great trading enterprises of the Peruzzi or Frescobaldi and therefore comparable to the Luccese business partnerships, had, in 1315, a capital of 10,000 pounds Florentine (divided between four shareholders) which, by 1321, had risen to 15,000 (when there were six) (ibid., 986–7).

[96] See my article on 'Lucchese commerce', 229–32, for an account of the early history of some of these smaller companies between 1316 and 1319 and for the expansion of their activities in the early 1320s.

[97] See ibid., 233–6, for an analysis of these sales and pp. 236–8 for an account of other transactions involving the Sbarra.

[98] L. Mirot, *Études lucquoises* (Paris, 1930), 40–1.

[99] ASL Diplomatico Sbarra, 7/5/1328 and 4/7/1328.

they bought 2,300 florins worth of raw silk from merchants resident in Pisa and Genoa.[100] After the death of Ciucco Rapondi, his brother Giovanni continued this trading activity in a less sustained way, experimenting with a series of new partners, such as Nicolao Scandaleone and Lando Schiatta, before settling into a more stable business relationship with Nicolao Pettinati in 1327–8.[101]

The scale of the Rapondi enterprise appears to have been smaller than that of the Sbarra and that of the Forteguerra perhaps smaller still, though the absence from his native city of the principal member of this last firm, Vanni di Jacopo Forteguerra, between 1319 and 1324, makes it difficult to estimate the total volume of its commercial dealings from Lucchese sources alone.[102] From 1325 onwards, however, when he was back in Lucca, it did carry on a brisk trade in silk, selling 1,500 florins worth of this in a period of just over four months in that year.[103] In all, the Sbarra, Rapondi, and Forteguerra companies, even on the basis of the fragmentary indications furnished by the surviving registers of the Lucchese notarial archive, can be shown to have sold 10,500 florins worth of silk between 1322 to 1328, besides lending, borrowing, and exchanging quite large sums of money at this period.[104] And, in addition to these, there were several reconstituted Guinigi partnershps[105] and various minor and middle-range business

---

[100] ASL Archivio notarile no. 72, cc. 104ᵛ., 230ʳ.

[101] On this, see my article on 'Lucchese commerce', 238–42.

[102] Ibid., 242–4.

[103] ASL Archivio notarile no. 74 at dates 20/6/1325, 25/6/1325, 28/8/1325, 23/10/1325.

[104] See my 'Lucchese commerce', 244.

[105] Ibid., 244–52. In February 1324 the main Guinigi firm was revived with an initial capital of £15,000, Lucchese *buona moneta* by five partners, Cecio Guinigi, Guarniero Guarnieri, Risico Risichi, Guido Sartori, and Francesco Burlamacchi but proved to be short-lived because of the death of Guido Sartori later that year and of Guarniero Guarnieri in the next (see ASL Archivio notarile no. 74, c. 181ʳ.–184ʳ., and at dates 27/12/1324 and 5/8/1325, 4/9/1325, no. 75, 5/4/1326). Its surviving members then formed new business associations, Cecio Guinigi with Filipuccio Spiafami, Francesco Burlamacchi with his kinsman Pelloro, and Risico Risichi with Bartolomeo Parenti (ibid., no. 75, 2/7/1326, 14/4/1326, 26/12/1326). The other Guinigi company, made up of Francesco, Lazzaro and Dino Guinigi also continued to function at this period, establishing new links with Lando Moriconi to replace those formerly existing with Ciucco Rapondi (ibid., no. 74, 20/4/1324, 27/3/1325, no. 75, 23/1/1326, 26/4/1326, no. 76, 16/8/1327, 26/10/1327, 31/10/1327, 14/11/1327). In the meantime, new partnerships were also formed between Nicolao and Pero Guinigi on the one hand and Bonaccorso and Lando Bettori on the other (ibid., no. 72, c. 278ᵛ., no. 73, c. 179ʳ.). It is clear from these indications that, while the Guinigi continued to be an important trading family in Lucca in the 1320s, its resources were at this stage split between several relatively minor trading enterprises.

firms[106] in the city which, between them, accounted for a substantial trade.

Foreign merchants present in Lucca under Castruccio appear also to have contributed to the revival of trade of the 1320s. Of these the most important were Florentine exiles such as Andrea and Filippo di Lapo Cipriani and Bartolomeo and Taldo di Mapheo Tedaldi.[107] In addition, Genoese financiers such as Lucchino Maniavacca,[108] though only occasionally resident in the city, played a significant part in stimulating the importation of raw silk into it or providing capital for its manufacturers.

The sources that we have are, of course, incomplete and therefore our knowledge of the trading activities of foreigners in Lucca must perforce remain fragmentary. Such indications as the documents give, however, reinforce the general impression, left by a study of Lucchese notarial registers, of an expansion of both Lucchese trade and the city's contacts with other places from the early 1320s onwards. The evidence contained in the material already used to give a general picture of Lucchese commerce at this period reveals the existence of links between local merchants and those in Pisa, Genoa, Siena, Milan, and Verona and indirectly in Florence, Venice, and Piacenza, not to speak of relations with non-Italians in France and England.[109]

---

[106] I have discussed these in 'Lucchese commerce', 252–6. As I have shown there, the most significant of these were the partnership of the Scortica brothers with Fredocchio del Gallo, that of Gialdello Sesmondi with his brother Dino, that of Matteo Brancali with Francesco Benettoni, that of Alluminato and Done Alluminati with Francesco, Guiduccio, and Coluccio Moccindenti, and that of Puccino and Nettoro Mattafelloni with Ceo and Armanno da Fondora and Jacopo Parenti.

[107] ASL Archivio notarile no. 68, 4/12/1319, no. 69, 23/2/1320, 23/8/1320, no. 72, cc. 41ʳ., 86ʳ., 104ʳ., 169ʳ., 390ʳ., no. 73, c. 110ʳ., no. 74, 21/4/1324, 25/10/1325, no. 75, 7/4/1326, 12/12/1326, no. 76, 15/9/1327. See also my 'Lucchese commerce', 257–8, for the activities of other foreign merchants in Lucca at this time.

[108] ASL Archivio notarile, no. 74, 5/1/1325, 4/2/1325, 13/2/1325, 30/9/1325. Other Genoese merchants recorded in substantial trading transactions with Lucchese merchants at this period were Cattanio di Ramondo, Michele Squarciafico, and Gabriele and Filippo da Prementario (ibid., no. 72, c. 230ʳ., no. 73, c. 103ʳ., no. 74, 1/2/1325, no. 75, 20/10/1326).

[109] See in particular, references in the two previous footnotes and ibid., no. 67, c. 162ᵛ., no. 69, 29/7/1319, no. 71, c. 119ʳ., no. 72, c. 151ʳ., no. 74, 31/12/1324, 7/4/1325, 11/5/1325, 13/6/1325, 30/9/1325, no. 75, 8/1/1326, 5/3/1326, 27/7/1326, 23/9/1326, 20/10/1326, no. 76, 13/5/1327, 30/7/1327, 16/8/1327, 18/10/1327, 30/10/1327, no. 77, c. 43ʳ. Contacts with Pisa have not been documented, being too frequent to be listed. On trading relations with south of France, particularly Montpellier, see K. L. Reyerson, 'Lucchese in Montpellier in the era of Castruccio Castracani: The mintmasters' penetration of Langueducian commerce and finance', *ACCC* 203–16. Families repre-

Whether this increase in business transactions involving foreigners is merely relative to the economically depressed years between 1314 and 1319, or whether it represents a growth with respect to the pre-1314 era, is of course another question which the current state of research on this subject makes it difficult to answer. The notarial records of the late thirteenth century studied by Blomquist[110] and what we know of the Ricciardi company in England at the same time[111] suggest that the scale of foreign operations of the Lucchese of the 1320s may well have been inferior to that of the late Duecento, though, had we adequate documentation on Lucchese trade with France, in particular in the Castruccian period, it might be found that what had occurred was not a diminution in the city's external commerce but its reorientation in the wake of the collapse of the Ricciardi's banking ventures in England. Certainly, the evidence on the financial value of raw silk sales in Lucca in 1322, 1325, 1326, and the first half of 1327,[112] on the basis of the records of only one notary, suggest that there had probably

sented at Montpellier in the early fourteenth century, according to Reyerson, included the Avvocati, Scatissa, Sbarra, Poggio, Del Drago, and Malagallia.

[110] According to Blomquist, 'Trade and Commerce', 95, Martinoso Bonanni in 1284 imported £16,830 12s.3d. worth of silk from Genoa and sold it in 52 lots to other merchants or craftsmen in Lucca. This is a figure comparable to those of the mid-1320s, on the assumption that he was responsible for a share of the silk trade in that year almost equal to that of the merchants using Ser Rabbito Toringhelli as a notary in the 1320s (see n. 112 below). In view, however, of the incomplete survival of sources from both periods, it would be risky to base any conclusion on the relative size of the Lucchese silk industry at these two times on the fragmentary indications these furnish. The main change between the pre-1294 and post-1314 eras would seem to have been the absence in the latter of a major commercial and banking company disposing of resources on the scale of those of the Ricciardi.

[111] The Ricciardi were the main Italian banking house concerned with the royal finances in the period between the 1270s and 1290s. Kaeuper has estimated their total advances to the king's 'wardrobe' over these two decades as £300,000 sterling (*Bankers*, 129), a truly enormous sum.

[112] I have calculated that the total silk sales recorded by Ser Rabbito Toringhelli, in the three complete years 1322, 1325, and 1326, amounted to £19,184, 7s. 3d., £31,754, 9s. 10d., and £27,807 15s. 1d. respectively, equal on the current rates of exchange (1 florin = in 1322 £2 19s. 4d., in 1325–6 £3) to 6,732½, 10,585, and 9,269 florins respectively. (I have taken Pisan money to be approximately equal to Lucchese at this period on the basis of ASP Archivio del Comune A92, C. 24ᵛ. which gives an exchange rate of £3 1s. Pisan to the florin in April 1327 Pisan style and ASL Archivio notarile no. 75, 13/3/1326 where 824 florins were to be exchanged for £2,500 Lucchese.) In the first five months of 1327, recorded silk sales in Toringhelli's register amounted to £13,348 4s. or 4,375 florins, while in the same period of 1328 only two sales, involving between them £3,381 11s. 6d. or 1,102 florins are noted (exchange rate of £3 1s. Lucchese to the florin used for these last totals). (Note years used above are Lucchese, beginning at the Nativity.)

been no falling off in the volume of these since the thirteenth century and, given that silk was essentially a commodity of international trade rather than of local consumption, this must have reflected the revival of a significant exporting activity.

Unfortunately, the gaps in the Toringhelli registers in the second halves of 1323 and 1324 make it difficult to chart the course of the upsurge of an extensive commerce at this period, but it would seem, from the surviving sources, that it reached its peak in 1325–6 and then, surprisingly, began to taper off from the middle of 1327 onwards. It may be that this apparent falling away in the last year or so of the Castruccian regime was due to a reduction in Ser Rabbito's notarial practice as he himself grew older; but it is more likely that it was connected with contemporary political events—the siege of Pisa, the transfer of at least some Lucchese commercial activity to that city after its capture by Ludwig of Bavaria, and perhaps the effects of an intensified war with Florence and the papacy. Whatever reasons lay behind it, it does not itself modify the overall picture of the 1320s as a time of economic revival, for the decline of that last year was relative to the high level of trade in the previous three and did not represent a decrease, in absolute terms, in the volume of financial transactions, with respect to the pre-1320 period.

In a wider context, the evidence of a thriving Lucchese commerce in the 1320s has implications bearing on the general character of Lucchese society under Castruccio and the nature of his regime. Ever since the nineteenth century there has been a tendency to assume that the mercantile spirit manifested itself in the Italy of the Trecento in republics, while tyrannies expressed a militaristic reaction to the bourgeois world of the communes. What the economic history of Lucca under Castruccio shows is that, in certain circumstances, a commercial ethos and despotism could not merely be compatible but could help to sustain each other. One has only to compare the names of the families supporting Castruccio with those of the leading merchants of the city[113] to realize how close were the links that bound

---

[113] In particular, the Guinigi, Rapondi, and Sbarra, and their associates the Bettori, Del Maestro, Burlamacchi, Sartori, Moriconi, and the Dal Portico, figure in the lists of *anziani* and *savi* and also among the leading merchants of the town. In addition, the Boccella, Boccadivacca, Dardagnini, Galganetti, Mangialmacchi, and Trentacosta were represented both among the *anziani* or *savi* and in minor partnerships discussed above, while the following families, members of which are known to have held office under Castruccio, also occur at the dates noted in Ser Rabbito Toringhelli's registers, as partners in lesser firms which I have not dealt with individually: Della Cappella 30/5/

the political oligarchy which collaborated with the lord of Lucca to the reviving commercial life of the town under his rule. In effect, the real conflict of interests in the Lucca of the early Trecento was not that between a militarily based tyranny and a mercantile polity, but between the artisan and lower middle-class dominated organization of the *popolo*, supported by the pro-Florentine Obizi-Bernarducci faction, on the one hand, and the socially prominent *casastici* and Ghibelline exiles on the other. Given that the great merchant families had been discriminated against by the Statute of 1308, their natural allies became those dedicated to overthrowing the regime that had inspired it. By the same token, the oligarchic nature of the new Castruccian constitution served their purposes well, giving them extensive representation in office and allowing them, through this, to participate in lucrative tax-farming and other government-related financial activities.[114] While the resurgence of Lucchese trade under Castruccio seems paradoxical in the light of the stereotyped images of merchant and tyrant derived from our own traditions of historical interpretation, it is not surprising, when one considers that Castruccio himself belonged to a once distinguished mercantile family, that he counted among his supporters nearly all the leading commercial dynasties of the town and that he had an interest in building up resources of capital in his city, upon which he could draw to help pay for the mercenary cavalry[115] on which his military success depended.

To some extent, an affinity existed, in the Lucca of the early Trecento, between the forces committed to its territorial expansion and those which aimed at its economic resurgence in that, in the

1326, Cassiani (or Casciani) 11/9/1321, Martini 10/1/1321, Pantassa 15/1/1325, Passamonti 3/5/1326, Schiatta 24/2/1325 and 5/2/1326, Spada 9/7/1326, and Tadolini 15/1/1325, 20/6/1326, 12/5/1327, 30/9/1327. In fact, the only first-rank Lucchese merchant family of this period absent from the suriving lists of officials is that of the Forteguerra which may not be represented in them only because its leading member, Giovanni, was out of Lucca between 1319 and 1324.

[114] Vanni Rapondi and Puccino Galganetti had tax-farms in 1316 (ibid., no. 65, c. 138ʳ.) but other surviving lists of tax-farmers from the Castruccian period (ibid., no. 93, 16/2/1317, 10/12/1319, 4/1/1320, 24/3/1320, 25/3/1320, and ASL Proventi no. 13) suggest that those engaged in this activity may have come from lesser merchant families, such as the Del Gallo, Sartori, Ceci, and Dombellinghi or from those who, to our knowledge, were not engaged in large-scale trade, though still belonging to what might broadly be described as the Lucchese merchant class.

[115] See ASL Archivio notarile no. 74, Reg. ii, cc. 158ᵛ.–160ᵛ. and Camarlengo generale no. 2, cc. 96ʳ., 99ʳ.–ᵛ., 100ʳ.–ᵛ., 107ᵛ., 110ʳ., 114ʳ., 116ʳ., for evidence of contributions made by members of the Lucchese merchant community to satisfy the needs of Castruccio's military expenditure.

commercial as in the military field, the city at this time essentially faced a problem of scale. Following the collapse of the Ricciardi company, the Florentines had gained an unchallenged pre-eminence in the international trade and banking in which the Lucchese had once rivalled them. This left the citizens of the smaller commune in the position of mere producers of a commodity, silk cloth, for the large-scale manufacture of which Florentine industry was not yet ready. Their ability to compete with their wealthier neighbour was, in terms of economic factors alone, likely to decline as advantages of skill and tradition gave way before the weight of superior resources. In the same way, the revolution in warfare which manifested itself in Italy after the death of Henry VII in the defeat of citizen troops by highly paid mounted mercenaries made the survival of smaller states depend on the acquisition of further territories which would enble them to sustain the cost of a viable professional army. The Guelph policy of pre-1314 Lucchese governments, if continued, would, in these circumstances, have made Lucca no more than a Florentine satellite, weakened by internal conflicts between factions and classes and vulnerable to absorption by the enlarged Tuscan state which would eventually have had to come into being to resist the power of the regional principalities arising in Lombardy. The Ghibelline alternative, exemplified by Castruccio's regime, aimed to compensate for the relative weakness of Lucca, first by superior skill in the handling of the new technology of war, then in the elimination of internal divisions through the limiting of political activity to the trusted sections of the merchant class, and finally through the extension of the size of Lucchese territory to rectify the existing imbalance in terms of resources between it and that controlled by Florence. The interests of the Lucchese trading community corresponded with those of Castruccio to the extent that it, too, found itself, with respect to its Florentine counterpart, at a disadvantage which it could overcome, not by economic means, but only through decisive political gains, such as the acquisition of Pisa, that would enable it to make up for its otherwise inferior position. The common aims of the lord of Lucca and of his merchant subjects and supporters would have been served by the creation of a regional state in north-west Tuscany around the twin focuses of Lucca and Pisa, commanding the coastal plain, the Val di Serchio, and the access of the Arno valley to the sea. The fact that this state, when transiently brought into being in 1327–8 (or, under Pisan rule, between 1314–16 and 1342–69), did not last does not diminish its significance as a potential objective of policy and the framework within which the aspirations of both Castruccio and the Lucchese merchant class might have been realized. In the event, a combination of accidental circumstances and underlying historical forces prevented it from enduring, and Lucca and Pisa, both overshadowed by their more powerful neighbour, went into a decline that eventually cost one city its independence and reduced the other to a buffer between Florence and Milan. But, in the perspective of the early fourteenth century when the political situation was still open, these developments could not have been anticipated (although they came in retrospect to colour later views of the Castruccian period), and the alliance between the lord of Lucca and its mercantile and administrative oligarchy could be established on the basis of a common concern for both territorial and commercial expansion, aimed at making the commune both a militarily viable state and one capable of further economic growth through the exploitation, to the benefit of its trading community, of the advantages deriving from its government's policies.

While the related goals of an enlarged Lucca and of a sustained revival of its economy were not in fact achieved, the coincidence, at this point in time, of the intersts of the Ghibelline regime with those of the city's merchant class did have enduring results in the shaping of the patrician society that was subsequently to dominate the town. It was the Castruccian era that brought to an end both the factionalism and the anti-aristocratic 'popular' movement of the thirteenth century. The families which had been pre-eminent in Lucca in the Duecento— the Obizi, Bernarducci, Cari (or Del Caro), Ciapparoni, Quartigiani, Ronzini, Tassignano, Arnaldi, Porta[116]—ceased, with the possible exception of the Interminelli, Martini, Mordecastelli, and Faitinelli, to be a significant force in Lucchese politics after the death of Castruccio Castracani; and with the exclusion from the *Anzianate* of the 'noble' houses of the Obizi, Quartigiani, Salamoncelli, Interminelli, and Poggio in 1372 when Lucca had recovered its independence, even some of these latter *consorterie* lost what was left of their former power.[117] In their place there rose to prominence the Guinigi, Sbarra, Forteguerra, and Rapondi who had been the leading merchants of the Castruccian period and whose close collaboration with the seigneurial government of that time had laid the groundwork for

---

[116] I have based this list on the names of fifteen families, each described as a 'Lucchese Geschlecht' in Schmeidler's edition of Ptolemy of Lucca's *Annals*, 325–71.

[117] C. Meek, *Lucca 1369–1400* (Oxford, 1978) 184.

their later political influence. If we consider the lists compiled by Meek and Berengo of the families most frequently represented in public office in Lucca in the late fourteenth and early sixteenth centuries,[118] we discover a considerable degree of continuity between these groups and those active in government or administration under Castruccio Castracani.

Lucca under his rule can therefore be said to have witnessed a return to an oligarchic regime which, after the recession in Lucchese trade following the sack of the city in 1314, favoured a revival in its commercial economy and which reversed the pro-Florentine 'popular' tendency of pre-1314 communal politics. As Castruccio himself came to rely more on military power and less on factional support and as some of the leading families originally committed to him were alienated by the tyrannical nature of his rule, he sought for new bases for his authority in the endorsement of foreign princes and in the establishment of a secure hereditary regional principality. But, notwithstanding this, his government remained dependent on the collaboration of large sections of the merchant class and the period in which he dominated Lucca had perhaps as its most enduring result the entrenchment of the position of a new aristocracy, drawn largely from the middle ranks of the *casastici* of 1308 but more mercantile in its orientation than the old nobility of the Duecento, which, after the city had passed through the century of crisis following his death, asserted itself as the ruling patriciate of the town.

[118] Ibid., 190–1 and M. Berengo, *Nobili e mercanti nella Lucca del Cinquecento* (Turin, 1965), 28, 30.

IV

War and foreign policy under Castruccio Castracani to the battle of Altopascio (1316–1325)

1. *The outbreak and early stages of Castruccio's war with Florence*

In May 1317, the conclusion of a general peace between the Guelphs and Ghibellines of Tuscany brought to a close the period of conflict in the region which had opened with the arrival in Italy of Henry VII. The way was now open for the consolidation of the new regimes which had emerged in Pisa and Lucca following the expulsion of Uguccione della Faggiuola and which needed a respite from war to reassert their control over their territories. The efforts of Castruccio Castracani, in particular, could now be directed to the establishment of his authority in Lunigiana and Garfagnana and to the securing of a *modus vivendi* with Pisa, so as to eliminate friction over rival claims to disputed lands. Good relations with Gaddo della Gherardesca, the new lord of Pisa, were especially important to Castruccio, in that his own city's resources were probably inadequate for the maintenance of the kind of mercenary force he needed to subjugate the Malaspina castles and villages in Lunigiana and for this purpose he therefore had to call on the aid of the German cavalry then still in Pisan service.[1]

In his policy of collaboration with Pisa to bring the northern limits of his state firmly under his control, Castruccio was helped by the rather clumsy attempts of Uguccione della Faggiuola to regain his former power over the two west Tuscan cities. Ever since his ignominious withdrawal from Lucca in 1316, Uguccione had been in Verona at the court of Can Grande della Scala. Securing the help of this ruler and conspiring with Marquis Spinetta Malaspina and the Lanfranchi in Pisa, he advanced (in 1319 according to Pisan sources, but in 1317 according to Villani[2]) into Lunigiana with an armed force. Before

---

[1] G. Villani, *Cronica*, ix. 86, 106.
[2] Ibid., ix. 86. For the Pisan sources, see Sardo, *Cronaca*, 75, and 'Cronica di Pisa',

he could reach Pisa, however, his plot with the Lanfranchi was discovered and four of that family killed, with the result that he had to abandon his intention of going on towards that city and returned to Verona, leaving his ally Spinetta Malaspina to face alone the fury of his enemies.[3]

This provided precisely the opportunity Castruccio needed to move into Lunigiana and complete the subjugation of that province. Since coming into power, his main preoccupation outside Lucca had been this region in which he still effectively enjoyed vice-comital jurisidiction.[4] In July 1316, he had gained possession of Massa by coming to terms with its marquises[5] and, after his rights over the neighbouring city of Sarzana (conceded in 1314) lapsed in the following December, he had tried to maintain his hold over it too. But, under pressure from Pisa, he had been forced to let the matter go to arbitration, as a consequence of which the town reverted to Pisan control although Castruccio retained the hill village and fort of Sarzanello above it.[6] Frustrated at this point, in mid-1317, in his efforts to complete his absorption of the whole of Lunigiana into the territory of Lucca, he turned his attention temporarily to Garfagnana, where he took Sommocolonia and Trassilico, expelling the Guelphs who held them.[7] Then, in June 1319, scrupulously observing a convention agreed upon at an earlier meeting with Spinetta Malaspina at Avenza, Castruccio gave the marquis ten days to hand over the lands in his possession or face attack, for, according to a judgement laid down by ten *savi* of Lucca, they belonged by right to the commune.[8] In the following

RIS, xv, vol. 997, and also Granchi, 'De proeliis', RIS (n. edn.), xi, pt. 2, pp 81–3 and notes.

[3] Sardo, *Cronaca*, and *RIS*, xv, col. 997. See also G. Villani, *Cronica*, ix. 86, U. Dorini, *Un grande feudatorio del Trecento: Spinetta Malaspina* (Florence, 1940), 76–7, G. Rossi-Sabatini, *Pisa al tempo dei Donoratico* (Florence, 1938), 89–95, Sforza, 'Castruccio . . . in Lunigiana', 331.

[4] Granted in July 1314 (Lazzareschi, 'Documenti', 291–2). By 1318, Pope John XXII, acting on behalf of the exiled bishop of Luni, Gherardino Malaspina, was seeking the restitution of the episcopal lands to the Church, but to no effect (see Sforza, 'Castruccio . . . in Lunigiana', 467–70).

[5] Sforza, 'Castruccio . . . in Lunigiana', 328–9 and 461–7.

[6] Ibid., 329–30 and G. Sforza, 'Della signoria di Castruccio e de' Pisani sul borgo e forte di Sarzanello', *Atti e memorie delle deputazioni di storia patria per le provincie modenesi e parmensi* (Ser. 1.), v (1870), pp. 22–4.

[7] BNF MS Palat. 571, c. 21ʳ.

[8] Sforza, 'Castruccio . . . in Lunigiana', 475–6, quoting ASL Atti di Castruccio no. 1, c. 31. A meeting the previous year between Spinetta Malaspina and the *podestà* of Lucca had established that the former should have ten days notice of his eviction from his land. (See S. Bongi, *Inventario del R. Archivio di Stato in Lucca*, (Lucca, 1872–88), ii, 313.)

August, with the support of Gaddo della Gherardesca and the help of his cavalry, the captain of Lucca systematically reduced a number of villages subject to the Malaspina and obtained the submission of their inhabitants.[9] In addition, he captured Verrucola and Fosdinovo, Spinetta's two strongholds in the area,[10] compelling the marquis to leave his lands and go into exile in Verona. Finally, between 7 and 11 September, he induced another of the Malaspina, Azzone, to yield up Ponzano to him, and its citizens to elect him as their lord.[11]

With this clean sweep of the hamlets in the mountainous extreme north-west of the territory of Lucca—which had been under its sovereignty in 1308 but which, owing to the subsequent weakness of the commune, had since passed into the hands of the Malaspina[12]— Castruccio re-established one segment of the former frontiers of his state. Uguccione's ill-advised descent into Lunigiana, whether it preceded this campaign by a few months or two years, undoubtedly provided not merely the pretext for the attack on and dispossession of Spinetta and his family, but also the means, in the form of Pisan co-operation, by which this reconquest could be effected. Castruccio profited by it, further, in the strengthening of his alliance with Gaddo della Gherardesca which he had been to such pains to maintain over these early years of his captaincy over the forces of his native city. Up to this time, Castruccio had done everything to placate the Pisans, not merely in the matter of Sarzana (in which he had shown himself conciliatory to the point of conceding to Conte Gaddo an already acquired territory, in contrast to the tenacious determination he was later to manifest in his efforts to hold what he had taken), but also in June 1318 when he yielded to the protests of the neighbouring commune and abandoned his intention of constructing fortifications near the mouth of the Magra river because the Pisan *savi* feared that these were works preparatory to the building of a port that might take trade away from their own.[13] Now this caution and willingness to compromise had borne fruit in the reconstitution of Lucchese territory, at least in its north-western quarter.

The question which Castruccio's apparent moderation of this period—together with its concomitant policies of peace with Florence

---

[9] Sforza, 'Castruccio ... in Lunigiana', 335–7 and 477–81.

[10] Ibid., 337–9 and 482–3 and G. Villani, *Cronica*, ix. 86.

[11] Sforza, 'Castruccio ... in Lunigiana', 339–40 and 484–9.

[12] Ibid., 327 and 333–4, Dorini, *Un grande feudatorio*, 77.

[13] Sforza, 'Castruccio ... in Lunigiana', 334 and 473–5 and ASP Comune A48, c. 119ᵛ.–120ᵛ.

and collaboration with Pisa—inevitably raises is why it did not continue to influence his actions. Until 1319, it seemed to have brought success and had allowed Castruccio and his Pisan counterpart, Gaddo della Gherardesca, to consolidate their regimes and overcome internal conspiracies, such as those of the Lanfranchi in Pisa and of the Avvocati in Lucca.[14] The answer to this question lies partly in the overall Italian political situation of the time and partly in Castruccio's own position as a ruler. The conflict between the Genoese Guelphs and Ghibellines, the former supported by King Robert of Naples, the latter by the great despots of northern Italy, had threatened the precarious peace of 1317 almost since this had been concluded and set off a chain reaction in which the major states of the peninsula—Milan, the papacy and Florence—were soon caught up. In this general political conflagration, Lucca, the frontiers of which adjoined the eastern Genoese Riviera, could not for long have remained uninvolved. Moreover, once Castruccio had consolidated his hold on his territories and reincorporated Lunigiana and Garfagnana in them, he could only further expand his state by infringing on areas where his interests would clash with those of the Florentines, for instance, in the small towns such as Santa Maria a Monte still held by Lucchese exiles under the terms of the treaty of Naples, or in those places on the Pistoian *contado* such as Serravalle which it had conceded to the Ghibellines. In the latter, in particular, the Lucchese tyrant was regarded as a natural protector of the imperialist faction in a region otherwise predominantly under Guelph administration. It was to him that the Pistoian Ghibellines appealed for support to ensure the enforcement in their favour of the peace of 1317;[15] it was he who helped them gain control of a number of villages on the western fringes of Pistoian territory in January 1318,[16] and he whom they elected, a year later, as captain-general of their party.[17]

His championship of the cause of the imperialist faction of the city immediately to the east of Lucca, while it doubtless created friction with Florence, did less to bring about war with that commune than the situation in Genoa. When, in July 1318, Robert was made lord of

<hr/>

[14] On the conspiracy of the Avvocati see Chapter III n. 43 above.

[15] See, in this connection, Davidsohn, *Storia*, iv. 869–70, and his sources ASP Comune A48, cc. 73ᵛ., 78ʳ., and ASL Atti di Castruccio no. 1, c. 7ʳ., the latter published in Lazzareschi, 'Documenti', 327–8.

[16] M. A. Salvi, *Delle historie di Pistoia e fazioni d'Italia*, (Rome, Venice, Pistoia, 1662–7) ii. 332–3.

[17] ASL Capitoli no. 1, cc. 14ᵛ.–15ᵛ.

Genoa and, in the following February, defeated the Ghibellines at Sesto, the position of the latter became more difficult; and it was probably at this stage that Castruccio first began to give assistance to them.[18] Certainly we know that, in May 1319, King Robert was putting pressure on the Florentines to mobilize their forces so as to make possible a diversionary attack from the east to draw the Lucchese away from involvement in the Genoese war.[19] Since, at this point, Castruccio made no effort to invade the Riviera, the plan was dropped, to be put into execution later, in 1320–1. Even so, these diplomatic moves, which entailed the writing of letters to subject communes to ask for troops, can hardly have escaped Castruccio's notice, and he must therefore have been well aware of the fragility of the peace, and of the possibility of it being broken at any time by the Guelphs if the exigencies of the Genoese campaign demanded it. For the next few months—from June to September 1319—he was occupied with the stabilization of his northern frontier through the conquest of the Malaspina lands in Lunigiana—something which, given the prevailing situation, he may well have undertaken to guard against a potential rebellion in that region in the event of a war with Florence. Then, the following spring, he suddenly attacked the Florentine outposts on his southern frontier, leading his men and the German mercenaries in Pisan service against these small towns and taking their garrisons completely by surprise.

According to Giovanni Villani,[20] his motives for thus abruptly violating the peace were connected with the turn hostilities between the Guelphs and Ghibellines were taking in northern Italy. In order to draw Matteo Visconti, who had intervened in support of the Spinola and Doria, away from his involvement in the Genoese war, Robert of Naples had organised a coalition against him, consisting of the French prince Philip of Valois and the Florentines, Bolognese and Sienese whose forces were to converge on Lombardy, compelling the Milanese to return there to defend their own territories. A contingent of a thousand knights from the Guelph communes had already reached Reggio in Emilia in April 1320 in accordance with this plan and (if the

---

[18] On these developments and their antecedents, see G. Villani, *Cronica*, ix. 84, 87, 90, 92, 93–5, 97–9, 103, Davidsohn, *Storia*, iv. 853–4, R. Caggese, *Roberto d'Angiò e i suoi tempi* (Florence 1922–30), ii. 31–9, G. Stella, 'Annales genuenses', *RIS* xvii, cols. 1031–42. On Castruccio's intervention, see G. Villani, *Cronica*, ix. 95 and Giovanni di Lemmo, 'Diario', 204.

[19] Davidsohn, *Storia*, iv. 858–9.

[20] G. Villani, *Cronica*, ix. 106.

Florentine chronicler is to be believed) Castruccio's assault on the Val d'Arno was intended, in response to pleas by Matteo Visconti and his north Italian Ghibelline allies, to check its advance. In other words, instead of waiting for the Florentines to make a diversionary attack on Lucca to force it to withdraw its troops from the Genoese Riviera, Castruccio chose to launch one of his own against them when their cavalry was committed to military action in Lombardy. To this reason for the Lucchese captain's unexpected descent upon the Val d'Arno, Villani added another: as a tyrant, Castruccio went to war because it would enhance his position while peace would have detracted from it. Whatever truth might lie behind this claim, it is likely to have been influenced more by its author's predilection for apt psychological judgements on the character of despots, than by direct knowledge. In point of fact, peace had served Castruccio well over the three years preceding the outbreak of hostilities in April 1320 and war, though bringing him military glory and historical fame, was to do more to undermine than to perpetuate the regime he sought to establish.

Castruccio later came to fit so closely the Machiavellian model of prince-general that it requires something of an effort of mind to cancel out that image and see him as he was in 1320 without the overlay of the impression produced by subsequent events. In the month in which he launched his attack on Florence, his four years' assiduous courting of the Emperor-elect Frederick of Austria had borne fruit in his election as lifetime captain and lord of his city and in his appointment as its imperial vicar-general. Benefiting from peace with Florence and from his alliance with Gaddo della Gherardesca, he had consolidated his own position and that of his commune, while studiously avoiding conflict with Pisa, the support of which was essential to him owing to the inadequacy of his own city's military resources. Only in association with that sister Ghibelline state and the other pro-imperial powers in northern Italy did he, in fact, venture to break the peace of Naples and then, in all likelihood, not anticipating that the future course of the war would make it eventually necessary for him to develop a sufficient territorial and financial base for him to be able to confront alone the superior might of Florence. His actions in the period leading up to the outbreak of war had been inspired not by a large-scale strategy of conquest but by the need to re-establish control over the territories of the state under his rule.[21] And even his campaign of April 1320 against

---

[21] In addition to restoring Lucchese control over the lands seized by the Malaspina in Lunigiana, Castruccio Castracani had re-established communal authority, in August

the Florentines appears to have had as its main aim—apart from its diversionary effect in the general context of Guelph-Ghibelline hostilities—the recovery of three towns, Cappiano, Montefalcone, and Santa Maria a Monte,[22] the reincorporation of which into the Lucchese *contado* restored the frontiers of 1314.

While it is unlikely that Castruccio was purposefully engaged up to this time in the building up of a major Signoria, there is no doubt that once he found himself at war with a richer and more powerful Florence—particularly after the death of Gaddo della Gherardesca in May 1320[23] robbed him of his most reliable friend in Pisa—he was led into a policy of territorial expansion and diplomatic intrigue in an effort to compensate for the relative inferiority of the state of which he had become ruler. As long as the Pisan alliance lasted and the Florentines and King Robert had other, more serious foes to contend with, Castruccio could make the most of the advantages his military skill gave him; but until he could count on revenues of his own sufficient to finance a viable military force, he remained vulnerable. Hence his driving urge, which became almost obsessive from this time onwards, to exploit military successes and divisions, among friends and enemies alike, to gain more territory.

The question of what revenues Castruccio Castracani had at his disposal from the resources of Lucca alone is one which the surviving sources do not permit us to answer accurately. However, their order of magnitude can be gauged roughly from the full records which exist from the 1330s and the partial ones which are available from the 1320s. In particular, by using the figures for civic revenue between November 1335 and April 1336[24] and those for tax-farms let in 1323 and 1326[25] one can arrive, on the assumption that the total amounts collected from the levies for which we have information for both the later and

1316, over Coreglia which had been seized for the Guelphs of Garfagnana on 1 July of that year by Count Nerone of Frignano (See BNF MS Palat. 571, c. 20ʳ., BSL MS 2588, ii. cc. 72ᵛ.–73ʳ.), and G. Lera, 'Francesco Castracani degli Antelminelli conte di Coreglia', *ACCC*, 405.

[22] G. Villani, *Cronica*, ix. 106, BNF MS Palat. 571, c. 21ᵛ., 'Storie pistoresi', 71–2, Mosiici, 'Ricerche', 34–5, Lazzareschi, 'Documenti', 325–7 (ASL Atti di Castruccio no. 1, cc. 36ʳ.–38ʳ.), and Granchi, 'De proeliis', *RIS* (n. edn.), xi, pt. 2, p. 45.

[23] 'Cronica di Pisa', *RIS*, xv, col. 997, G. Villani, *Cronica*, ix. 122, Sardo, *Cronaca*, 76. The last source gives the date as May 1322 (Pisan style) (= 1321); but the other two accord on the year 1320, though Villani gives no indication of the month. According to Tronci, *Annali pisani*, iii. 104–5, Gaddo della Gherardesca's tombstone in the church of San Francesco in Pisa gives the date of his death as 1 May 1321 (Pisan style) (= 1320).

[24] ASL Proventi no. 1.

the earlier period were proportionate to the total for those not represented in the latter, we arrive at an estimate of about £225,000 *buona
moneta* or 75,000 florins for the annual value to the commune of the
various *gabelle* and *proventi* it raised in the city and in the *contado* in
1323 and 1326.[26] The salaries of officials, including Castruccio's own
allowance, set in 1317 at 4,000 florins per year,[27] have to be deducted
from this to determine the amount available for other expenses. In
1327, these wages accounted for just over £25,000 *piccoli* or rather more
than 7,000 florins in Lucca and its *contado* (not including the province
of Luni, the eastern Genoese Riviera, or Pontremoli) without taking in
the *podestà*'s stipend which, on the basis of figures for 1335–6, may be
estimated at about 1,400 florins per annum.[28] In addition, the cost of
officials' horses, not covered by their salaries, would have absorbed

[25] Ibid., no. 13.

[26] Bongi in his *Inventario*, ii. 28, on the basis of ASL Proventi no. 1, estimated the
revenues for the whole year 1335–6 at £325,910 12s. *piccoli* by multiplying what he took
as the amount collected for 4½ months by 8/3. However, the total he used for this purpose
in fact included some income which was, strictly speaking, not revenue, failed to take in
revenue which had been paid directly to Pietro dei Rossi, then vicar of Lucca, and
covered collections for the *gabelle* and *proventi* for periods varying from four to six
months, but mostly of 5½, not 4½ months. Instead of taking his figure, I have therefore
gone through the total for the several *gabelle* and *proventi*, estimating annual yields for
each. Doing this, I have arrived at a total of £143,171 5s. 4d. *piccoli* for the taxes in
Proventi no. 1, cc. 1–7 (not farmed), of £101,429 12s. 6d. for those in Proventi no. 1,
cc. 8–17 and 19ᵛ.–20ᵛ. (tax farmed in Lucca), £20,219 8s. 10d. for the vicariates, and
£35,764 8s.10d. for the *taglia* of the £57,000, giving totals of £264,820 6s. 8d. without the
taglia and £300,584 14s. 6d. with it (75,663 or 85,881 florins). In order to arrive at estimates of revenue for 1323 and 1326, I have compared the annual tax-farms for these two
years with the estimated yields of the corresponding duties in 1335–6. Of nineteen of
these for which the figures survive for 1335–6 and for 1323 or 1326, eleven are common
to the last two years, producing on both occasions approximately the same total (£15,575
and £15,470 respectively). Assuming on the basis of this a rough equality between the
average level of tax-farms in these two years and comparing the sum of the nineteen
gabelle or *proventi* occurring in one or other of them with the yield of the same taxes in
1335–6, one arrives at a ratio of about 66 *piccoli* in 1335–6 to 50 *buona* or *nuova moneta* in
1323/1326 for duties which, between them, accounted for a quarter of the revenue
collected in 1335–6, other than in the *taglia*. Applying this to the other taxes levied in
1335–6, one can calculate the total probable revenue of Lucca in 1323 and 1326 at about
£200,469 or 66,823 florins without the *taglia* or £227,543 or 75,848 florins with it. Given
the margin of error likely in this expansion and assuming equal proportions for different
taxes, it is best to state these as approximations around the round numbers of £200,000
or £225,000 *buona moneta* or 66,667 or 75,000 florins.

[27] Lazzareschi, 'Documenti', 309.

[28] ASL Libri di Corredo no. 4, cc. 2–37. The figures given in this document are for
the last six months of 1327 and I have multiplied them by two to produce annual totals
(in some cases monthly rates are given). The salary of the *podestà* is given in ASL
Proventi no. 1, c. 27ʳ. as £2,244 7s. 6d. *piccoli* for 5½ months (mid-November 1335–1 May
1336), which equals £4,896 16s. 2d. or 1,399 florins for the whole year.

approximately a further 2,000 florins in a full year according to the records we have for the second half of 1327.[29] Between mid-November 1335 and the end of April 1336, the sum spent on officials was only £5,468 12s. 8d. *piccoli* (giving an annual rate of £1,848 15s.), but this did not include the salaries of the vicar and several others whose wages were listed in the sources for late 1327, so that the discrepancy, of the order of 4,000 florins, is less marked than at first appears.

Accepting the figures for the expenses for officials for 1327 and subtracting them from an estimated revenue of around 75,000 florins, we are left with a residue of just over 60,000 florins, the bulk of which would have gone to the payment of troops. In $4\frac{1}{2}$ months, between mid-November 1335 and the end of March 1336, these were to cost the commune just under 20,000 florins, giving an annual rate of almost 53,000 florins, of which roughly 70 per cent was taken up by the cost of cavalry and 30 per cent by that of infantry.[30] If the same proportions of revenue had been devoted to mercenaries in the 1320s, less than 47,000 florins a year would have been spent on them. However, since, in the 1330s, Lucca was under foreign domination and some payments were made out of public funds to various individuals, it is likely that less was available then for the payment of troops than would have been the case during Castruccio's war against Florence.[31] It is probable therefore that a sum of the order of 50,000 florins per year could have been committed from the income of Lucca and its *contado* to the hiring of mercenaries in the 1320s though it is unlikely, in view of the maximum of not far over 60,000 florins a year for expenditure other than the salaries of officials, that more than 55,000 florins could have been set aside for this purpose. Assuming that the ratio of 7:3 for the cost of cavalry to that of infantry held in the 1320s as it did a decade later, this

[29] See Libri di Corredo no. 4, cc. 63^r.–67^r. and cc. 24^v., 30^r. I have calculated the combined out-payments and monthly allowances for horses for six months to have been £3,516 18s. *piccoli*, giving an annual rate of £7,033 16s. or just over 2,000 florins.

[30] ASL Proventi no. 1, cc. 34^v.–36^v. I have excluded the figures for a few days in the first half of November 1335. Eliminating these, one arrives at an expenditure of £48,847 15s. 7d. *piccoli* for cavalry and £20,722 0s. 11d. for infantry in $4\frac{1}{2}$ months or £130,260 (= 37,217 florins) and £55,258 (= 15,788 florins) respectively at a proportionate yearly rate.

[31] Of the total yield for taxes in late 1335 and early 1336, over £17,000 had gone directly to Pietro dei Rossi. Other sums, amounting to over £18,500 *piccoli* went to various individuals. On the other hand, of course, these out-payments (amounting to over 10,000 florins over a full year) would have been partly compensated for in 1327 by Castruccio's allowance and the higher sums paid as salaries to officials (over 6,500 florins between them).

would have set the total pay an unexpanded Lucchese state could have afforded for its mercenary cavalry at somewhere around 35,000 florins.

Just how large a force could have been maintained with such a sum would have depended, of course, on whether it was hired for the whole year, or only for the duration of a limited campaign. The figures we have for the pay of troops in Pisa and Florence in the years between 1317 and 1328 and in Lucca in the 1330s indicate that the cost per month of a foreign knight varied from 6 to 24 florins with *caporali* of *bandiere* being paid considerably more, from 20 to 75 florins per month. The standard pay in Florence for foreign mounted mercenaries in 1319 was 9 florins per month for members of *bandiere* and up to 35 florins per month for *caporali*, depending on the size of the *bandiera*.[32] By 1320, this had risen to 10 florins[33] and by 1325 to 13 or 14 florins per month for ordinary knights and 18 for 'milites de corredo'.[34] In Pisa, in August 1328 (when the city was under Castruccio's rule), the basic rate was 12 florins per month.[35] In Lucca in 1334 the cost per head of mercenaries averaged just under 15 florins per month, including that of *caporali* of whom the proportion seems to have been high and the salary substantial (between 40 and 75 florins a month).[36] By 1339–40, Lucchese rates of pay appear to have been reduced to 6–9 florins for knights with *caporali* receiving only about twice this.[37]

Taking these indications together, one can say that the probable cost of a foreign mercenary knight in the 1320s would have been between 10 and 12 florins per month, with the pay of *caporali* and other supplementary members of the troop adding another florin per man on average to this figure. In addition, in time of war, there would have been the expense of compensation for horses wounded or killed in battle which, according to the Pisan records for 1328,[38] amounted to 1,182 florins for 351 men in $1\frac{1}{3}$ months, though admittedly in August–September of that year, at a time of heavy fighting against the Floren-

---

[32] ASF Provvisioni no. 16, cc. 34ᵛ., 76ᵛ., 93ʳ.–94ᵛ. ASF Provvisioni Protocolli no. 7, cc. 34ʳ.–35ᵛ.

[33] ASF Provvisioni no. 17, c. 20ᵛ.

[34] Ibid., no. 21, c. 91ʳ. and ᵛ. and c. 101ʳ.

[35] ASP Comune A93, cc. 33ᵛ.–34ᵛ.

[36] ASL Condotta no. 1.

[37] ASL Condotta no. 2.

[38] ASP Comune A93, cc. 36ʳ.–38ᵛ. Florentine records (ASF Provvisioni no. 15, c. 186ᵛ., no. 20, c. 186ᵛ.) indicate rates of compensation ranging from 16 to 40 florins each for chargers and 8 to 16 florins each for pack horses, though, on 17 September 1324, Amerigo dei Donati was paid as much as 120 florins for the loss of his horse (ibid., no. 21, c. 43ʳ.).

tines. The period of enlistment of mercenaries in the records surviving from this period was generally from four to six months between April and September,[39] but there are enough exceptions to this to suggest that at least some *bandiere* were kept in service through the winter.[40]

The 32,000–38,000 florins a year which Castruccio is likely to have had available to him from the revenues of Lucca and its *contado* alone would, on the basis of what we can discover about the cost of mercenaries in the 1320s in Tuscany, have enabled him to engage about 250 knights for a full year, about 500 for 6 months, or about 750 for 4 months. When one considers that, in order to defeat the Florentines at Altopascio in September 1325, he had to get together a force of over 2,000 knights, the significance of the limitations imposed on him by the paucity of the financial resources of his native city becomes immediately evident. In 1320 Castruccio found himself at war with a Florence which had a population and income approximately four times those of Lucca,[41] and alliances with the kingdom of Naples, the Church, and the Tuscan and Emilian Guelph cities. Against this imposing array of forces he could count only on the temporary support of Pisa and the possibility of help from the Lombard Ghibelline states. The only strategy which would enable him to overcome the natural disadvantages of his position was one of piecemeal conquest of a more extensive territory to enlarge the economic base of his military power. This he could achieve both through successful border warfare against Florence and the exploitation of divisions in the neighbouring cities of

[39] These were the months for which the commune of Lucca hired knights in 1334 (ASL Condotta no. 2). In 1319, the Florentines engaged their mercenaries from 17 April for 4 months (ASF Provvisioni no. 16, c. 93ᵛ.) and in 1325 from 15 April to 14 December (ibid., no. 21, c. 101ʳ.). The Pisan records, referred to above, (ASP Comune A93, cc. 36ʳ.–38ᵛ.) specify payments to mercenaries for the period from 1 August to 10 September 1328.

[40] ASF Provvisioni no. 17, c. 20ᵛ. mentions the engagement of 50 knights for 6 months from 10 September 1320 to 9 March 1321. ASL Proventi no. 1, cc. 34ᵛ.–35, shows that more than 4,000 florins were spent in a month on mounted mercenaries in Lucca in each of January, February, and March 1336, while ASL Condotta no. 2 records payments to mercenaries in the same city between November 1339 and June 1340.

[41] The revenues of Florence in 1339 are known to have been 343,300 florins (see Ildefonso di San Luigi, *Delizie degli eruditi toscani* (Florence, 1779), xii. 349), which was four times the estimated revenue of Lucca in 1335–6 (see n. 26 above). The Florentine 'gabella salis' yielded 30,000 florins per year from August 1324 to June 1326 (ASF Provvisioni no. 22, c. 66ʳ. and ᵛ.), while the Lucchese 'dogana salis' was let in 1335–6 for £21,600 + £10,700 + £750 piccoli, equal to 9,443 florins (ASL Proventi no. 1, c. 2ᵛ.). Applying the multiplier I have used to derive an estimate of Lucchese revenues in the 1320s from those of 1335–6, this is reduced to 8,338 florins or 27.8 per cent of the yield of the corresponding Florentine tax.

Pisa and Pistoia with the aim of adding them to his dominions by means of an interplay of military pressure and political intrigue.

In the period between the outbreak of fighting in April 1320 and the decisive battle of Altopascio in September 1325, Castruccio's war policy has consequently to be seen has having two aspects: first, the conduct of minor hostilities designed to hold the Florentines at bay and, if possible, make small gains at their expense, while also softening up Pistoia, in particular, to political penetration; secondly, the undertaking of a secret diplomacy for the purpose of facilitating his plans for territorial expansion through conspiracy or collusion with those whose interests happened to coincide temporarily with his own. What gave Castruccio the time for this was the continued involvement of the Lucchese–Florentine conflict within a wider confrontation between Guelph and Ghibelline forces in Italy. This assured him not merely of the help of Ghibelline allies but also of the division of the resources of his Guelph enemies between three theatres of operations—Lombardy, Liguria, and Tuscany—of which the third, in which he was primarily involved, had, at least to begin with, the lowest priority in the eyes of his foes. Thus, Castruccio had a breathing-space, particularly valuable after the cooling of his relations with Pisa, in which to lay the foundations of a state of his own, strong enough, when need arose, to withstand the full force of the Guelph alliance when it was eventually directed against him.

The course of hostilities between Lucca and Florence over these years can, in fact, only be understood by placing them against the background of the general conflict of which they formed part. Its wider Italian dimension Castruccio could, at least for a time, exploit. When the Milanese induced Philip of Valois to withdraw from northern Italy while the troops of the Tuscan Guelph communes were still in Reggio,[42] Castruccio not only had a free hand in his incursions into the Arno valley but also was able, later that year, to resume his intervention in the eastern Genoese Riviera.[43] In order to draw him away from these, the Florentines were compelled to launch an attack on the Lucchese frontier in the Val di Nievole. When Castruccio returned rapidly from Liguria and repulsed them,[44] they induced Spinetta Malaspina, with three hundred cavalry and five hundred infantry in Florentine pay, as well as a hundred knights of his own, to try to

---

[42] G. Villani, *Cronica*, ix. 110.

[43] Ibid., ix. 111.

[44] Ibid., ix. 115.

regain, in the early months of the following year,[45] the places in Lunigiana which had been taken from him in 1319. Castruccio thus found his territories attacked at both ends. Despite the death of Gaddo della Gherardesca in the previous May he still disposed of a contingent of Pisan troops with the result that, besides his own, he had under his command about twelve hundred knights and a considerable force of infantry. Nevertheless, finding himself opposed by a Florentine army of roughly the same size, and with four hundred cavalry and five hundred foot-soldiers under Spinetta Malaspina invading Lunigiana, he was at a distinct disadvantage, unable on the one hand to relieve the castle of Montevettolini which the Florentines were by this time besieging and, on the other, to send sufficient troops to deal with Spinetta without risking a defeat in the Val di Nievole.

His response to this dilemma was to build up his forces with contingents of troops not only from Pisa but also from the Lombard cities of Milan, Piacenza, and Parma and from Arezzo which was then also Ghibelline under the rule of its bishop, Guido Tarlati. By this means he acquired a temporary superiority in cavalry over the Florentines with a total of more than 1,600 knights.[46] Characteristically, he did not divide his army at this point to fight on two fronts but, leaving Lunigiana for the time being undefended, concentrated his full power on driving back the Florentines. The Guelph commander, Guido della Petrella, taken by surprise at the sudden increase of his enemy's forces, retreated from the siege of Montevettolini and, after a skirmish which Castruccio would have won had it been prolonged into a battle, escaped unnoticed at night by leaving his camp-fires burning. He then distributed his troops as garrisons in Fucecchio, Carmignano, and other fortified frontier towns. Castruccio was meanwhile left free to ravage the surrounding countryside while the Florentines, finding their territory suddenly open to attack, hastened to recall their troops from Lunigiana. This, of course, reduced Spinetta's army to a mere handful, making it easy for Castruccio, as soon has he had thoroughly intimidated the Florentines by his show of force in the Val di Nievole and the middle Val d'Arno, to recapture the villages the Malaspina marquis had just taken.[47]

Whilst this campaign left the situation much as it had been before it started and, in one sense, was therefore inconclusive, it had proved

[45] Ibid., ix. 127.
[46] Ibid., ix. 115, 127.
[47] Ibid., ix. 127 and Davidsohn, *Storia*, iv. 881–3, 888–92.

Castruccio's ability to meet a serious threat from an initially superior
opponent by means of a skilful tactical manœuvre. Its significance lay
not only in the indication it gave of the interdependence of military
operations in different areas but also of the Lucchese commander's
capacity to exploit interior lines of communication to secure a critical
short-term advantage by a rapid movement of troops from one theatre
of war to another. He was later to employ the same device, in circumstances which permitted him to achieve a far more decisive result, in
the battle of Altopascio in 1325.

It is also worth noting that he was able to neutralize a dangerous
double-pronged Florentine attack while at the same time continuing
to make gains in Liguria and maintaining access to reinforcements
from Lombardy which could give him a temporary tactical superiority
in Tuscany when he needed it. For, despite his departure from the
Genoese Riviera di Levante to meet the Florentine threat in the Val di
Nievole, he continued to deploy enough troops there to gain control of
the eastern extremity of Liguria and also to acquire Pontremoli, the
key point on the road between his territories and Parma, and, beyond
it, Milan. His tactics, based on the interchange of critical numbers of
troops, went hand in hand, in other words, with a policy of acquiring
strongholds which gave access to other Ghibelline-dominated areas.

The history of his penetration both of the eastern Riviera and Lunigiana (in which Pontremoli stands) is sufficiently important in itself to
deserve to be dealt with at greater length. While in a sense it began in
1318 with Castruccio's first intervention in favour of the Genoese
Ghibellines, it soon went beyond this and, in the summer of 1320,
turned into a systematic attempt to impose political control in these
regions. On 19 July of that year, the legates of the council of the
imperial party of Genoa were empowered formally to appoint him
vicar-general of the eastern Genoese Riviera for six months,[48] an election which was ratified in Lucca on 8 August.[49] At this point, then,
Castruccio obtained a title to jurisdiction over the Riviera di Levante
analogous to that he already enjoyed as protector of those parts of the
contado of Pistoia under Ghibelline rule. He lost no time in seeking to
make his newly acquired authority real in terms of actual control of
part of the territory it covered. While the Florentine attack on the Val

[48] ASL Atti di Castruccio no. 1, cc. 65ᵛ.–66ʳ. published in Lazzareschi, 'Documenti',
328–30.

[49] Ibid., cc. 66ʳ.–67ʳ., 70ᵛ.–71ᵛ., and pp. 330–5. On 26 August his title was changed to
captain.

LUNIGIANA AND THE EASTERN EXTREMITY OF THE GENOESE RIVIERA

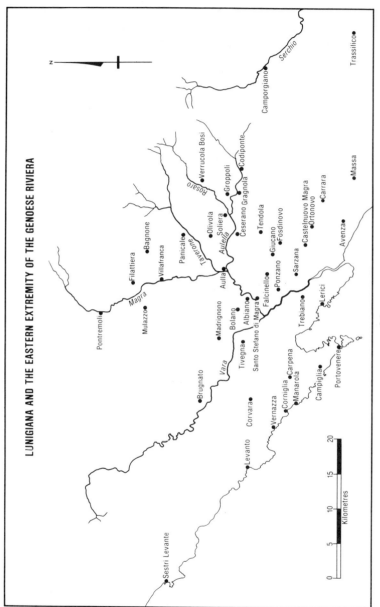

Map I.

di Nievole which forced him to leave Liguria late in 1320 prevented him from participating in the Ghibelline attack on Genoa launched by Frederick of Sicily in July of that year (which lasted till February of the following one),[50] it did not materially interfere with the more modest campaign Castruccio had undertaken in September against a group of townships on the eastern extremity of Liguria, immediately adjoining his own territories. This appears to have been carried on, even in his absence—for, while two of these places, Levanto and Corvara, submitted to him on 15 and 16 September, two others, Corniglia and Manarola, held out until 18 November and the following 12 February respectively.[51] It is a testimony to his determination to acquire a foot-hold in Liguria that, in a militarily difficult situation, he was willing to spare forces to secure his gains in this region; and it may well be that his intervention in Genoese affairs, at least at this stage, had as its real aim these minor but attainable additions to his own territories, rather than support for the Ghibelline attack on Genoa itself, the pretext for his election as vicar-general and captain of the eastern Riviera but, in the light of his very limited penetration into this area at this time, not apparently a serious goal of his strategy.

The tendency which was evident here to concentrate on small-scale, slow accumulation of border villages or towns adjoining his state manifested itself at roughly the same period in his acquisition of the 'borgo di sotto' of Pontremoli and his Pistoian policy. In the case of Pontremoli, he did not even need to resort to military action. A long-standing feud between those of the lower and upper halves of the town, supported, on the one hand, by Franceschino Malaspina, marquis of Mulazzo, and Ghiberto da Correggio of Parma and, on the other, by Cardinal Luca de' Fieschi and another branch of the Malaspina under Moroello, opened the way for Castruccio's intervention when the inhabitants of the 'borgo di sotto' rebelled against an attempted reconciliation between these rival overlords and called him in as its protector.[52] On 27 May 1321, he accordingly accepted lordship

[50] G. Villani, *Cronica*, ix. 112, 116, 117, 118.

[51] Sforza, 'Castruccio . . . in Lunigiana', 342–7 and 496–503. By 1327, Castruccio had in his hands the following villages on the Riviera di Levante: Carpena, Corvara, Manarola, Corniglia, Vernazza, Monterosso, Levanto, Tivegna, Sestri and Trebiano (ASL Libri di Corredo no. 4, cc. 43^r.–46^r.). Except for Sestri, these must all have been acquired as a result of the campaign of 1320–1.

[52] For an account of the complicated antecedents of Castruccio's acquisition of Pontremoli, see G. Sforza, *Memorie e documenti per servire alla storia di Pontremoli* (Lucca, Florence, 1887–1904) (also published as *Storia di Pontremoli dalle origini al 1500* (Florence, 1904)), i. 168–94.

over that part of the town for five years[53] and then used it as a base to gain control of the upper town as well by the following February.[54] Interestingly, Castruccio appears to have gained control over Pontremoli without apparently antagonizing Ghiberto da Correggio, whom he displaced as its governor, but who, as lord of Parma, must nevertheless, if Villani is to be believed, have simultaneously allowed him the use of some of his knights in the campaign against the Florentines of June 1321. The key to the ease with which he took over the town without offending its previous ruler lies most probably in the special relationship he had built up with the dominant family of Lunigiana. For, despite his previous expulsion of Spinetta Malaspina from his lands, Castruccio took pains to stay on good terms with other branches of this aristocratic dynasty whose continued acquiescence he needed not only to hold Pontremoli but also to preserve the position he had originally acquired in 1314 as viscount of the bishopric of Luni.

Following the death of Gherardino, the bishop who had first empowered Castruccio to administer the secular affairs of that diocese, his successor Bernardone, a member of another branch of the Malaspina, chose likewise to come to terms with the lord of Lucca, whom he allowed from April 1321 onwards to exercise vice-comital jurisdiction on his behalf in his lands.[55] This renewal of Castruccio's authority, with the blessing of Bernardone, over the episcopal territories of Luni, of course preceded by a month his appointment as governor over the Ghibelline lower town of Pontremoli, a circumstance which is indicative of his cultivation of the Malaspina in the period immediately prior to his election. His influence with the family continued to grow over the ensuing year and a half, judging by his close collaboration over that time with the new bishop of Luni and his brother Nicolao, called Marchesotto. On 24 August 1321, after having been granted the village and citadel of Castiglione di Terserio by

[53] ASL Atti di Castruccio no. 1, cc. 52ᵛ.–53ᵛ., published in Lazzareschi, 'Documenti', 337–9.

[54] Ibid., cc. 55ᵛ.–56ʳ. The election of Castruccio as lord of the 'borgo di sopra' on 18 February recorded in this document was preceded five days earlier by the renewal of his authority over the 'borgo di sotto', free of the conditions imposed on him the previous May (ibid., cc. 53ᵛ.–54ᵛ., published in Lazzareschi, 'Documenti', 347–9). On 20 February, both 'borghi' combined to appoint Castruccio lord of a now united town (ibid., cc. 56ᵛ.–58ʳ.).

[55] The document which survives, dated 6 April 1321, is, in fact, an authorization by Castruccio to Banoso di Gubbio and Ser Lazzaro Saggina, empowering them to accept the vice-comital jurisdiction on his behalf (ibid., c. 44ʳ. and ᵛ. published in Lazzareschi, 'Documenti', 336–7). His formal reinvestiture presumably occurred shortly afterwards, later in the month.

Bernardone, Castruccio promptly handed them back, for nine years, to Nicolao who was to administer them but return them in the event of any conflict between the bishop and the lord of Lucca.[56] On the following 31 October, Nicolao further agreed not to permit anyone who was Castruccio's enemy entry to his lands,[57] while on 16 August 1322, together with his brother, he swore fealty to Castruccio.[58] It is evident from the documents recording these events that the favour of these two Malaspina was secured by guaranteeing them in turn the military and political protection they needed to exercise their authority in this area. In this way, two purposes were served: Castruccio became in name as well as in fact overlord of Lunigiana and the bishop and his brother were allowed to enjoy the use of some of the lands under his now legally endorsed jurisdiction. He appears both then and later to have further strengthened his links with other branches of the Malaspina, to buttress his position on the northern frontiers of his state, notably by the marriage of his daughter Caterina to Marquis Giovanni Malaspina in November 1326.[59]

The success with which Castruccio had established his control over Lunigiana and the eastern tip of the Genoese Riviera in 1320–1 left him free thereafter to devote his energies to the war with Florence, fought along the eastern and south-eastern frontiers of his state. He was aided here by the continuing involvement of the Guelph coalition in hostilities in Lombardy directed against the Visconti.[60] He himself contributed to the further embroilment of his enemies in this fighting across the Apennines by sending six hundred knights (in Lucchese and Pisan pay) to Galeazzo Visconti to enable the latter to win a decisive victory over the army of the Church at Val di Taro late in November 1321 and to take Cremona at the beginning of the following January.[61] By dispatching these troops, Castruccio also repaid a debt to his Lombard ally who had come to his help with a force of five hundred cavalry the previous June, as well as making it easier for him to call on assistance from the Visconti in the future.

---

[56] Ibid., cc. 50ᵛ.–51ʳ. and pp. 340–1.

[57] Ibid., c. 46ʳ. and pp. 341–3. The terms agreed on, to apply, like Nicolao's tenure of Castiglione di Terserio, for nine years, also stipulated that no enemy of Castruccio's was to be sold or leased any land in Lunigiana nor given any advice, help, or favour.

[58] Ibid., cc. 46ᵛ.–47ʳ. and pp. 350–1.

[59] Lazzareschi, 'Documenti', 400, Sforza, 'Castruccio . . . in Lunigiana', 353, 504–7.

[60] G. Villani, *Cronica*, ix. 129. The Florentines, Sienese, and Bolognese had to send a thousand knights to reinforce the papal armies here in the autumn of 1321.

[61] Ibid., ix. 129–30.

The concentration of the efforts of both Guelphs and Ghibellines on the war in Lombardy led to a lull in hostilities on the Val d'Arno front where the Florentines, having engaged a hundred and seventy Friulan knights and as many bowmen, were able to check further Lucchese incursions beyond the Usciana.[62] Castruccio, for his part, was content to allow fighting to die down in this area in order to enable him to direct his whole attention to his designs against Pistoia. He began at this time a slow infiltration of its territory that was to culminate, three years later, in his acquisition of that city. Exploiting his title as captain-general of its Ghibellines, he had already, in 1320 and 1321, come to the aid of his partisans, entrenched in villages to the southwest of Pistoia, when they had clashed with the Guelphs around the abbey of San Baronto[63] and had later contested with the Florentines possession of the adjoining region around Vinci and Cerreto Guidi.[64] Now, in the months leading up to Easter 1322, Castruccio followed up these earlier skirmishes with military operations on the *contado* of Pistoia,[65] the purpose of which was to put pressure on that city's government. At this stage, he embarked on a two-pronged policy of armed harassment and diplomatic cajolery that was intended to achieve a *modus vivendi* with its rulers.

The technique he employed in achieving this aim was one of disruption of movement, trade, and agriculture around Pistoia by continual, devastating attacks through its countryside. His purpose was to make conditions sufficiently difficult for the inhabitants of town and *contado* alike for the most amenable of them to come to terms with him. He evidently succeeded in terrorizing the peasantry, to judge by the testimony of the 'Storie pistoresi', as a result of his massacre of the defenders of a fortified stronghold at Piuvica who had refused to yield to him, to such effect that many of them were prepared to pay him protection money to safeguard their lives and property.[66] He thus gained a considerable degree of control over the Pistoian and Pratese countryside. His main aim, however, was to exploit the inconvenience this caused to the citizens of Pistoia itself in order to arrive at an accommodation with the faction among them most willing to treat with him. He was favoured in this design by the divisions in the town: ever since the

---

[62] Ibid., ix. 135.
[63] 'Storie pistoresi', 72–3.
[64] Ibid., and G. Villani, *Cronica*, ix. 127.
[65] G. Villani, *Cronica*, ix. 146, 'Storie pistoresi', 74.
[66] 'Storie pistoresi', 74.

Black Guelphs had reduced it into a powerless protectorate in 1306, its leading families had learnt to bend to the prevailing political winds, though some inclined to a pro-Florentine and others to a more in-dependent, neutral stance. Now that Castruccio had suddenly shown himself to be more of a threat than the previously dominant Guelph forces in Tuscany, the way was opened for sections of the Pistoian ruling group publicly to affirm their support for peace in preference to continued, enforced alliance with Florence in the anti-Lucchese war.

According to the author of the 'Storie pistoresi', even King Robert of Naples's vicar in the city was privy to the first approaches made to Castruccio at Serravalle with the aim of arriving at a truce with him.[67] Whatever the truth of this perhaps rather dubious claim, it is certain that the faction led by the Tedici family, which enjoyed considerable artisan and popular support, took the initiative in steering Pistoian public opinion towards an acceptance of an accommodation with Lucca. The head of the Tedici house, Ormanno, the abbot of Pacciana, must, in the light of subsequent events, have had as his main motive the enhancement of his own personal power and the eclipse of that of his enemies who were closely identified with the prevailing pro-Florence policy of the commune.[68] His method of arriving at his goal was, on the one hand, to play upon the attractiveness of peace with Castruccio to gain popularity among the mass of his war-weary fellow-citizens and, on the other, to temporize with the Florentines in order to keep them guessing as to his own intentions long enough to prevent any effective countermove on their part before terms for a truce could be arranged with Lucca. While the artisans and 'popolo minuto' were worked up to agitation with the catchword 'Truce, truce', which the Guelph families found it impolitic to oppose, Flor-ence, alarmed at the reported negotiations with Castruccio, dis-

---

[67] Ibid., 74–5. According to this source, the vicar Pino della Tosa, who had earlier clashed with Castruccio's army at Lo Sperone near Pistoia and had been compelled to retreat because of the superior numbers of the Lucchese force, was involved in these negotiations. On this point, however, there is some doubt since Pino's vicariate could not have lasted beyond February 1321 (J. M. Fioravanti, *Memorie storiche della città di Pistoia* (Lucca, 1758), 271) or, at the very latest, August of that year when that office is recorded as held by Pietro della Torre of Orvieto (F. A. Zacharia, *Anecdotum medii aevi*, (Turin, 1755), 263). Davidsohn, *Storia*, iv. 930, concludes that it was Bavigliano Manetti and not Pino della Tosa to whom the 'Storie pistoresi' refer, since he was withdrawn as vicar on 21 April 1322 (Zacharia, op. cit., 39) at the time of the conclusion of the truce with Castruccio, which accords with the statement in the 'Storie' that Pino was recalled because of that agreement.

[68] 'Storie pistoresi', 76.

patched six ambassadors to promise Pistoia military assistance as a means to ending his depredations on its *contado*. Ormanno Tedici cunningly kept up appearances with these envoys, making a semblance of listening sympathetically to their proposals while at the same time hastening both his negotiations with the Lucchese and the mobilization of his supporters in both town and country for a seizure of power in the city.

On the Easter Monday, 12 April 1322, he assembled a council in the palace of the *anziani* to discuss how a truce with Lucca might be concluded, pretending at this stage that he was prepared to take the advice on this question of the Guelphs in the city and of the ambassadors who were present at this assembly. Then, having arranged for the discussions on this matter to be resumed in the afternoon in the Franciscan church, he let his opponents go to lunch, while he mustered his supporters and took control of the streets. His principal enemies, Ettolo Taviani and Bonifazio Ricciardi, realizing what was happening, took refuge with the Florentine ambassadors under whose protection they were safe. In the meantime, however, Ormanno seized the palace of the *anziani*, the gates, and the cathedral campanile. That evening, another meeting was called in an attempt to obtain ratification of the abbot's actions, followed the next morning by further negotiations with the Florentine emissaries. The situation, nevertheless, remained to some extent in the balance until Castruccio's army appeared, doubtless at Ormanno's prompting, at San Pantaleo, half a mile from the city. Fearful lest the Tedici, frustrated in their bid to expel their enemies, might admit this force through one of the gates they held, the Florentine envoys judged it best to depart, taking Ettolo Taviani and Bonifazio Ricciardi with them, and abandoning the faction favourable to them. This permitted Ormanno Tedici to reform the government in his favour, to have himself elected 'captain of the people', to expel the remaining members of the Taviani and Ricciardi families, and to resume negotiations with Castruccio for settling the final terms of the truce.[69]

The exact date when it was concluded remains in doubt, but it must have been between April and December of 1322.[70] Under it, Castruccio

[69] Ibid., 77–9, G. Villani, *Cronica*, ix. 146.

[70] For a discussion of the question by S. A. Barbi, its editor, see 'Storie pistoresi', 79, n. 2. According to Villani, the truce was signed immediately after the April 1322 disturbances. Barbi cites the evidence of papal letters in May and November urging the Pistoians to settle their differences and preserve the Florentine alliance in support of his view that it was concluded in November or December 1322. However, as Davidsohn

was to receive a tribute of 3,000 florins a year[71] and presumably was to
desist from military operations against Pistoia, though evidently not
against some of its possessions in the mountains to the north of the city,
which he assailed in the next two winters, on the pretext of retaliation for
help to rebels in the Lucchese dependency of Lucchio.[72]

The events which occurred in April 1322 were, in the long run, to
prove a decisive turning-point in Castruccio's plans for territorial
expansion, marking as they did the first step towards his acquisition of
Pistoia. At the time, however, their significance appeared to be far
more limited. Under Ormanno Tedici, who had originally been a
staunch supporter of the Black Guelphs, that city did not pass, in any
real sense, into the Ghibelline camp. While the abbot of Pacciana's
personal enemies and rivals for power were exiled when he became
captain of the people, many prominent Guelphs remained in the town
and neither the papacy nor Florence lost hope of a return of the commune to the party of the Church.[73] What the revolution of April 1322
did, however, achieve was a definite displacement, both in the internal
and external situation of the city, of the previously prevailing balance
of power. Pistoia moved, under Ormanno Tedici, from being an ally of
Florence to being a buffer between it and Lucca and, internally,
acquired a ruler whose position had been gained and would have to
continue to be maintained through Castruccio's good will, political
manipulation, and armed support.

On the face of it, the lord of Lucca obtained relatively little from his
truce with Pistoia, abandoning what had until then been for him a
highly successful sphere of military operations in return for fairly
small tribute and the disengagement from the Guelph coalition of one
of its minor members. Nevertheless, what had happened had fundamentally strengthened his position. His captaincy of the Pistoian
Ghibellines combined with the dependence on him of the Tedici
made him the key figure henceforth in the affairs of the vulnerable city
to his east, capable of increasing his influence over its government

has shown (*Storia*, iv. 935–7), even after the truce, Pistoia was by no means considered
by the Guelphs and the papacy in particular as irredeemably lost to their cause; consequently this evidence is not conclusive.

[71] G. Villani, *Cronica*, ix. 146.

[72] On 24 February 1323 Castruccio wrote complaining to Abbot Ormanno Tedici of
the help given to Lucchio by the inhabitants of mountain villages under Pistoian jurisdiction (ASL Atti di Castruccio no. 1, c. 38ᵛ. published in Lazzareschi, 'Documenti',
352).

[73] See, in this connection, Davidsohn, *Storia*, iv. 935–7.

without fear of Florentine interference. Castruccio needed only to work on the divisions both in the commune and in its ruling family to bring about the complete take-over he sought.

2. *The rift with Pisa and the acquisition of Pistoia*

The process by which he achieved this was, however, to be a slow one and he did not complete it for three years. In the meantime, he had to pass through what was one of the most critical phases in his political life. In the first two years of his war with Florence he had been singularly fortunate in his struggle with a potentially superior enemy: he had re-established the southern frontiers of his state and strengthened his line of defence in that quarter against a possible Guelph counter-offensive from the Val d'Arno, he had extended his control over the eastern tip of Liguria and Pontemoli, he had dislodged the Florentines from Pistoia, and, by assuming the leadership of that city's Ghibelline exiles, had entrenched himself along the western edge of its *contado*. Above all, he had skilfully resisted Florentine attempts to break through his defensive perimeter in the Val di Nievole and to raise revolts in his rear, by drawing on timely support from his allies and isolating Spinetta Malaspina through the cultivation of other branches of that magnate's family. What Castruccio had achieved, however, had depended very much on the prevalence of a certain set of conditions—ability to call on help from Pisa and the Lombard Ghibellines to offset his own relative military weakness, and the continued absorption of the bulk of the Florentine mercenaries in the political morass of the Church's war against the Visconti. This conflict not only enabled Castruccio to overcome any inferiority to which he might otherwise have been subject in his armed struggle with the Guelphs of Tuscany, but it also gave him the means for claiming assistance from Lombardy when he required it because of the Visconti's reciprocal need for his support when they themselves were under threat.

In the eighteen months from April 1322 to October 1323 these conditions continued apparently to prevail but their foundations were undermined and, in the following year and a half, from late 1323 on, they ceased to hold. The key factors which eventually changed Castruccio's position were, firstly, his breach with Pisa and, associated with it, the war between that city and Aragon for the control of Sardinia, and, secondly, the emergence of Ludwig of Bavaria as the effective emperor-elect in place of Frederick of Austria, with all the implications which that had for the Guelph–Ghibelline conflict in

northern Italy. A new set of strategic considerations came to govern
north and central Italian politics as a result. The Guelph–Ghibelline
confrontation centred uneasily on Milan and Genoa was to be
replaced by a more complex combination of political alignments.
Papal–imperial antagonism, muted between the Habsburg–Angevin
marriage alliance of June 1316 and Ludwig's victory at Muhldorf in
September 1322 by the temporary reconciliation of the ruling houses
of Austria and Naples, revived after the latter date and became the
dominant factor in the overall Italian situation. In Tuscany, Pisa's
trading interests and its preoccupation with retaining Sardinia, in the
face of Aragonese and Lucchese efforts effectively to partition its territories, drew it out of the Ghibelline league. This was to mean, by the
end of 1323, that Castruccio was far more isolated than he had been at
the outbreak of the war against Florence in 1320 and therefore far
more dependent upon the protection of the two distant sovereigns,
James II of Aragon and Ludwig of Bavaria, as well as upon his capacity
to defend his state alone against his Guelph enemies.

In the summer of 1322, this transformation of the Italian political
scene lay, however, some way into the future and, while certain forces
were working towards it, they had not yet altered the basic conditions
in which Castruccio operated. He was still able to make use of Pisan
mercenaries right up to August 1323, and to count on the Florentines'
involvement in the war against the Visconti to hold his front against
them in the Arno valley. But he ceased, at this point, making significant gains through minor hostilities and hence faced the risk of being
left the ruler of a small state confronted by one with superior
resources, unless he moved beyond a strategy dictated by his limitations to one aimed at overcoming them.

The campaigns which Castruccio fought between mid-1322 and late
1323 clearly indicate a slowing down of the momentum of his military
operations. After a succession of skirmishes at the end of 1322,[74] he
found himself compelled to put down a rebellion in Lucchio in the Val
di Lima which he did not quell till 17 March 1323.[75] Since the inhabitants of neighbouring hamlets in Pistoian-held territory smuggled
supplies into this village while he was besieging it, Castruccio felt

---

[74] These had included supporting the Genoese Ghibelline attack on Portovenere in
September (G. Villani, *Cronica*, ix. 170).
[75] Ibid., ix. 193. He had been engaged in besieging the place since before 24 February
(see n. 72 above).

justified in invading and occupying these places to isolate Lucchio and so bring about its surrender.[76]

While Castruccio was still in the Val di Lima the Florentines plotted unsuccessfully to seize Ponte a Cappiano,[77] and the next summer conspired with some of the citizens of Buggiano in the Val di Nievole to have that town betrayed to them. When their plans misfired because Castruccio got wind of them and when two hundred of the Florentines' Friulan mercenaries deserted to him because of dissatisfaction with their pay and the offer of more money from Lucca, a plan for a concerted attack on that city by the Genoese Guelphs in the west and the Florentines in the south had to be abandoned.[78] Castruccio, his army reinforced and his enemy's weakened by the defection of the latter's Friulan cavalry, went on the offensive for the first time in more than a year. With eight hundred knights and eight thousand infantry, drawn both from Lucca and Pisa, he crossed the Usciana at Ponte a Cappiano on 13 June, and assailed the Florentine positions at Fucecchio, Santa Croce, Castelfranco, Montopoli, and San Miniato. He ravaged the surrounding country but did not remain in the area to attempt to take any of these places, returning to Lucca on the twenty-third, a mere ten days after the opening of the campaign.[79]

After invading the *contado* of Prato at the beginning of July and being driven off by superior Florentine forces,[80] he resumed his attacks on the Val d'Arno on 24 August, once again laying waste the land around Montopoli, Castelfranco, and Santa Croce.[31] But when he returned to the same area on 19 December in an attempt to seize

---

[76] Ibid., and 'Storie pistoresi'. According to Villani, Pistoia, alarmed by Castruccio's invasion of its territory, feared further breaches of the truce and requested Florentine aid, which arrived in the form of seventy-five knights and four hundred infantry. This is confirmed in Florentine records referring to the payment of troops sent towards Lucchio in March 1323 (ASF Provvisioni no. 19, c. 87ʳ.).

[77] G. Villani, *Cronica*, ix. 193. See also ASF Provvisioni no. 19, c. 87ʳ. According to Davidsohn, *Storia*, iv. 950, the Florentines succeeded in taking Ponte a Cappiano in May, but his source for this is a letter in which the year is not specified. In view of the absence of any confirmatory information on the recapture of this fortified bridge which we know to have been in Castruccio's hands in 1325, the report of the taking of it cannot be assigned with certainty to this period. Furthermore, Villani (ix. 209) states that on 13 June 1323 Castruccio crossed the bridge at Cappiano without mentioning any resistance to him here, which is not consistent with it having been captured the previous month by the Florentines.

[78] G. Villani, *Cronica*, ix. 208. The date when the Friulan troops passed over to Castruccio's side was 7 June 1323.

[79] Ibid., ix. 209.

[80] Ibid., ix. 214.

[81] Ibid., ix. 220.

Fucecchio, he very nearly came to grief. Admitted to the town one rainy night by some dissatisfied poorer citizens, he managed to bring into it fifty knights and five hundred infantry. With these men, he seized control of the streets and all of the citadel except for one tower. Signal fires on top of this soon, however, brought to the scene Guelph reinforcements from neighbouring villages which, together with the townsmen, drove him back in fierce fighting in the early morning. In the ensuing retreat, Castruccio was wounded in the face and lost a hundred and fifty men.[82]

This near disaster brought home to him the risks inherent in such lightning strikes into enemy territory. In the face of Florentine preponderance in real armed strength, they could not achieve lasting gains, since he always found himself obliged to retreat from them when the bulk of the Guelph army moved against him. His problem, at this time, was essentially that the war in Lombardy was no longer proving enough of a distraction to keep more than a fraction of the Florentine mercenaries out of Tuscany. In fact, in the first half of 1323, Ghibelline Milan, which had fought a successful campaign against the Church in the previous summer, reached the nadir of its military and political fortunes. Its general, Marco Visconti, defeated the papal captain, Ramon de Cardona, on 6 July 1322 at Bassignano,[83] but was himself routed on the following 25 February on the Adda and on 19 April at Gargazzola.[84] As a consequence, Milan was besieged on 11 June and might have fallen had it not been for intervention in its favour by Can Grande della Scala of Verona, Passerino Bonaccolsi of Mantua, and the marquis of Este, who brought with them Ludwig of Bavaria's ambassadors.[85] The troops sent by these other Lombard lords to relieve the city forced Ramon de Cardona to raise its siege on 28 July and to withdraw to Monza which was then, in turn, invested by the now strengthened Ghibelline army on 8 August.[86]

While the Florentines, as before, maintained a contingent of two hundred knights in the Church's army throughout these months, the absence of any need to reinforce it before August 1323[87] meant that

[82] Ibid., ix. 223.

[83] G. Villani, *Cronica*, ix. 160.

[84] Ibid., ix. 191, 199. In the meantime, the Visconti had been expelled from Milan in November 1322, only to return there the following month (ibid., ix. 181, 184).

[85] Ibid., ix. 211, 212.

[86] Ibid., ix. 212, 213.

[87] Ibid., ix. 187, 199. See also ix. 211, referring to the presence of Florentine mercenaries at the siege of Milan. According to a letter sent by the Florentines to Pope John

they could keep in Tuscany forces sufficient to contain Castruccio's forays beyond his defensive perimeter. That they did not use these to launch a major offensive themselves may be due partly to the internal divisions to which Giovanni Villani attributed their failure to follow up their repulse of Castruccio from the outskirts of Prato,[88] but also to hostilities against the Aretines (to whom the Pisans and Lucchese had lent a hundred and fifty of their mercenaries in May 1322[89] and from whom the Florentines took Caposelvi in Val D'Ambra in September of that year[90]) and against the Tolomei, allies of Guido Tarlati, the bishop of Arezzo, who raised a revolt on the *contado* of Siena between December 1322 and February 1323.[91] The defection of their Friulan mercenaries in June and the failure of the various plots to gain possession of villages in Lucchese territory, as well as Castruccio's seizure of the military initiative in the summer of 1323, clearly also played a part in their maintenance of a defensive posture right through that year when, in fact, conditions might have favoured their taking a more aggressive stance.

The general position in which the Lucchese tyrant found himself was, in any case, deteriorating, so they could afford to wait. In February 1323, the Genoese Ghibellines had suffered a decisive defeat which had compelled them to abandon the siege with which they had persevered for so long, and to retire to Savona and Voltri.[92] This left Castruccio once again exposed to an attack from the rear. At the same time, he could count on no help from Lombardy where, until the end of July, the Visconti were more hard pressed than he. Nor could he render them much assistance, fully occupied as he was with the rebellion of Lucchio in the winter, preparing to meet an expected joint Florentine and Genoese Guelph offensive in the spring, and campaigning in the Val d'Arno and Pratese *contado* in the summer. By

XXII on 24 August (ASF Capitoli no. 16, c. 5ʳ.), reinforcements were requested for these troops because of losses due to sickness.

[88] G. Villani, *Cronica*, ix. 214. According to this chronicler, the Florentine magnates who served in the civic cavalry objected to the proposed invasion of Lucchese territory because they resented the Ordinances of Justice. They also apparently encouraged exiles to attempt to re-enter the city, causing further commotion and inducing the army to return to Florence by 20 July. On 10 August the exiles approached the city again at night, causing more nervousness on the part of the Signoria which feared a conspiracy involving the magnates in the city and the exiles outside it (ibid., ix. 219).

[89] Ibid., ix. 151.

[90] Ibid., ix. 151, 166.

[91] Ibid., ix. 183.

[92] Ibid., ix. 188. See also Finke, *Acta*, i. 388–9.

autumn, he might have been able to join the Ghibelline forces in Lombardy, but the shortness of the time between his return from Montopoli at the end of August and the raising of the siege of Monza on 1 October makes Davidsohn's suggestion that he did so open to question.[93]

Whether he did so or not, he did not share with the Visconti the sudden upturn of their fortunes late in 1323. For to his already precarious military position was added, in late October, the further blow of his rift with Pisa. His relations with this city had been difficult for some time, probably ever since his abrupt and unwelcome appearance with his army at San Giuliano during the civic disturbances of May 1322. On that occasion, according to Villani, 'the Pisans, fearful of his coming lest he and his men should overrun and plunder the city, forbade him to advance'.[94] For all their suspicion of him, however, the Pisans had not, at that stage, suspended their alliance with him. For his part, the lord of Lucca remained as careful as ever to avoid offending the interests of the neighbouring city, the military support of which was so vital to him. When further friction arose in late 1322 between Pisan-held Sarzana and Lucchese-dominated Sarzanello, he proved to be as pliable as he had been in 1317 in yielding to the demands made on him.[95] He must by this time have been aware of the possibility that the growing divergence between his interests and those of his closest ally might eventually cost him its military support which was so essential to him.

Pisa in fact derived no real advantage from its war with Florence, which, besides, used up resources that, from 1323 onwards, were needed for the defence of its most valuable possession, Sardinia. As events in 1322 revealed, it still depended upon Florence commercially, despite the state of hostilities with that city, for, when it attempted in the August of that year to raise its duties on Florentine goods, retaliation in the form of a withdrawal of trade by the leading user of its port

---

[93] Davidsohn, *Storia*, iv 944. On the basis of a papal letter of 30 April 1325, Davidsohn actually places Castruccio's arrival on the scene in July at the time of the raising of the siege of Milan. But this letter only accuses him of besieging the papal inquisitors in Monza at an unspecified date, which could equally refer to the second siege, between Ramon de Cardona's defeat on 29 February and 28 March 1324, or the third between September and December 1324 (G. Villani, *Cronica*, ix. 244, 270).

[94] Ibid., ix. 153.

[95] Sforza, 'Della signoria' 10–12 and 24–29, and ASP Comune A49, cc. 45ʳ.–71ᵛ. Sforza dates the documents on pp. 24–9 in Pisan style as 1323; but it is clear from the heading of register A48 and from the text he himself quotes on p. 29 that all were drawn up in 1322 in Lucchese and modern style.

had forced a cancellation of the increase.[96] If this was a disturbing portent for Castruccio, an even more alarming one must have been King Robert of Naples's request, made to the Pisans about the same time, on 9 August 1322, for five galleys for his fleet.[97] Though this was rejected, the very fact that it was submitted, and then considered by the Pisan *anziani*, created the possibility of a clash of interests between Castruccio, who, the following month, participated in the Genoese Ghibelline attack on Portovenere, and those who had been asked to supply ships for the navy which raised the siege of that town. The prospect of an Aragonese attack on Sardinia made a reconciliation between Pisa, on the one hand, and the pope, King Robert of Naples, and the Genoese Guelphs, on the other, in any case not unlikely.[98]

The diplomatic situation in 1322 and 1323 was becoming more fluid and such changes in alliances could therefore not be ruled out. Not only was it feasible that Pisa might switch sides in a desperate effort to hold Sardinia; but, indeed, Castruccio, with Pisan mercenaries no longer available to him because they were needed for the defence at that island, might choose to enter an anti-Pisan coalition in common with Aragon and Florence, thus easing himself out of a war which was bringing him no further gains and which he could no longer fight on equal terms. Alternatively, he could exploit dissatisfaction in Pisa with Nieri della Gherardesca's rule and the weakening of that commune as a result of the attack on Sardinia to bring about a change in its government which would ultimately work to his advantage.

The Aragonese project for the conquest of the large Mediterranean island from which Pisa drew about two-fifths of its revenues[99] acted in fact as a solvent of existing relationships, confusing the previous demarcation between Guelph and Ghibelline forces. The claim which James II of Aragon asserted to Sardinia at the Cortes of Gerona in

[96] Davidsohn, *Storia*, iv. 924, and *Forschungen*, iii. 157–8, G. Villani, *Cronica*, ix. 165, G. Volpe, 'Pisa, Firenze, impero al principio del 1300 e gli inizi della signoria civile a Pisa', *Studi storici*, xi. (1902), 314–6. See also ASP Comune A90, C.78ʳ. for reference to terms on which Florentine and Sienese merchants traded on 22 December 1323, presumably under the conditions established towards the end of the previous year.

[97] ASP Comune A49, cc. 58–60. See also ibid., c. 54ʳ., where the *anziani* of Pisa used as excuses for not sending help to Guido Tarlati in Arezzo the cost of defending Sardinia against a possible Aragonese attack and the obligation to furnish galleys to King Robert of Naples (23 July 1322).

[98] G. Villani, *Cronica*, ix. 170. On this, see also Finke *Acta*, i. 390, and ii. 578.

[99] Volpe, 'Pisa, Firenze, impero . . .', 310.

1322[100] went back to 1297 when Pope Boniface VIII, in an effort to facilitate the recovery of Sicily by the Angevin kingdom of Naples, had promised Sardinia and Corsica to the Aragonese in return for their abandonment of their support for Frederick of Sicily.[101] Since these islands were, in reality, under Pisan and Genoese rule, the grant of them by the Church represented no more than a justification for their seizure by force. It was, however, a perfect pretext for aggression, even though, at the time when the claim was revived, the papacy no longer supported it and was, indeed, taken completely by surprise by its reassertion. Neither John XXII nor his close ally Robert of Naples had anything to gain by James II's sudden intrusion into Italian politics. Despite this, since Aragon's quarrel was with Pisa, it was logical that it was to the maritime republic's principal enemy, the commune of Florence, that the Aragonese ambassadors, seeking support for their king's enterprise, should first turn. Accordingly, in January 1323, a certain Tuccio Aldobrandini pleaded on that monarch's behalf for a subsidy of 50,000 florins from the leading Tuscan Guelph city.[102] He seems to have received only promises, amounting to half that amount, for in September another envoy, Alberto de Gatello, who was also sent to Florence, complained of that commune and of Siena, Pistoia, and Bologna that none of them had fulfilled their undertakings to provide 25,000 florins each.[103] Interestingly, in his report he also included a reference to the non-payment of the same sum by the commune of Lucca.[104] Was this, one wonders, a mistake on his part, or did it indicate secret contacts even at this stage between Castruccio and the Aragonese emissaries? If it did, then it would confirm the assertion of the Pisan chroniclers that the lord of Lucca, in common with malcontents in Pisa, had been responsible for urging the Sardinian venture on the Aragonese Crown.[105]

Whatever the truth as to this intriguing possibility, there is no doubt that Castruccio, like the enemies of the Gherardesca in the neighbouring city, was playing a double game. According to Rossi-Sabatini, a

[100] R. Muntaner, 'Cronica' ch. 271 in *Les Quatre Grans Croniques*, ed. F. Soldevila (Barcelona, 1971), 910.

[101] V. Salavert y Roca, *Cerdeña y la Expansion mediterranea de la Corona de Aragon* (Madrid, 1956), 114–20.

[102] A. Arribas Palau, *La conquista de Cerdeña por Jaime II de Aragon* (Barcelona, 1952), 276.

[103] Ibid., and ACA Cancelleria Reg. 341, ff. 147–50.

[104] ACA Cancelleria Reg. 341, fo. 148ᵛ.

[105] See Sardo, *Cronaca*, 77, 'Cronica di Pisa', col. 998, BNF MS Palat. 571, c. 22ᵛ.

group of Pisan aristocrats was at this time dissatisfied with Nieri della Gherardesca because he had failed to reward them adequately for their support during the disturbances of May 1322. Hankering after the influence they had enjoyed under Uguccione della Faggiuola, they were prepared to intrigue with the lord of Lucca in the hope of regaining their former power under his protection.[106] Their opportunity came in 1323 when the rebellion of the 'judge' of Arborea (overlord or viceroy over one of the four administrative sub-divisions of Sardinia) provoked the immediate dispatch to the island of an Aragonese expeditionary force under James II's son, the Infante Alfonso.[107] During the ensuing siege of Iglesias by the invaders between 28 June 1323 and 7 February 1324, the Pisans attempted to relieve this city and also Cagliari which was likewise under attack. In October 1323, a fleet of galleys was sent out but, when it was confronted by an Aragonese squadron of roughly equal size, was compelled to turn back. It was while this was away that the conspirators planned to act. The captains of four of the German mercenary companies remaining on the mainland were won over by Betto Malepa Lanfranchi who planned to kill Nieri della Gherardesca and then, with the help of Castruccio and the troops under these bribed commanders, to seize power. Unfortunately for him and his fellow-plotters, two Florentine Ghibelline exiles, Bonifacio de' Cerchi and one of the Guidi, who were living in Lucca but at times resident also in Pisa, got wind of the conspiracy and betrayed it. On 24 October, Nieri was therefore able to arrest and execute Betto Lanfranchi, discharge the treacherous mercenaries, and exile several leading citizens, including Lippo da Caprona. Castruccio, whose part in the aborted coup was discovered in the ensuing investigations, had a price of 10,000 florins put on his head. The rift between him and Nieri della Gherardesca was therefore complete, as was that between the cities of Lucca and Pisa, between which all contact ceased.[108]

The breach with the neighbouring commune politically isolated the tyrant of Lucca, but also left him free openly to pursue the anti-Pisan

---

[106] Rossi-Sabatini, *Pisa al tempo dei Donoratico*, 143–4.

[107] G. Villani, *Cronica*, ix. 198, 210, V. Balaguer, *Historia de Cataluña y de la corona de Aragon* (Barcelona, 1962), iii. 107–11. The rebellion of the 'judge' of Arborea occurred in April. The Aragonese fleet of 300 ships, including 70 galleys, left Barcelona under Alfonso at the end of May, and arrived in Sardinia in June.

[108] G. Villani, *Cronica*, ix. 230. Finke, *Acta*, iii. 419–20 (dated in that edition 29/12/1322, but, in fact, from its context—the original lacking any indication of year—almost certainly 29/12/1323 (see Chapter III n. 62 above), ACA CRD Ap 91.

policy which he had concealed during his intrigues with the Lanfranchi. Taking advantage of his former association with Cardinal Napoleone Orsini,[109] James II of Aragon's 'friend' at the papal court, he was now able to offer his full co-operation to that monarch in a joint attack on Pisa.[110] Going beyond this, Castruccio even suggested accepting Aragonese overlordship in return for financial support to keep his army in the field. In an undated note in the Aragonese archives which must, however, belong to this period,[111] he also floated the idea of a truce with Florence. His go-between in these extraordinary endeavours to enlist Aragonese support, Cardinal Napoleone Orsini, could hardly contain himself for joy at the prospects he believed they opened up for his royal protector, James II: all manner of territorial acquisitions in Italy, capped perhaps even by the title of king of the Romans which Napoleone could use his influence at the papal court to have confirmed![112] One suspects that Castruccio was more realistic in his assessment of what he could expect from Aragon and more modest in his aims. At this time, he found himself in a very difficult position. The rift with Pisa left him very vulnerable to Florence and he had somehow either to make peace with his principal enemy or to obtain some alternative means of financial or military support against her. Furthermore, the Sardinian war provided him with an opportunity to gain what the failure of the Lanfranchi plot had denied him by using James II of Aragon, in the way he was later to use Ludwig of Bavaria, as the instrument for the conquest of Pisa.

As it happened, he met in the Aragonese monarch a man as shrewd as himself who had no mind to be deflected from his main goal, the reduction of Sardinia, by military adventures which would serve

[109] Finke, *Acta*, ii. 607.
[110] Ibid., ii. 607, 609–11.
[111] Ibid., 622, summarizes ACA CRD 940 Caja 77; an undated note brought back from Italy by Alberto de Gatello which must have been written some time after September 1323 when we know (see n. 103 above) that this envoy was in Florence, and, judging by the third condition stipulated in it, after the exile of Castruccio's supporters from Pisa following the discovery of the Lanfranchi plot. The three demands it records Castruccio as making are as follows: (i) that the Aragonese intercede with the pope and King Robert of Naples to enable a truce to be concluded between the Florentines and the lord of Lucca; (ii) that the king of Aragon stipulate how many knights he intends to keep in Lucca at his expense till the end of the war; (iii) what the position of the lord of Lucca and of his Pisan exile friends would be at the end of the war. See also ACA CRD 4203 (in Finke, *Acta*, ii. 619–21, 623). For a discussion of this question, see Arribas Palau, *La conquista*, 278–9.
[112] Finke, *Acta*, ii. 607. See also C. A. Willemsen, *Kardinal Napoleon Orsini* (Berlin, 1927), 99, Arribas Palau, *La conquista*, 277.

Castruccio's interests rather than his own. Nevertheless, he welcomed the Lucchese tyrant's overtures since, clearly, any threat to the Pisans from the landward side would create a diversion that could only aid Alfonso in his attacks on Iglesias and Cagliari.[113] Castruccio, for his part, even if he derived no tangible benefits from his negotiations with Aragon, at least gained time through the confusion created by his unexpected diplomatic alignment with James II. While he was, in a sense, under that monarch's protection, his position and intentions would remain sufficiently uncertain for his enemies to wait to see in what direction he would move before they combined against him. Castruccio even went to the trouble of getting the Infante Alfonso to send him a set of conditions of vassalage,[114] presumably in the hope that this would commit the Aragonese crown prince to defend his lands against any one who tried to take them from him. At the same time, he was at pains, through his ambassador, to point out to Cardinal Napoleone Orsini that James II need not avoid alliance with him for fear that this might alienate the pope: he (Castruccio) was all too willing to remove any objection on that score by making peace with Florence, so releasing Guelph forces in Tuscany to fight for the Church in Lombardy.[115]

It is hard to know how much of this elaborate smokescreen the lord of Lucca actually believed, and how far he was merely trying to buy friends and fend off enemies with empty threats and false promises. While fighting continued in Sardinia, the possibility of a wider co-operation between Lucca and Aragon remained, and probably Castruccio did hope for some joint venture involving the army of the one and the navy of the other, or at least for financial subsidies to enable him to assail Pisa by land while the bulk of her forces were away defending her island colony. However, the speed in which the conquest of Sardinia was completed dispensed with the need for such diversionary attacks. The Pisans, who had failed to relieve Iglesias in October 1323, finally did manage to dispatch a large fleet in defence of their possessions on the island the following January, carrying five hundred knights and two thousand archers under the command of Nieri della Gherardesca's son Manfredi. But this was held up by bad weather and, on reaching its destination on 25 February, found that Iglesias had been forced to capitulate eighteen days before. Worse

---

[113] Finke, *Acta*, ii. 622–3.
[114] Ibid., ii. 624.
[115] Ibid., ii. 623.

still, when the disembarked Pisan army met Alfonso's forces at the battle of Lupocisterna shortly afterwards, it was routed and compelled to seek refuge in the besieged stronghold of Castel Castro, overlooking the Bay of Cagliari. In the meantime, the Aragonese fleet succeeded in driving off the Pisan ships, so isolating the garrison of this embattled outpost and denying it relief or supplies from the mainland. When a desperate sortie from the beleaguered town failed in May and when no further help from Pisa had come by June, its defenders surrendered on terms which gave sovereignty over Sardinia to king James II of Aragon but allowed the Pisans to retain Castel Castro as his vassals, against the payment of a tribute of two thousand Genoese pounds a year.[116]

By June 1324, the expedition had therefore been brought to a victorious conclusion. While relations between Castruccio and the Aragonese monarch continued to be cordial, there was now clearly no call for an active alliance between them. The Lucchese tyrant may have attempted to prolong James II's involvement in Italian affairs by suggesting that he press on with his conquests by attacking Corsica, to which he had a claim dating back to the same papal donation that had prompted his acquisition of Sardinia.[117] But such an invitation, even if made, clearly did not meet a positive response and Castruccio was therefore left in mid-1324 with the avenue to expansion westward blocked by the failure of the Lanfranchi coup and the Aragonese withdrawal from Italian politics, and more than ever vulnerable to Florence because of the transformation of Pisan support into hostility, intensifed by that city's reconciliation, at this time, with King Robert of Naples. In May 1324, that monarch had called in at Pisa on the way home from Avignon and had been received there with great favour and honour.[118] In these circumstances, Castruccio was forced to think in terms of an eastward expansion of his territories. Pistoia now remained his only hope and he began once again to interfere in the politics of that town. In the first half of 1324, Ormanno Tedici retained his power there, but was increasingly overshadowed by his nephew Filippo, who aspired to supplant his uncle. Castruccio at this point appears to have chosen as the instrument of his policy this young man who was likely to be both more Ghibelline in temper and more open to the Lucchese tyrant's overtures by reason of his own ambition than the

---

[116] G. Villani, *Cronica*, ix. 237, 251, 259, Balaguer, *Historia*, 111–13.

[117] This was suggested by the sixteenth-century Aragonese historian Zurita y Castro in his *Anales de la corona de Aragon* (Saragossa 1610), iii. 62. It is possible that he may have had access to sources now lost.

[118] G. Villani, *Cronica*, ix. 249.

abbot of Pacciana. Ormanno Tedici had, in fact, agreed early in the year to the readmission of King Robert of Naples's vicar and seemed to be moving towards closer links with the Guelphs.[119] It was Filippo Tedici, presumably at Castruccio's instigation, who, according to Villani, stopped this official from reaching Pistoia by having his party waylaid by an armed band at Tizzana on 3 March 1324.[120] This action not merely revived tension with Florence but provoked another incident, even more damaging to relations with that city. Conte Novello, the Florentine commander, decided on his own initiative to retaliate against the assault on the Neapolitan vicar by attacking and taking the Pistoian village of Carmignano on 21 April. This left Ormmano Tedici with no choice but to call on Lucchese help to defend his territories. Castruccio was only too willing to intervene and hurried to Serravalle with five hundred knights. In the meantime, however, the Florentines, alarmed lest the Lucchese tyrant might use this pretext to seize Pistoia, ordered Conte Novello to withdraw from Carmignano.[121] For the time being, appearances were saved and Castruccio was held in check. But Pistoian suspicion of Florentine intentions nevertheless remained and was to prove an important factor in ensuing developments in the city.

Filippo Tedici, though at this time, according to the author of the 'Storie pistoresi', already intriguing with Castruccio, carefully concealed his hand, exploiting not merely the Lucchese tyrant's secret support but also, paradoxically, the discontent of the town's Guelphs with his uncle's policies.[122] In the climate of uncertainty prevailing in Pistoia, it was possible for him to be all things to all men in his efforts to ease himself into Ormanno's position. Assured as he was of Castruccio's military backing should he need it, he could afford to allay the fears of the Florentines and their Pistoian sympathizers by pretending that he wanted to readmit those whom his uncle had exiled. Whether there was any complicity between the abbot of Pacciana and his nephew in the pursuance of this double-faced policy, as Villani suggests, or whether the former was merely hoodwinked by the latter as the author of the 'Storie pistoresi' asserts, the fact remains that, on 23 July 1324, Filippo seized power as a result of an uprising of

[119] Davidsohn, *Storia*, iv. 937.

[120] G. Villani, *Cronica*, ix. 240.

[121] Ibid., ix. 247. However, Carmignano did voluntarily become a Florentine possession the following January. See ibid., ix. 279, and its act of submission on 4 January 1325 in ASF Provvisioni no. 21, cc. 77ʳ.–79ᵛ.

[122] 'Storie pistoresi', 81.

the Guelphs which his uncle either could not or did not choose to put down. Ormanno, however, was not harmed, being allowed to remain in the city as an honoured kinsman of its new ruler.[123] The truce with Lucca was confirmed by the incoming regime which, despite the political sympathies of some of those responsible for installing it, outwardly retained a neutral rather than a pro-Guelph stance.

It is difficult to determine whether, at this stage, Filippo was already secretly committed to come out eventually on Castruccio's side, or whether he was trying only to play off Florence against Lucca in an effort to consolidate his own position. Whatever the true motivation of his two-faced policy, there is no doubt that his actions were, in August and September 1324, precipitated on the one hand by the resumption of Lucchese military activity on the Pistoian *contado* and, on the other, by his uncle's intrigues with the Florentines. On 31 August, Castruccio suddenly appeared with his troops in the immediate vicinity of Pistoia, seizing Brandelli which overlooked not merely that city but also Florence and to which he therefore gave the name Bellosguardo. Filippo Tedici responded to this invasion of his territory by asking for Florentine help; but when this was granted only on condition that the Guelph army be allowed to enter Pistoia, he demurred. The Florentine forces therefore turned back at Prato and Filippo came to terms with Castruccio, increasing the tribute due to the Lucchese tyrant under the previous truce.[124] In the meantime, however, Ormanno Tedici had opened negotiations with the Florentines and, together with a Gascon mercenary captain serving in Pistoia, agreed to open one of the gates of the city to them. If the 'Storie pistoresi' are to be believed, he also induced them to send an embassy, ostensibly for the purpose of effecting a reconciliation between him and his nephew. Filippo received this, but his discovery of the plot hatched by Ormanno put him on his guard against the intended treachery. The walls were consequently guarded, the abbot of Pacciana seized, and the Florentine ambassadors expelled. The troops which had approached the city, hoping to enter by the Porta San Pietro, immediately withdrew and Filippo remained, for the time being at least, securely in power.[125]

---

[123] Ibid., 81–2, and G. Villani, *Cronica*, ix. 261.

[124] G. Villani, *Cronica*, ix. 269. See also ASF Provvisioni no. 21, c. 70ʳ., which confirms that Florentine troops were sent towards Pistoia and against Castruccio between 31 August and 2 September 1324.

[125] G. Villani, *Cronica*, ix. 269, and 'Storie pistoresi', 83–4. According to Villani, it was the Gascon who betrayed the plot, but the latter source suggests it was rather a Floren-

But he continued to be fearful of possible Lucchese or Florentine designs against Pistoia and, about this time, appears to have made up his mind to yield the city to one or other of those who were trying to seize it before it was taken from him, thus deriving some profit from its loss. What is unclear is whether he had already decided, despite his pretence of an even-handed policy, to favour Castruccio and deceive the Florentines, or whether that resolve came later and was inspired by his dissatisfaction with Florentine assurances. It is also uncertain whether there was any collusion between Filippo Tedici and Castruccio when, in the following February, the latter again invaded Pistoian territory, this time striking, as he had done two years earlier, in the mountains north of the city, where he took Sambuca.[126] Filippo responded to this Lucchese intrusion as he had done to the last by asking for help from the Florentines and, on this occasion, did admit their troops, on 7 April. While on the face of it, this made it seem that he was inclining their way, Villani and the author of the 'Storie pistoresi' agree that he was, by this time, negotiating with Castruccio. According to the latter source, his intermediary was Frate Gregorio Ottantauno of the order of the Eremitani. Filippo was also, of course, simultaneously engaged in finding out from the Florentines what they would offer him for Pistoia. Again according to the 'Storie pistoresi', they agreed to knight his son Carlino, dowry his daughters, and marry them to leading Florentine citizens, as well as paying him three thousand florins. Castruccio, on the other hand, promised him his daughter Dialta in marriage and ten thousand florins. The latter offer was clearly the more attractive and Filippo accepted it, undertaking to admit the Lucchese through the Porta del Prato in the early hours of 5 May. That morning, therefore, Castruccio was able to enter Pistoia with his troops, surprise the Florentine garrison, and seize the city.[127]

tine friend of Filippo Tedici who alerted him to the conspiracy, the implicated mercenary revealing it only when challenged with the evidence supplied by this informant. Villani gives the date of these events as 22–23 September.

[126] According to Villani (ix. 285) with the collusion of Filippo Tedici, but, according to the 'Storie pistoresi' (p. 86), of one of the two commanders of the citadel of Sambuca, a brother-in-law of Filippo Tedici, who was a Ghibelline.

[127] G. Villani, *Cronica*, ix. 285, 294, 'Storie pistoresi', 85–8. It is Villani who claims Filippo Tedici was paid 10,000 florins. The Pistoian chronicler merely states that he received the captaincy of the city and a share of its revenues amounting to £1,200 a month (about 4,500 florins a year). He also adds that Castruccio bribed Filippo's adviser Messer Cremona and others involved in the plot with sums of money amounting in all to 6,000 florins and made Frate Gregorio prior of San Frediano (*sic*) (in fact, probably San Giorgio) in Lucca (see *RIS* (n. edn.), xi. pt. 5, p. 85, n. 1). The anonymous author of BNF MS Palat. 571 (c. 23ʳ.) raises the sum paid to Filippo Tedici to 20,000 florins.

Thus, Castruccio finally succeeded in his long cherished aim of adding another major commune to his state. It was a welcome triumph, for, in the preceding year and a half since his rift with Pisa, his fortunes had been at their lowest ebb. Following his near disaster at Fucecchio in December 1323, his troops attempted, with an equal lack of success, to take Castelfranco the following 22 May, being defeated once again by the garrison, thanks to the prompt arrival of reinforcements from Fucecchio.[128] This had confirmed the effectiveness of the Florentine line of defence along the Arno and discouraged further Lucchese attacks on this front. The war had henceforth bogged down, except for Castruccio's thrusts into neutral Pistoian territory in August–September 1324 and February 1325, in the course of which he did not have to contend with opposition by the Florentines, owing either to Filippo Tedici's diffidence in inviting their intervention, or to his own ability to withdraw before they arrived. The lord of Lucca's policy at this stage seems to have swung away from direct military action to intrigue. In addition to pursuing his carefully contrived secret negotiations with Filippo Tedici, he also attempted to hatch plots in March and April 1325 in both Pisa and Florence. On 20 March, according to Villani, he sent assassins to kill Nieri della Gherardesca,[129] while in April he sought to corrupt some French mercenaries in Florentine service and gain control of Capraia and Montelupo through the treachery of Tommaso Frescobaldi, and of Prato through that of Vita Pugliesi.[130] None of these conspiracies came to anything but Castruccio's resort to them on the eve of his acquisition of Pistoia is testimony to his desperation just before this coup enabled him to resolve the impasse in his war with Florence.

It was indeed fortunate for him that, over this period, he had had to face no serious enemy attack and that his diplomacy had the edge on that of his adversaries in the contest for possession of Pistoia. He succeeded where the Florentines failed because, even though he was militarily contained, he was able to take the initiative in exploiting both the vulnerability and cupidity of the Tedici regime. Whereas the Florentines were too much afraid of throwing Pistoia into the arms of Castruccio to exert pressure through force, the lord of Lucca skilfully alternated between threats and blandishments, being more dangerous in the one and more tempting in the other than his rivals. As before,

---

[128] G. Villani, *Cronica*, ix. 252.

[129] Ibid., ix. 289.

[130] Ibid., ix. 292.

the Florentines failed to take advantage, throughout the period leading up to the Lucchese acquisition of Pistoia, of their military
superiority over Castruccio, their forces being at this time engaged not
only in Lombardy, where the fighting had taken a turn for the worse
for the Guelphs,[131] but also in campaigns against Arezzo and Città di
Castello.[132]

3. *The Altopascio campaign*

Castruccio's seizure of Pistoia in May 1325, however, jolted the
Florentines out of their complacent conduct of the war. The shock of
its loss was all the greater for being so unexpected and occurring at a
time when the presence of their troops in the city seemed to promise
its return into the Guelph fold. The chronicler Villani has left a
description of the receipt of the news in Florence: it arrived during a
banquet in the church of San Pietro Scheraggio, held to celebrate the
knighting of the executor of the Ordinances of Justice and of the
German *condottiere* Urlimbach, later to be captured by Castruccio.
Everyone immediately rose, armed, and set off towards Prato, hoping
that Pistoia might still be recovered by a prompt relief of the Florentine garrison. When further messengers arrived while the hastily
gathered host was already on its way, announcing the irrevocable loss
of the town, the citizens returned home 'with great grief and fear'.[133]

The following day, that is, on 6 May, the Catalan captain and
former commander of the papal forces in Lombardy, Ramon de
Cardona, arrived in Florence from Avignon. He had been captured by
the Visconti in the February of the previous year, had escaped, gone to
the papal court, and there had been approached by a Florentine
embassy which had offered him the position of captain-general of the
city's forces for a year. He had accepted on terms that gave him a
salary of twelve florins a day, with the right to bring with him twenty
'cavalieri di corredo', eighty other knights, and fifty men-at-arms.[134] In
addition to these troops, he would have had, of course, at his disposal

---

[131] On 29 February 1324, the papal commander, Ramon de Cardona, was defeated
and captured by the Milanese at Vaprio (ibid., ix. 239); the Guelphs suffered another
reverse on the following 8 June (ibid., ix. 258), and lost Monza in September (ibid., ix.
270) and Borgo San Donnino on 15 March 1325 (ibid., ix. 288).

[132] Ibid., ix. 215, 226, 253, 286, ASF Provvisioni no. 21, c. 43ʳ.

[133] G. Villani, *Cronica*, ix. 294. See also ASF Provvisioni no. 21, c. 106ʳ. for the resolution that Urlimbach be knighted.

[134] Ibid., no. 21, c. 91ʳ. and ʳ. The entry is dated 18 March 1325 but refers to the terms
indicated as already concluded at this date. The ambassadors had received their commission the previous 3 December (ASF Provvisioni Protocolli no. 6, c. 126ʳ.).

the other mercenaries in Florentine pay, including five hundred French knights who had reached Florence on the previous 20 November.[135] His timely arrival therefore made possible the undertaking of immediate military operations under his command, with the aim of making good some of the losses suffered through Filippo Tedici's surrender of Pistoia. Sworn in as captain-general on the evening of the day he entered Florence, he promptly led the city's army out to besiege the Pistoian possession of Artimino, which he took on 22 May.[136] He then returned in triumph to prepare for a campaign which had as its aim the invasion of the heartland of Lucca through an advance across the Val di Nievole.

In the meantime, Castruccio was consolidating his hold on his newly acquired territories. Even before he gained control of Pistoia on 29 April 1324, he had obtained from Ludwig of Bavaria the grant of an imperial vicariate over the city.[137] After his assumption of effective power, Castruccio added substance to this legal right to rule by convoking Pistoia's General Council of the Commune and People on 9 and 12 May and having it make peace with him, with Lucca, with the exiled Pistoian Ghibelline faction and, by implication, with the Empire.[138] In this way, without any radical change of government in the town, he quietly assumed control over it, observing the appropriate legal forms. At the same time, he was under no misapprehension as to the true base of his power and, immediately he had taken the city, began building a citadel and putting his own sympathizers into key positions in both town and *contado*.[139]

With Pistoia firmly in his grasp, Castruccio was free to confront the Florentine counter-offensive, which was aimed not only at wresting his newly acquired possessions from him, but also at striking at Lucca itself and dealing once and for all with the threat he posed to the Guelphs. Ramon de Cardona had at his disposal an army of over two thousand four hundred knights and fifteen thousand infantry.[140] To

---

[135] G. Villani, *Cronica*, ix. 276. This number contained more than sixty 'cavalieri di corredo'.

[136] Ibid., ix. 298.

[137] ASL Capitoli no. 4, cc. 48^r.–49^v., published in Lazzareschi, 'Documenti', 352–6.

[138] ASL Atti di Castruccio no. 1, cc. 60^v.–64^v., published in Lazzareschi, 'Documenti', 356–64.

[139] G. Villani, *Cronica*, ix. 294, 'Storie pistoresi', 88.

[140] G. Villani, *Cronica*, ix. 300. Over nine hundred of these knights were Florentines and fifteen hundred mercenaries. Of the latter, six hundred were French, two hundred German, a hundred Burgundian, one hundred and thirty Catalan, and four hundred

begin with, he moved this force directly towards Pistoia, stopping at
Prato (which he reached on 12 June), apparently with the intention of
drawing the Lucchese army forward to the eastern frontier of the
Pistoian *contado*. In fact, Castruccio had taken up a defensive position
on 11 June at Montale to block the Florentine advance.[141] Once he had
done so, however, Ramon de Cardona brought his numerically
superior army south of that stronghold on 17 June to attack and lay
waste the surroundings of Agliana and then approached Pistoia from
the south-east. Castruccio was compelled by this flanking movement
to withdraw from Montale to that city itself, from behind the walls of
which he, his seven hundred knights, and his infantry had to look on
helplessly as the Florentines ravaged the surrounding country and, on
St. John's Day, as a gesture of defiance and contempt, ran a *palio* (with
a prize of samite velvet) within sight of the town gates. According to
one chronicler,[142] another race took place the following day, after
which the attacking force moved on to Piuvica, Quarrata, and Tizzana.
The last of these villages, which lay on the edge of Pistoian territory
just north-east of Florentine held Carmignano, was besieged on 4 July.
The direction in which Ramon de Cardona took his army brought him
to the point from which he could easily reach the cluster of Guelph
outposts near the junction of the Arno and the Elsa—Fucecchio, Santa
Croce, and Castelfranco.

The general line of his strategy now began to reveal itself: his
advance on to the Pistoiese was, in fact, a feint, the aim of which was to
keep Castruccio's troops tied down in the east while he led his army
south to attack the enemy on the exposed Arno–Usciana front. While
siege works were begun at Tizzana to create the impression that it was
the capture of this fortified village which was his immediate object, the
Catalan commander sent his marshal to Fucecchio five days later with
five hundred of his best knights. Simultaneously, to give further cover
to this deception, he dispatched another body of cavalry to harass the
outskirts of Pistoia. The Florentine troops who had gone to Fucecchio
were joined there by a hundred and fifty Lucchese exiles and the levies
from the towns and villages of the Val d'Arno commanded by Ottaviano Brunelleschi and Bendino de' Rossi. On the night of 9–10 July,
this combined force stealthily approached the Usciana between Ponte

and fifty in companies of mixed origin, including French, Gascons, Flemings, Proven-
çals, and Italians.
[141] Ibid., and 'Storie pistoresi', 89.
[142] BNF MS Magliabechiano xxv, 19, c. 29[r].

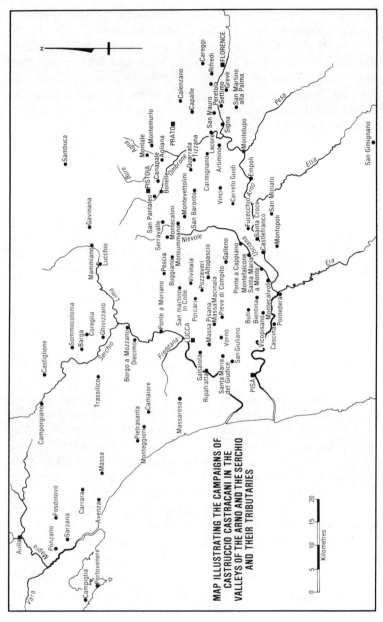

MAP ILLUSTRATING THE CAMPAIGNS OF
CASTRUCCIO CASTRACANI IN THE
VALLEYS OF THE ARNO AND THE SERCHIO
AND THEIR TRIBUTARIES

Map 2.

a Cappiano and Montefalcone, placed a previously constructed wooden bridge over this narrow stream and crossed undetected into Lucchese territory. The next morning Ramon de Cardona struck camp and marched the bulk of his army to this breach in Castruccio's defences, leaving only a small body of men around Tizzana. The garrison of Cappiano and its fortified bridge had been taken completely by surprise by the sudden appearance of an attacking force and was unprepared for the siege that began on the evening of the tenth when the main body of Florentine troops had successfully passed the Usciana. The soldiers holding the bridge, in fact, gave in three days later, and those in the castle and village of Cappiano after a further six days. Ramon de Cardona then, on 21 July, turned his attention to Montefalcone which surrendered on the twenty-ninth. The capture of this last Lucchese stronghold on the southern approaches to the Val di Nievole then opened the way for Ramon de Cardona's advance into this key valley through which the road to Lucca ran.[143]

Castruccio, when he received the news of what had happened, must have been greatly alarmed by it. He had clearly assumed up to this point that the Florentines were primarily concerned with the recapture of Pistoia and its *contado*. Now it became evident that in Ramon de Cardona he had an opponent whose strategic skills were a match for his own and who had chosen, instead of attempting to slowly chip away at Lucchese-held territory, to use his military superiority in an effort to cut Castruccio off from the centre of his state, or at the very least attack that centre itself instead of the periphery of his dominions. Immediately he heard that the Florentines had established themselves north of the Usciana, the lord of Lucca withdrew his army from Pistoia, leaving only a small garrison to hold the place, and encamped at Vivinaia on the heights above the plain of Altopascio, near the present site of Montecarlo. He sent appeals for help to his allies and eventually received reinforcements consisting of three hundred knights from Arezzo, two hundred from the Romagna and the Marches, and a hundred and fifty from various minor Ghibelline lords. Because of his rupture with Pisa, no help was, of course, available from that quarter. Nevertheless, by extending the resources of Lucca and Pistoia to the full and filling out the nucleus of the mercenaries he could afford to pay for from the revenues of those two cities,

---

[143] G. Villani, *Cronica*, ix. 301, 302, 'Storie pistoresi', 89–90. The latter source dates the capture of Cappiano on 18 July, Villani on the nineteenth. Otherwise there is substantial agreement between the two accounts.

with civic mounted levies, Florentine and other Ghibelline exiles, and the allied detachments just mentioned, he managed to build up his cavalry to almost fifteen hundred men. With infantry from both the communes now under his rule he would probably have had a force nearly equal in numbers, though greatly inferior in cavalry, to that under Ramon de Cardona who, after the fall of Montefalcone, began to make his way slowly north, towards Altopascio.[144]

The Catalan commander thus appeared to have the advantage, at least in the crucial element of mounted knights, over his opponent. Against this must, however, be set the fact that he had arrived in Tuscany only very recently and had no real understanding of the terrain he was now entering. Castruccio, by contrast, was a master in the tactical exploitation of the peculiar features of the natural amphitheatre formed by the marshy plain around Altopascio and its horseshoe of surrounding hills. His preferred strategy had always been a defensive, positional one, based upon a command of heights and passes and aiming at the establishment, at the critical moment, of a military superiority which would confront his adversary with the choice of retreat or encirclement. The area into which the Florentine army was now advancing was ideal for the application of such methods. Across it ran the road from Cappiano to Altopascio flanked by swamps and the hills on which Castruccio had erected his hastily constructed fortifications at Vivinaia and Il Cerruglio. Beyond it to the west lay the pass into the Lucchesia between the abrupt eminence of Porcari and the Bientina marshes, with the Monti Pisani rising further to the south-west.

Once the Florentines had penetrated his defences on the Usciana, Castruccio realized that there was no point in denying them control of the valley beyond. He did, however, put a garrison of five hundred men in Altopascio itself with enough supplies for two years, in the hope of delaying their advance for some time. He also planned diversionary attacks on the *contado* of Prato in an effort to draw away some of the Florentine troops and so reduce the discrepancy between the

---

[144] The figures for Castruccio's army are from Villani, ix. 301. BNF MS Magliab. xxv, 19, c. 30ᵛ., estimates it to have had only 1,200 knights but Villani's total includes allied contingents, all of which may not have arrived at the time to which the anonymous author of that chronicle refers. The latter writer put the size of the infantry under the Lucchese tyrant's command at 20,000 which would seem to be quite a generous estimate, even allowing for the inclusion in it of both the Lucchese and Pistoian civic levies. The Florentine army, according to the same source, was made up of 2,600 cavalry and 12,000 infantry.

size of their forces and his. His main concern, nevertheless, was to hold the heights above the plain so as to be able, from virtually impregnable positions, to watch his enemy's movements and to attack him when a suitable opportunity offered.

For the time being, however, circumstances remained unfavourable to him. The Florentine breakthrough on the Usciana encouraged the other members of the Guelph league to send contingents of troops to swell Ramon de Cardona's army: the Sienese dispatched five hundred knights, six hundred archers, and a hundred men-at-arms, the Bolognese two hundred cavalry, Perugia two hundred and sixty, and Camerino, Gubbio, Grosseto, Montepulciano, Colle, San Miniato, San Gimignano, Volterra, Faenza, Imola, and various Guelph lords a further four hundred and seventy horsemen between them, as well as five hundred infantry. These additions increased the numbers under the Catalan captain's command to three or four thousand mounted and seventeen thousand foot soldiers.[145] On 3 August, this huge force, which must have greatly outnumbered Castruccio's, laid siege to Altopascio. The Lucchese tyrant, unable to relieve that town, could only send a detachment of his own troops, a week later, to ravage and loot the outskirts of Prato and then sweep down to Lecore on the eastern edge of the Florentine *contado*. When this had no effect, he decided to try to draw part of the Guelph army out of the plain of Altopascio with an attack on Carmignano. On 23 August, he consequently dispatched a hundred and fifty of his knights and a thousand infantry to surprise that place. But though this force succeeded in entering the village, it was not able to take it, for the defenders were rapidly reinforced by a party of Bolognese cavalry which had been stationed in Florence. In the ensuing fighting, the assailants were driven back, four hundred and fifty of them being killed and some others captured.[146] These were losses that Castruccio, short as he was of troops, could ill afford. But an even worse reverse followed close on the heels of this defeat. The garrison of Altopascio, hard pressed by a persistent Florentine bombardment and attempts to mine the town's walls, lost heart when the news reached them, on 25 August, of the Lucchese rout at Carmignano. Despite having two years' provisions, those in it chose to

---

[145] Ibid., ix. 302, 303, 'Storie pistoresi', 90–1. BNF MS Magliab. xxv, 19, cc. 30ᵛ.–31ʳ. estimated the Florentine army after the fall of Altopascio as 3,200 knights and a large number of infantry.

[146] G. Villani, ix. 302. BNF MS Magliab. xxv, 19, c. 30ᵛ. states that Castruccio sent 100 knights to Carmignano and lost 10 of these together with 600 infantry of whom 380 were killed.

negotiate with Ramon de Cardona, and agreed to surrender the place
on condition that they themselves were allowed to go free.[147]

Thus, in the space of two days, Castruccio not only lost five or six
hundred men but was disappointed in his expectation of holding up
the advancing Florentine army till he was in a position to attack it.
Ramon de Cardona's troops were now able to move on to the next
stage on the road to Lucca, the abbey of Pozzeveri, half way between
Altopascio and Porcari. This being unlikely to prove a major obstacle
to them, they were literally on the threshold of the Lucchesia and had
only the castle of Porcari to overcome before they emerged from their
vulnerable situation in marshy terrain into the plain of Lucca itself.
Surprisingly, however, it was at this point, when they were on the
verge of penetrating into the heart of Castruccio's state, that the
Florentines began to waver in their purpose and, instead of pressing
quickly towards the logical goal of their strategy—the conquest of
Lucca—were daunted into irresolution.

It was now nearly September and their army, though victorious, had
suffered severe losses from sickness. Illness had spread through their
ranks already during the siege of Montefalcone in July. In the assault
on Altopascio, the common medieval practice of catapulting refuse,
excrement, and dead animals into the town in order to bring about a
quick surrender through the spread of pestilence, while it had probably contributed to the early submission of the place, also led to the
spread of infection into the besiegers' camp. As a result, many in the
Guelph army sickened, some died, and many more left, it being one of
the problems of citizen levies and allied detachments at this period
that it was difficult to hold such forces together long in adverse conditions. Indeed, if Villani is to be believed, Ramon de Cardona had been
allowing some of his troops to leave, in return for the payment of a
fee.[148] Castruccio had, in addition, been doing his utmost to corrupt
and win over the mercenaries in Florentine service. Two French
knights, had, in fact, been secretly in contact with him, one of whom,
being on the point of death, admitted his treachery, at which the other
was expelled and eventually joined the Lucchese forces.[149]

Despite the tactical superiority of the Guelph army, its leaders were

[147] G. Villani, *Cronica*, ix. 303.
[148] Ibid.
[149] G. Villani, *Cronica*, ix. 302. The account of the catapulting of refuse into Altopascio is based on 'Storie pistoresi', 90 and that of the spread of sickness in the Florentine camp on Villani, ix. 303.

therefore nervous at the prospect of a prolonged campaign, fearing the continued effects of sickness, possible defections, and a bogging down of the offensive in the attack on Pozzeveri and Porcari owing to the onset of autumn and winter rains. It was in these circumstances that disagreement arose between Ramon de Cardona and some of the prominent citizens (*savi*, as Villani describes them) in the field and in Florence. The latter, arguing that Castruccio's defences were too strong to be penetrated, urged an attack on Santa Maria a Monte, which in effect would have implied a return of the army from the plain of Altopascio to the Arno–Usciana front, west of Montefalcone. They believed that town could easily be taken, so re-establishing the Florentine frontier which Castruccio had overrun in 1320. In other words, they were committed to the limited objective of militarily containing the Lucchese tyrant, by reducing his territories, rather than to that of attempting there and then decisively to defeat him by an assault on Lucca. The chronicler Giovanni Villani, whose point of view at this time presumably reflected that of many influential Florentines, favoured this course or, alternatively, an immediate thrust through the pass north of Porcari which, by driving a wedge between that fortress and the main body of Castruccio's army, would, he thought, have brought about the latter's destruction.[150]

In fact, neither of these proposals made much military sense. The withdrawal to Santa Maria a Monte would have robbed of its point a campaign which from the beginning had had as its *raison d'être* a direct attack on Lucca, and wasted the gains made so far, aside from the marginal ones achieved through a pushing of the frontier back a few miles. The suggested attack north of Porcari would, on the other hand, have been extremely hazardous, the Lucchese being entrenched in strong defensive positions on either side of the proposed line of advance of the Florentines whose flanks would therefore have been exposed to them. Not surprisingly, Ramon de Cardona and the other Guelph commanders rejected this advice from their militarily incompetent paymasters and insisted on the continuation of the drive towards Lucca. In the process, however, of the discussions between the Florentines and their generals in the field, valuable time was lost. Altopascio had capitulated on 25 August but it was not until 9 September that the Guelph army encamped before the abbey of Pozzeveri, the next obstacle it had to overcome in its advance.

---

[150] G. Villani, loc. cit.

In the meantime, Castruccio had not been idle. The fall of Altopascio had made clear to him that he could not delay much longer a
trial of strength with the Florentines. If they succeeded in taking
Pozzeveri and Porcari, he would be forced to retire from the positions
he held on Il Cerruglio and at Vivinaia in order to defend his capital.
In the open country surrounding it, he would not enjoy the advantages
of the hilly and marshy terrain around Altopascio. It was therefore
urgent that he obtain reinforcements which would enable him to
match the Florentines at least in cavalry. So he began to negotiate with
the Lombard Ghibellines for the dispatch of a force of a thousand
knights, eight hundred of whom were in Borgo San Donnino under
Azzo Visconti and two hundred in the cities of Modena and Mantua,
then held by Passerino Bonaccolsi. He would have liked to have had
these troops on the basis of a reciprocal exchange; but his own inability to intervene in Lombardy in favour of the Visconti over the
recent past made it difficult for him to claim them on these terms. This
left him with a problem: his lack of financial resources for the payment
of such a substantial body of cavalry for even a short period.

While he pondered on this, events began to move fast in the plain of
Altopascio. On 21 September, nearly two weeks after the Florentine
army had advanced to the abbey of Pozzeveri, Ramon de Cardona—
perhaps influenced by those of his advisers who believed he ought to
attempt to break through the gap between Porcari and Il Cerruglio—
sent a party of knights to probe the Lucchese defences in that quarter
under the command of his marshal and of the German mercenary
Urlimbach. When Castruccio, on his vantage point in the hills above,
saw the approach of this force which Villani estimated at a hundred
horse but which the Aragonese ambassador in his dispatch numbered
at five hundred cavalry and five hundred infantry, he sent down a
detachment of his own men (according to the latter source of four
hundred knights and two thousand infantry) to block its advance. On
Villani's testimony, another two hundred cavalry then reinforced the
original Guelph contingent, while Castruccio also sent more troops
down to match and then outnumber the forces opposing him (according to Villani by two to one). The resulting skirmish lasted for several
hours. In the end, despite Castruccio being unhorsed, the Ghibellines
were victorious, the Florentine troops being driven back to their camp
with forty of their best knights killed or captured. Among the prisoners
were Urlimbach, two leading Florentine citizens, Francesco Brunelleschi and Giovanni della Tosa, and eighteen other knights. Ramon de

Cardona, Villani claimed, might have averted this set-back, had he intervened in the engagement with the bulk of his army; but he chose not to so do for fear of risking a decisive battle on ground unfavourable to him.[151]

This victory, though minor and inconclusive in itself, was an invaluable psychological fillip for Castruccio. Ramon de Cardona's failure to bring up the main body of his troops in support of his outnumbered knights confirmed for Castruccio the Guelph commander's reluctance to risk a pitched battle and so made it clear that, for the first time, the military balance was tilting in the Lucchese tyrant's favour. The Florentine army had by now been much reduced in numbers by sickness and by the departure of those to whom the Catalan captain and his marshal had given exemptions from service in return for money. While Giovanni Villani was probably exaggerating when he claimed that its size had been cut by more than half,[152] there is no doubt that its numerical advantage over Castruccio's forces had been substantially reduced. The strain of a long campaign in the unhealthy plain around Altopascio had also clearly affected the Florentines' morale. It is significant that, after the skirmish of 21 September, Castruccio's main worry became, not an enemy attack on Pozzeveri and Porcari, but the retreat of the Guelph host before he could force it to a decisive engagement. His fear that the latter might happen appears indeed to have been his motive for urging on the arrival of reinforcements from Lombardy, which must, by this time, have already been on the way.

These, under Azzo Visconti, appear to have arrived in Lucca just before 22 September.[153] Here, however, they remained for that day, while their commander refused to move until he was paid, or promised more money. According to Villani, he had already been given 10,000 florins but was only induced to add his contingent of

---

[151] Giovanni Villani (*Cronica*, ix. 305) and 'Storie pistoresi', 93 place this skirmish on 11 September, but a surviving letter by Castruccio Castracani to John the Apothecary and Master Henry, Ludwig of Bavaria's ambassadors, published in G. B. Verci, *Storia della marca trevigiana e veronese* (Venice, 1786–91), ix, *Documenti*, 90–1, and dated 22 September 1325, describes it as having occurred on the previous day. On the question of the dating of this engagement, see also Davidsohn, *Storia*, iv. 1013, n. 1. A further contemporary account exists in a letter from the Aragonese ambassador in Avignon to the Infante Alfonso of Aragon (published in Finke, *Acta*, i. 416–17). This bears the date 26 September 1325 but Finke considers that this may possibly be mistaken. BNF MS Magliab. xxv, 19, c. 31ᵛ. estimated the number of knights engaged in both sides in this skirmish as 800 in all.

[152] G. Villani, *Cronica*, ix. 303.

[153] According to G. Villani, *Cronica*, ix. 306, the Florentines learnt of his arrival on that day.

knights to the Lucchese army by the pleas of the city's women and the undertaking that another 6,000 florins would be found for him, partly in cash and partly in the form of assurances of future payment by the town's merchants.[154] The Lucchese archival records provide partial confirmation of the Florentine chronicler's claims which, however, they also reveal to have been inaccurate in detail. The amount they show to have been raised as loans underwritten by a large group of Lucchese businessmen was 10,500 florins; and the date on which this money was borrowed was just over a week later than the Sunday when Villani alleges Azzo Visconti was in Lucca.[155] It is probable, on the basis of this evidence, that the Milanese commander was given some kind of assurance on the twenty-second of a payment of 10,500 florins, subject perhaps to the successful outcome of the projected battle (which was fought on the next day); but that it was not until the following Monday that the authorizations to raise the money were drawn up.[156] Whether Azzo was also advanced 10,000 florins as Villani alleges before he would leave Lombardy is open to question; but it is possible that 6,000 florins were sent to him then and that the Florentine chronicler confused the two sums in his account; taking 10,000 florins to have been paid earlier and 6,000 later, when in fact the opposite was the case. Whatever the truth on this matter, it is clear that, in order to establish a temporary superiority over the Florentines in the brief climax of this campaign, Castruccio needed 10,500 florins more than he could raise from the revenues of Lucca and Pistoia combined and that he had consequently to resort to what was, in effect, a forced gift from the mercantile community of his native city.

It is also interesting to note the nature of the group who, whether they liked it or not, were induced at this time to come financially to the

[154] G. Villani, *Cronica*, ix. 304, 306.

[155] ASL Archivio notarile no. 74, Reg. ii, cc. 158ᵛ.–160ʳ. The money was actually handed over to the communal treasury on 11 October (ibid., c. 160ᵛ.), which presumably paid Azzo Visconti shortly afterwards.

[156] The most probable reading of the evidence is that the Lucchese merchants involved in authorizing the loan of 10,500 florins on 30 September had, on the twenty-second of the month, undertaken to raise this sum within a specified time, perhaps two or three weeks. In the interval between these two dates, they would have made enquiries in Pisa as to the availability of finance there and, by the thirtieth, located 8,753 florins available from one Piacentine and two Genoese bankers resident in that city. They would then have gone ahead with the delegation to one of their number of the task of borrowing this sum and finding the shortfall between 10,500 florins and this amount. After another twelve days, when the remaining sum had been found and all the 10,500 florins raised, they would have fulfilled the obligation, entered into on or just after 22 September, to pay it into the Lucchese treasury.

aid of the lord of Lucca. It consisted, in fact, of the leading merchants and bankers of the town who had benefited from the revival of trade then in progress and who, in many cases, had also held various offices under Castruccio.[157] It is indeed significant that it was they, as much as foreign mercenary cavalry, who were responsible for swinging the balance in favour of Castruccio at this crucial stage in his war with Florence.

Once Azzo Visconti's services and those of his eight hundred knights were secured, Castruccio could move decisively against the Florentines. According to Villani,[158] the numbers of the Guelph cavalry had by this time been reduced to about two thousand and their infantry to eight thousand; for the first time in the campaign, therefore, the Lucchese enjoyed a tactical superiority over their enemies. On 22 September, immediately he heard of the arrival of Milanese reinforcements in Lucca, Ramon de Cardona realized the danger of his position and began withdrawing his army from the abbey of Pozzeveri towards Altopascio. Meanwhile Castruccio, who had ridden on that day back to his capital to induce Azzo Visconti to bring his men up as quickly as possible, learnt of the Florentine retreat and recognized the need for rapid action if his enemies were not to escape from the trap he had set for them. Fearing that the Guelph forces would slip away from their vulnerable situation in the valley around Altopascio, he moved the main body of his cavalry without delay along the ridge of hills that ran along its northern edge. Leaving the eight hundred Milanese knights to follow, he brought his own fifteen hundred horsemen to a point where the elevation of the Cerbaie curved back to the plain just west of Altopascio. Here, he confronted the troops of his adversary which Ramon de Cardona had hurriedly drawn up in battle array to meet him. Having prevented any further Florentine withdrawal, Castruccio was thus able, on the morning of Monday 23 September, to attack his enemy on his own terms as soon

---

[157] It included Giovanni Rapondi, Jacopo Sbarra, Gialdello Sesmondi, Puccino Galganetti, Lazzaro Guinigi, Nicolao Baratella, Parello Passamonti, Nicolao Busdraghi, and Benettuccio Arnolfi. A further group of merchants who associated themselves with this financial grant on 2 October had in it Vanni and Ser Orlando Forteguerra, Mingo Spada, Ghirarduccio Streghi, Matteo Brancali, Dettoro del Lieto (ASL Archivio notarile no. 74, Reg. ii, cc. 158ᵛ.–160ᵛ.).

[158] G. Villani, *Cronica*, ix. 306. The same source gives the size of Castruccio's cavalry force at Altopascio as 2,300, including the knights under Azzo Visconti.

as Azzo's men, coming up close behind his own, arrived upon the scene.[159]

The Florentine army, weakened not only by sickness but also, if the 'Storie pistoresi' are to be believed, by the departure of the troops sent on ahead to escort the baggage train in the expectation of a general retreat,[160] appears to have met the Lucchese assault in a battle formation consisting of two forward lines of 'feditori', backed by the main body of cavalry and infantry under Ramon de Cardona's immediate command. Its vanguard was, according to Villani, made up of a hundred and fifty French and Florentine knights, with seven hundred others under Borgnes, Ramon's marshal, behind them, shielding the remaining eleven or twelve hundred horsemen and eight thousand infantry from the impact of the first charge. Again according to the Florentine chronicler, while the one hundred and fifty knights in the forefront of the Guelph army fought well and turned the flank of Azzo Visconti's advancing cavalry, the seven hundred under Borgnes directly behind them gave way and pulled back at their first contact with the enemy, Villani alleges, because the marshal leading them chose not to resist Azzo, from whose father Galeazzo he had, years before, received his knighthood. Whatever the truth of this explanation (which fits too neatly this author's tendency to attribute disasters to appropriate human failings to be entirely credible), one can accept, on the basis of his otherwise well-informed account, that it was the failure of the second line of the 'feditori' to check the Lucchese assault, after the first had deflected it, which swung the battle in Castruccio's favour. For Ramon de Cardona, when he saw his marshal's standards veer round and the knights around them pull back, was not prepared to risk counter-attacking the approaching enemy cavalry force with one only half its size. He himself stood his ground and was eventually captured, but many of his troops, particularly those on horseback who were better able to get away, panicked at the retreat of the front ranks of their army, turned, and fled. The infantry, finding it harder to escape, resisted, but could do little to save the day once the onslaught of Milanese and Lucchese knights had broken up the Florentine cavalry formations.[161]

---

[159] G. Villani, *Cronica*, ix. 306. Villani states that Azzo reached the battlefield at the third hour, that is, about nine in the morning.

[160] 'Storie pistoresi', 93.

[161] G. Villani, *Cronica*, ix. 306 and 'Storie pistoresi', 93, BNF MS Magliab. xxv, 19, c. 31ʳ., BNF MS Palat. 571, c. 23ʳ. and ·., Giovanni da Bazano, 'Chronicon mutinense',

The casualties suffered in the battle itself seem to have been relatively low, but the losses on the Guelph side in the course of the mopping up and flight were considerable. Castruccio had had the presence of mind to send two detachments of Azzo's German mercenaries to cut off the enemy's line of retreat by seizing the bridge at Cappiano. This did not prevent about half the Florentine troops from escaping either by passing the Usciana before this advance party could gain control of this fortified river-crossing or by struggling over this stream or the nearby hills and marshes before being overtaken by the pursuing Ghibelline cavalry. But probably four or five thousand of them were either killed or captured,[162] some of the former drowning in the Usciana as they tried to cross it in heavy armour or were cut down by the Lucchese infantry which, though it had taken no active part in the battle, spread over the field in the wake of the Florentine rout to pick off unhorsed knights or scattered men-at-arms.[163]

Among the captives taken by Castruccio were not only the Guelph commander Ramon de Cardona and his son, but a substantial number of French knights and leading Florentine citizens.[164] There was also

RIS xv, col. 586, and (n. edn.), xv, pt. 4, p. 92, 'Chronicon estense', *RIS*, xv, col. 386, and (n. edn.), xv, pt. 3, p. 95, G. Stella, 'Annales genuenses', *RIS*, xvi, cols. 1053–4, Granchi, 'De proeliis', *RIS*, xi, cols. 330–1, 'Cronaca senese dei fatti', *RIS*, (n. edn.), xv, pt. 6, p. 130, 'Chronicon parmense ab anno 1038 usque ad annum 1338', *RIS* (n. edn.), ix, pt. 9, pp. 179–80, 'Annales parmenses maiores', *Monumenta Germaniae historica scriptores*, xviii (1863), 758, Finke, *Acta*, i. 416–17, 633–4. There is some variation between these sources as to details, the size of Azzo's relieving force being given as 800 in Villani, Giovanni da Bazano, BNF MS Magliab. xxv, 19, and 'Chronicon estense', 1,000 in 'Storie pistoresi', 600 in BNF MS Palat. 571, 300 in 'Annales parmenses maiores' and 'Chronicon parmense', and 1,200 in Giorgio Stella. (I have accepted 800 as the figure both finding confirmation in most independent accounts and lying roughly midway between the other estimates.)

[162] The chroniclers differ to some extent on the exact losses suffered by the Florentines. The 'Storie pistoresi' put them at more than 3,000, including those killed and captured, the 'Annales parmenses maiores' and 'Chronicon parmense' at more than 5,000; Giovanni da Bazano gave the number of prisoners at more than 2,000 and those killed at more than 3,000, while BNF MS Palat. 571 states that the number of knights taken was more than 2,000. Putting these indications together, one can conclude that Florentine casualties were probably in the region of 5,000 of whom about 3,000 were killed and perhaps 2,000 captured, though this latter figure probably would also have included those within the fortified places taken after the battle (see n. 164 below).

[163] G. Villani, *Cronica*, ix. 306, 'Storie pistoresi', 93.

[164] G. Villani, *Cronica*, ix. 306, Davidsohn, *Storia*, iv. 1018, n. 3. See, in particular, the 'Libro del Mazzinghi', (ASF Archivio Bardi nos. 78 and 88) published in Ildefonso di San Luigi, *Delizie*, xii. 268–87, which reproduces lists of Florentine citizens and *contadini* captured at Altopascio as does BNF MS Magliab. xxv, 19. From these it would appear that the prisoners included upwards of 200 men from the city (199 in the 'Libro del Mazzinghi' list, 217 in the other) and over 500 from the Florentine territories (583 in

much booty captured, owing to the rapid abandonment of the Florentine camp. In the wake of the victory, further prisoners were taken in
the fortified strongholds held by the Guelphs north of the Usciana.
First Cappiano and Montefalcone fell on the day of the battle and
then, on 6 October, Altopascio itself; and from these places five hundred men were led to join those already in captivity in Lucca.[165] Thus,
the Florentines suddenly found their army scattered and their territories defenceless while Castruccio, having quickly mopped up
pockets of resistance in the area he now controlled, was ready to
invade the Florentine *contado*. The prisoners in his hands gave him the
possibility, through their ransoms, of paying the debts he had incurred
in the course of the campaign and of leaving some money over (if
Villani is to be believed in his assertion that the lord of Lucca made
nearly 100,000 florins out of his captives[166]) to continue hostilities
against his arch-enemy.

   The ravaging of the country around Florence was to yield further
plunder to enrich the victors. Having taken and demolished the fortifications of Cappiano and Montefalcone in the wake of the battle and
leaving Altopascio to be besieged by a detachment of his army,
Castruccio moved the bulk of his forces to Pistoia. From here, he
advanced on Carmignano, where Filippo Tedici and his Pistoian levies remained to invest the place while, with the main body of his
troops, Castruccio continued on into the Florentine *contado* which he
entered at Lecore on the twenty-ninth. On the following day, he

the former and 475 in the latter). The discrepancies suggest that neither list is complete,
which is confirmed by the mention in Charles of Calabria's correspondence (R. Bevere,
'La signoria di Firenze tenuta da Carlo figlio di Re Roberto negli anni 1326 e 1327',
Archivio storico per le provincie napoletane, xxxiv (1909), 627) of a prisoner captured at Altopascio, Giovanni di Albizzo de' Medici, not mentioned in these lists (Davidsohn,
Storia, iv. 1018, n. 3, however, also asserts that Piero Forese's name was omitted, which,
in fact, it is not; see Ildefonso di San Luigi, *Delizie*, 272). Given that there were about
fifty French knights captured (G. Villani, *Cronica*, ix. 306) and prisoners also from the
forces of the Florentines' allies as well as some Lucchese Guelph exiles (BNF MS
Palat. 571, c. 23ᵛ.), one could estimate the total number of prisoners at over a thousand.
To these should be added the garrisons of strongholds captured after the battle which,
according to Villani, consisted of 500 men in all. Including these, the number of
prisoners must have been at least 1,300 and was probably a little higher than this, in the
range of 1,500–2,000.

   [165] G. Villani, *Cronica*, ix. 306, and BNF MS Magliab. xxv, 19, c. 31ʳ., 'Storie
pistoresi', 94. The date for the fall of Altopascio is from Villani, the Magliabechiana
chronicle (c. 31ᵛ.) giving it as two days later on the eighth.
   [166] G. Villani, *Cronica*, ix. 323.

captured Signa, the defenders of which abandoned that town and fled at his approach.[167]

Since his victory over the Guelphs at Altopascio, he had moved with great speed to implement a strategy, the aim of which was to strike directly at his principal objective, the city of Florence. Avoiding the temptation to pursue the retreating remnants of Ramon de Cardona's army across the Usciana into the marshes around Fucecchio, he had chosen instead to bring his men straight from the battlefield through the pass of Serravalle to Pistoia and then lead them along the Ombrone to its junction with the Arno near Signa. In so doing, he had skirted the barrier of the Monte Albano hills, bypassed the Florentine strongholds of Fucecchio, Empoli, and Montelupo, and now, by taking Signa by surprise, had opened the road to Florence itself. Advancing quickly into the plain on which it lay, he encamped at San Mauro on 1 October and, after burning and plundering the villages of Campi, Brozzi, and Quaracchi, set up his headquarters at Peretola, in Geri Spini's villa, which he fortified. Here, he was within sight of the walls of Florence and could send his cavalry riding up to them at will. For the next three days, his troops systematically pillaged the hamlets and country houses that lay to the west of the city, between the river and hills around Rifredi and Careggi. The Florentines, terror-stricken, did not venture to oppose him despite having, according to Villani, 'many knights and innumerable infantry' within the walls, for they feared not only risking combat with an apparently invincible enemy, but also the possibility of treachery among their own citizens.[168]

While they kept careful watch day and night, Castruccio continued with his depredations. To add insult to injury, on 4 October he arranged for three *pali* or races to be run within sight of the city, as a contemptuous manifestation of his control over its surroundings and as a taunt to its timid defenders. One of these was a horse-race for his cavalry, another a foot-race for his infantry, while the third, the most pointed mockery of all, was for the prostitutes among the camp-followers of his army. His gesture of defiance made, Castruccio on the following day moved his camp from Peretola (the site of the finishing post of the races), burning the villa which he had earlier taken over, together with its outhouses and the villages of Capalle and Calenzano which lay to the north. Having completed the devastation of the sector

---

[167] Ibid., ix. 317, 'Storie pistoresi', 95.
[168] Ibid.

of country north-west of Florence, he returned to Signa, crossed the Arno and began laying waste the area south of the river. On 6 October, he put to the torch Gangalandi, San Martino alla Palma, and the settlements on the plain around Settimo. By the eighth, the main body of his troops had reached Greve, while the knights of his vanguard swept forward to San Pietro a Monticelli. This brought them close to the as yet unwalled *borghi* of San Pietro Gattolino and San Frediano on the Oltrarno, much to the alarm of the Florentines who hastily fortified these with wooden *steccati*. While these defensive works continued day and night, Castruccio's forces extended their plunder and destruction westwards into the lower Val di Pesa which they laid waste right up to Montelupo on the Arno. Wherever they went, the Lucchese did not merely burn farms and villages, but seized whatever animals and booty they could lay their hands on. Virtually the whole of the western outskirts of Florence were stripped bare, with immense consequent losses of wealth and agricultural productivity, affecting for years the economy of the city's surroundings.[169]

One can only speculate as to the reasons for Castruccio's decision to lay waste his enemy's territories in this way. Villani[170] attributed it to his inability to pay his troops and his need therefore both to make good from plunder what he lacked in ready cash and to prolong the campaign till further sums could be raised to defray his expenses. This may well have been a motive, but other psychological and strategic factors would, in all likelihood, also have influenced him in the extraordinary harshness which he displayed. It was essential for him to bring home to an otherwise stronger foe the full force of his victory at Altopascio, to demonstrate beyond doubt the military advantage which he had gained, to demoralize the Florentines and weaken their capacity to oppose him. That the severity he showed made him loom more fearful in Florentine eyes than the once dreaded Henry VII is attested by Giovanni Villani's remark that the siege and laying waste of Florence by that emperor had been almost as nothing compared to Castruccio's.[171]

In fact, of course, however great the terror he inspired in the Florentines, the Lucchese tyrant lacked the resources for a protracted investment of their city, let alone its capture. Having produced the desired psychological effect on his enemy, he was content to withdraw

---

[169] G. Villani, *Cronica*, ix. 318.
[170] Ibid., ix. 319.
[171] Ibid., ix. 218.

to Signa. From here he moved north to ravage the outskirts of Prato,[172] returning to Signa to rendezvous with Azzo Visconti who had in the meantime been to Lucca to collect the money Castruccio had raised to pay him.[173] On 26 October (or perhaps on the thirtieth) the two commanders brought their reunited forces once again towards Florence, along the north bank of the Arno, though this time only for the ritual purpose of holding another *palio* at Rifredi, to avenge, on this occasion, the insult done to Milan by Ramon de Cardona when he had had a race run, within sight of the walls of that city, during his siege of it on St. John's Day in 1323.[174] Following this, Azzo Visconti and his Milanese knights withdrew from the campaign, returning to Lombardy by way of Lucca. Castruccio meanwhile persisted a little longer in his devastation of Florentine territory, laying waste the Val di Marina in the direction of Prato on 5 November before discharging the three hundred Aretine cavalry in his service, leaving a garrison of Florentine Ghibellines in Signa, and taking the bulk of his forces back to Lucca for the feast of that city's patron saint, St. Martin.[175]

While these operations had been proceeding around Florence itself, the detachments left in the Ghibelline army's rear during its advance on Florence had gone on with the reduction of the strongholds which had not fallen to the Lucchese during the pursuit of the retreating Guelph troops. The village of Altopascio which had given its name to Castruccio's victory had yielded on 6 October. On the eleventh of the same month the citadel of Carmignano, which had held out since 27 September, at last capitulated, as did the nearby Strozzi castle of Torrebecchi and the village of Artimino.[176] These minor conquests in Castruccio's rear consolidated his hold over the Pistoian *contado* and the Val di Nievole and hence strengthened the eastern approaches to the now enlarged Lucchese state. With the acquisition of Signa, they established a defensive perimeter consisting of the Usciana, the Monte Albano hills, the Arno, the Ombrone, and Agna. It is significant that Castruccio was content to hold this line and

---

[172] Ibid., ix. 322. There is some discrepancy in dates between Villani, ix. 319 and 322, the latter having Castruccio encamped outside Prato from 19 to 26 October, then returning to Pistoia on the twenty-eighth, coming back to Signa on the twenty-ninth, and not reaching Rifredi till the thirtieth, while in the former chapter Azzo and Castruccio are recorded as bringing their forces to Rifredi on the twenty-sixth.

[173] See n. 155 above and G. Villani, *Cronica*, ix. 319.

[174] Ibid., ix. 211, 319.

[175] Ibid., ix. 322, 323.

[176] Ibid., ix. 306, 318; 'Storie pistoresi', 94–5.

did not seek permanently to occupy any of the territory he had overrun around Florence.

At the same time, he was well aware of the psychological capital to be made from both the rout of the Florentines at Altopascio and their humiliation in the wake of their defeat. The two races run outside Florence and later, on the eve of his departure from the Florentine *contado*, the coining of a new form of Lucchese money, the 'Castruccini', at Signa in what had been Florentine territory,[177] were minor gestures of contempt which pointed up the weakness of the once great city on the Arno. But the most effective of Castruccio's demonstrations of the completeness of his victory was to be left until his return to Lucca when, on St. Martin's day, 11 November,[178] what later historians have described as his 'triumph' was held. In fact, at the time, it was probably conceived more as a chivalric pageant, but Castruccio's Renaissance biographers Tegrimi and Manucci quite clearly endowed it with the character of a Roman triumphal procession which it has retained in the later Castruccian historiography. The form of the ceremonial entry of the lord of Lucca into his city, as described by the contemporary Giovanni Villani, did undoubtedly contain many of the features of a classical celebration of victory, so that this subsequent historical elaboration of it is not altogether inappropriate. According to this chronicler, Castruccio was met, on approaching the city, by the whole body of its citizens and their wives, as though he were a king. As a sign of disdain towards the Florentines, he was preceded by their *carroccio* captured at Altopascio, drawn by oxen draped in the Florentine arms, and bearing their bell which was rung regularly as the procession advanced. Behind this cart, symbolic of Guelph military might, from which hung Florentine and Angevin emblems on inverted banners, came the leading prisoners taken in the battle, including their commander Ramon de Cardona, all carrying lit tapers as offerings to the patron saint of Lucca, St. Martin. These fifty or so prominent captives were later entertained at a banquet—before being brutally returned to their cells where ill treatment and sometimes torture were used, according to Villani, to exact speedy payments of their ransoms. Evidently, once the well-orchestrated performance had

[177] G. Villani, *Cronica*, ix. 323. On the 'castruccino', see *Corpus nummorum italicorum*, xi (Milan, 1929), 78–9.

[178] G. Villani, (*Cronica*, ix. 323) gives the date 10 November for Castruccio's triumphal entry into Lucca but specifies that it was on St. Martin's Day that this occurred which is, in fact, the eleventh of that month.

had its desired theatrical effect, the more practical consideration of meeting the costs of the campaign overcame the impulse to chivalric spectacle and courtesy! This short account of Castruccio's celebration of his victory was so extensively elaborated by Tegrimi[179] and Manucci[180] that it is difficult, in assessing its significance now, to disentangle contemporary fact from later legend. That it was more than merely the ceremonial offering of the spoils of war to the patron saint of his town by a grateful lord of Lucca is, however, evident even from Villani's description of it. With his public display of the Florentine *carroccio*, the inversion of the captured flags, the humiliation of his leading prisoners, Castruccio seems clearly to have wanted to impress both his Lucchese subjects, who were ordered out *en masse* to meet him, and foreign powers whose spies or envoys would have reported on the proceedings of the day.

Castruccio's triumphant homecoming had a symbolic importance in signalling that a new phase had begun in his long struggle with Florence. Up until September 1325, his had been a precarious position; now he had convincingly proved his superiority on the field of battle, had consolidated his hold over his recent acquisition of Pistoia and its *contado*, had unnerved and demoralized his enemies, and, above all, had established his credentials as one of the leading Ghibelline lords of Italy, so earning, in the eyes of Ludwig of Bavaria and of the other anti-Guelph powers in the peninsula, the undisputed right to act as the champion of the imperial cause in Tuscany. This, in turn, would enable him, in the remaining three years of his life, to extend his dominions, at the expense of foes and former allies (such as the Pisans) alike, and to secure a legally more secure, hereditary title for his authority.

How, one may ask at this point, had he succeeded in so short a time in so effectively enhancing his position? If we examine Castruccio's conduct of his war with Florence, it becomes clear that he owed this achievement to a combination of remarkable diplomatic and military skills. In the first place he had outmanœuvred his rival in the struggle for the control of Pistoia and, in the second, he had, once this gain was made, cunningly exploited the terrain of the territory lying between Florence and Lucca first to immobilize the forces opposing him and then to trap and destroy them. Having done this, he followed up his victory in such a way as to derive the maximum impact from it,

[179] N. Tegrimi, *Vita*, 138–51.
[180] A. Manucci, *Le azioni*, 95–103.

through a direct thrust at his antagonist's capital and the devastation of its outskirts. By consolidating his hold over his own recently expanded state while engaged in this foray into his enemy's heartland and through the psychological advantage he gained by thus bringing the war to the very walls of Florence, he effectively ensured the retention by military shock tactics of what intrigue and bribery had originally given him.

The two most notable aspects of the overall strategy he employed in leading up to the Altopascio campaign, as well as during and after it, were its economy and timing. His alternation between armed threat and financial inducement in his carefully laid plans to acquire Pistoia, his mastery of positional tactics in using the terrain of the plain of Altopascio to hold the vast Guelph host at bay, his skilful exploitation of a temporary tactical advantage in the ensuing battle and his subsequent ability to encircle and destroy the bulk of the Florentine army, his promptness in following up his victory with an attack on his enemy's territory—all these mark him as a general of genius. Whatever faults Castruccio Castracani may have had as a ruler, there can be no doubt that as a military commander and as an organizer of the straitened means at his disposal for war and the acquisition of territory, he displayed an extraordinary brilliance. Above all, he understood how to adapt to his purpose what was available to him—the potential advantages for a defensive strategy of hill and marshland and for an offensive one of heavily armed mercenary cavalry, the possibility of calling upon the financial reserves built up by the merchants of his city and, with victory in sight, of anticipating what it would yield in plunder and ransoms, to secure the means of achieving it. Everything must clearly have been finely calculated to offset what was initially a highly disadvantageous position and convert it, through carefully contrived psychological effects, into the appearance of effortless mastery.

V

Castruccio Castracani at the height of his power (1325–1328)

1. *Towards a dynastic principality: Castruccio as landholder, patron, and family head*

The victory of Altopascio opened for Castruccio a period of consolidation and enhancement of his authority. His war with Florence
continued to claim his attention, but in a less pressing way, at least in
the immediate aftermath of the battle when his great enemy was still
demoralized by defeat. At home, he could therefore work more
securely to transform his elective lordship into a hereditary principality, taking advantage of the imperial favour which his military
distinction brought him and using it not merely to ground his own
power in Lucca on surer foundations, but also to continue with his
expansionary policy, aimed at the creation of a regional state under his
rule.

From being the mere defender and leader of the Ghibelline faction
in the two cities he controlled, he could now move towards the establishment of a personal and dynastic authority, endowing his own
family with wealth and social eminence and attempting to establish
the right of his heirs to succeed to his position. Already, well before
1325, he, his wife, and her brothers had set about acquiring extensive
property holdings which were to become the nucleus of a considerable
family fortune.

As has already been mentioned, after the building of the fortified
enclosure of the Augusta, Castruccio purchased within it the Dal
Portico palace in which he had been living and some of the land and
houses in the adjoining area. It is not clear how far these structures,
grouped around what was then already known as the Cortile del
Signore, were transformed by Castruccio into a seigneurial residence
in the remaining years of his life. Aldo Manucci, at the end of the sixteenth century, described a recently demolished building around the
then still existing courtyard, with a turret, gates back and front, and

rooms decorated with paintings bearing Castruccio's arms.[1] But neither the 1324 description of the Dal Portico palace nor that in the 1412 Guinigi *terrilogio* mention these particulars which may therefore be either inventions of Manucci's fertile imagination or features of later constructions within the circuit of the Augusta.

Whatever their nature at the time, there is no doubt that a significant complex of buildings, probably eventually intended as the site of a ruler's palace, at the western end of the Augusta enclosure did pass into Castruccio's hands between 1323 and 1325.[2] It is also clear that Pina, Castruccio's wife, accumulated land in the parish of San Giovanni in Escheto in Massa Pisana on the outskirts of Lucca between 1321 (or possibly 1319) and 1323, on which Castruccio's famous villa was to be erected, though it is not certain how much of the structure and grounds described in the 1412 Guinigi *terrilogio* existed at the time of his death. In 1412, the estate contained a large tiled palace with great hall, upper and ground-floor rooms, and portico, together with a garden, vineyard, orchard, courtyard with a well, one half-tiled and one fully tiled outhouse, another tiled house and stable, and a further garden with vines and fruit trees—covering in all nine acres of arable land and ten of vineyard. This extensive property had been built up, as the *terrilogio* indicates, from five separate land purchases,[3] the details of three of which fortunately survive in the register of Ser Nicolao Boccella.[4] Just when the Castracani villa was built on this land is, however, a matter for speculation. Aldo Manucci, in his biography, asserts that it was erected in 1318, which clearly cannot have been the case; but his description of it may faithfully reflect the nature of the building as it was in the late sixteenth century. According to him, it was decorated with paintings, including one, at the head of the great hall, representing the imperial coronation of Ludwig of Bavaria, with Castruccio included in the picture as a participant in that ceremony in Rome. Unfortunately, however, it seems from his account that this 'adornment' as he calls it was not visible when he wrote since he speaks of it having been overlaid by the later

[1] Manucci, *Le azioni*, 69–70.

[2] ASL Fortificazioni no. 1, cc. 92ʳ.–95ʳ., 104ᵛ.–105ᵛ., Archivio notarile no. 94, Reg. i, cc. 88ʳ., 108ᵛ., and 132ᵛ., Archivio Guinigi no. 130 bis, c. 39ʳ.

[3] ASL Archivio Guinigi no. 130 bis, c. 41ʳ. The first sale contract is dated 1329, but this is almost certainly a scribal error for 1319 given that the other contracts, which this one precedes, are in date order. (Another description of this estate, as it was in 1400, is given in ASL Raccolti Speciali San Frediano no. 252, c. 12ʳ.)

[4] ASL Archivio notarile no. 94, Reg. i, cc. 20ʳ., 92ʳ., 101ʳ.

construction of rooms along that side of the building.[5] There are, as I have argued elsewhere,[6] reasons for supposing that this fresco was not painted until after Castruccio's death, so its existence does not in itself prove that the building which it decorated was erected in his lifetime. We do, however, know from various chroniclers that it was standing in 1355,[7] and from one of them, Matteo Villani, that at this date it had been unoccupied for seventeen years. Furthermore, Bongi discovered a reference to it in the *Estimo* of 1333, when it was already known as 'the palace of the duke'.[8] These indications do make it appear likely that it was constructed either in the last five years of Castruccio's life or very shortly afterwards and certainly within the decade 1323–33.

In addition to his palace within the Augusta and his family's villa at Massa Pisana, Castruccio and his wife acquired land and houses both in the villages around Lucca and in the city itself.[9] His brothers-in-law the Streghi were, in the meantime, establishing themselves as land-lords around Pietrasanta, Camaiore, and Massa in Lunigiana.[10] Castruccio's son Arrigo also developed property interests in the outer reaches of the same sector of the Lucchese state by acquiring a half share of a palace and a house in Pontremoli.[11]

These purchases would have made Castruccio and his relatives into substantial property holders in Lucca and in surrounding districts. Together with such Castracani assets as he had been able to recover on his return to the city from exile in 1314, they would have elevated Castruccio and his Streghi brothers-in-law to a prominent rank among Lucchese landowners. However, it is worth stressing that what

[5] Manucci, *Le azioni*, 65.

[6] See my article, 'Il problema', 375–7. The case for supposing that this fresco existed is stated by P. Campetti, 'Ritratti di Castruccio Castracani', *Atti della R. Accademia Lucchese* (NS), iii (1934), 268–70, and is based on miniatures in BSL MS 1661, c. 36ʳ. and MS 2629, c. 178ᵛ., which however, give what I have argued is an anachronistic representation of the crowning of Ludwig of Bavaria in Rome in 1328.

[7] Sercambi, *Croniche*, i, c. 146 (vol. i, p. 112), M. Villani, *Cronica*, ed. F. G. Dragomanni (Florence, 1846), v. 37, Sardo, *Cronaca*, 126.

[8] See S. Bongi, *Di Paolo Guinigi e delle sue ricchezze* (Lucca, 1871), 9, ASL Estimo no. 13, c. 193ᵛ. (not 213 as misprinted in Bongi's footnote). In 1333, however, the Castracani villa, unlike most of the adjoining land then still in the hands of Castruccio's heirs, appears to have been ceded to Neruccio Bottacci, though later it returned into the possession of the former duke's sons.

[9] ASL Archivio Guinigi no. 130 bis, cc. 40ʳ.–46ʳ., 49ᵛ., 94ᵛ., Archivio notarile no. 94, Reg. i. cc. 207ᵛ., 133ᵛ.–136ᵛ., 145ʳ.–146ᵛ.

[10] See Chapter II n. 100 above and ASL Diplomatico Archivio dei notari, 30/10/1323, Spedale, 13/8/1324 and 4/4/1327.

[11] ASL Archivio Guinigi no. 130 bis, c. 94ʳ. and Archivio notarile no. 94, Reg. i, cc. 117ᵛ.–119ᵛ.

he had acquired had come to him as a private citizen, buying what he obtained through normal channels, and not as lord of Lucca, and that, in its extent, what he had accumulated in no way amounted to a princely fortune. One should guard against the temptation to see this process of property acquisition as necessarily implying the establishment of the landed base for a dynastic authority. At the time, Castruccio moved gradually and cautiously and the impression that his aim was the creation of lordly magnificence may well be the result of hindsight.

The same is probably true of the impressive building programme with which Tegrimi[12] and the biographers who followed him credited the Lucchese tyrant. According to these later writers, this involved the construction of an array of castles, bridges, and roads.[13] While some of these, such as the tower at Pontremoli, can be shown, on the basis of contemporary inscriptions, to have been erected in Castruccio's time[14] and others may, in the light of circumstantial evidence, be attributed to the same period,[15] his responsibility for the remainder finds no confirmation in any of the extant sources. In some cases, as in those of the fortifications in Monteggiori[16] and Sarzanello,[17] it can be definitely excluded in that documents attest to their existence before he came to power. Though it is possible that Tegrimi may have had information now lost on the Lucchese ruler's building activities, it is more likely that he ascribed to the illustrious subject of his biography any notable structure dating from the century or so on either side of that despot's lifetime. It is interesting and perhaps significant that he fails to mention castles and gates which, according to contemporary writers,

---

[12] Tegrimi, *Vita*, 44–52.

[13] For instance, the citadels of Sarzanello, Nozzano, Monteggiori, Castello Ghibellino, San Martino in Colle, Bargiglio, the tower at Pontremoli, the walls of Ghivizzano, the bridges at Pescia, Ponte a Moriano, Castelnuovo in Garfagnana, and those on the Serchio between Barga and Perpoli, on the Lima at the Bagni di Corsena (now Bagni di Lucca), and the road and bridge between Viareggio and Montramito.

[14] See U. Mazzini, 'L'epigrafe pontremolese di Castruccio', *Giornale storico della Lunigiana*, iii (1911), 151. The same may also be true of the bridge at Pescia, the marble foundation stone of which Tegrimi claims to have seen (*Vita*, 50), but which is now destroyed.

[15] For instance, the Bargiglio which was not listed in the Statute of 1308 as a citadel to be garrisoned by the commune (Bongi and Del Prete, 'Il statuto', 276, 318) but which was granted by Ludwig of Bavaria to Castruccio's widow and sons three months after his death (ASL Diplomatico Tarpea, 15/12/1328).

[16] Bongi and Del Prete, 'Il statuto', 276, 318.

[17] Sforza, 'Castruccio . . . in Lunigiana', 414–26, and F. Bonatti, *Castruccio Castracani degli Antelminelli in Lunigiana* (Pisa, 1981), 51–61.

Castruccio did erect, for instance the Rocca Arrighina and Porta Ghibellina at Pietrasanta,[18] the fortress of Bellosguardo at Brandelli near Pistoia,[19] and the citadel Bella Ispera over that city's Porta Lucchese.[20] He also does not record the digging of the moat around Lucca in 1318 and the provision of water-mills on it six years later.[21]

Whatever the extent of the public building projects undertaken by Castruccio, it would seem that their purpose was largely utilitarian or political. There is little evidence of his use of the scarce resources at his disposal for the raising of monumental structures such as the lavish palaces of later tyrants or impressive churches or family chapels. In the light of the building activities of later rulers, this may seem surprising; but one should recognize the differences between their circumstances and those of a despot of Castruccio's era. Up until 1320, the future lord of Lucca was preoccupied with consolidating his authority and securing his election to the permanent governorship of the city. Thereafter, his time and energies must have been largely devoted to the prosecution of his war with Florence. The strain on his financial resources which this imposed, at least until 1325, would have permitted him to spend money only on such projects as were militarily necessary or politically prudent. It was solely those buildings, such as his *palazzo* within the Augusta or (if indeed he was responsible for it) his villa at Massa Pisana, which he paid for from his own growing personal fortune, that could fulfil more than these functional ends and give expression to his seigneurial aspirations.

The information which survives on Lucchese culture under Castruccio is even more meagre than that which we have on his private and public building activity. It is probable, in the light of this, that the preoccupations of war and diplomacy prevented this early tyrant not only from sponsoring extravagant architectural projects, but also from engaging in that patronage of the arts which was to distinguish some of the later Italian despots. Unfortunately, however, the destruction of the Augusta and the villa at Massa Pisana and the failure of the other structures from Castruccio's period to endure to the present time make it impossible to establish even this conclusion with any degree of certainty. Their disappearance means that we simply lack the evidence for assessing his contribution to the furtherance of

---

[18] BNF MS Palat. 571, c. 22ᵛ.

[19] Ibid., c. 23ʳ., G. Villani, *Cronica*, ix. 269, 'Storie pistoresi', 86.

[20] BNF MS Palat. 571, c. 23ʳ.

[21] Ibid., cc. 21ʳ., 23ʳ.

the arts in his age. Deodato Orlandi, the one notable Lucchese
painter of the period, almost certainly went into exile when the
Guelph regime was overthrown in 1314.[22] Apart from Manucci's references to the execution of a fresco in the tyrant's palace in the Augusta
and in his villa at Massa Pisana, no traditions have come down to us
linking his name with particular paintings. There is, however, one
surviving example of sculpture which can be related to him: that
adorning the tomb of his son Guarnerio in the church of San
Francesco in Sarzana. This was executed, almost certainly in 1328, by
the Pisan sculptor Giovanni di Balduccio[23] and was a work of some
artistic significance. It consisted of a stone coffin resting on two
crouching lions, surmounted by an effigy of the dead boy, over whom
two inclined angels supported a statue of the Madonna and child, the
whole group being set in an elaborate Gothic surround jutting from
the wall of the church. This architectural frame was, in turn, crowned
by a gabled cusp or roof which had, at its apex, a figure holding a
shield decorated with the imperial eagle and, at its base, above the
Wittelsbach and Castracani arms, two other statuettes, one in an attitude of prayer. Adorning the front of this canopy which rested on two
slender columns was a relief of a haloed Christ or God the Father and,
supporting it and the tomb it enclosed, was a projecting base, featur-
ing once again the Wittelsbach and Castracani emblems as well as two
ornamental lion's heads. On the front of the stone coffin appeared
three further reliefs: a Jesus in the centre displaying the nail-wounds
in his hands, flanked by the Virgin Mary and St. John. The whole
work, in addition to its impressive overall design, expressed, in the
fineness of its rendering of the faces of the dead child and his atten-
dant angels, a tenderness and pathos characteristically conveyed by
the best Gothic sculpture of the period.[24] Admirable though this
monument is from an aesthetic point of view, it is unlikely to have
been commissioned from purely artistic motives. Castruccio Castracani would have seen it rather as an expression of his personal grief
and, at the same time, as an indication of the dynastic aspirations of
his family and its close links with the reigning imperial house. Its erec-

---

[22] See P. Campetti, 'Deodato Orlandi', *Atti della R. Accademia Lucchese* (NS), v (1942),
145–58.
[23] On this work and its dating, see C. Benocci, 'La tomba di Guarnerio Castracani
degli Antelminelli nella chiesa di S. Francesco a Sarzana: ricerche e contribuiti', *Rivista
di archeologia, storia, costume del Istituto Storico Lucchese*, ix (1981), 9–22.
[24] For illustrations of this tomb, see Bonatti, *Castruccio*, 71–80, and for bibliographies
of works on it, ibid., 80, and Benocci, 'La tomba', 21–2.

tion is thus attributable not so much to its patron's interest in art as to his determination to commemorate the passing of one of his sons in a manner fitting to his newly acquired ducal dignity.

Altogether, therefore, however it was that Castruccio sought to establish his prestige and authority in his city in the last three years that he ruled, it was not by extensive public building programmes nor by attracting artists to his court to give lustre to his regime. Such considerations do not appear to have influenced him, preoccupied as he was with pursuing his political and military aims and furthering the interests of his family. Indeed, in the last few years of his life, his main concern, apart from his war with Florence and his designs against Pistoia and Pisa, would seem to have been the establishment, for himself, of a secure title to rule and, for his sons, of the right of succession to his lordship. After the defeat of Frederick of Austria by his rival Ludwig of Bavaria at Muhldorf in September 1322, the vicariate over Lucca and its dependencies which Castruccio had been granted in 1320 by the Habsburg prince was in need of confirmation by the man who had effectively replaced him as emperor-elect. That the lord of Lucca did not apply immediately to the new incumbent of the imperial throne for the endorsement of his rights over his city may have been due to a lingering loyalty to Frederick, though it is more probable that it was the temptation to seek an alternative protector in James II of Aragon which delayed his approach to Ludwig till May 1324.

When, however, the success of the Infante Alfonso's expedition against Sardinia had eliminated the possibility that Lucca might claim support from the Aragonese in return for an alliance against Pisa, Castruccio lost no time in asking for and obtaining from the emperor-elect his authorization as vicar, not only over the territories with which Frederick had invested him in 1320, but also over his later acquisitions of Pontremoli and the lands of the diocese of Luni (on both banks of the Magra) and, more remarkable still, over the as yet to be acquired city and *contado* of Pistoia.[25] The conferral of these imperial prerogatives opened the way for the close co-operation between the lord of Lucca and the Bavarian emperor-elect which was to persist for the next four years. He was to exploit it not only to legitimize the power he enjoyed over the territories under his control, but also to gain prior justification for his expansionist schemes, as a result of Ludwig's

[25] ASL Capitoli no. 4, cc. 48ʳ.–49ᵛ., published in Lazzareschi, 'Documenti', 352–3, 354–6.

acceptance of Castruccio not merely as a fervent Ghibelline partisan but as a ruler with the power to outmatch his Guelph enemies and therefore as an essential support for the emperor's own Italian ambitions.

Having secured the re-endorsement of his vicariate over Lucca and a notional jurisdiction over Pistoia which he soon translated into an actual one, the Lucchese tyrant turned his attention next to ensuring that his enlarged dominions should pass without hitch to his descendants. On the eve of the Altopascio campaign on 17 June 1325, as Ramon de Cardona's forces were leaving Prato and about to invest Agliana in the first stage of their attack on Lucca, Castruccio assembled the *anziani* and *savi* of the city to obtain from them the nomination of his son Arrigo as captain-general and rector of the commune, associating his heir with himself in the government of his state. On the following day, this election was ratified in a public parliament by the general council.[26] Thus, presumably to provide against the contingency of his own death in the coming hostilities, the lord of Lucca made formal provision for the automatic succession of his eldest son to his position.

It is from this point that one can date the attempted foundation of a dynasty by Castruccio. His victory at Altopascio which followed quickly afterwards, by consolidating his hold on his city and on his recent acquisition of Pistoia, confirmed his control over what was virtually a territorial state, maintained by force of arms and by virtue of a delegation of imperial authority, transcending the limits of a mere elected lordship and coming to be regarded as a hereditary possession of his family. This family itself, which was beginning around this time to aspire to the princely status to which Ludwig of Bavaria's elevation of Castruccio to his dukedom was to give official recognition two and a half years later, was a numerous one, the eldest members of which had either come of age or were approaching maturity. Unfortunately for their father, his first four children were daughters. While this carried with it one advantage, that he was able, through them, to establish marriage alliances which suited his policies, it meant that his prospective successor, his son Arrigo, was a minor. The exact birthdate of Castruccio's heir is unknown, but the fact that he was named after the Emperor Henry VII[27] (who had entered Italy in 1310) and that he had

[26] ASL Atti di Castruccio no. 1, cc. 24ᵛ.–26ʳ.
[27] See Winkler, *Castruccio*, 10, I. del Lungo, *Dino Compagni*, vol. i, pt. 2, p. 1002.

not yet come of age in December 1327[28] indicates that he could not
have been more than fifteen in 1325, and might well have been a year
or two younger. His three brothers, Vallerano, Giovanni, and Guarnerio, named respectively after Henry VII's brother and son and his
marshal Werner von Homburg, were smaller still. The last of these,
Guarnerio, was to die while still a child, probably in 1327.

By that time, three of Castruccio's daughters had been married to
husbands evidently chosen as a means of forging links between the
Castracani family and the ruling houses of territories which had
recently come into its possession (or might later do so). The eldest,
Dialta, became the wife of Filippo Tedici in May 1325, so sealing the
bargain by which Lucca gained control of Pistoia. The second,
Caterina, in November of the following year wed Giovanni, marquis of
Mulazzo, a member of the Ghibelline 'spina secca' branch of the
Malaspina, whose guardian Castruccio had been since 1320 and who,
in 1323, had acted as *podestà* and captain of Lucca.[29] Castruccio's third
daughter Bertecca, was married to Fazio, the son of Gaddo della
Gherardesca, probably at the end of 1327.[30]

The marriages of the first three Castracani daughters seem to
reflect the three directions of their father's expansionist policies, east
to Pistoia, north to Lunigiana, and west to Pisa, and to underline the
increasingly dynastic character of his authority over what was becoming more a regional than a city state. Curiously, Castruccio's fourth
daughter Jacopa, instead of becoming the wife of yet another young
noble from a neighbouring territory on which he had designs, was
allowed to take the veil, entering the convent of Santa Chiara at Gattaiola near Lucca, some time between November 1326 and December
1327.[31] This presumably established a useful link with the local

---

[28] Lazzareschi, 'Documenti', 401. Castruccio's last will, dated 10 July 1328, included
an earlier one of 20 December 1327, to which it was in effect a codicil (ibid., 402).

[29] Sforza, 'Castruccio . . . in Lunigiana', 351–2, S. Bongi, *Bandi lucchesi*, 241.

[30] In Castruccio's will, she is merely described as countess of Donoratico.
(Lazzareschi, 'Documenti', 400). But her husband can be identified as Fazio della
Gherardesca from a passage in his testament (published in M. Maccioni, *Difesa del
dominio dei conti della Gherardesca sopra la signoria di Donoratico, Bolgheri, Castagneto, etc.*
(Lucca, 1771), i. 94) in which Castruccio's sons are described as his brothers-in-law
('cognati nostri'). Given that Bertecca was Castruccio's third daughter, it is improbable
that she would have been of marriageable age before his rift with Pisa in October 1323
and it is therefore likely that her wedding took place between the fall of Pisa to Ludwig
on 11 October 1327 and the following 20 December.

[31] Jacopa's name is omitted from a list of the nuns of Santa Chiara at Gattaiola dated
21 November 1326 (ASL Archivio notarile no. 96, c. 57ᵛ.), but she had become 'Soror

church, while leaving Verde, still a minor at the latter date, available
for a possible future political marriage.

In addition to the nine legitimate children he had in 1325 (reduced
to eight two years later with the death of Guarnerio), Castruccio in his
will acknowledged two 'natural' ones, a son Ottino (later known as
Altino) and a daughter Marchesana. The latter was married to a
certain Moreccio simultaneously with her half-sister Caterina's
wedding to Giovanni Malaspina.[32] It is not clear whether this illegi-
timate offspring formed part of Castruccio's household. Even without
them, however, it would have been a large one, particularly early in
1325 before the departure of Dialta for Pistoia. Unfortunately, the surviving sources do not provide us with information concerning the
private life which the lord of Lucca led with his wife Pina and their
children. In the public sphere, however, his family became increasingly significant as it assumed a political role of greater importance,
particularly from about 1325 onwards. As he himself moved towards
the establishment of a territorial state, so also did his preoccupation
grow with the perpetuation of his authority through hereditary succession and its enhancement through dynastic alliances.

The final stage of Castruccio's twelve-year spell of political power
which opened with his successful conclusion of the Altopascio campaign was distinguished, however, not merely by the assumption of
greater prominence by his family. It was also marked by the formation
of closer links with the Emperor-elect Ludwig of Bavaria for the
purpose of legitimizing both his recent territorial acquisitions and the
hereditary nature of his lordship. And this, in turn, was to bring him
into sharper conflict with the papacy, which had already been
antagonized by his part in the theft of the pontifical treasure from San
Frediano in 1314 and by his support of Lombard Ghibellinism, but
which came to regard him, after 1325, as a serious threat to its political
position in Italy and, eventually, as the principal ally of its main adversary, the Rome-bound Ludwig.

2. *Castruccio and the Lucchese church*

Castruccio's relations with the Church thus deteriorated, around 1325,
from a state of mutual hostility to one of active opposition. Curiously,

Jacoba' of that convent in Castruccio's will of 20 December 1327 (Lazzareschi,
'Documenti', 400).

[32] Lazzareschi, 'Documenti', 400–1.

however, at least until Ludwig of Bavaria's appearance in Italy forced on the local clergy a choice between pope and emperor, this did not seem to have produced any real rift between him and the Lucchese ecclesiastical establishment. This, to all appearances, went on functioning as before despite the growing tensions between their Ghibelline lord on the one hand and Pope John XXII and his Italian allies on the other. That this should have been the case would seem to have been due in part to the circumstance that, when Castruccio first came to power in 1316, he had delivered his city from Uguccione della Faggiuola, then the principal threat to the Guelphs, and had presided over a government which had made peace with Florence and King Robert of Naples. By the time war had broken out with them again, in 1320, his position in Lucca was well established, as were his links with the town's leading families, as well represented in the cathedral chapter as among the citizens who elected him their lord in that very year. Another reason, however, for the absence of friction between his regime and the leading members of the Lucchese clergy was the tendency of the composition of the cathedral chapter to be affected by the political changes which the city underwent in the period from 1301 to 1314. This clearly contributed, after the latter year, to the loyalty of the majority of the canons to the Ghibelline government of Lucca, at least up to the time when the presence of the excommunicated Ludwig of Bavaria in Italy aggravated the problem faced by its churchmen in reconciling their allegiance to temporal and spiritual authority. As Benedetto has shown,[33] the expulsion by Pope Boniface VIII in 1301 of six of the canons of San Martino who were closely linked with the exiled White faction and their replacement by men from Black Guelph families created a precedent which resulted in 1314 in the withdrawal from the chapter of those associated with the now banished Obizi faction and the return to it of three of the former 'Ghibelline' partisans excluded in 1301.

Notwithstanding this, however, there was still a considerable degree of continuity in the composition of the chapter between the first decade of the fourteenth century and the early years of the post-1314 regime which persisted into the Castruccian era, to be modified significantly only after 1325. Twelve of the sixteen canons of 1313 were listed as members of the chapter after 1314, and these included three

---

[33] See G. Benedetto, 'I rapporti tra Castruccio Castracani e la chiesa di Lucca', *Annuario della biblioteca civica di Massa* (1980), 82–6.

of those appointed in 1301 in place of exiled Whites.[34] The apparent willingness of these clerics to work with the new government must be attributed to the strong representation among them of men of leading urban families which had either gone over to the regime or approved of its abrogation of the anti-*casastici* provisions of the Statute of 1308. In fact, if we examine the names of these twelve survivors, we find that half of them came from houses which had been dubbed *potenti* in 1308, two were foreigners, one was from the *contado*, and three of solid, Lucchese merchant stock.[35] Since all of the three returned White canons[36] belonged to *casastici* families, nine in all of the post-1314 chapter would have come from this top layer of Lucchese society.

Those who were elected to it while Castruccio Castracani was in power in fact included a lower proportion of members of these aristocratic houses and more foreigners and men from the *contado*; three of the new canons of this period were of *casastici* lineages, three foreigners, three from the *contado*, and one from an ordinary Lucchese merchant family.[37] Despite this, the chapter under his rule reflected, as it had done earlier, the predominance in the Lucchese Church of the city's patriciate. Nor is there any indication of any rapid turnover in its composition in the first few years of his term in office, only four canons ceasing to attend its meetings between 1317 and 1321,[38] and four between 1322 and 1324.[39] The attenuation of the original membership of the chapter over this period follows a pattern consistent with the natural rotation of men in this kind of body and does not suggest any drastic alteration over these years in its general composition.

In the remainder of the Castruccian period, its character seemed to change more quickly, partly because of the withdrawal of some of the

[34] I have accepted Benedetto's reconstruction of the full chapter for 1313 ('I rapporti', 76–7) and have derived my lists of its members after 1314 from ACL LL 49 cc. 60ᵛ., 78ᵛ., 150ᵛ., LL 52 cc. 1ʳ., 21ʳ., LL 54, cc. 75, 28ᵛ., 120ᵛ.

[35] The Simonetti (a branch of the Quartigiani), the Del Gallo, the Malagallia, the Della Rocca, the Brancasecca, and the Faitinelli had all been designated *casastici* in 1308. Jacopo Barghini of Florence and Francesco Cortevecchia of Pisa were foreigners, Guidotto da Fosciano came from the Lucchese *contado*, while Lamberto Gracci, Pietro de' Schiava, and Filippo Arnolfini belonged to substantial Lucchese *popolani* families.

[36] Guglielmo and Giovanni degli Interminelli and Bongiorno dei Flammi.

[37] The first group contained Ubaldo Spoletini, Soffredo Malisardi, and Ciato Savarigi (from a branch of the Interminelli), the second Jacopo Gucci da Prato, Giovanni da Cerreto, and Andrea Sapiti da Firenze, the third Nicolao da Buggiano, Latino da Coreglia, and Enrico da Camaiore.

[38] Jacopo Barghini, Giovanni Interminelli, Filippo Arnolfini, Arrigo del Gallo.

[39] Raniero della Rocca, Guglielmo Interminelli, Pietro de' Schiava, Guidotto da Fosciano.

older canons and partly because of the introduction into it of new men who were less broadly representative of the old Lucchese aristocracy. Problems also began to arise at this time over the legitimacy of elections, particularly in the last two years of the Lucchese tyrant's life. The position of the leading churchmen in the city clearly became more difficult at this time for a number of reasons. First, their long-lived bishop, Enrico del Carretto, who had held his see since 1300 and been in exile since 1314, died in 1323, leaving it vacant.[40] Since this event more or less corresponded with the deterioration of relations between Lucca and the papacy, there could be no early replacement of him by a successor. Under pressure from Castruccio's vicar, Matteo of Assisi, the canons agreed on 5 July 1324 to elect an administrator of the bishopric and vicar of the episcopal chapter from among the clergy of the diocese, choosing Albizzo da Brancoli, prior of the church of Santa Maria Forisportam and a protégé of the lord of Lucca, to hold this position.[41] In this way, the secular authorities were satisfied, but the problem of maintaining good relations with the papacy was exacerbated by John XXII's denunciation of Castruccio in the letter 'Angit nos', dated 30 April 1325.[42] The Lucchese tyrant had, of course, earlier incurred papal censure, by implication, in the pontifical missive of 31 March 1317, deploring the looting of the sacristy of San Frediano in 1314, in which he had participated,[43] and even been

[40] ASL LL 52, c. 22ʳ., and ᵛ. Enrico del Carretto, a Franciscan, appointed by Pope Boniface VIII in 1300 (F. Ughelli, *Italia sacra; sive de episcopis Italiae* (Rome, 1644), vol. i, col. 881), had been in residence at the papal court in Avignon for some time before his death (see R. Manselli, 'Lo sinodo lucchese di Enrico del Carretto', in *Italia sacra*, xv (1970), 198–202, and E. Coturri, 'La chiesa lucchese al tempo di Castruccio', *ACCC* 113–24.

[41] ACL LL 52, c. 26ʳ. On Albizzo da Brancoli and his relationship with Castruccio, see Benedetto, 'I rapporti', 93–4. For further evidence of Castruccio's influence on the deliberations of the chapter see ACL loc. cit., in which it resolves that the disposition of the prebend of the late canon Guglielmo degli Interminelli will only be made with the approval of the lord of Lucca.

[42] ASV Reg. Vat. no. 114, ff. 188ᵛ.–189ᵛ., published in German translation in W. Preger, 'Die Verträge Ludwigs des Baiern mit Friedrich dem Schönen in den Jahren 1325 und 1326', in *Abhandlungen der historishe Klasse der königlich bayerischen Akademie der Wissenschaften* xvii (1883), 169–72, and in an abridged form in Ficker, *Urkunden*, 21–2. A shortened version of this letter was sent out to various Italian dioceses. G. Mollat in his *Lettres communes des papes d'Avignon analyseés d'après les registres dits d'Avignon et du Vatican: Jean XXII (1316–1334)* (Paris, 1904–47), v. 452, 466–7, and vi. 308 summarizes and abstracts these.

[43] ASV Reg. VAT no. 63, fo. 352ᵛ., published in S. Riezler, *Vatikanische Akten*, 19–20. Another letter, written on the same day, condemned the slightly later theft by Francesco della Faggiuola of the treasure from San Romano (published in Baluze, *Vitae*, ii, col. 305).

excommunicated, together with the Lucchese *anziani* and other officials, in September 1318 for his continued administration of the lands
of the bishopric of Luni after the lapse of his vicariate over it.[44] But, in
the former of these two condemnations he had not been explicitly
named (although his part in the theft of the papal treasure on that
occasion was to be one of the grounds of his later excommunication),
and, in the latter, he had had his sentence imposed on him not directly
by the pope, but by the bishops of Florence and Fiesole. In 1325, however, the full force of the pope's anger was directed at Castruccio in a
manner that made it difficult for the local clergy to maintain its *modus
vivendi* with him without risking papal disapproval. Not only was the
Lucchese tyrant blamed for his appropriation of part of the pontifical
treasure in 1314, for not allowing letters stating the Church's case
against Ludwig of Bavaria to be read in Lucca, for giving comfort and
aid to excommunicates such as the Visconti of Milan and Lippaccio of
Osimo in the March of Ancona,[45] but he was also accused of imprison-
ing messengers sent to the city to proclaim the charges against
Ludwig, of arresting and despoiling travellers going to and from the
papal see, of intercepting, opening, and tearing up papal correspondence, of seizing Church property in the bishoprics of Lucca and
Luni, including goods belonging to monasteries and hospitals, of
imposing taxes on the clergy, of expelling churchmen from their
livings and replacing them with others of his own choosing whom he
then protected and defended, of violating interdicts, and of compelling rites and offices to be performed in defiance of them.

It is not clear how many of these charges in fact had substance, but if
there is any truth in them at all, they throw a different light on the
relations between Castruccio and the Lucchese clergy from that which
is shed by the episcopal chapter records. They illuminate the dilemma
of the local ecclesiastics, caught between, on the one hand, a ruler who
rode roughshod over clerical immunities, drew on the financial
resources of the Church when it suited him to do so, and insisted that
the religious like the secular among his subjects should do his will
and, on the other, the pope, at odds with their city on political grounds

---

[44] R. Piattoli, 'Documenti per la storia di Castruccio Antelminelli e delle sue
imprese', in *Bollettino storico lucchese*, xv (1943), 14–21.
[45] In August 1322, Lippaccio, lord of Osimo, had started a rebellion against the
government of the Church which had taken over his city in the previous May. (G.
Villani, *Cronica*, ix, 142, 161). He was aided, according to the Florentine chronicler, by
the city of Fermo and other Ghibellines, including evidently Castruccio Castracani.

and as insistent as Castruccio on exacting from them their due obedi-ence. Just how churchmen coped with the conflicting demands made on them in these circumstances is a question to which the available sources do not give a direct answer, though there are indications in them of various forms of evasive action which would seem to be aimed at minimizing their responsibility for a situation they could not control. For instance, in November and December 1327 the cathedral chapter chose to fill two vacant canonries through indirect election, in a manner which made allowance for the possibility of challenges to the appointments so made. The method adopted was that of delegating to one of its members the task of nominating the new incumbent to the office, whose relatives and friends were then formally asked to under-take to support the chapter in the event of that elector's choice being disputed. Why it acted in this way is not certain, but it was probably with the intention of limiting its liability for making an appointment in defiance of a papal request the previous March that the next vacant canonry in Lucca be assigned to another candidate.[46] It is perhaps also significant that, on the first occasion on which this procedure was followed, on 10 November 1327, the canon who was being replaced was Opizo Simonetti dei Quartigiani whose death was, in all likeli-hood, the result of Castruccio's suppression, earlier in June, of the conspiracy hatched by his family.[47] The second time a canon was chosen in this way, Giovanni Parghia, the first person selected, declined the invitation to join the chapter after consulting with his family and friends.[48] The position was then offered to a member of another branch of the Interminelli clan, Ciato Savarigi, who, having gained the support of his kinsmen and associates, accepted it.

The evident reluctance of members of the Lucchese clergy to take on canonries at this stage is in itself an indication of the state of the Lucchese Church in 1327. Another is the change in the complexion of the chapter since 1324. In the intervening three years, three of the older canons had left, two had died, and new men had come in to take

[46] ACL LL 54, cc. 81ᵛ.–82ᵛ. On 8 March 1327 the archpriest Nicolao da Buggiano presented to the chapter a letter from Guglielmo de'Goghi of the bapistry in Parma informing it of John XXII's grant of a canonry in Lucca to Addighiero di Polacio degli Addighieri of Parma. Although the appropriate papal bull had not yet been sent, the chapter was asked to assign the next vacant canonry to the papal nominee.

[47] Ibid., cc. 106ʳ.–109ʳ. The canon elected to replace him was Soffredo, the son of the prominent Lucchese citizen Burnetto di Opizo Malisardi.

[48] Ibid., cc. 113ʳ.–116ᵛ. He was elected on 11 December 1327 and renounced his canonry on the eighteenth, being replaced by Ciato Savarigi on the twenty-fourth.

their place.[49] The greater instability in the membership of the chapter is testimony to the tensions and pressures to which it was subject in the closing years of Castruccio's period in power, though notwithstanding these its composition continued to a modified degree to maintain its traditional balance between men from prominent Lucchese families and outsiders.

Despite the growing difficulty of preserving their loyalty to both the Pope and the lord of Lucca—the latter now in effect under the ban of the Church—the canons seem to have kept up their contacts with the papacy, through direct or indirect channels, at least up to about March 1327.[50] However, their relations with John XXII undoubtedly suffered a severe blow when they failed to accept his nomination of Addighiero Addighieri to their chapter in November of that year. When, in March 1328, they were forced, under pressure from Castruccio, to allot the prebend held by the absentee canon, Giovanni da Cerreto to Ludwig of Bavaria's protégé 'Volcoldo' (Volkhardt?) of Nürnberg at the emperor's request,[51] they must have fallen even further out of papal favour. Already, in June 1327, John XXII had complained of the inability of the rector he had appointed to the church of San Pietro Somaldi to take up his benefice 'on account of the tyranny of Castruccio degli Interminelli';[52] and later records indicate that other pro-papal clergy were, in like manner, either excluded or expelled from their livings within the territories controlled by the lord of Lucca or by his imperial protector in 1327 or 1328.[53] In these circumstances, the position of those churchmen who were permitted

---

[49] In addition to Soffredo Malisardi and Ciato Savarigi, these were Jacopo Gucci da Prato (ibid., c. 107ᵛ.), Andrea Sapiti da Firenze, and Giovanni da Cerreto (ibid., c. 120ʳ.). The first two of these came from *casastici* houses and the remaining three were foreigners.

[50] See n. 46 above and ACL A11, c. 69ᵛ.

[51] ACL LL 54, cc. 126ᵛ.–127ʳ.

[52] ASV Reg. Vat. no. 84, ff. 50ᵛ.–51ᵛ. (résumé in Mollat, *Lettres communes*, vi. 562).

[53] There are references in the Vatican archives to Bartolomeo, abbot of San Paolo a Ripa d'Arno in Pisa, who was expelled from his monastery and imprisoned by Castruccio (ASV Reg. Vat. no. 93, fo. 98ʳ.), to Nicolao Bulgarini, prior of San Giovanni e Reparata in Lucca, who was deprived of his rectorate of the hospital of San Leonardo in Treponzio (ibid., no. 92, fo. 188ᵛ.), to Pietro di Castellano who was driven from his parish of San Stefano di Feletria in the diocese of Luni (ibid., fo. 227ʳ. and ᵛ.), to John, bishop of Massa, whose revenues from that episcopate had been confiscated after he had been forced to abandon his see (Mollat, *Lettres communes*, viii. 19), and to Federigo da Fosdinovo who was imprisoned and deprived of his office as canon of the church of Santa Maria Forisportam (ibid., no. 118, ep. 35). Only two of the clerics referred to in these records were, however, in the diocese of Lucca.

to continue with their ecclesiastical duties cannot have been a very happy one. Castruccio had left the court of Ludwig of Bavaria before the latter made Pietro da Corvara antipope with the title of Nicholas V in May 1328, and it was not until after the Lucchese tyrant's death that the city was compelled to accept that prelate's authority and the bishop he appointed.[54] Nevertheless, the progress of the papal case against Castruccio to the point of formal proclamation of his excommunication[55] and the emergence of Lucca as one of the principal bastions of Ghibellinism in Italy after Ludwig's entry into Tuscany in September 1327 would have made it impossible for the town's remaining clergy to maintain the token obedience to both State and Church which had enabled them, up to about 1325, to live with Castruccio without breaking with John XXII. While an open schism was not to divide the Lucchese Church until Ludwig imposed his antipope upon it on his return to the city after the duke of Lucca's death, the claims which Castruccio made on its property and his imprisonment of at least one of its members[56] must in effect have brought about a political, if not an ecclesiastical rift within it.

Notwithstanding this, the majority of the higher echelons of the Lucchese clergy, as represented by its cathedral chapter, seems to have chosen, for reasons of expediency if not of conviction, to remain in Lucca under him, and some later even to accept the authority of an excommunicated emperor and his schismatic pope.[57] There is no question that, in 1327–8, this result was brought about in significant measure by duress on the part of Castruccio who, having nothing

[54] On 28 January 1329, Rocchigiano Tadolini was appointed bishop of Lucca by Nicholas V. He was subsequently forced to renounce his see in 1330 (ibid., Ughelli, *Italia sacra*, cols. 881–2) after Ludwig of Bavaria's departure from Italy and the abdication of Nicholas V.

[55] Although the papal case against Castruccio had been instituted in April 1325, it was not until 1 April 1328 that a bull was issued pronouncing his excommunication (ASV Documenti di Castel S. Angelo, Armadio C, no. 1064). See also G. Villani, *Cronica*, x. 78, who dates the excommunication 30 March 1328. Another version of the bull of excommunication, which coupled the condemnation of Castruccio with that of Ludwig of Bavaria, was issued by Pope John XXII on 5 April 1328 (Lazzareschi, 'Documenti', 382–94).

[56] See n. 53 above and ASV Reg. Vat. no. 90, fo. 113ᵛ. and no. 118, ep. 702.

[57] The register of the Antipope Nicholas V (Reg. Vat. no. 118) contains letters dating from 1329 to three of the cathedral canons of the end of the Castruccian period, Bongiorno dei Flammi (ep. 501, 657), Giovanni da Sorbano (ep. 501), and Ubaldo Spoletini (ep. 653). It also records the replacement of three of the absentee canons of 1328, specifically designated as loyal to Pope John XXII, namely Rosso Faitinelli (ep. 693), Andrea Sapiti of Florence (ep. 688), and Enrico da Camaiore (ep. 529).

further to lose through further papal condemnation, could freely dispense with clerical immunities and impose his will by force on his ecclesiastical no less than on his lay subjects. Earlier, however, the principal factor conditioning the attitude of the Lucchese clergy appears to have been not so much the ruthlessness of his treatment of it (of which there is evidence only towards the end of his life) as the need to preserve the position of the city's Church as a reflection of the prevailing social structure and political order. As Benedetto has shown,[58] clerics who belonged to the Interminelli *consorteria* or to families favourable to Castruccio were able to acquire a number of key benefices in the Lucchese diocese in the period up to 1322, while the appointment in the following year of Albizzo da Brancoli as administrator during the vacancy of the see placed the government of the Church in the bishopric of Lucca in the hands of one of his supporters. The influence of his own partisans among the local clergy would undoubtedly have contributed to the attitude taken by it towards the city's lord, at least up until about 1327. The acquiescence, however, of others not so clearly committed to his faction would also have played a part in the avoidance of any violent clash between State and Church under his rule. The social origins of those who held high ecclesiastical office in Lucca and the custom of removing from their benefices those most closely identified with exiled *consorterie* ensured a large measure of tolerance, on the part of the clerics, to the prevailing government, even when this was politically hostile to the interests of the papacy.

In the history of Castruccio's relations with the local ecclesiastical establishment and with the Church as a whole there seem to be two distinct turning-points. The first occurred around 1325 when the excommunication proceedings against him began and when the issue of conflicting loyalties therefore first confronted the Lucchese clergy. The second came late in 1327 when Ludwig's entry into Tuscany encouraged in the newly created duke of Lucca a more high-handed attitude towards clerical persons and property that resulted in an effective subjugation of Church to State and so severed the last remaining links between the city and Pope John XXII. These turning-points correspond with critical changes also in Castruccio's political position, the first with his seizure of Pistoia and his subsequent consolidation of that gain as a result of the Altopascio campaign, the

---

[58] Benedetto, 'I rapporti', 88–94.

second with the final realization of his ambitions to secure his authority by hereditary title and to acquire Pisa. The sharpening of his
conflict with the papacy and the forcing of the local Church into submission were but the translation into the ecclesiastical sphere of his
policy of territorial expansion and of the building up of a dynastic
state. Underlying developments in both of these areas of his activity
was the forging of his special relationship with Ludwig of Bavaria, at
once the instrument for the achievement of his political designs and
the precipitating factor in the last, most arbitrary stage of his dealings
with the Church.

3. *Castruccio, protégé of Ludwig of Bavaria and antagonist of Charles of Calabria*

The context of Castruccio's close involvement with the Emperor-elect
was to be the situation which followed Altopascio, one in which the
Florentines, with the aid of their Neapolitan allies, were to seek to
regain their pre-eminence in Tuscany, so inducing the Lucchese
tyrant to call once again on help from outside to restore the advantage
which that battle had given him. On the eve of that engagement, he
had already communicated with Ludwig's ambassadors in a letter
describing his success in the skirmish which preceded it. His contact
with them, at this stage, underlines the importance he attached to the
support of his imperial protector.

It was, however, to be some time before the Bavarian prince's favour
could be of practical assistance to him in the face of the military
resurgence of Florence. For while, in the immediate aftermath of Altopascio, Castruccio had continued to harass this enemy's *contado* from
his forward base at Signa,[59] it was not long before the balance of forces
which had tilted in his favour with that decisive victory began to
redress itself as a result of intervention in support of the beleaguered
commune by its traditional ally, the kingdom of Naples. Already, on 1
December 1325, three hundred knights dispatched by King Robert
had reached the city, of whom half were in his pay and half were taken
into Florentine service.[60] When these proved inadequate either for
relieving the siege of Montemurlo or for keeping Castruccio's troops
from riding with impunity right up to the gates of the city, it was
resolved, on 23 December, to invite the Neapolitan monarch's eldest

---

[59] G. Villani, *Cronica*, ix. 329, 332.
[60] Ibid., ix. 330, ASF Provvisioni no. 22, c. 11ᵛ.

son Charles, duke of Calabria, to come to Florence as its lord for ten years. The conditions of his appointment were to be that he should, in return for an annual grant of 200,000 florins, maintain at least a thousand knights (all of whom should be foreign) and, after the termination of hostilities, four hundred knights under the command of his vicar, in return for 100,000 florins a year. He should further undertake to respect the laws and statutes of the commune during the period of his lordship.[61] Ambassadors promptly conveyed this offer to Naples where it was accepted on 13 January 1326.[62]

The appointment of Charles of Calabria as lord of Florence and commander of what was in effect a new army to defend it against Castruccio provided a long-term answer to the military threat confronting the city. In the meantime, however, more urgent measures had to be put into effect to cope with its predicament until Charles and his forces should arrive. On 1 January, Pierre de Naix, a French knight who had fought and been captured at Altopascio but who had since been released, was elected Florentine war-captain[63] and immediately set about bolstering the commune's defences. His installation in this office came too late to save the beleaguered stronghold of Montemurlo which fell to the Lucchese on 8 January;[64] but he did display considerable energy over the next few weeks in efforts to wrest the military initiative from Castruccio. He began by trying to bribe some of the latter's mercenaries to betray their commander, kill him, surrender Carmignano and Signa, and come over to the Florentine side with two hundred knights. When this plot was discovered and two Burgundians, one Englishman, and six Germans were executed for complicity in it,[65] Pierre de Naix attempted a direct attack on Signa. He expected to encounter little resistance because Castruccio had just discharged some of his mercenaries whose loyalty the recent conspiracy had made him doubt. The Lucchese tyrant, however, evidently determined to make one last show of strength before Charles of Calabria's arrival, suddenly appeared on the scene with seven hundred cavalry and two thousand infantry. With these he not only

---

[61] Ibid., c. 54ʳ. and ᵛ., G. Villani, *Cronica*, ix. 333.

[62] R. Bevere, 'La signoria di Firenze tenuta da Carlo figlio di Re Roberto negli anni 1326 e 1327', *Archivio storico per le provincie napoletane* xxxiii (1908), 441, BNF Magliab. xxv, 19, c. 32ʳ., G. Villani, *Cronica*, ix. 333.

[63] G. Villani, *Cronica*, ix. 336. I follow Davidsohn, *Storia*, iv. 1039 n. 1 in rendering the chroniclers' Piero di Narsi as Pierre de Naix.

[64] G. Villani, *Cronica*, ix. 329.

[65] Ibid., ix. 336.

relieved Signa four days after Pierre de Naix had laid siege to it, but also struck south at the Val di Pesa on 19 February and, on the twenty-fifth, with an army increased by reinforcements, swept once again along the north bank of the Arno to Peretola. Having thus demonstrated his continuing mastery over the military situation, he withdrew, not merely from the outskirts of Florence but back to more easily defensible positions on the Pistoian *contado*. On 28 February he abandoned Signa, razing that town, destroying its bridge across the Arno, and withdrawing with his men to Carmignano.[66]

Pierre de Naix, foiled so far in his efforts to gain a victory against Castruccio, attempted one more coup in May, to vindicate his reputation before he lost his command to Charles of Calabria's vicar. In so doing, he fell into a trap, neatly laid for him by his adversary. Lured to Carmignano on 14 May by the prospect that it would be surrendered to him by some of Castruccio's remaining Burgundian mercenaries, he found himself and his detachment of two hundred cavalry and five hundred infantry ambushed by a superior Lucchese force. Captured together with two other constables, eleven knights, forty squires, and many foot-soldiers, he was taken to Pistoia where Castruccio had him beheaded, allegedly because he had broken his word, given on his release from prison, not to engage in further hostilities against the lord of Lucca.[67]

The blow of Pierre de Naix's débâcle before Carmignano was softened for the Florentines by the arrival in their city some days later of Charles' vicar Walter of Brienne, with his escort of cavalry and infantry.[68] His master, the duke of Calabria, was to leave Naples at the end of May and proceed by slow stages to his destination in Florence which he did not reach till the end of July.[69] Castruccio had, therefore, considerable time to prepare for the change in the military situation in Tuscany which the Neapolitan prince's entry into the region would

[66] Ibid., ix. 338–9.

[67] Ibid., ix. 350, and BNF Magliab. xxv, 19, c. 33ʳ.

[68] G. Villani, *Cronica*, ix. 351, and BNF Magliab. xxv, 19, c. 33ʳ. Walter of Brienne was appointed vicar and captain of war in Florence on 26 April (Bevere, 'La signoria', xxxiii. 448–9), when the force under his command was to consist of 100 cavalry and 50 infantry. Villani states, however, that he reached Florence with 400 knights. There is also some disagreement as to the exact date of his arrival, given by Villani and BNF MS Palat. 571, c. 23ᵛ. as 17 May and by BNF Magliab. xxv, 19 as the twenty-third of that month.

[69] He appears to have left Naples on 31 May and arrived in Florence on 30 July (Bevere, 'La signoria', xxxiii. 451–3, and G. Villani, *Cronica*, ix. 333 and 421). He had reached Siena much earlier on 10 July (G. Villani, *Cronica*, ix. 356), but had remained there till the twenty-eighth (Bevere, loc. cit.)

bring. His response to this new challenge seemed at first uncharacter-
istically defensive and conciliatory. He dismantled his most exposed
fortresses along his frontier with his enemy and, when the papal legate
Cardinal Giovanni Orsini visited Pisa at the end of June 1326, he
attempted to use this prelate as an intermediary in peace negotiations
with the Florentines.[70] Understandably distrustful of his intentions,
they, however, rebuffed these initiatives. Doubtless they recalled not
only his recent devastation of their *contado*, but also his election,
earlier in the year, as captain of their city's exiled imperial faction.
For, even as Castruccio had been preparing to withdraw from Signa
and to burn it at the end of February, the Florentine Ghibellines had
met there on the twenty-fourth of that month to offer him the office of
their leader which he had formally accepted in Lucca on 7 March.[71]
Therefore, while on the one hand making peace overtures to his
enemies, he had also been at the same time laying the foundations of
future claims to their territories.

The ambivalence of the Lucchese tyrant's actions at this stage
reflected the growing difficulty of the situation in which he found himself. While militarily still fairly secure, thanks to the careful guard kept
over his frontiers, he was once again compelled to recognize the
disparity between the resources at his disposal and those available to
his two formidable opponents, Florence and the kingdom of Naples.
The range of operation of the powers with which he was confronted
was brought home to him when, at the beginning of July 1326, a
Neapolitan fleet suddenly appeared off the Ligurian coast and
assailed his outposts on the eastern extremity of the Genoese Riviera.
Levanto and Lerici were attacked and burnt down by this naval
expedition which also lingered some time in the Gulf of La Spezia,
contemplating a landing in Lunigiana. At the begining of September
this plan was abandoned as too risky because that region was amply
garrisoned by strong detachments of both cavalry and infantry.[72]
Nevertheless, the fact that it was considered underlined the vulner-

---

[70] G. Villani, *Cronica*, ix. 353. Cardinal Orsini arrived in Pisa on 23 June and went on
from there to Florence which he reached on the thirty-first of that month.

[71] ASL Capitoli no. 4, cc. 50ʳ.–52ʳ. and Atti di Castruccio no. 1, cc. 74ᶜ.–76ʳ.,
Lazzareschi, 'Documenti', 367–72.

[72] G. Villani, *Cronica*, ix. 352, BNF MS Magliab. xxv, 19, c. 33ʳ. The fleet which had
left Naples on 22 May had earlier landed troops on the Maremman coast. From there it
sailed to Portovenere, then still held by the Genoese Guelphs, and on along the Riviera
di Levante, returning to the Gulf of La Spezia in August and leaving it at the beginning
of September.

ability of Castruccio's position. The lack of co-ordination between this projected sea-borne assault and the movements of Charles of Calabria's land-based forces, then still stationed in Florence, had neutralized the effectiveness of what might otherwise have been a double-pronged offensive, forcing the Lucchese ruler to divide his meagre forces to defend simultaneously the opposite ends of his territories. But the danger remained of the revival of such a potentially serious threat to him. He could meet it, in fact, only by putting into effect two seemingly contradictory strategies, in the short term resorting to defensive, delaying tactics, but in the long run aiming to counterbalance the advantage the Florentines had gained in enlisting the support of the Neapolitan monarchy by seeking comparable outside aid for himself, which in fact could only come from his imperial protector, Ludwig of Bavaria. Until that ruler could be induced to enter Italy, he had to hold out as best he could and might need to make concessions to preserve his previous gains. If, on the other hand, Ludwig could be persuaded to come to his assistance, then another alternative set of policies could be put into operation in which Castruccio could play the role of the protagonist of the imperial power in central Italy; and this contingency demanded the continued assertion of his claims as the champion of Ghibellinism in that region.

Fortunately for him, the problems that he faced were largely resolved by the dilatoriness and ineffectuality as a military commander of his new opponent, Charles of Calabria. Roughly a year was to separate that prince's election as lord of Florence from the parliament of Trent at which Ludwig of Bavaria agreed to embark on his Italian expedition. Yet, in that period, little was done by the Guelphs to exploit Castruccio's vulnerability. Charles himself, from his entry into Tuscany on 10 July, appeared to be more concerned with extending his authority over the communes he had come to defend than with vigorously prosecuting the war against his enemy.

Negotiations over questions of jurisdiction and the reconciliation of the Salimbeni and the Tolomei delayed him for eighteen days in Siena.[73] When he finally reached Florence, on 30 July, he left his forces inactive while he bargained with the commune over his right to appoint civic officials and to readmit rebels and exiles to the city.[74] This delay in pressing home the advantage his superior numbers gave

---

[73] G. Villani, *Cronica*, ix. 356.
[74] Ibid., x. 1-2.

him was all the more surprising in that it occurred in August, the very month in which Robert of Naples's fleet was standing by in the Gulf of La Spezia waiting to land troops in Lunigiana and in which, according to Giovanni Villani, Castruccio lay seriously ill with an infected leg.[75] It was not until after Charles of Calabria's demands had been met and he had formally been installed as lord of Florence on 1 September[76] that he began to make preparations for hostilities against the Lucchese tyrant.

With a thousand of his own knights, five hundred from Florence, and contingents of three hundred and fifty cavalry from Siena, three hundred from Perugia, two hundred from Bologna, a hundred each from Orvieto and Faenza, not to mention infantry levies from Florence and its *contado*,[77] he had a formidable army at his disposal. It was characteristic of him that he chose to begin his campaign not by using it in a frontal attack on his enemy but with two diversionary attacks in Castruccio's rear carried out by others. In October, he induced Spinetta Malaspina, exiled lord of part of Lunigiana, to attempt to recover his lost territories, providing him for that purpose with three hundred knights paid for by Florence, two hundred from the forces of the papal legate in Lombardy, and a hundred lent him by Can Grande della Scala at whose court that marquis had lived since being expelled from his lands. With these troops, Spinetta crossed the Apennines and laid siege to his former castle of Verrucola Bosi. The preceding September,[78] Charles had also instigated the seizure by some of the Pistoian Guelphs of two mountain villages north of Pistoia, Gavinana and Mammiano. The duke's plan was evidently to tie Castruccio's forces down, dealing with these outbreaks of resistance to him in Lunigiana and in the Apennine foothills, so weakening the Lucchese line of defence between Montemurlo and Carmignano towards which the bulk of the Florentine army could then advance. This strategy of dividing the enemy's resources before attacking him,

[75] Ibid., x. 16.

[76] Ibid., x. 2. See Bevere, 'La signoria', xxxiii. 459–64, and ASF Provvisioni no. 23, c. 1ʳ. and ᵛ. for the final terms of his appointment, decided on 29 August, for the period of ten years from 1 September 1326.

[77] G. Villani, *Cronica*, x. 1.

[78] Mammiano was already besieged by Castruccio on 2 October (Bevere, 'La signoria', xxxiii. 654) and would have been invested long enough at that date for messengers to have gone there and back from Florence by that date. The rebellion of the Pistoian Guelphs who held it and Gavinana must therefore have begun in September. (This is confirmed by BNF MS Magliab. xxv, 19, c. 33ᵛ.). Mammiano was still under siege on 9 October (Bevere, 'La signoria', xxxiii. 657).

though sound in theory, was, however, flawed in practice because it took insufficient account of Castruccio's ability to exploit both his internal lines of communication and the qualities of the terrain. While holding off the main Guelph thrust before Pistoia with relatively small garrisons entrenched in strong defensive positions, he could deal one by one with the other sectors where his power was challenged. Their topographical isolation was such that there was little danger of effective Florentine support to the rebels in either area, all the more so since the delays in Charles's initiation of the campaign made its beginning coincide with the onset of winter which made impassable the mountain roads leading to where Spinetta Malaspina and the Pistoian Guelphs were fighting. Whilst Castruccio had easy access to Verrucola Bosi along the Magra river and its tributaries and to Gavinana and Mammiano from the Val di Lima, the duke of Calabria could only send supplies and reinforcements to his remotely placed allies across major natural obstacles or through passes held by his enemies.

Having provisioned Verrucola for a long siege, the Lucchese tyrant turned his attention first to Mammiano and Gavinana around which he put 'battifolli' or stockades. Their defenders immediately appealed to the Florentines for help; but attempts to get this through to them proved unsuccessful. First, Biagio dei Tornaquinci was despatched with three hundred knights and five hundred infantry to relieve the two besieged villages, but, while attempting to cross the mountains, he and his men were forced back by early winter snows. Then, the main body of the duke's army moved to Prato and from there sent another slighly larger detachment of three hundred cavalry and a thousand foot-soldiers to penetrate the Lucchese defences north of Pistoia. But these also encountered the most inhospitable weather, ran short of food, and, fearful of being ambushed or having their line of retreat cut when Castruccio seized the passes in their rear, withdrew rapidly across the Apennines, leaving their baggage train behind, and made for Bologna. In the meantime, Charles of Calabria had marched with the remainder of his forces to the gates of Pistoia and then east to encamp before the Lucchese-held village of Montale. They remained there for three days before being washed out by heavy rain and lashed by furious winds—after which they promptly returned to Prato. Failing to get help and hearing of the retreat, of both the two relief expeditions and the bulk of the Florentine army, the defenders of Mammiano and Gavinana lost heart and decided to abandon their strongholds, fleeing under cover of night. In the subsequent pursuit, most of them were captured or killed by the Lucchese who commanded the passes. Castruccio was therefore easily able to crush all resistance to him in the area and leave a small garrison to hold the Pistoian foothills. He was then free to descend the Val di Lima and make his way up the Serchio towards the mountains where Verrucola was still holding out against Spinetta Malaspina. When that marquis heard of his approach, he raised the siege of his former castle and withdrew towards Parma before his opponent could cut his line of retreat into Lombardy.[79] On his arrival at the scene, the Lucchese tyrant consequently found that his enemy had retired without a fight.

When Charles of Calabria ingloriously returned to Florence on 20 October, he was thus compelled to recognize the complete failure of the strategy on which he had based his campaign. He had been defeated partly by the weather, in small measure by Castruccio himself, but most of all by his own lack of understanding of the physical environment in which he had chosen to fight. His adversary was a past master in exploiting mountainous terrain, in bottling up the separate detachments of enemy forces between natural obstacles, to passage between which he held the key, and then repulsing or eliminating each body of troops by establishing a local tactical superiority over it, while holding his front in other sectors through carefully thought out defensive dispositions. The duke had played into Castruccio's hands in adopting tactics that suited his opponent's favoured form of warfare. In so doing, he had, besides, lost the opportunity to mount an effective offensive against his enemy before the winter rains set in, leaving himself with the prospect of resuming the war the following spring when, in all likelihood, the balance of power in Italy would have changed to the benefit of the Ghibellines as a result of the entry of Ludwig of Bavaria into the country. None of these considerations seem, however, very much to have preoccupied Charles of Calabria who continued, through the early months of his lordship over Florence, to concern himself primarily with the consolidation of his position as ruler over Guelph Tuscany and the securing of its defences. On 14 September he set about rebuilding the fortresses to the west of his capital, such as Signa,[80] which Castruccio had demolished in the course of his

[79] The above account is based on G. Villani, *Cronica*, x. 6, backed by BNF MS Magliab. xxv, 19, c. 33ᵛ.–34ʳ. and BNF MS Palat. 571, c. 24ᵛ. Giovanni Villani was elected one of the *ufficiali per le gabelle* in Florence on 13 September 1326 (Bevere, 'La signoria', xxxiii. 645) and would therefore have been relatively well informed on government business at this period.

[80] G. Villani, *Cronica*, x. 5.

strategic withdrawal the previous February. In January and February 1327, Prato and the Val d'Elsa towns of San Miniato, San Gimignano, and Colle were induced formally to accept the duke's authority, which completed his acquisition of legal sovereignty over all the non-Ghibelline Tuscan communes.[81]

At roughly the same time, on 21 January, a minor expedition was mounted against Pistoia, through the Val di Bure, by a force of eight hundred knights under the command of Count Guido Novello. This reached the gates of that city, destroying a barbican and then devastating the country and wrecking mills on its way back to the Florentine lines.[82] Apart from such token hostilities against Castruccio, Charles of Calabria remained militarily inactive through the winter, so much so that his opponent was left free to undertake one or two minor ventures of his own. At the beginning of 1327, on 5 January, the latter attempted to seize Vicopisano from the Pisans by sending a hundred and fifty knights, led by one of their rebels, Benedetto Maccaioni de' Lanfranchi, to surprise the place. These troops were admitted to it through treachery, but later driven out by its inhabitants and defenders.[83] Early in February Castruccio was more successful in a similar collaboration with exiles sympathetic to his cause, when some Genoese Ghibellines with his support took Sestri Levante, which he then incorporated within his Ligurian dominions.[84]

Charles of Calabria thus proved as ineffective in restraining Castrucio's military ventures as he did in attacking him. For all that, the duke's presence in Tuscany continued to be essential to the Florentines as a means of protection against the Lucchese tyrant. Sensing this, the Neapolitan prince exploited their fear of Castruccio by extracting more money from his new subjects, receiving a further 30,000 florins from them to raise 800 more knights to serve under him.[85] Between him and his Castracani enemy there developed in fact a kind of symbiotic relationship: he needed the threat the lord of Lucca posed to the Florentines as a means of putting pressure on them to get what he wanted,[86] while Castruccio for his part owed the

[81] Ibid., x. 14.
[82] Ibid., x. 15, Bevere, 'La signoria', xxxiv. 602.
[83] G. Villani, *Cronica*, x. 13.
[84] Ibid., x. 16, Finke, *Acta*, ii. 637.
[85] G. Villani, *Cronica*, x. 10, Bevere, 'La signoria', xxxiv. 210–12, Ficker, *Urkunden*, 27–8.
[86] The exploitation of Florentine tax resources by Charles of Calabria has been ably described by Davidsohn (*Storia*, iv. 1061–7) and by B. Barbadoro in his *Le finanze della*

continued preservation of his state, at least for the time being, to the studied half-heartedness of the duke's conduct of hostilities. The Lucchese ruler realized, however, that he could not permanently count on the dilatoriness of his enemy's prosecution of the war against him. Sooner or later, the greater weight of resources available to the Guelphs would overwhelm him unless outside help allowed him to redress the balance. For this reason, in the winter of 1326–7, the prospect of Ludwig of Bavaria's arrival in Italy became more and more attractive to him.

Already in December 1326, when the emperor-elect was at Innsbruck, Castruccio had, if one can believe a Florentine report, dispatched an envoy to that city to urge the German ruler to cross the Alps,[87] and certainly the Lucchese tyrant's ambassadors were present in February 1327 at the parliament at Trent at which the Ghibelline princes of Italy obtained from Ludwig an undertaking, in return for a grant of 150,000 florins, that he would enter Italy and proceed to his imperial coronation in Rome.[88] Unlike Can Grande della Scala of Verona, Azzo and Marco Visconti of Milan, and Rinaldo and Opizo d'Este of Ferrara, Passerino Bonaccolsi of Mantua, and Guido Tarlati of Arezzo, Castruccio appears not to have attended this meeting in person[89] and, at this stage, his standing among Ludwig's Italian supporters would have been inferior to that of the great Lombard despots. Nevertheless, the fact that it was primarily as a counterpoise to Charles of Calabria that the Bavarian monarch had been invited to Italy already placed the lord of Lucca in a key position as potentially at least Ludwig's most effective ally in his Italian venture. It would be some time before the emperor-elect could come to Tuscany since observance of the ritual stages of his coronation demanded that he should be crowned in Milan before being finally invested with the

---

repubblica fiorentina (Florence, 1929), 381–400, 551–71). On this question, see also Bevere, 'La signoria', xxxiii. 658, xxxiv. 202–4, 212, 219, 612–14, 618, 629, xxxv. 33, 222, xxxvi. 273–5, ASF Provvisioni, no. 23, cc. 9ᵛ., 11ᵛ., 23ᵛ., 65ᵛ., 99ʳ.–100ᵛ., ASF Liber Fabarum no. 13, c. 18ʳ., G. Villani, *Cronica*, x. 30.

[87] Davidsohn, *Storia*, iv. 1088, E. A. Winkelmann, *Acta imperii inedita saeculi xiii et xiv* (Innsbruck, 1880–5), ii. 306.

[88] G. Villani, *Cronica*, x. 18, gives 16 February as the date of Ludwig's formal promise to come to Italy. On the twenty-fourth of the same month, he wrote to Frederick of Sicily announcing his decision to that ruler (J. F. Boehmer, *Fontes rerum germanicarum* (Stuttgart, 1843–68), i. 195).

[89] At least according to G. Villani, *Cronica*, x. 18. Cortusio, 'Historia', *RIS*, xii. col. 839 and Albertino Mussato, 'De gestis italicorum', *RIS*, x. col. 770, do, however, list him among those at Trent.

imperial insignia in Rome. But when he did, his presence in the region would serve no one's interests better than Castruccio's. The latter had only to wait for his protector's arrival, through the spring, summer, and early autumn of 1327, trying over that period to fend off the Florentines as best he could until Ludwig came to his aid and enabled him to resume his expansionist policies. In these critical months the Lucchese ruler reverted to his classic defensive strategy. He conserved his limited resources by abandoning and dismantling exposed fortresses to avoid wasting troops on garrisoning them. Thus, at the end of 1326, he withdrew from Montefalcone on the Usciana and Montale near Pistoia.[90] At the same time he reduced the number of castles he kept manned in Lunigiana. With Ludwig still in Milan between March and August,[91] he was vulnerable to a large-scale Florentine attack through the summer of 1327, and he countered this threat, as he had done in 1325, by holding the heights above the Val di Nievole, hoping that his enemy might once again be trapped there.

But Charles of Calabria, who lacked the boldness of Ramon de Cardona and, in 1327, was advised by two prudent marshals, Filippo di Sangineto and Guglielmo di Agello of Salerno,[92] preferred a more cautious mode of warfare. Despite intensive military preparations between March and May,[93] the duke's first serious move against Castruccio in the summer of 1327, like that of his campaign of the previous year, was to attempt to instigate a rebellion in his enemy's rear and then to intervene in support of it. On this occasion, it was the disgruntled Lucchese *consorteria* of the Quartigiani who were persuaded to rise against the tyrant whom they had helped to instal in power in 1316. The plot hatched with them was, however, soon discovered and the attack on Lucca associated with it abandoned.[94]

Foiled in his efforts to overthrow Castruccio by stealth, Charles of Calabria was compelled to resort to open warfare. But he took the field

[90] G. Villani, *Cronica*, x. 6.

[91] Ibid., x. 18, 19. The emperor left Trent on 13 March and went from there by way of Como to Milan which he did not leave until 12 August. See also J. F. Boehmer, *Fontes*, i. 169, for a letter written by Ludwig to William of Holland from Trent on 13 March.

[92] Filippo di Sangineto was appointed on 30 December 1326 and replaced by Guglielmo di Agello on 16 April 1327 (Bevere, 'La signoria', xxxiv. 320, xxxv. 11). Sangineto, who left Florence for Lombardy, was urged to return to the duke's service on 21 May (ibid., xxxv. 38) and presumably did so shortly afterwards since his presence was then urgently requested.

[93] Ibid., xxxiv. 634–5, 637, xxxv. 4–5, 15–19, 21, 24–31, 40.

[94] G. Villani, *Cronica*, x. 25, BNF MS Palat. 571, c. 24ᵛ. On this conspiracy, see also pp. 96–7 above.

with his customary tardiness. His preparations for the summer
campaign which had in effect begun in late March were prolonged
until his large army was ready to leave Florence on 25 July. More than
a month earlier, on 22 June, the infantry levies from the *contado* had
been summoned to Florence.[95] Five days later, the duke's officials
were given authority to requisition food to supply his troops.[96] On 5
July, the French and Provençal mercenaries who had come by sea and
travelled over Sienese territory arrived in Florence.[97] By the time
everything was ready for the attack on Castruccio, Charles had
assembled a force of thirteen hundred of his own cavalry, together
with three or four hundred mounted Florentine mercenaries and eight
thousand infantry. He reviewed these troops in the Piazza Santa
Croce and then ordered them to march to Signa, near which they
encamped for three days. He evidently intended to give the impression that he was about to invade the Pistoian *contado*. In fact, however,
the movement in this direction was a feint to cover an attack on Santa
Maria a Monte, south of Lucca. Leaving their tents up to deceive the
enemy, his men slipped out of their camp at nightfall and marched
through the hours of darkness by way of Montelupo towards their
destination. A body of four hundred knights from the Val d'Elsa joined
them north of Fucecchio and together they crossed the Usciana the
following day on a wooden bridge which had been put up by a forward
party during the night.

From here, it was a relatively short distance to Santa Maria a Monte
which was promptly invested. The besieging force was soon reinforced by another three hundred and fifty cavalry sent in aid of the
Florentines by the Bolognese and the papal legate in Lombardy.
Infantry levies from allied communes also swelled the Guelph army
until it numbered nearly two and a half thousand horse and twelve
thousand foot. With a force of this size surrounding the town, the
Florentines could be confident that Castruccio would not be able to
relieve it. The Lucchese tyrant remained meanwhile on the heights of
Vivinaia above Altopascio, expecting Santa Maria e Monte to hold out
for some time and so tie down his enemy's forces. The place was well
defended, being amply provisioned, having a garrison of five hundred,
and boasting three concentric rings of fortifications. But the energy of
the Florentine attack on it took him by surprise. This was conducted

[95] Bevere, 'La signoria', xxxv. 214–15.
[96] Ibid., xxxv. 217.
[97] BNF MS Magliab. xxv, 19, c. 35ʳ.

not by Charles of Calabria who, as Giovanni Villani disarmingly put it, had remained in Florence since it was 'beneath the dignity of a duke to besiege a mere castle', but by his captain, identified by the chronicler as 'Conte Novello di Monte-Scheggioso e d'Andri' but in fact Bertrand de Baux, count of Monte Caveoso and Andria. Under the direction of this obscure and underrated commander, the normal procedure of trying to force the surrender of a castle by besieging it was abandoned in favour of a direct assault. On 2 August, the third circuit of walls, enclosing the *borghi*, was stormed by a combined force of dismounted knights, infantry, and archers who then moved directly to the second, from which they also drove the defenders after having scaled the ramparts with ladders. The garrison and surviving inhabitants withdrew into the citadel which held out for a further eight days before surrendering on terms when it became clear that there was no prospect of their being relieved.[98]

The taking of the *rocca* of Santa Maria a Monte on 10 August alarmed Castruccio because of the speed with which it had been accomplished. However, remarkable though it was as a feat of arms, the capture of the town did not serve any strategic purpose since the road to Lucca lay not through it but through the Val di Nievole, access through which Castruccio still commanded by virtue of his control over the strong points that dominated it. (The Bientina marshes, lying behind the ridge on which Santa Maria a Monte stood, cut it off from the Lucchese plain.) Symbolically, its recovery by the Florentines was significant, for it was one of the places left in the hands of the Lucchese exiles by the treaty of peace between King Robert of Naples and Lucca in 1317 which Castruccio had taken in 1320 at the very time when he had first assumed lordship of his town and gone to war with the Guelphs. But militarily, its acquisition merely strengthened the line of Florentine defences north of the Arno without immediately threatening Lucca.

Its captors, following their victory, at first appeared to be making a direct thrust at their enemy's capital. On 18 August they marched to Fucecchio, remained encamped outside it for two days, then suddenly recrossed the Usciana into the plain of Altopascio where they drew themselves up in battle order at Galleno, trumpeting and challenging Castruccio to descend from the hills to fight them. The latter, who had

[98] Ibid., G. Villani, *Cronica*, x. 29, BNF MS Palat. 571, c. 24ᵛ. For the identification of Bertrand de Bauce (or Baux), who was appointed captain on 4 June 1327, see Ficker, *Urkunden*, 40, Bevere, 'La signoria', xxxv, 247, 617 and xxxvi. 12.

only eight hundred knights and ten thousand infantry to his enemy's two and a half thousand cavalry and twelve thousand foot-soldiers, chose wisely to stay where he was and the Florentines, perhaps remembering their rout two years earlier, a mere mile or two along the road towards Lucca, retreated three days later. By this time Ludwig of Bavaria had left Milan and had reached the Po[99] and the danger that, like Azzo Visconti in 1325, he might quickly cross the Apennies to give Castruccio the tactical superiority he needed for victory doubtless made them pause. So they once again withdrew south of the Usciana, passed around the Monte Albano hills, and besieged Artimino, a fortified village which, together with Carmignano and Tizzana, guarded the south-eastern approaches to Pistoia.

On 26 August, the third day of their investment of this place, the duke's forces stormed it: in the course of an assault lasting from noon to evening they failed to take it but burnt its wooden defences and gate. This left the town so exposed that those holding it surrendered the following morning.[100] The capture of Artimino crowned the campaign with a second victory within the space of three weeks; but it was to be the last for some time. Hearing that Ludwig of Bavaria was approaching Pontremoli, Charles of Calabria recalled his army to Florence on 28 August. His troops had distinguished themselves in the two brief sieges and assaults in which they had participated, but the gains they had made had not seriously weakened Castruccio's position nor threatened either of the cities the latter controlled.

Disturbed though he almost certainly was by the loss of Santa Maria a Monte and Artimino, the Lucchese tyrant must have been relieved that these Florentine successes were not followed up by a reduction of Carmignano and Tizzana and an attack on Pistoia. With Ludwig about to enter Tuscany, he had in fact escaped fairly lightly, thanks to the slow start of Charles of Calabria's campaign against him. This had cancelled out the effects of the emperor's prolonged delay in

---

[99] On 23 August, when the Florentine army withdrew from Galleno, Ludwig crossed the Po between Cremona and Borgo San Donnino (G. Villani, *Cronica*, x. 32). Charles of Calabria took some pains to have his movements watched, as is evident from his payment of spies, who had sent back reports on Ludwig's progress through Lombardy (Bevere, 'La signoria', xxxiv. 631, 635, xxxv. 8, 21, 437, 438, 441, 443, 448, 451, 607, 616, 617, 622–3. See also Ficker, *Urkunden*, 38–40 for references to Ludwig's journey across Lombardy in letters addressed to Charles of Calabria and the pope).

[100] G. Villani, *Cronica*, x. 30, BNF MSS Magliab. xxv, 19, c. 35ʳ. and Palat. 571, c. 24ᵛ. Where these sources differ as to dates I have accepted Villani's chronology because of the greater detail and circumstantiality of his narrative.

Milan, due to his involvement in that city's politics. After the Bavarian prince had been crowned there on 31 May, he had demanded from Galeazzo Visconti that tyrant's share of the 150,000 florins promised him at Trent and, on being refused immediate payment, began to intrigue with Galeazzo's enemies to such effect that on 6 July he managed to depose him and his family from power. This done, he was able to extract 50,000 florins from the new Milanese regime which he installed, as a reward for its establishment, and was promised a further 25,000 (of which 16,000 was paid) by Luchino and Azzo Visconti as the price of their liberation from the prison to which, with Galeazzo, he had confined them. Having now enough money to pay his troops, he called another parliament of Lombard and Tuscan Ghibelline rulers to justify to them his actions in Milan. This met at Orcinuovo near Brescia on 13 August and was attended by Can Grande della Scala, Passerino Bonaccolsi, Rinaldo d'Este, and Guido Tarlati, as well as by Castruccio's ambassadors. Because by this time Lucca appeared to be in some danger, owing to the successful Florentine attack on Santa Maria a Monte, and perhaps because the fate of the Visconti had somewhat cooled the eagerness of the other Lombard tyrants to have him visit their cities, it was resolved at this congress that the emperor should go directly to Tuscany and receive a further subsidy of 200,000 florins to meet the cost of maintaining his army there. His forces were to consist of fifteen hundred knights of his own, together with contingents of two hundred and fifty from Verona, a hundred and fifty from Mantua, and one hundred from Ferrara, making two thousand cavalry in all. After having passed through Cremona, Borgo San Donnino, and the *contado* of Parma, Ludwig reached Pontremoli with this body of troops on 1 September to be met there by Castruccio.[101]

The emperor's entry into the Lucchese state at this frontier outpost gave the Ghibellines, for the first time since Charles of Calabria's arrival in Florence, a tactical advantage in Tuscany. With Ludwig's two thousand knights, Castruccio's eight hundred, and detachments from Arezzo and other allied powers, they disposed of over three thousand cavalry which more than matched the strength in mounted troops of their Guelph enemies. Instead, however, of directing this force against Florence, Ludwig and Castruccio chose to employ it, paradoxically, against that traditional Tuscan bastion of Ghibellinism,

[101] G. Villani, *Cronica*, x. 32. BNF MS Magliab. xxv, 19, c. 35ʳ. gives the number of knights as 2,500. Sardo, *Cronaca*, 80, states that the amount Ludwig of Bavaria demanded from Galeazzo Visconti was 50,000 florins. See also 'Storie pistoresi', 112–14.

Pisa. The circumstances that led to this surprising turn of events are complex but may be attributable to three principal factors—first, Castruccio's ability to use Ludwig in the furtherance of his own designs over the maritime city, secondly, the emperor's ever-present need for money, and, thirdly, the virtual policy of friendship with Naples and Florence which the Pisans had pursued since their rupture with Lucca and the Aragonese attack on Sardinia. Although their ambassadors had been present at Trent among the leaders of the other Ghibelline powers of Lombardy and Tuscany, their main purpose at the parliament held there had been to try to bribe Ludwig not to enter their city if he came to Italy.[102] Furthermore, when the emperor was crowned in Milan and news of that event had been celebrated in Pisa by Ghibelline exiles, some sections of the lower classes, and Castruccio's supporters, the 'popolani ricchi' dominating the government had, according to Giovanni Villani,[103] become alarmed and had expelled from the town those elements of the population suspected of putting loyalty to the emperor above obedience to the prevailing regime, including the German mercenaries in the republic's pay. Whatever the truth of this claim, there is no doubt that, under the semblance of a traditional Ghibelline posture, the rulers of Pisa had for some time maintained a policy of friendly neutrality, verging on alliance, with the Guelphs, and therefore found the prospect of Ludwig's imminent arrival at their gates acutely embarrassing. Their *entente* with Naples and Florence had grown up gradually and almost imperceptibly within the general texture of an Italian political scene still dominated by Guelph and Ghibelline rivalries. As early as mid-1323, the visit to Pisa of the prince of Taranto, brother of King Robert of Naples, signalled the beginning of a shift in the city's diplomatic position,[104] confirmed the following May when the Neapolitan monarch himself called in at Porto Pisano, on his way home from Genoa.[105] Charles of Calabria's correspondence, while lord of Florence, bears witness to his intimate relations with Pisa.[106] Of parti-

[102] G. Villani, *Cronica*, x. 18.
[103] Ibid., x. 24.
[104] Finke, *Acta*, iii. 444–5.
[105] Caggese, *Roberto d'Angiò*, i. 71. The stay of the king in Pisa occurred between 22 April when he was in Genoa and 5 June when he was already back in Naples. (See also G. Villani, *Cronica*, ix. 249, who gives the date of Robert's visit as May 1324.)
[106] On 6 September 1325, Charles of Calabria wrote to the commune of Pisa to ask for payment of money promised three years earlier. On the same date he asked the Genoese to restore to the Pisans a ship which they had captured from them (Bevere, 'La signoria', xxxiii. 641–2) while on 25 November (and again on the following 13 January)

cular interest is his letter of 17 May 1327 to that commune, informing it of Ludwig of Bavaria's intention to visit it and explicitly suggesting that that ruler be denied entry.[107]

It is clear from these contacts that an understanding had grown up between the Neapolitan royal family and the Pisans that each would aid and neither would offend the other. This, however, stopped short of an alliance, involving the obligation militarily to support each other, as had been made clear in February 1325 when King Robert of Naples had unsuccessfully asked the Pisans to contribute five galleys to the fleet which he was equipping for an expedition against Sicily[108] and later in April 1326 when that monarch declined an offer from Pisa to assume sovereignty over Sardinia and declare war on Aragon in return for a subsidy of 200,000 florins. King Robert's response to this latter suggestion—that he *would* lend fifty galleys to the Pisans if they made him their lord[109]—exposed the essential weakness of the tactic of trying to use the Neapolitans against the Aragonese. The price demanded, the sacrifice of communal liberty, was too high for the anticipated benefit of help against Aragon.

The maritime republic at this juncture found itself in a difficult position, compromised with the Ghibellines because of its overtures to King Robert of Naples, yet unable to count on his aid without losing all it might hope to gain with his support. Castruccio was well able to exploit the predicament in which the Pisans lay: if the approaches made to King Robert were known to the Aragonese, as they were, it is highly unlikely that the lord of Lucca would have been unaware of them. He, in turn, by intimating to Ludwig how things lay, could arouse that ruler's suspicions of the former Ghibelline commune which its unwillingness to admit him within its walls would only increase. Hence, the scene would be set for the siege of the city and its capture. The motives which led Ludwig so readily to fall in with the plans of the Lucchese tyrant are more difficult to fathom. He had no

the Genoese and the town of Portovenere were requested to free the Pisan merchants taken with this ship which had been carrying grain belonging to the commune of Pisa but destined for Provence (ibid., xxxiv. 201–2 and 416). In January 1327, there were, on the other hand, complaints to the Pisans at their seizure of a Genoese galley and demands that they suspend reprisals against Genoa (ibid., xxxiv. 419–20). On 14 March the commune of Pisa was thanked for ceding Montemassi and Marittima to Charles (ibid., xxxiv. 626).

[107] Ibid., xxxv. 34–5 and Ficker, *Urkunden*, 39–40.
[108] ASP Comune A50, cc. 70ᵛ.–71ᵛ.
[109] Finke, *Acta*, i. 421–2.

real interest in making Pisa subject to Lucca, as did Castruccio. His
actions seem rather to have been governed by considerations of short-
term expediency. He had originally left Trent, in Villani's words,
poor, 'with few of his troops, and short of money',[110] and had to make
his Italian venture finance itself. Having deposed the Visconti and
been dispatched south by the other Lombard despots, who were disin-
clined to give him much further monetary support, he in fact needed
Castruccio as much as Castruccio needed him, to secure his passage,
through hostile lands, to Rome and back. As for Pisa, his stay in Milan
had taught him something which both he and his successor Charles IV
were to put to good use in their journeys across the Alps, namely, that
the way to extract the most money from an Italian city was to change
its government. What those already enjoying power refused to part
with, those who owed their newly established authority to imperial
intervention would gladly hand over.

At the beginning of September 1327, when Ludwig and Castruccio
had left Pontremoli and reached Pietrasanta on the road to Lucca,
ambassadors were sent to Pisa to request that city to admit him. As
Giovanni Villani put it, the emperor 'did not wish to enter Lucca if he
did not first have the city of Pisa', which, however, according to that
chronicler, was ruled by the rich, the powerful, and the enemies of
Castruccio who did not want to obey Ludwig for fear of Castruccio
and the likely financial burdens imposed by Ludwig's visit, and so
refused entry to his envoys in order, allegedly, not to offend the
Church or to violate the peace with King Robert of Naples and the
Florentines. The Bavarian ruler took their reaction as an affront, as he
did their preparations to defend themselves against him, and determined to curb the recalcitrant city to his will. The veteran Tuscan
Ghibelline leader, Guido Tarlati, bishop of Arezzo, then sought to
mediate between Pisa and the emperor. Going to Ripafratta on the
northern confines of the Pisan state, he invited ambassadors to come
to him from the commune to resolve differences by negotiation. Three
distinguished citizens, Lemmo Sismondi, Albizzo da Vico, and Ser
Jacopo da Calci were duly sent to present the republic's proposals,
which were that Ludwig should be paid 60,000 florins in return for a
promise not to come to Pisa. Their failure to make any concessions on
the essential point of the emperor's entry into their city spelled the
doom of their mission and played into Castruccio's hands. No sooner

---

[110] G. Villani, *Cronica*, x. 18.

were the negotiations broken off than the Lucchese tyrant brushed aside the guarantees of safety granted to the ambassadors and seized them as they were returning home. His troops, along with Ludwig's, then crossed the Serchio and, on 6 September, laid siege to Pisa.[111] Guido Tarlati, discredited by the collapse of his efforts to reconcile the city with the emperor and mortally offended by Castruccio's violation of the safe conduct he had given the envoys, remained with the imperial army for the time being, but, having failed to regain his influence over the emperor, left it in disgust after the capture of Pisa. Before doing so, he traded insults with the Lucchese ruler in an exchange reported by Villani in which each accused the other of betraying the true cause of Ghibellinism.[112]

Pisa, against which Castruccio had so skilfully set the emperor, did not long hold out against the combined imperial and Lucchese armies. The speed with which the siege was laid prevented any effective Florentine aid. Charles of Calabria did transfer 3,000 florins to the Pisan government on 30 September to help pay its mercenaries, through the agents of the Bardi and Acciaiuoli companies in the city,[113] but otherwise contented himself with provisioning and repairing the fortifications of Santa Maria a Monte and other Florentine frontier posts.[114] The dispositions of the besieging forces would in any case have made it difficult to relieve the city. Ludwig placed his troops around the Borgo San Marco, south of the Arno, blocking the road to Florence, while Castruccio spread his from the Porta San Donnino to the Porta della Legazia north of the river and built two wooden bridges (one of them a pontoon) up and downstream from the city to allow for rapid transfers of soldiers from one bank to the other. Within a few days, the Lucchese and imperial forces were entrenched all around Pisa, while its *contado*, including Porto Pisano, was occupied by Ludwig's and Castruccio's men. With the support of exiles from the city sympathetic to their cause, they even managed to recruit infantry levies from subject villages to swell the numbers of the besieging army. Prosecuting the siege with great energy, they attacked the town's gates, attempted to undermine its walls, and employed various

[111] Ibid., x. 33, BNF MSS Magliab. xxv, 19, c. 35ᵛ., Palat. 571, cc. 24ᵛ.–25ʳ., Sardo, *Cronaca*, 80. See also 'Storie pistoresi', 114, which erroneously places Ludwig's visit to Lucca before the siege of Pisa.

[112] G. Villani, *Cronica*, x. 35. Guido Tarlati died in the Maremma, on his way home to Arezzo, on 21 October 1327.

[113] Ibid., x. 34, Bevere, 'La signoria', xxxv. 618.

[114] Bevere, 'La signoria', xxxv. 453–6, 448–9, 616, 625–7, 631–2.

engines of war against the city's defences. Their best weapon, however, turned out to be the divisions among Pisa's citizens whose
resolve to resist the emperor weakened with time and with the growing
awareness of the commune's political isolation. The architect of the
policy of outright opposition to Castruccio and of friendship with the
Guelphs, Nieri della Gherardesca, count of Donoratico, had died
some time earlier, probably in December 1325,[115] and Fazio, who had
replaced him as head of that dominant Pisan family, was the son of
Castruccio's former ally Gaddo and was soon to become that ruler's
son-in-law. He was the natural focus for a party which began, during
the siege, to press for accommodation with Ludwig. He was supported
by Vanni Buonconte, whose father Banduccio had been executed by
Uguccione della Faggiuola in 1314, and probably also by the pro-
Castruccian faction which had begun to emerge in the city as early as
the closing stages of Nieri della Gherardesca's life.[116] As a result of the
influence exerted by this segment of civic opinion, it was decided to
reopen negotiations with Ludwig and to offer him 60,000 florins,
together with the right to enter the city, in return for his promise to
preserve its communal institutions and to admit Castruccio and its
exiles only with the consent of its elected government. On 8 October,
the emperor formally accepted these terms and, three days later, on
Sunday 11 October, made his triumphant entry into Pisa, to be
welcomed at a mass in its cathedral by its citizens.

In just over a month the siege was thus concluded and the city
delivered to Ludwig, apparently without the dreaded change of
regime. But the Bavarian ruler, sworn though he was to maintain the
constitution of the republic and exclude its enemies from its capital,
found ways, as he had done in Milan, of slipping out of his promises
and professions of support to its governors through the simple device
of a carefully orchestrated revolution. Within three days of his admission to the city, fearful as much of a rising by the 'popolo minuto' as of
the imperial army, the Pisan authorities cancelled the conditions they
had earlier imposed on the emperor, proclaimed him their lord, and
allowed entry into the city by Castruccio and its exiles. Ludwig
responded to this generous capitulation by executing one of his own

[115] According to Sardo, *Cronaca*, 79, he died on 13 December 1325 (1326 Pisan style).
There is supporting evidence for this in a letter by P. de Abbacia to James II of Aragon
of 10 November 1325 which described Nieri as being mortally ill at that time (Finke,
Acta, ii. 640). On this, see also G. Rossi-Sabatini, *Pisa al tempo dei Donoratico*, 154–5.
[116] Finke, *Acta*, ii. 640.

constables who had killed the communal *bargello* in the course of the preceding disturbances, so playing Cesare Borgia to his unfortunate subordinate's Raniero d'Orca, and establishing his credentials as a rigorous and impartial defender of civic justice. He also opened the port of Pisa to merchants of all cities and countries, requiring only the payment of a duty of 8*d*. in the pound on all merchandise shipped through it. Attracting a certain measure of popularity by these gestures to good government and the encouragement of commerce, he was able to obtain in return from the commune, in addition to the 60,000 florins promised in the terms of surrender of the city, a further 100,000 (on Villani's reckoning) to pay for his journey to Rome, together with a subsidy of 20,000 florins from the Pisan clergy.[117]

With Pisa securely in Ludwig's hands, he was able to proceed to Lucca which he entered on 4 November 1327. According to Villani, he was received there with great honour and celebration and then taken by Castruccio on a tour of inspection of the eastern frontiers of the state the lord of Lucca had built up. The intention of this journey was evidently to bring home to the emperor the vulnerability of Florence to attack from the Lucchese strongholds on the Pistoian *contado* which dominated the plain on which that bastion of the Guelph cause stood. Ludwig was presumably duly impressed for, on 17 November, six days after returning to Lucca for the feast of St. Martin, its patron saint, he conferred on its lord, already imperial vicar over it and Pistoia, the further title of duke, not merely over those two cities but also over Luni and Volterra.[118] The last of these places was not, in fact, in Castruccio's possession, as Pistoia had not been when Ludwig had, earlier, in 1324, extended his authority over it, but lay beyond the eastern fringes of the Pisan *contado* in a direction where the Lucchese

---

[117] The foregoing account is mainly based on G. Villani, *Cronica*, x. 34, 37, and 48, Sardo, *Cronaca*, 80–1, BNF MSS Magliab. xxv, 19, c. 35ᵛ. and Palat. 571. c. 25ʳ. On the question of exactly how much Ludwig was paid by the Pisans, there is some discrepancy even in Villani's *Cronica*, since in x. 48 he speaks of a total of 200,000 florins, which the emperor extracted from them, though the three grants Villani specifically mentions of 60,000, 100,000, and 20,000 florins add up to only 180,000 florins. The Pisan records which note amounts levied by the commune in *prestanze* to raise the sum promised to Ludwig on 22 October 1327, but do not disclose that sum itself, suggest that 140,000 or 150,000 florins were collected in November and December of that year from the citizens of Pisa. (See ASP Comune A93, c. 2ʳ., 13ʳ., 18ᵛ., 23ᵛ., 24ᵛ., 33ʳ. and ᵛ.).

[118] G. Villani, *Cronica*, x. 37 which, however, states that Castruccio was proclaimed duke on St. Martin's day, that is, 11 November. The text of the imperial diploma granting the title which has survived in two versions (ASL Capitoli no. 4, cc. 15ʳ.–17ᵛ. and Diplomatico Tarpea, 17/11/1327) and is published in Lazzareschi, 'Documenti', 372–6, gives the correct date of 17 November.

tyrant's ambitions might next draw him. As yet, nothing was granted to him of Pisan territory, though on 3 December the emperor did transfer Sarzana and Rotina in Versilia and Montecalvoli and Pietracassa in the lower Val d'Arno from Pisan to Lucchese jurisdiction.[119] (It was not until the following May that Castruccio obtained from the emperor his vicariate over Pisa.) Nevertheless, despite this omission, Ludwig's elevation of the former *signore* of Lucca to the rank of duke (in return, so Villani claimed, for a grant of 50,000 florins,[120] but also in recognition of his part in the successful siege of Pisa and of his creation of a powerful Ghibelline state in Tuscany) was for Castruccio a critical step in his transformation from an elected to a dynastic ruler. The ducal title was a personal one and depended directly from the emperor; it was also hereditary and passed automatically down the male line. It conferred special rights and powers to appoint officials in all cities and towns within the duchy, to enact municipal statutes, provided they were consistent with divine and natural law, to have jurisdiction over rivers, ports, and the sea coast as well as over mineral-bearing deposits, to coin money, to enfeoff vassals, to grant knighthoods, to authorize judges and notaries, and to legitimize natural offspring.[121] Subject to homage to the emperor on the part of himself and his heirs, it gave Castruccio and his successors legal sovereignty in the territories he controlled, together with a presumptive claim to Volterra. Only the papacy's refusal to recognize the validity of his dukedom[122] detracted from the princely dignity he had acquired by virtue of this imperial privilege.

Having granted Castruccio his title, Ludwig returned to Pisa the following day[123] to prepare for his journey to Rome. There he found Jacopo Sbarra, the Lucchese merchant whom he had appointed his treasurer, busily collecting the money which the commune had promised him on 22 October,[124] and his *podestà* and governor, Baverio de' Salinguerra of Gubbio,[125] who was, on the emperor's departure, to become vicar-general on his behalf, both making good the effects of

[119] G. Villani, *Cronica*, x. 46.
[120] Ibid., x. 37.
[121] Lazzareschi, 'Documenti', 373.
[122] Ibid., 389.
[123] BNF MS Palat. 571, c. 25ʳ.
[124] ASP Comune A93, cc. 2ʳ., 13ʳ., and 18ᵛ.
[125] Baverio was *podestà* and governor-general of the city and *contado* of Pisa from the beginning of November till 17 December 1327 when he became imperial vicar-general in the city (ibid., cc. 1ʳ., 21ʳ., 23ᵛ.).

the siege and preparing for Ludwig's stay in the city.[126] By 15 December, the imperial army was ready to leave, but Castruccio, committed though he was to accompanying the emperor in return for the extraordinary favours received from him (which had been granted, one suspects, to bind the Lucchese ruler to lending his support to the Roman expedition) was reluctant to set forth. He found himself in a dilemma, owing as he did an immense obligation to Ludwig which he could not justifiably fail to fulfil, yet at the same time being well aware of the vulnerability of his state to both internal dissension and Florentine attack. He finally resolved his problem by deciding to wait in Lucca till he had news that Charles of Calabria, with the bulk of his army, was following Ludwig south into central Italy, and then to leave most of his troops guarding his dominions while he himself, with a picked force of three hundred knights and a thousand crossbowmen, caught up with the more slowly moving imperial host. Thus, the emperor's journey was delayed by Castruccio's unwillingness to come with him until he had, by his departure, set in motion also the duke of Calabria, drawing the latter away from Florence and so freeing Lucca from immediate military danger. Ludwig, not understanding his ally's careful tactical calculations, waited for six days at the abbey of Santo Remedio, three miles from Pisa, for Castruccio to appear. In the meantime, he sent forward parties ahead to seize the Maremma passes and when, on 21 December, there was still no sign of the Lucchese ruler, the emperor advanced south towards Rome. Hearing that Ludwig was already in the Maremma, Charles then announced on 24 December that he was about to return to the kingdom of Naples and four days later left Florence.[127] Castruccio was now free to move and did so rapidly: leaving a thousand knights to hold Lucca, Pistoia, and Pisa, he led his small force of thirteen hundred men in quick pursuit of Ludwig's much larger army, of which the cavalry alone numbered

---

[126] The record of communal expenditures for November–December 1327 refers to repairs to bridges (ibid., cc. 12ʳ., 19ᵛ., 21ʳ., 22ᵛ.), gates (c. 15ᵛ.) and towers (c. 26ʳ.) damaged during the siege and payments made to refurbish the emperor's quarters, as well as money spent to equip him with horses and their fodder (c. 3ʳ.). In addition there were many expenses associated with embassies (cc. 4ʳ., 14ᵛ., 17ᵛ.) and hospitality for both Ludwig and Castruccio (cc. 15ᵛ., 19ᵛ., 23ᵛ.).

[127] G. Villani, *Cronica*, x. 49. See also Bevere, 'La signoria', xxxvi. 262–3, for arrangements being made on 17 December to choose and pay councillors from Prato to accompany the duke on his journey to Naples, ibid., 271–2, for advances of nearly 22,000 florins from the Bardi and Acciaiuoli companies to finance the journey and the hiring of troops, and ibid., 426–7, for the appointment on 14 December of Filippo di Sangineto as captain and vicar-general in the duke's absence.

three thousand. He overtook it at Viterbo which the emperor, after a difficult passage over the Ombrone near Grosseto, had reached on 2 January 1328.[128]

He found the emperor negotiating with the Romans. The situation in the Eternal City at this stage favoured the Ghibellines. Early in 1327 the leading pro-Angevin nobles Napoleone Orsini and Stefano Colonna had been expelled in a coup which had brought to power the latter's brother Sciarra, who had been elected captain of the people and who ruled in association with a council of fifty-two 'popolani'. Later, in July, King Robert of Naples had tried to bring Rome back into the Guelph fold by dispatching his brother, the prince of Morea, to exert pressure on its inhabitants with his army of a thousand knights. But the ravaging of the city's surroundings and the imposition of a blockade on it had served only further to alienate the Romans. An attempt by the papal legate Cardinal Giovanni Orsini to mediate between them and King Robert at the end of August had proved unsuccessful, as had an assault on the city through the Vatican quarter, which was repulsed by Sciarra Colonna's partisans on 28 September.[129] Having reached the point of armed conflict with the prince's and the legate's forces, Sciarra's faction now therefore needed imperial support in case of further attacks by their Orsini enemies backed by Angevin troops. Hence, they had written to Ludwig while he still lay encamped at the abbey of Santo Remedio and, according to Villani, it had been their pleas to him to hasten to Rome before that city was surprised by Guelphs which had been responsible for his departure from there on 21 December.[130]

Ludwig was therefore entitled to expect an invitation to enter Rome. He had, however, to wait on the deliberations of the Council of Fifty-two which reflected the views not merely of the Colonna party but of other citizen groups. In it, opinion was divided between those who were unqualified advocates of the emperor's coming, those who were doubtful about it because it would incur the disapproval of the Church, and those who were prepared to allow his admission on terms dictated by the council. Eventually, it was resolved to send an embassy to Ludwig to lay down the conditions for his entry. But Sciarra and his

[128] G. Villani, *Cronica*, x. 48. BNF MS Magliab. xxv, 19, c. 30ʳ. gives Ludwig's date of departure from Pisa as 11 December as against the fifteenth according to Villani. Ludwig left Viterbo on 5 January (G. Villani, *Cronica*, x. 54), so Castruccio must have joined him between the second and fourth of that month.

[129] G. Villani, *Cronica*, x. 20, 21.

[130] Ibid., x. 48.

associates effectively undermined this decision by secretly com-
municating with the emperor and urging him to ignore the ambassadors and confront the fifty-two with a *fait accompli* by immediately
marching on Rome. This advice was taken and, as soon as the ambassadors had presented their proposals, Castruccio, acting on Ludwig's
behalf, ordered trumpets to be sounded to signal the advance of the
imperial army on the Eternal City and informed the embassy that this
was his reply to their demands. The envoys were then taken into
custody, all roads to Rome cut, and travellers proceeding there
detained to prevent news of Ludwig's approach reaching the city
before him. When he appeared with his forces outside its walls on 7
January, Sciarra Colonna's partisans opened the gates to him so that
he was able to make an unimpeded entry into the Vatican quarter.
Four days later, he crossed the Tiber to take up residence at Santa
Maria Maggiore and to be officially welcomed to the city by a parliament of his adherents on the Capitol. At this, it was resolved that his
coronation would take place the following Sunday, 17 January, in St.
Peter's.[131]

The ceremony was elaborately prepared to impress the Roman
populace and allay the doubts of those among them who might have
questioned its legitimacy in the absence of the pope. Roman senators,
including Sciarra Colonna, knights, the Council of Fifty-two, the
prefect of the city, judges, and nobles, all sumptuously robed,
advanced in solemn procession from Santa Maria Maggiore to the
Vatican along richly decorated streets. Once in St. Peter's, they and
the assembled public witnessed the investiture of Castruccio as count
of the Lateran Palace and the conferral of knighthoods on him and on
various other dignitaries. Then Ludwig was anointed, consecrated,
and crowned. As count of the Lateran Palace, Castruccio supported
Ludwig during the unction with holy oil and later held the golden
imperial crown, but he almost certainly did not place it on the
emperor's head as he is represented as doing, together with Sciarra
Colonna, in manuscript drawings allegedly based on a lost fresco in
the Castracani villa in Massa Pisana.[132] Villani's account implicitly
excludes this, and another chronicler[133] states that this culminating act

[131] Ibid., x. 54.
[132] Ibid., x. 55, *Monumenta Germaniae Historica Legum*, Sectio iv. vol. vi., pt. 1
(Hanover, 1914–27), pp. 285–6. On the fresco in the villa at Massa Pisana, see references
in n. 6 above.
[133] BNF MS Magliab. xxv, 19, c. 36ᵛ.

of the coronation was performed by four *sindachi* of the commune of Rome, presided over by Sciarra. The notion that the new duke of Lucca crowned Ludwig probably originates, therefore, in a confusion between him and one of these four men and a telescoping of his role as holder of the crown (by virtue of his position as Lateran count) with that of the representatives of the Roman republic who, by placing the symbol of *imperium* on his head, transmitted to the emperor the authority once vested in their ancient state.

Notwithstanding this, Castruccio undoubtedly played a crucial part in the ceremony in St. Peter's. He and Sciarra Colonna had clearly been the chief officiating figures at it, overshadowing by their presence the schismatic bishops responsible for Ludwig's consecration. It was only fitting, therefore, that during the ensuing festivities on the Capitol, the union of the families of the emperor's two leading supporters should have been foreshadowed by the announcement of the betrothal of Castruccio's eldest son Arrigo to Sciarra's daughter.[134] The prominence of the duke of Lucca among Ludwig's associates was further emphasized when to his already numerous titles were added those of senator of Rome and the emperor's standard-bearer, or lieutenant.[135] Over the next few days, if we can believe Villani, the honours heaped on the Lucchese tyrant began to turn his head and led him to behave with an ostentation untypical of his earlier, more down-to-earth habits as a ruler. He had, according to this writer, a mantle made for him of crimson samite, on the front of which was embroidered in gold, 'What God wills is', and on the back, 'What God shall will, shall be'. The presumptuousness of this garment drew from the Florentine chronicler his usual moralizing comment: unwittingly Castruccio's pride made him prophesy his own fall. For the 'will of God which was to be' was soon made evident, a mere fortnight after Ludwig's coronation, when news reached Rome that Pistoia had been captured by the Guelphs.[136]

Once he had learnt of the loss of this city, Castruccio shook himself free of the ceremonial atmosphere which had enveloped him during the preceding weeks. Though, as Villani put it, he was 'lord and

[134] BNF MS Palat. 571, c. 25ᵛ. *Monumenta*, Sectio iv, vol. vi, pt. 1 p. 286.

[135] *Monumenta*, Sectio iv, vol. vi, pt. 1, p. 285 and G. Villani, *Cronica*, x. 55. The former source confirms the conferral on him at this stage of the title 'Romani imperii vexillifer', which Villani does not mention.

[136] Ibid., x. 59, 'Storie pistoresi', 116–18, BNF MS Magliab. xxv, 19, c. 36ᵛ., Sardo, *Cronaca*, 81–2, Ficker, *Urkunden*, 55, ASF Missive I Cancelleria no. 3, c. 8ᵛ. For an account of the Florentine capture of Pistoia, see text below.

master of the emperor's court and more feared and obeyed than the Bavarian',[137] the true foundation of his power, as he himself well understood, lay in the lands he ruled. Ludwig's favours had been of invaluable assistance to him in giving a dynastic base to his authority and legitimizing his territorial claims. But they were no substitute for control over the cities from which he drew his strength and which gave him the ability to attract imperial largesse. Hence his position was clear: he must return to Tuscany and attempt to recover Pistoia even at the risk of offending the emperor. Yet, in doing so, he could not but have been painfully aware of the dilemma confronting a new ruler of his type who was, sooner or later, bound to be torn between the exigencies of maintaining power and the demands of those whose authority could sanction it. Castruccio's knowledge of the precariousness of his state had made him reluctant to follow Ludwig to Rome; yet the advantages to be gained by the emperor's dependence on him had been such as to appear to justify the risks of a temporary absence from Lucca. Now, however, the costs of such a course became clear and forced him to change direction, so ironically imperilling much of what his close association with Ludwig had gained for him. For, without Castruccio, the emperor would have to forfeit an expedition against Naples that might otherwise have been feasible and which could have weakened Guelph power in Italy sufficiently to permit a later attack against Florence. And since, without Pisa, Pistoia was unlikely to be retaken, the recovery of the latter city might have to be bought at the price of offending the prince in whose hands the former commune still nominally lay.

4. *The recovery of Pistoia and the death of Castruccio*

The fall of Pistoia thus represented for Castruccio more than a temporary reverse, despite his brilliant recapture of it a few months later. By its timing, it brought to a head one of the fundamental difficulties he faced, that of reconciling considerations of immediate political power with the long-term consolidation of his regime. It forced him to a choice which, a few months later when the emperor had left Italy, might have been avoided. In this sense, it represented a critical turning-point in his fortunes. At the time, however, he reacted to it with his customary energy, seeking rather to repair the damage caused by his absence from Lucca than consciously to consider its ultimate consequences. He took leave of the emperor on 1 February, four days

---

[137] G. Villani, *Cronica*, x. 59.

following the fall of Pistoia and the morning after news of its loss had
reached Rome by sea. Eight days later, he arrived in Pisa with an
escort of only twelve cavalry, having left the remainder of his troops,
supplemented by a detachment of cavalry under Azzo Visconti,[138] to
follow in easier stages.

Once back in Tuscany, he was better able to assess the situation. He
had expected that, with the departure of the duke of Calabria with
fifteen hundred knights at the end of December, the Florentines
would have reverted to a defensive posture and that his territories
would therefore have been safe from attack by them. However, before
leaving for the kingdom of Naples, Charles had entrusted to his
former marshal, recently appointed captain and vicar-general in his
stead,[139] the command of a sizeable army which was to be built up by
the enlistment of five hundred knights in Lombardy and six hundred
in Provence.[140] By late January 1328, the new Guelph general was,
thanks to the arrival of these reinforcements, in quite a strong military
position and was able to provide adequate armed support for the
daring coup against Pistoia. The moving spirits behind this would
appear to have been—besides Filippo di Sangineto himself—two
Pistoian exiles, Jacopo di Braccio Bandini and Baldo Cecchi,[141] and

[138] According to Villani, he had gone to Rome with three hundred knights and a
thousand crossbowmen and returned with two hundred additional cavalry (Cronica, x.
48, 59). Florentine official sources, however, claimed, on the authority of Malia of
Grosseto, that on 8 February Castruccio, accompanied by Azzo Visconti, had crossed
the Ombrone with six hundred knights, to be followed a day later by the count of
Chairamonte with a further eight hundred cavalry (ASF Missive I Cancelleria no. 3,
c. 12ʳ.). The most probable conclusion to be drawn from these reports is that Castruccio
brought back from Rome not only the three hundred knights he had taken there but
further contingents under Azzo Visconti and other commanders. The information
received by the Florentines would seem to have been mistaken in implying that
Castruccio was with his troops when they crossed the Ombrone (given that he arrived in
Pisa the following day, this appears unlikely), and also in alleging that the count of
Chairamonte led the second detachment of knights who passed through Grosseto on 9
February (since this noble is recorded as witnessing an imperial diploma in Rome on
the fifteenth of that month) (Lazzareschi, 'Documenti', 380), but was probably accurate
as to the dates on which Castruccio's and Azzo's men, and the reinforcements in their
rear, forded this river.
[139] Filippo di Sangineto had been appointed to these offices on 15 December 1327
(Bevere, 'La signoria', xxxvi. 425–7).
[140] Under the terms of his appointment, Filippo was to have one thousand knights at
his disposal (ibid.). Three days before he took over his positions as captain and vicar-
general, commissioners were elected to recruit five hundred knights in Lombardy for
service in Tuscany and elsewhere in Italy, while on 17 December arrangements were
made for the enlistment of 600 knights in Provence (ibid., 255–9, 457–8).
[141] G. Villani, Cronica, x. 58, and Bevere, 'La signoria', xxxvi. 278–9. Both of these
Pistoian Guelphs, together with Giovanni Cancellieri, whose role in the enterprise was

the Florentine patrician Simone della Tosa. The plan these four men devised for the recapture of the neighbouring city involved entering it under cover of darkness, using a transportable bridge to cross its moat and ladders to climb its walls at a point where they were known to be badly guarded. Once in the town, the attackers would breach its defences with battering rams to admit Filippo di Sangineto's cavalry and take the nearby Porta San Marco to enable the rest of their army to follow its vanguard into the town.

The equipment required to carry out this carefully calculated design was assembled, in great secrecy, in Prato and, on the evening of the 27 January, the expedition which was to give effect to it left Florence for that city. It consisted of Filippo di Sangineto, six hundred mercenary knights, and Simone della Tosa but no other Florentines since, for reasons of security, it had been decided to conceal the whole project from them. This attacking party reached Prato before midnight and there was joined by a mule and wagon train bearing the pieces of the transportable bridge, ladders, and battering rams, as well as by two thousand infantry from that town's garrison. With these troops, Filippo di Sangineto marched straight to Pistoia where he arrived well before dawn. Here, guided by the two exiles who had helped hatch the plot (and perhaps, if the author of the 'Storie pistoresi' is to be believed, by some conspirators within the city[142]), the Guelph army was led to an unguarded tract of the walls near the Porta San Marco. The two Pistoians, Bandini and Cecchi, were able to cross the moat at this point for, in what had been a particularly severe winter, it had frozen over, and then confirm the absence of defending troops there by scaling the ramparts and raising on them the banners of the commune of Florence and of the duke of Calabria. A hundred infantry followed them and, while these were entering the city, the transportable bridge was assembled and the battering rams were brought over it to break down the walls from both sides. Soon a breach had been made and Filippo di Sangineto, with a hundred and fifty knights, was able to ride though it. In the meantime, however, the Guelphs already in Pistoia encountered a patrol from the defending garrison which was on a routine inspection round. The members of this were overwhelmed and killed by the attackers but not before they had raised the alarm.

not specified, were later granted pensions by Charles of Calabria in recognition of their part in the taking of Pistoia.

[142] 'Storie pistoresi', 117.

In a short time, the troops left in the city by Castruccio were roused and marshalled in the city's main square. Numbering a hundred and fifty cavalry and five hundred infantry, they moved quickly towards the Porta San Marco which still held out against the assaults of Filippo di Sangineto's men, despite the burning of its forward defences and drawbridge. This Ghibelline force then counter-attacked but was repulsed by the Guelph commander and his knights. It also found its movements impeded by spiked metal 'brambles' which the invading soldiers had scattered in the surrounding streets. With the charge of Castruccio's men thrown back, the Guelphs finally succeeded in breaking the resistance of the remaining defenders of the Porta San Marco and so admitting the rest of their army. Once it became clear that this was in the city, the Ghibellines withdrew from it into the citadel—Bella Ispera—which Castruccio had begun to build by its western gate, the Porta Lucchese. In this were the two eldest of Castruccio's sons, Arrigo and Vallerno, who woke to discover that the city which their father had entrusted to their keeping had been lost. They attempted to retrieve their position at break of day by ordering their German knights to attack the nucleus of the Florentine army which had gathered in the *prato* beside the Porta Lucchese while the rest of it had scattered through the captured town to loot it. But when this final assault failed to dislodge the Guelphs and when the numbers of the latter grew as some of their plundering comrades rejoined their ranks, the younger Castracani resolved to abandon their half-built citadel which they judged would not be able to withstand a sustained attack and leave with their mercenaries while a line of retreat still lay open to them. So the Lucchese withdrew from both the city and the castle of Pistoia, preferring not to risk the loss of further men and of the surrounding villages in a desperate effort to maintain their foot-hold there till help could be brought in from the outside. Filippo di Sangineto was thus able to occupy both in the one day, unleashing his troops on a $1\frac{1}{2}$ week sack of the town and rewarding them further with an additional month's pay for their part in its capture.[143]

By the time Castruccio returned to Pisa, the Guelph commander was back in Florence which he had entered in triumph on 7 February. Simone della Tosa remained in Pistoia as captain of the city with two hundred and fifty knights and a thousand infantry under his com-

---

[143] See references in n. 136 above. The payment of an additional month's stipend to the troops engaged in the capture of Pistoia is recorded in Bevere, 'La signoria', xxxiii. 277–8.

mand. The position of the Florentines in the city was not, however, as strong as the size of its garrison and the ease of its recent capture might indicate. The Lucchese continued to hold Serravalle, Carmignano, Montemurlo, and Tizzana, a ring of fortified villages which provided a base for their subsequent encirclement of the town. Filippo di Sangineto had neglected to follow up his triumph in Pistoia with a reduction of these places and Castruccio therefore had open to him the possibility of attempting to retake it once he had the armed forces to hold off any Guelph relieving expedition. Furthermore, in the following three months, the Florentines were to fail adequately to provision Pistoia, largely because of the serious financial problems then facing their city.

Reading the apprehensive and petulant letters their government dispatched to Charles of Calabria in Naples, one is struck by the difficulties they experienced in finding the money to hold their latest conquests because of the sums already expended on their lord and his troops. Even before the taking of Pistoia, the strain of maintaining the garrison of Santa Maria a Monte, which Charles of Calabria had captured before Ludwig of Bavaria's arrival in Tuscany, had been causing the Florentines such concern that, on 23 January 1328, they had proposed that this stronghold be abandoned and demolished since its site was unhealthy and holding it served no military purpose.[144] According to the representations made by the communal authorities at this time, the income from the *gabelle* was no longer sufficient to cover the expenses occasioned by the war, with the result that a further levy of 60,000 florins had been raised, together with 120,000 florins in forced loans—which left still unpaid 15,000 florins required to maintain troops in Santa Maria a Monte, Signa, and Artimino and 4,000 for the continuing work on the city's walls.[145] The financial position of the commune had deteriorated to the point where there were no longer funds to pay civic officials, or to spend 8,000 florins in buying grain at a time when it was in such short supply in Florence that its price had risen to between 16 and 18 *soldi* a *staio*.[146]

[144] ASF Missive I Cancelleria no. 3, cc. 4ʳ.–5ᵛ., 6ʳ.

[145] Ibid., c. 4ᵛ. Barbadoro, *Le finanze*, 552, records only one *prestanza*, that of 60,000 florins, during the duke's government of Florence, but this letter probably refers also to the forced loans, levied just before his arrival in the city, which between them raised 91,000 florins.

[146] ASF Missive I Cancelleria no. 3, c. 5ʳ. On 12 February, King Robert was asked to send 2,000 sacks of grain to relieve the shortage in Florence and to waive payment for them, in view of the financial difficulties of the commune (ibid., c. 12ᵛ.).

On 30 January, in its instructions to Filippo di Sangineto after the capture of Pistoia, the Florentine Signoria urged him to discover how much money could be raised from that city and its surrounding villages to enable its fortifications to be set in order and suggested once again that Santa Maria a Monte should be abandoned,[147] presumably to effect savings that could be put to better use in securing the commune's latest conquest. On 13 February, in a postscript to the letter to King Robert of Naples informing him that Castruccio's troops had crossed the Ombrone, the priors told that ruler that Pistoia needed to be provisioned but claimed that the cost of this was beyond the means of the Florentines. They therefore 'reverently' asked how much the king or duke might see fit to contribute to these expenses.[148] On 1 March they wrote again to Robert lamenting their financial position and the heavy fiscal burdens the city was carrying because of the payment of Charles of Calabria's 200,000 florins' annual salary and the additional expense of keeping garrisons in several fortified places,[149] complaints that were repeated in another letter nine days later, which protested their inability to allot further funds to supplying Pistoia until financial assistance was forthcoming from their allies.[150] According to Giovanni Villani,[151] what underlay this persistent correspondence was a dispute which erupted between Filippo di Sangineto and the Florentines as to whether the cost of provisioning captured places should be met from the money already allocated to the duke by the commune or from further funds which it was the responsibility of the latter to find. The chronicler echoed the grievances of his compatriots when he stated that their commander had stripped Pistoia bare when it was sacked and then refused to provision it with the money that remained to him, choosing instead to send it to the duke of Calabria in Naples.

The disagreements which arose between the Florentines and their captain and the failure to attend adequately to the defences of Pistoia which followed from them offered Castruccio an opportunity, but it was one which he was, initially at least, in no position to exploit. Having just lost one of the two cities he had held, he lacked the means to wrest it back from the Florentines without the full commitment to

---

[147] Ibid., c. 7ʳ., and ᵛ.
[148] Ibid., c. 14ᵛ.
[149] Ibid., c. 15ᵛ.
[150] Ibid., c. 18ʳ.
[151] G. Villani, *Cronica*, x. 84.

that task of the power and wealth of Pisa. This commune, however, not only regarded him with considerable fear and distrust, but was also still technically under the rule of the emperor, represented locally by his vicar-general Baverio de' Salinguerra. Before he could harness its resources for the purpose of retaking Pistoia, Castruccio needed therefore to secure his control over the city. According to the testimony of the chroniclers,[152] he began appropriating its revenues and acting as its lord immediately he returned from Rome. In fact, however, he did not move to formalize his authority over it until some time later when he was about to take the field against the Florentines and therefore needed to have a secure legal basis for his use of Pisan troops in the siege of Pistoia.[153] Until then, he appears to have played a waiting game, hoping that Ludwig would countenance his effective seizure of power in the town, in view of the military situation in Tuscany and the emperor's own financial problems.

Despite his disappointment at Castruccio's departure from Rome, the emperor continued to shower his protégé with favours in the six weeks after he left, renewing the commission granting him a dukedom on 15 February[154] and, on 14 March, confirming and vesting as a hereditary possession the dignity of count of the Lateran Palace which had originally been conferred on him immediately before the imperial coronation.[155] The evident persistence of Ludwig's goodwill left Castruccio free, in the two months following his return, to take stock of the situation in Tuscany and assure his position in Pisa before the resumption of major hostilities against the Florentines. He profited by this respite not only to prepare for the coming siege of Pistoia but also to embark on some minor military ventures, intended to test the strength of the Guelph defences and his ability to rely on his reluctant Pisan allies, soon to become his even more reluctant subordinates.

[152] Ibid., x. 59, BNF MSS Magliab. xxv, 19, c. 37ʳ. and Palat. 571. c. 25ᵛ.
[153] The Pistoian campaign began on 13 May (G. Villani, *Cronica*, x. 84, ASF Missive I Cancelleria no. 3, c. 33ᵛ.). According to Villani, Castruccio then committed to it a thousand knights and a great number of infantry including the Pisans with their 'Carroccio', 'most of them against their will'. He himself arrived, with further troops, in Villani's account, on 30 May, but according to official Florentine records (ASF Missive I Cancelleria no. 3, c. 40ᵛ.) on 3 June.
[154] Lazzareschi, 'Documenti', 376–80. It is not clear why the privilege granting Castruccio his dukedom was reissued at this time; but the probable reason, in view of the one substantial discrepancy between its earlier and later texts (ibid., 375 and 379), was that it was thought proper to renew it after the imperial coronation had endorsed the authority from which it derived.
[155] Ibid., 380–2.

Following the arrival of the bulk of his troops from Rome, he attempted to take Montopoli by treachery. Since this town adjoined Pisan territory, his move against it could be seen as serving the interests as much of the city the goodwill of which he was courting as of his own. When his designs against Montopoli failed, he decided to probe the strength of the Florentine positions around Pistoia, leading an expedition on to its *contado* on 1 March. This met with very little resistance and he was therefore able to reprovision the isolated Ghibelline outpost of Montemurlo which was to play a key part in his subsequent campaign against Pistoia.[156] Finally, on 10 April, profiting by the opposition of some Maremman nobles to their Sienese masters, he managed to provoke the rebellion of Montemassi and to penetrate the Guelph encirclement of that village in order to supply it with enough food for it to hold out till the end of August.[157] While these limited military operations achieved no lasting gains, they served their purpose by exposing weak points in his enemies' defences or by creating a diversion which could pin down some of their troops while Castruccio pursued his main aim, the recovery of Pistoia.

His principal preoccupation, however, over these two months of preparation and preliminary skirmishing must have been the dilemma of Pisa. Without its men and revenues, he could not hope to regain Pistoia; yet, could he be assured of these without taking steps that risked offending the emperor? Eventually Castruccio was to resolve this problem by securing his authority over the city through the mediation of imperial ambassadors and by exploiting Ludwig of Bavaria's ever-pressing need for money. According to the story told by Giovanni Villani[158] (and in part by two other chroniclers[159]), he seized power in the city after the emperor, on receiving complaints from some prominent Pisans, had assigned it to his wife. She had allegedly despatched a Count Ortinghe there as her vicar, but Castruccio, after having graciously received him, bribed him to leave and, on 29 April, made himself lord of Pisa and arrested the previous imperial vicar,

[156] G. Villani, *Cronica*, x. 59.

[157] Ibid., x. 80, 99. It was eventually retaken by the Sienese and Florentines on 27 August.

[158] Ibid., x. 82.

[159] BNF MSS Magliab. xxv, 19, c. 37ʳ., and Palat. 571, c. 26ʳ. The second of these chronicles appears to contain a mere repetition of Villani's account. The first diverges from it in making the emperor rather than the empress the proposed ruler of Pisa, in naming the imperial envoy count of Lunzinborgo and not Ortinghe, and in commenting that many Florentines saw in the turn of events a stratagem contrived by Castruccio and Ludwig, intended presumably to deceive their enemies.

Baverio de' Salinguerra, together with several of the city's leading citizens. This intriguing tale cannot, however, be accepted since the documentary sources make it clear that the Lucchese tyrant acquired authority over Pisa not as its lord but as Ludwig's vicar, an office which he was granted on 29 May by imperial ambassadors.[160] These were Frederick of Nürnberg and Meinhardt von Ortenburg who had been dispatched by the emperor on the sixteenth of that month[161] and, in investing Castruccio with that title, acted with their master's consent. As for Baverio de' Salinguerra, he had been replaced as imperial vicar-general in Pisa earlier in May[162] by Giovanni da Castiglione,[163] one of Castruccio's supporters. Furthermore, documents in the Lucchese archives, detailing loans made to Castruccio by his friends in May and June 1328,[164] leave little doubt that the Lucchese ruler was able to obtain the acquiescence of Ludwig in his assumption of the vicariate over Pisa in effect by buying it from him. There is therefore no substance in Giovanni Villani's claim that Castruccio made himself lord of Pisa by force, never having even held that title which, in all the Pisan sources of the period, is accorded to the emperor.[165] The Florentine chronicler's account of this episode is clearly based on a misunderstanding of the actual events surrounding Castruccio's assumption of power in Pisa. It does appear to be true that the Lucchese tyrant offended some Pisan notables late in March 1328,[166] and interestingly also that Meinhardt von Ortenburg (who must be seen as the original of Villani's Ortinghe[167]) was briefly imperial vicar in Pisa immediately before Castruccio was elevated to

[160] Lazzareschi, 'Documenti', 394–6 and *Monumenta*, Sectio iv, vol. vi, pt. 6, pp. 380–1.
[161] ASP Comune A94, c. 53ʳ. and ˅.
[162] Ibid., A214, c. 58˅.
[163] He was one of the witnesses to Castruccio's will (Lazzareschi, 'Documenti' 406) and one of those friends who lent him money (in his case 300 florins) to enable the duke of Lucca to buy his vicariate over Pisa from Ludwig of Bavaria (ASL Camarlengo generale no. 2, c. 110ʳ.).
[164] Ibid., c. 114ʳ., 'pro solutione que fieri debuit Serenissimo Principi et domino domino Romanorum Imperatori pro gratia ipsi domino duci concessa vicariatus civitatis et comitatus Pisarum'. See also ibid., c. 110ʳ., 116˅., and ASL Anziani avanti la libertà no. 9, pp. 91, 98.
[165] ASP Comune A 94 c. 14˅., 27˅; A214, c. 59˅.
[166] ASF Missive I Cancelleria no. 3, c. 23˅.
[167] 'Ortinghe' has also been identified (by Davidsohn and others) with Friedrich von Oettingen who became Ludwig's vicar-general in Tuscany between November 1328 and March 1329 (ASL Curia dei Rettori no. 1, p. 213, and Diplomatico Tarpea, 30/11/1328). For a discussion of this point, see Winkler, *Castruccio*, 126–7.

that dignity.[168] But the assumption underlying the Florentine chronicler's narrative that there was a rift between the duke of Lucca and
Ludwig of Bavaria at this time finds no support in the available documents and is probably attributable to the impression produced later
by the emperor's treatment of Castruccio's sons. When these were
deprived of their dukedom very shortly after their father's death (for
having taken over control of Pisa without Ludwig's consent), their
disgrace was put down to an antagonism towards the Castracani which
the Bavarian prince had supposedly conceived when the Lucchese
tyrant had become his regent in that city. All the indications furnished
by the archival sources, however, make it clear that, when Castruccio
received his vicariate there, no open breach had developed between
him and his patron. Such evidence as there is can only lead one to the
conclusion that it was the combination of Ludwig's need for money
and the Lucchese ruler's dependence on the resources and manpower
of Pisa for the reacquisition of Pistoia that explains the latter's
appointment as imperial vicar in that commune on 29 May. The
timing of his elevation to this office is clearly closely connected with
the progress of the military campaign against Pistoia which had
opened on 13 May and which Castruccio was to join at the beginning
of June. With his position in Pisa assured, he could concentrate his
energies and the considerable forces he had assembled on the siege of
the city he had so suddenly and unexpectedly lost four months earlier.

That the moment was right for an attack upon that city must by now
have been apparent to Castruccio. Not only did he hear that the
Florentines had not provisioned it adequately,[169] but he could also
have been aware of discontent among its inhabitants on account of the
looting which it had suffered in the aftermath of its capture. According
to the author of the 'Storie pistoresi', this had continued even beyond
its ten-day sack, when 'there had remained neither Ghibellines nor
Guelphs, neither Blacks nor Whites who were not robbed'.[170] The
appointment as captain and *podestà* of Pistoia of Simone della Tosa
whom its citizens had expected to halt this plunder had only, in the
opinion of the same chronicler, worsened it, for now the Florentines

---

[168] See ASP Comune A94, c. 56ʳ., where he is referred to as 'tunc vicario pro
imperiale maiestate pisana civitate'. Since Meinhardt was still in Rome on 16 May 1328
when he and Frederick of Nürnberg received their commissions as ambassadors from the
emperor there, he could only have held this office briefly, immediately before he passed
it on to Castruccio.

[169] G. Villani, *Cronica*, x. 84.

[170] 'Storie pistoresi', 118.

joined their mercenaries in participating in it.[171] This had created such disorder in the city that 'each took from another what he could without any payment'.[172] In this situation, there were some who saw the prospect of a return to Lucchese rule as the lesser of two evils and were therefore prepared to advise Castruccio, through his son-in-law Filippo Tedici, how Pistoia might most quickly be restored to the Ghibelline fold. The plan which these citizens proposed, according to the 'Storie pistoresi',[173] was that the town be very closely besieged, in which circumstances they believed it would, in view of the lack of order which prevailed within it, fall within two months. (In fact, its surrender was to take place after just three weeks more than this predicted period.)

Castruccio, who had been preparing for some time[174] to exploit such an opportunity, moved to invest Pistoia on 13 May. In the preceding weeks, the Florentines had become increasingly desperate in their efforts to raise money to equip that city to face such an eventuality but, because of their financial difficulties, had achieved little to improve the military situation of the recently captured town.[175] When, on 12 May, reports came in warning of an impending Lucchese attack, appeals were promptly dispatched to all allies, asking them to send troops as quickly as possible to repel 'the army of the tyrant Castruccio' which was approaching Florentine territory.[176] On 14 May further letters went out to the members of the Guelph League confirming this news and adding the further details that, on the previous day, the enemy forces, bringing with them ladders and other wooden and iron equipment, had established a camp at Bonelle, a mile from Pistoia on the road to Carmignano.[177] These, according to reports sent out two days later and also chronicle evidence,[178] proceeded to lay waste the immediate surroundings of the besieged city where, however, nothing remained to be destroyed, after the ravages of previous campaigns, but the grain in the fields.

The troops which thus cut off Pistoia from Florence and then

---

[171] Ibid., 119.

[172] Ibid., 120.

[173] Ibid.

[174] The Florentines, writing to the pope as early as 4 April, had informed him of Castruccio's military preparations (ASF Missive I Cancelleria no. 3, c. 23ᵛ.).

[175] Ibid., cc. 31ʳ., 32ʳ.

[176] Ibid., c. 33ʳ.

[177] Ibid., c. 33ᵛ.

[178] Ibid., c. 34ᵛ., 'Storie pistoresi', 120.

devastated the land around it consisted, Villani estimated,[179] of a
thousand knights and a large number of infantry, but did not include
Castruccio nor the whole of his army. It was only later, at the end of
May or the beginning of June, that the Lucchese tyrant, having
secured his vicariate over Pisa, felt able to leave that city for an
extended period to direct the operations against Pistoia in person.
Until then, he appears to have entrusted the command of the besieging forces to Filippo Tedici.[180] Once he himself arrived on the scene,
however, he brought with him additional men who swelled the
numbers of his cavalry to 1,700[181] and increased his infantry by drawing on the levies of both Lucca and Pisa. The size of his army enabled
him to put into effect the plan proposed by his Pistoian advisers of
blocking all movement in and out of the encircled town by establishing several fortified camps clustered tightly around it. In place of
the original encampment at Bonelle, a mile from the city, no fewer
than six fort-like enclosures were erected much closer in, dominating
the gates and posterns and the roads issuing from these. By maintaining close guard from each of these, the besiegers were able to intercept
all movement in and out of Pistoia, while the proximity to the city
enabled a bombardment of it by catapults to be kept up day and night.
The defenders were compelled to put up wooden towers of their own
from which they could hurl missiles at the Ghibellines and so prevent
the Lucchese siege engines from being pushed right up to the town's
battlements. They also made sorties, one of which succeeded in
setting fire to the Pisan camp, while another destroyed the covered
way built out from Castruccio's headquarters at the Ranolmi mill,
under which miners had been tunnelling towards the city's moat and
walls.[182]

---

[179] Villani, *Cronica*, x. 84.   [180] 'Storie pistoresi', 120.

[181] The figure once again is Villani's. The same chronicler stated that Castruccio,
when leaving for Rome to follow Ludwig of Bavaria there, left 1,000 knights to guard
Pisa, Lucca, and Pistoia, taking 300 cavalry with him (x. 48). In addition to these 1,300
knights he would have brought additional troops back from Rome, estimates of which
ranged between Villani's 200 cavalry and 1,000 crossbowmen and the 1,100 knights
deducible from a report made by Malia of Grosseto to the Florentines (see n. 138
above). (The discrepancy between these figures may be due to the fact that the crossbowmen were mounted.) Allowing for forces to garrison Lucca, Pisa, and various other
fortified places, it would seem likely that Castruccio would have had at his disposal
nearly 2,000 cavalry at the height of the Pistoian campaign. Some of this number would,
however, have been mounted levies from Lucca and Pisa, so that the total of mercenary
knights in his service would probably never have exceeded 1,500 and may well have
been only about 1,200.

[182] 'Storie pistoresi', 121.

Thus, fighting proceeded at close quarters, accompanied by the barbarities usual in the sieges of the period. When Castruccio took the Guelph outpost at Pieve a Monte Cuccoli, which had been holding out two miles from his camp, he decided to make an example of the garrison by hanging the Pistoians in it and, after having mutilated the foreigners, had them led to the gates of Pistoia. Incensed by these atrocities, those in the besieged city, led by the relatives of those who had been killed, dragged out of confinement those who had been captured in sorties against Castruccio's army and executed eighteen of them, suspending their bodies from the battlements and catapulting the dismembered remains of two of these victims who had been drawn and quartered straight into the Lucchese commander's camp. According to the author of the 'Storie pistoresi', this grisly action had a salutary effect on him, for he never afterwards harmed a prisoner![183]

The outcome of the siege was not, however, to be determined by the ferocity of the skirmishing outside Pistoia nor by savage executions of luckless captives. What would decide it was rather the capacity of the encircling forces to hold off any relieving expedition until the exhaustion of the city's meagre reserves of food compelled it to surrender. The result would depend, on the one hand, on the effectiveness with which Castruccio could use the fortified villages in his possession, such as Montemurlo, Carmignano, and Tizzana, and any other defences he could improvise, to halt the eventual Guelph attack from Prato and, on the other, on his ability at the same time to maintain his siege of Pistoia.

To do this he would have needed considerable financial resources, given that the cost of mercenary knights in Pisan service at this period averaged about 12 florins per month[184] (without counting compensation for horses killed in battle) and that the probable number of professional cavalry under his command during the Pistoian campaign would have been between 1,200 and 1,500.[185] To meet these expenses, Castruccio would have had access to the ordinary revenues of Lucca and Pisa, such additional moneys as he could extract from his citizens, and forced loans from the Pisans. Before leaving for Rome, Ludwig of Bavaria had imposed a *prestanza* of six *soldi* in the *lira* on

[183] 'Storie pistoresi', 122.
[184] ASP Comune A94, cc. 28ʳ., and '., 33'.–34'. The compensations for horses lost (ibid., cc. 36ʳ.–38'.) average out at 3.27 florins per man; presumable for the 1½ months for which the records detail the payment of the *bandiere* concerned.
[185] See n. 181 above on the likely number of mercenary cavalry in Pisan and Lucchese service at this time.

them, which was expected to yield 140,000 florins.[186] Not all of this was collected at the time and his ambassadors returned to the city in May to recover such moneys as were still owing to him. It is not clear whether Castruccio would have had access to any of this, but we do know that at least two other smaller forced loans were raised, one when he was vicar, and one when Meinhardt of Ortenburg briefly held that office.[187] Both of these were presumably to meet military expenses during the Pistoian campaign. Given that no more than about 50,000 florins a year would have been available from the Lucchese *gabelle* for hiring mercenary troops[188] and that only just over 350 foreign knights appear to have been supported from the ordinary revenues of Pisa in July and August 1328,[189] Castruccio must have found means of extracting further funds from both cities to maintain an army of the size with which the chroniclers credit him.

This may have been done partly by siphoning off some of the yield of the *prestanza* of 140,000 florins, but it also required the levying of forced loans from his Lucchese supporters, and in particular from those who stood to gain from his expansionist policies by obtaining administrative positions in his new territories. For instance, we know that he borrowed 7,244 florins in the course of 1328 from Jacopo Sbarra,[190] who had become Ludwig of Bavaria's treasurer in Pisa,[191] and 1,660 florins and £65 15s. 6d. *buona moneta lucchese* between December 1327 and June 1328 from Dettoro del Lieto[192] who, together with his brother Jacopo, acted as an official for the payment of troops in that city.[193] In all, in the last nine months of his life, Castruccio is recorded as having received over 20,000 florins in such loans from Lucchese merchants who, in addition to the two already mentioned, included Lazzaro Guinigi, Jacopo Galganetti, Nicolao Busdraghi, Nuccio, Guido, and Benettuccio Arnolfi, Giovanni Rapondi, Guelfo and Lemmo Casciani, and his predecessor as vicar of Pisa, Giovanni

---

[186] ASP Comune A93, c. 33ʳ. and ˅.

[187] ASP Comune A94, cc. 56ʳ.–57ʳ., 64˅.–67˅. They were, however, for the rather small sums of 3,032 and 3,150 florins respectively.

[188] See p. 131 above.

[189] ASP Comune A94, cc. 28ʳ., 29ʳ., 33ʳ.–35˅. Their pay was drawn directly from the *gabelle*, not from forced loans.

[190] ASL Camarlengo generale no. 2, c. 96ʳ., Anziani avanti la libertà no. 7, p. 39.

[191] ASP Comune A93, cc. 18˅., 20˅., 23˅., 25ʳ.

[192] ASL Camarlengo generale no. 2, c. 116ʳ., Anziani avanti la libertà no. 9, p. 91.

[193] ASP Comune A94, cc. 31˅., 54ʳ.

da Castiglione.[194] Given, however, that a considerable part of this sum would have gone towards grants made to Ludwig of Bavaria for the favours he granted to the Lucchese tyrant and to expenses incurred in the course of the siege of Pisa at the end of 1327, there would still have been considerable difficulties in meeting the financial demands created by the Pistoian campaign which would have had to be met from the resources of Pisa and its dependencies such as Elba[195] and from exactions from the clergy.[196] Just how long Castruccio could have continued satisfying them if Pistoia had not fallen at the beginning of August is hard to tell, but judging by what we know of the cost of mercenaries and of the strains imposed on the treasuries of both Lucca and Pisa by Ludwig's needs and those of the war against Florence, it would seem that there was a certain urgency for him to achieve his objective as quickly as possible.

The critical point in the siege of Pistoia came when the Guelphs mounted the counter-attack intended to relieve the city. From the middle of May onwards, the Florentines had been pleading with Charles of Calabria, Robert of Naples, the pope, his legate in Bologna, and various allied and subject cities to send troops which would permit an offensive against Castruccio to be undertaken. With three hundred knights surrounded in Pistoia, only eight hundred remained in Florence under the command of Filippo di Sangineto.[197] This force would clearly need to be reinforced before it could move against an enemy with roughly twice that number of cavalry. Consequently, help from other members of the Guelph league was essential as the Florentine Signoria did not tire of reminding its correspondents, with all the more insistence when it appeared that Ludwig of Bavaria might soon be leaving Rome and bringing his army northwards towards Tuscany. The papal legate in Lombardy, from whom military support had been sought as early as 14 and 16 May, when Castruccio's forces first

---

[194] ASL Archivio Guinigi no. 72, c. 63^r., Camarlengo generale no. 2, cc. 96^r., 99^r. and ^{v}., 100^r. and ^{v}., 107^v., 110^r., 114^r., 116^r., Anziani avanti la libertà no. 7, pp. 34, 44; no. 9, pp. 91, 98.
[195] G. Volpe, 'Pisa, Firenze, impero', 310, estimated (on the basis of a document in W. Doenniges, *Acta Henrici VII*, ii. 95) that the revenue of Pisa in 1312 was 224,196 florins of which 91,196 florins were provided by Sardinia and 60,000 by Elba. Since the former was lost to the Pisans by 1328, this would have left a total income from the *gabelle* of Pisa and its *contado* and from the iron-mines of Elba of about 140,000 florins in the latter year, on the assumption that levels of revenue had remained roughly the same as in 1312.
[196] See nn. 53 and 56 above.
[197] Villani, *Cronica*, x. 85. The garrison of Pistoia had presumably been reinforced by fifty cavalry between when it was first captured and when the Lucchese besieged it.

encamped around Pistoia,[198] continued to be bombarded with appeals for troops.[199] When the request for these was not immediately met, further letters were sent later in the month to Charles of Calabria and the pope, underlining the gravity of the position of the besieged city and urging that pressure be put on the legate to supply prompt assistance.[200] Other pleas for help went out a little later, on 2 June, to San Gimignano, Gubbio, Perugia, Montepulciano, Ascoli, Camerino, Foligno, the bishop of Florence, and several lords from Tuscany and the March of Ancona.[201] Two days later, news was transmitted to King Robert of Naples of Castruccio's arrival at the siege of Pistoia with more troops[202] and, on the same date, the legate was asked to preach, and Charles of Calabria to support the crusade against the Lucchese tyrant ordered by the pope.[203] At the same time, the Sienese were exhorted to suspend, as far as possible, their trade with Pisa.[204] On 6 June, the Florentines, in submitting their usual request to the papal legate to dispatch a contingent of knights to Tuscany, insisted that this should not be placed under the command of Guglielmo da Rosso Monte who was suspected of being secretly in league with the enemy.[205] The specific nature of this demand would appear to suggest that, by this time, some undertaking, if only in principle, had been made by Bertrand de Poujet, the legate in Lombardy, to supply troops for service in Tuscany. Certainly, the Florentines seem henceforth to have acted on the understanding that they could proceed with their offensive against Castruccio. On the following day, they called up

---

[198] ASF Missive I Cancelleria no. 3, cc. 33ᵛ., 34ᵛ.–35ᵛ.

[199] Ibid., cc. 38ʳ., 39ʳ. and ᵛ., 41ʳ., 45ʳ., 46ʳ., 47ʳ.

[200] Ibid., cc. 36ʳ., 37ʳ.–38ᵛ.

[201] Ibid., cc. 39ʳ., 40ʳ.

[202] Ibid., c. 40ᵛ.

[203] Ibid., c. 39ʳ. and ᵛ.

[204] Ibid., c. 42ʳ. There was technically supposed to be an embargo on trade with the Ghibelline states which was never, however, very effective because of the possibility of working through intermediaries. (See, on this, particularly A. Sapori, 'Firenze e Castruccio: tentativi di guerra economica', in *Atti della R. Accademia Lucchese* (NS), iii (1934) 59–72). Pisa was, of course, not covered by this, strictly speaking, but the Florentines evidently expected not only their own citizens but also their allies to avoid any city under Castruccio's control. The ineffectiveness of Florentine attempts to cordon off their enemies economically may be illustrated by Ludwig of Bavaria's instructions to Jacopo Sbarra, his treasurer in Pisa, on 30 April 1328 to pay Pietro and Chiaro di Dino Peruzini (Peruzzi?) of Florence 4,000 florins which he had borrowed from them (ASL Diplomatico Sbarra, 30/4/1328).

[205] ASF Missive I Cancelleria, no. 3, c. 41ʳ. Two of his associates had evidently been captured while fleeing to Pisa, some days previously.

infantry levies from some small towns in the mid-Arno valley.²⁰⁶ And on 9 June they informed the cities of Parma, Piacenza, and Reggio and the sons of Orlando de' Rossi and Ghiberto da Correggio that Filippo di Sangineto had decided to attempt to relieve Pistoia. Five days later, the new Florentine ambassador to Bologna was instructed to convey the same message to the legate and ask for troops to be sent as quickly as possible.²⁰⁷ On 17 June, after an appeal had been made to the pope on the previous day, the same request was transmitted directly to Bertrand de Poujet.²⁰⁸ Simone della Tosa, the Florentine vicar in Pistoia, had evidently managed to smuggle out a letter to the Signoria on the sixteenth,²⁰⁹ asking that efforts be made to raise the siege as early as possible since the city could not hold out for long. In response to his plea, the Florentines pressed on with the recruitment of knights in Lombardy and attempted to compose the differences between the papal legate and Alberghettino Manfredi, captain of Faenza, which were responsible for the former's reluctance to allow his troops to cross over into Tuscany.²¹⁰

In the meantime, reports that Castruccio was about to seize Pistoia and that Ludwig of Bavaria was preparing to leave Rome began to alarm the Florentine authorities. The fear that the Lucchese ruler would storm the besieged city on 26 June led Filippo di Sangineto to rush with his forces to Prato in an attempt to avert its possible fall.²¹¹ Three days later, on the twenty-ninth, the Florentine Signoria, relaying information it had received from Silvestro Manetti, told Charles of Calabria that Ludwig, frustrated in his intention to invade the kingdom of Naples, was about to return to Tuscany and asked the Neapolitan prince to send his army to Spoleto from where it would be able to intercept the Bavarian's troops, whether these moved north, south, or remained in Rome.²¹² On 2 July, further letters went out appealing for help both from the duke and from his father, King Robert of Naples.²¹³

²⁰⁶ Ibid., c. 42ᵛ.
²⁰⁷ Ibid., cc. 43ʳ., 45ʳ.
²⁰⁸ Ibid., cc. 45ʳ., 46ʳ.
²⁰⁹ Ibid., c. 46ʳ. and ᵛ. We know of this letter only from the reply to it, dispatched by the Signoria on 18 June and promising help as soon as it could be sent.
²¹⁰ Ibid., cc. 48ᵛ.–51ʳ.
²¹¹ On 25 June, writing once again to its ambassadors in Bologna, the Florentine signoria noted that Castruccio was expected to try to take Pistoia the following day and that consequently Filippo di Sangineto had gone to Prato with all his forces to do what he could to prevent this (ibid., c. 49ᵛ.).
²¹² Ibid., c. 50ʳ.   ²¹³ Ibid., cc. 52ʳ.–53ᵛ.

The fears gripping the Florentine priors at the many dangers that they felt beset them were somewhat allayed over the next few days by information that the papal legate in Lombardy, won over by 10,000 florins now advanced to him for their pay, had finally agreed to send down to Florence the eight hundred cavalry which had been so insistently demanded over the previous six weeks. While, on 2 June, these had not been expected till the twelfth, by the fifth news had come through that they were on their way and would 'infallibly' arrive by the seventh. Filippo di Sangineto could thus, it was maintained, take the field as early as the tenth.[214] As a result of the cumulative efforts of several weeks, the Florentines were at last able to start assembling the formidable army with which they hoped to raise the siege of Pistoia. It was to consist of Filippo di Sangineto's eight hundred knights, of another eight hundred provided by the legate, of four hundred and sixty just enlisted in Florence and Piacenza, and five hundred supplied by Siena, Volterra, San Gimignano, Colle, Prato, and the Conti Guidi—in all between 2,500 and 2,600 cavalry together with a large body of infantry estimated by one chronicler at 8,000.[215] To bring this force together, the Florentines had needed to find at least another 16,000 florins[216] beyond their projected military expenditure and had done this by raising a forced loan of 20,000 florins. Half of this sum, however, was to cover the advance paid to the legate at Bologna to induce him to send his eight hundred knights, which he undertook to repay later to the commune of Florence.[217] In order to help finance the

---

[214] Ibid., cc. 52ᵛ., 54ᵛ. In fact, according to BNF MS Magliab. xxv, 19, c. 38, the legate's knights did not arrive in Florence until 12 July.

[215] G. Villani (*Cronica*, x. 85) estimated the number of knights from Bologna as 900, including 500 from the legate and 400 from the commune of Bologna. I have, however, taken the figure of 800 from the Florentine official sources referred to above. (Eight hundred is also the figure given in BNF MS Magliab. xxv, 19, c. 38ʳ.) Villani's total of 2,600 cavalry is fairly close to that arrived at by the addition of the numbers given above. His estimate of 460 for the combined size of the two detachments of knights enlisted in Florence and Piacenza also would appear to be accurate, given that we know that 200 were taken on in the former city and 4,100 florins paid to recruit those in the latter (ASF Missive I Cancelleria no. 3, cc. 48ᵛ.–51ʳ.). The number of *pedoni* is given as 8,000 in BNF MS Magliab. xxv, 19, c. 38ʳ. which also estimates the total number of Guelph cavalry at 2,500.

[216] Ten thousand to the legate, 4,100 to pay troops engaged in Lombardy, and an estimate of at least 2,000 florins per month for the 200 knights enlisted in Florence. Later, in August 1328, the Florentines were to claim that the Pistoian enterprise had cost them 60,000 florins (ASF Missive I Cancelleria no. 3, cc. 65ʳ., 68ᵛ.) but this presumably included the cost of taking the city as well as that of trying to save it from recapture.

[217] ASF Liber Fabarum no. 13, cc. 122ʳ., 128ʳ.

attack on Castruccio, the outpost of Santa Maria a Monte had finally been abandoned on 15 June, but the savings made by the withdrawal of its garrison were cancelled out by the costs of dismantling its fortifications.[218]

In fact, it took a little longer than the Florentines had hoped to launch their attack against Castruccio. Although a general muster was to have been held on Sunday 10 July,[219] it was not until two days later (probably because of the late arrival of the legate's eagerly awaited knights) that Filippo di Sangineto was able to leave Florence for Prato with most of his troops, after they had been blessed in the Piazza Santa Croce and given the banner of the church to bear before them. Even then, not all the allied contingents had reached Florence and they had to follow the main body of the army to Prato over the next two days. It was only on the eighteenth[220] that all the forces under Filippo di Sangineto's command were able to set forth from the latter city on the first stage of their advance against Pistoia. This took them just beyond the bridge at Agliana where they camped that night. On the next day they pressed on to a place Villani called Cappanelle, which was probably Canapale and which lay a short distance from Castruccio's camp.[221]

The Lucchese commander had, according to the author of the 'Storie pistoresi', been observing their approach with apprehension. Reducing his camps around Pistoia from six to one, he brought the main body of his troops forward and set them up in strong defensive positions to block the advance of his enemy. He ordered his men to dig ditches and build obstacles from cut-down trees to impede the

---

[218] ASF Missive I Cancelleria no. 3, c. 28ʳ., Provvisioni no. 24, cc. 53ʳ., 67ʳ.

[219] ASF Missive I Cancelleria no. 3, cc. 55ᵛ., 56ᵛ. All villages and communes within the Florentine *contado* were to forward 2 florins by that date for each of the *pedoni* they were expected to maintain in the general levy.

[220] G. Villani (*Cronica*, x. 85) gives the date 13 July for the departure of Filippo di Sangineto from Florence and the nineteenth for the advance of his army from Prato to Agliana; but he also says that the former day was a Tuesday and the latter a Monday. In fact the twelfth not the thirteenth was a Tuesday in 1328, and the eighteenth, not the nineteenth, a Monday. The date eighteenth is given in BNF Magliab. xxv, 19, c. 38ʳ. for the march from Prato to Agliana and the twelfth for the arrival of the legate's eight hundred knights in Florence. That the general manifesto opening the campaign against Castruccio was issued by the Florentines on 18 July (ASF Missive I Cancelleria no. 3, cc. 57ᵛ.–58ʳ.) also suggests that their forces left Prato on that day.

[221] G. Villani *Cronica*, x. 85, and BNF MS Magliab. xxv, 19, c. 38ʳ., 'Storie pistoresi', 123. According to ASF Missive I Cancelleria no. 3, c. 58ᵛ., the Florentine camp was, on 23 July, one mile from Pistoia. This is consistent with its being at Canapale which is, besides, on the side of the town from which the Florentine army was approaching.

movement of cavalry. Castruccio's control of Montemurlo to the north and Carmignano and Tizzana to the south in effect restricted the Guelph army to a single route which ran roughly beside the Ombrone along the main road from Prato to Pistoia. Recognizing the numerical superiority enjoyed by the Florentines, the duke of Lucca was determined at all costs to avoid a pitched battle, but at the same time tried so to dispose his troops that the enemy could not dislodge them. The narrowness of the corridor along which the latter had to move made it possible, by improvising fortifications on either side of the Lucchese positions and placing these where a frontal attack upon them could be repulsed, effectively to hold back the larger Guelph forces with a smaller body of men.

Finding Castruccio so well entrenched, Filippo di Sangineto resorted to an appropriately fine chivalric gesture. He formally challenged his opponent to battle by sending him the customary gauntlet. This Castruccio courteously accepted, replying to Filippo's invitation to fight with a rhetorical letter[222] declaring himself to be an offshoot of the tree of the invincible Emperor Henry VII ready, with the help of his champions Galeazzo Visconti and his son, valiantly to pit against the leonine strength of the duke of Calabria the beak and claws of the imperial eagle. Having satisfied the demands of knightly protocol with this barrage of words, the Lucchese commander then proceeded to sit tight while the Guelph forces stood below his camp for a whole day, drawn up in battle formation, waiting for him to engage them in the promised combat. It soon became clear that, whatever weight Castruccio might place in theory on chivalric convention, he was not prepared to risk his army or the chance of retaking Pistoia in a set-piece feat of arms. He managed, however, to go on dangling the prospect of one before the Florentines for another two days until they were finally convinced that he would not leave his lines to venture his fortune on the field of battle. Then Vergiù di Landa, joint commander of the mercenaries who had recently been enlisted in Lombardy, decided to attempt to force a way through Castruccio's defences. For a whole day his knights attacked but met such resistance that they were eventually compelled to retreat. The Lucchese dispositions were so well placed that there was no breaking through them.

Faced with his inability either to lure Castruccio into a conventional military engagement or to penetrate the Lucchese lines, Filippo

---

[222] Published in W. Doenniges, *Acta*, ii. 253, and in *Monumenta*, Sectio iv, vol. vi, pt. 1, pp. 382–3.

di Sangineto withdrew to the Bure a little to the east of his previous camp. He remained here till the twenty-eighth, sending out parties of troops to probe the enemy's defences, gaining ground in the daytime which was lost at night, quarrelling with the commanders of the legate's troops as to what strategy should be followed, and eventually falling ill.[223] In the meantime, the Florentines wrote, on 23 July, to Charles of Calabria, complaining that Castruccio had deceitfully pretended that he was prepared to come to battle but instead had retreated behind the fortifications he had erected, and was waiting for five hundred knights whom Azzo Visconti was recruiting for him in Cremona and who were expected soon to come to his aid. Once again, the duke was asked quickly to send troops from the kingdom of Naples to meet this new danger.[224] It may well be that the real or imagined threat of a repetition of what had happened at Altopascio, when Castruccio had remained on the defensive for a time only to strike a devastating blow at his enemy as soon as he had acquired a tactical military superiority, began at this stage to influence the Guelph commanders. According to Villani, differences developed between them, some wanting to persist with the attempt to relieve Pistoia while others held that the Ghibelline forces besieging it could be drawn away by a diversionary attack on Pisa, thus permitting the encircled city to be more easily reprovisioned from Prato. The marshal in charge of the legate's knights was, besides, anxious to end the campaign quickly so as to be able to return across the Apennines to deal with problems which had arisen in the Romagna. He was consequently making difficulties, demanding an advance from the commune of Florence of a further two florins for each of his men. This money was found for him, although in sending it the priors voiced their usual complaints as to the dire state of their government's finances.[225] There were also doubts about the loyalty of his German knights who had been fraternizing with those in Castruccio's service, raising fears of possible defections or treachery. In fact, one squadron of the cavalry supplied by the Sienese had gone over to the enemy,[226] so nervousness on this score was not entirely unjustified.

Having failed either to win a decisive victory or to break through the

---

[223] G. Villani, *Cronica*, x. 85, 'Storie pistoresi', 124. Filippo's illness is confirmed in ASF Missive I Cancelleria no. 3, c. 62ᵛ.
[224] ASF Missive I Cancelleria no. 3, c. 58ʳ. and ᵛ.
[225] Ibid., c. 59ᵛ.
[226] Ibid., c. 62ʳ.

Lucchese defences, the Florentine commanders seem suddenly to
have lost their confidence and resolve. Frustrated and disappointed,
they chose what Villani described as the 'lesser evil',[227] namely withdrawal to Prato and a diversionary thrust on to the Pisan *contado*. At
least this was the course that Filippo di Sangineto opted to take: the
Florentines were evidently not happy with their captain's decision[228]
and at first questioned it but were eventually won over by his argument
that it would ultimately be to the advantage of the besieged Pistoians,
since without the presence of Pisan troops their encirclement could
not be sustained. Evidently, there was an expectation that Castruccio
would not be able to keep his army where it was if Lucca or Pisa were
threatened by the Guelphs. When, on 28 July,[229] Filippo di Sangineto's
men, having for the last time and without effect 'trumpeted and challenged Castruccio to battle',[230] withdrew to Prato, they left there some
of their number to escort supplies to Pistoia should its siege be raised.
The greater part of the Florentine forces, however, including the
legate's knights whose marshal assumed command of the expedition,
rode to Signa and thence, after a feint across the Usciana to make it
seem as though an attack were planned on Lucca, down the Arno to
Pontedera. This town was taken and burnt, as was Cascina, by Guelph
troops who encountered resistance only from the local villages and
were therefore easily able to sweep across an otherwise undefended
countryside to the very gates of Pisa, looting and laying waste everything in their path.

Despite the reports he received of the devastation of the lower Val
d'Arno by the Florentines, Castruccio, contrary to their expectations,
did not allow any of his men to leave the siege of Pistoia. After the
departure of the Guelph forces, he had instead had the positions
formerly taken up by his troops around the encircled town reoccupied.
Seeing this and learning with dismay of the withdrawal of the Florentine relieving expedition, its vicar Simone della Tosa wrote to the

---

[227] G. Villani, *Cronica*, x. 85.
[228] ASF Missive I Cancelleria no. 3, c. 62[r]. For further Florentine efforts to bring the
legate's knights back from the *contado* of Pisa, see also ASF Missive I Cancelleria no. 3,
c. 63[r].
[229] This date is given in both G. Villani, *Cronica*, x. 85, and BNF MS Magliab. xxv, 19,
c. 38[r].
[230] G. Villani, *Cronica*, x. 85. Where other sources are not given, the above account of
the closing stages of the siege of Pistoia is based largely on this chronicler,
supplemented by the letters of the Florentine signoria referred to above, the 'Storie
pistoresi', 123–5 and Sardo, *Cronaca*, 82.

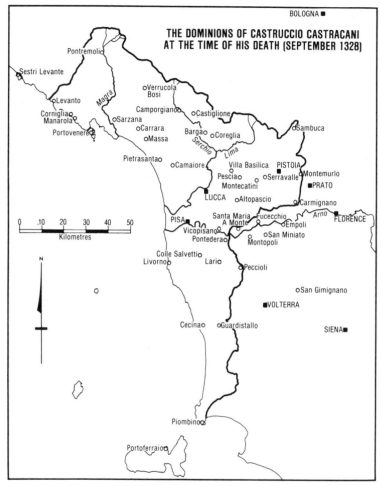

BOLOGNA ■

THE DOMINIONS OF CASTRUCCIO CASTRACANI
AT THE TIME OF HIS DEATH (SEPTEMBER 1328)

Pontremoli○

Sestri Levante○

○Verrucola
Bosi

○Levanto

Corniglia○
Manarola○

Portovenere○

Camporgiano○○
○Sarzana
○Castiglione

○Carrara
○Massa

Bargao○ ○Coreglia

○Sambuca

Pietrasanta○

○Camaiore

Villa Basilica   PISTOIA ■
○
Pesciao   ○Serravalle○Montemurlo
Montecatini   ■PRATO

LUCCA   ○Altopascio
○Carmignano

PISA■

Santa Maria   Fucecchio
A Monte○   ○Empoli   Arno   FLORENCE ■
Vicopisano○
Pontedera○   ○San Miniato
Montopoli

Colle Salvettio
Livorno○   Lario○

○Peccioli

0   .10   20   30   40   50
Kilometres

N

○

○San Gimignano

■VOLTERRA

Cecina○   ○Guardistallo   SIENA■

Piombino○○

Portoferraio○

Map 3.

Signoria on 30 July to inform it that, unless Pistoia was resupplied, it
could only hold out for another fifteen days and did not have even
enough horseflesh to last three weeks.[231] Replying on 1 August, the
priors promised that Pistoia would be relieved 'infallibly' and, in the
meantime, urged its defenders to fight on with valiant heart and their

[231] The text of this letter does not survive but its contents can be deduced from the
priors' reply to it on 1 August and their report of the same date to Charles of Calabria
which summarizes them (ASF Missive I Cancelleria no. 3, cc. 59ᵛ., 61ʳ.).

habitual constancy, so earning a fame and glory that time would not efface.[232] These hollow-sounding exhortations fell, however, on deaf ears. Making the best of the desperate situation, Simone della Tosa and the Pistoians negotiated with Castruccio the terms of their surrender, by which those who wished would be allowed safely to leave the captured town, taking with them what they could carry, and those who wished to stay could remain to enjoy full rights of citizenship. These conditions having been accepted (doubtless with alacrity) by the duke of Lucca, the city admitted him and his troops on the morning of 3 August.[233] Thus, Pistoia, passed once again into Lucchese hands.

Its recapture was a heavy blow for the Florentines and a triumph for their great enemy. As Villani put it, it was 'almost incredible that it could come to pass that Castruccio should maintain the siege with sixteen hundred knights or thereabouts, and that the Florentines who had in their army and in Pistoia three thousand horsemen or more of excellent quality and very many infantry could not force him to withdraw'.[234] It was an extraordinary result and one which, at first sight, might seem difficult to explain. The reasons for it were, however, fairly clear. On the one hand, what had helped to bring it about was the ineptitude of the Florentines and the difficulties they had experienced in working with their allies. Pistoia had fallen as soon as it did because of misunderstandings as to who was financially responsible for defending and supplying it. The forces intended to relieve it had been assembled too slowly because the papal legate in Lombardy would only commit his troops to the enterprise if money were first advanced to him to enable them to be paid. Once the Guelph army had taken the field, the lack of any carefully thought out military strategy agreed upon by the commune of Florence and its commanders, compounded by the illness of Filippo di Sangineto at the most critical stage of the campaign, produced first vacillation and then the futile diversionary attack on Pisa.

While these weaknesses in the prosecution of hostilities by the Guelphs contributed in significant measure to their loss of Pistoia, it was Castruccio's ability to exploit them which decided the fate of that city. Unlike the Florentines, the Lucchese commander appreciated

[232] Ibid., c. 59ʳ.

[233] Ibid., c., 63ʳ., G. Villani, (*Cronica*, x. 85), BNF MS Magliab. xxv, 19, c. 38ᵛ., and 'Storie pistoresi', 125 all also agree on this date.

[234] G. Villani, *Cronica*, x. 85.

the essentially positional character of early fourteenth-century warfare. He knew that, while superior numbers of professional cavalry were the key to victory, they could be effectively used only on favourable terrain. Hence, by following a defensive strategy, it was possible to put an opposing army in the position where it had either to withdraw or risk a disastrous defeat if its original tactical advantage were neutralized.

It was probably the prospect of such an eventuality that induced the Guelph commanders to pull their troops back to Prato ten days after these had originally advanced on Pistoia. Their ensuing tactic of an attack on Pisa was not itself entirely lacking in justification in military terms. Its ineffectiveness was essentially due to its timing. Had the Florentines provided one more months' supplies for Pistoia and had they brought their army together a month earlier than they did, a devastation of the Pisan *contado* and perhaps even a thrust up the Serchio towards Lucca would eventually have drawn Castruccio and his troops away from the siege of Pistoia to the defence of their own territories. But the lateness of this last desperate effort to save the encircled city foredoomed it to failure.

With Pistoia retaken, Castruccio hastened back to Lucca and from there went on with his troops to Pisa, from the *contado* of which the Guelphs withdrew at his approach.[235] He was now master, at one and the same time, of three city-states, of Lucca and Pistoia by virtue of his dukedom and recent military successes, of Pisa thanks to his imperial vicariate. The territories which power endorsed by legal title had brought under his rule made up a regional principality sufficiently large and wealthy for him to meet the Florentines on equal terms. Controlling the Mediterranean littoral from eastern Liguria to Piombino and Elba, the heights of the Apennines from Pontremoli to Sambuca, the Val d'Arno to Pontedera, the Val di Nievole north of the Usciana and the Fucecchio marshes, the Pistoiese flanked by its mountain forts of Tizzana, Carmignano, and Montemurlo, and his heartland of the Lucchesia and Garfagnana in the Val di Serchio, he disposed of a state of imposing dimensions and with resources adequate to the maintenance of a viable mercenary army.[236] The

---

[235] G. Villani, *Cronica*, x. 86 and 'Storie pistoresi', 125–6.
[236] According to Florentine sources, (ASF Missive I Cancelleria no. 3, cc. 74ʳ., 77ᵛ.) at the time of his death at the beginning of September 1328, 1,500 knights were in the service of the three cities of Pisa, Lucca, and Pistoia. Therefore, despite the financial strains of the previous months, the revenue of the three cities and their dependencies

question that remained to be answered concerning it was whether he
would be able to hold it together and whether, in particular, he could
consolidate his dominance over Pisa, a city the inhabitants of which
were, in the main, hostile to him, to which he had the weakest legal
title, and which was the most vulnerable, as recent events had shown,
to attack from Florence. Indissolubly linked with this question was, of
course, another: that of his relations with the emperor. Ludwig of
Bavaria finally left Rome on 4 August and was to arrive in Pisa on 21
September.[237] The attitude that he would take to the claims of
Castruccio and his heirs to rule the latter city would obviously play a
large part in determining whether they would be able to fuse it with
their other territories or continue to hold it only precariously by force.
According to Villani, the emperor had conceived a 'veiled resentment'
against the Lucchese tyrant when the latter had gained control of
Pisa.[238] Since some of the details of the incident which allegedly
provoked the emperor's hostility are, as described by the Florentine
chronicler, demonstrably false, it is difficult to know what to make of
this assertion. There can be no doubt as to the legality of the grant of
the vicariate over Pisa to Castruccio, nor is there any evidence that, in
the Lucchese tyrant's lifetime, the emperor made any effort to revoke
it. If he did feel privately displeased, his need for further funds to pay
his troops[239] would have made it awkward for him to sever his links
with the one Italian source from which money was still easily available
to him, if perhaps not as abundantly as he might earlier have hoped.
His financial dependence on Pisa, and to a lesser extent on Lucca,
probably provides the key to the enigma of his relationship with his
former protégé. Had Castruccio lived, therefore, it seems possible that
he might have been able to exploit the emperor's shortage of money to
secure an extension of his vicariate and perhaps even Ludwig's
consent to the absorption of Pisa within his dukedom, thus making it
part of the hereditary possessions of his family.

would have been sufficient to support what was, in early fourteenth-century terms, an
effective military force.

    [237] Ibid., cc. 64'., 77'., G. Villani, *Cronica*, x. 94, 100.
    [238] G. Villani, *Cronica*, x. 82.
    [239] On 20 August 1328, the Florentines reported that Castruccio had raised 20,000
florins destined for Ludwig of Bavaria by obtaining an advance on his *gabelle* (ASF
Missive I Cancelleria no. 3, c. 68'.). If this information was correct, it would seem that,
at this stage, the duke of Lucca was already preparing to meet the emperor's financial
needs, in return presumably for Ludwig's continued endorsement of his position in
Pisa.

Hopes such as these, however, if he ever entertained them, were soon to be dashed by his illness. The Pisan chroniclers were later to attribute this to poisoning: according to them he sickened after having eaten peaches offered to him during a *palio* held in Pisa on the occasion of the ceremony of thanksgiving to the Virgin Mary, presumably on the feast of her assumption, 15 August.[240] Probably. however, Villani and the author of the 'Storie pistoresi' were closer to the truth in their belief that the complaint from which Castruccio died was brought on by the rigours and exhaustion of the Pistoian campaign.[241] But the most likely cause of his fatal illness was some kind of epidemic which affected those who had been involved in the recent hostilities, including Galeazzo Visconti whose death occurred shortly before that of his former commander.[242] (The ailment from which Filippo di Sangineto suffered late in July during his attempt to relieve Pistoia may have been a result of the same infection, as may the fever which was to carry off Charles of Calabria on 9 November in Naples.[243])

Whatever the origins of his illness, there is general agreement that he contracted it probably within about a fortnight of his recapture of Pistoia.[244] While he lay sick in Lucca, his condition deteriorated and the likelihood of his death made it necessary to make some provision for that eventuality. According to Villani, secret negotiations had been opened with the Florentines to explore the possibility of a peace with them. There is no reference to these in any of the surviving official sources which instead appear to have assumed that Ludwig of Bavaria and Castruccio were planning a concerted attack on Florence,[245] but the emperor was, it seems, later convinced that they had taken place, so there may have been some preliminary discussions with individuals, if not at government level, to examine the prospects of an accord. If there were, however, they came to nothing because of the Lucchese ruler's illness. The lack of time to arrive at an accommodation with his

---

[240] Sardo, *Cronaca*, 83, 'Cronica di Pisa', *RIS*, xv, col. 1000. That the date of this *palio* was that of the feast of the Assumption of the Virgin Mary, namely on 15 August, is suggested by ASP Comune A94 cc. 20`., 22`. and `., 23`., which records the spending, on the twelfth and thirteenth of that month, of money in preparation for two *pali*.

[241] G. Villani, *Cronica*, x. 86, 'Storie pistoresi', 126.

[242] G. Villani, *Cronica*, x. 86.

[243] Ibid., x. 107, Bevere, 'La signoria', xxxv. 432, Ficker, *Urkunden*, 107.

[244] The 'Storie pistoresi', 126, speaks of him sickening shortly after the retaking of Pistoia, which is consistent with his falling ill on or soon after 15 August.

[245] See ASF Missive I Cancelleria no. 3, c. 65`., 68`., 70`. The references in Villani to the alleged negotiations between Castruccio and the Florentines are in *Cronica*, x. 86, 104.

enemies therefore left Castruccio with no choice but to advise his heirs to do their best to hold what they had. He suggested that, in the event of his death, news of it should be withheld for a week so as to permit Lucca, Pistoia, and Pisa to be well enough garrisoned with troops to prevent any uprising against his successors.

He died on 3 September, the same day of the year as that later self-made ruler and general of genius, Oliver Cromwell.[246] His eldest son Arrigo, who inherited his dukedom, kept the event secret, as he had been instructed, until the tenth, in the meantime securing his control over the three cities his father had left him. Then, on the fourteenth, true to the provisions of Castruccio's will, he had the body of the deceased duke, robed in Franciscan habit, buried in the church of San Francesco in Lucca, after an appropriately grand and impressive funeral.[247] Although excommunicated, this great enemy of the Church had died piously, confessing himself and receiving the sacrament of extreme unction, and was now interred as a member of an order distinguished at this time both for its spirituality and for the opposition of its foremost minds[248] to the papacy which had also been Castruccio's antagonist. In choosing his last resting-place, the Ghibelline captain saw to it that, in death as well as life, he should remain a true imperialist.

As he lay dying, he is reported to have said 'I see myself dead and when I am gone, you will see all overturned.'[249] Whatever might have been meant by this prediction, there is no doubt that, without him, the state which he had painstakingly built up began quickly to crumble. His decease had, in fact, come at a time singularly unpropitious for a

---

[246] G. Villani, *Cronica*, x. 86, 'Storie pistoresi', 126, BNF MS Palat. 571, c. 26ʳ. BNF MS Magliab. xxv, 19 gives 4 September as the date of Castruccio's death, but this would appear to be a scribal error. The decease of the duke of Lucca was not reported in official sources till it became public knowledge, in Pisa on 10 September (ASP Comune A214, c. 59ʳ.) and in Florence on the thirteenth (ASF Missive I Cancelleria no. 3, c. 73ᵛ.).

[247] G. Villani, *Cronica*, x. 86, 'Storie pistoresi', 126, Lazzareschi, 'Documenti', 397.

[248] This was, of course, the period of the Franciscan schism when the majority of the order, under its general Michael of Cesena, had fallen out with Pope John XXII over the issue of the poverty of Christ. Michael of Cesena and William of Ockham had, in fact, fled from Avignon at the end of May and arrived in Pisa on 9 June 1328 (L. Baudry, *Guillaume d'Occam: sa vie, ses œuvres, ses idées sociales et politiques* (Paris, 1949), i. 114–16). In Italy, they were joined by other Franciscans, such as Marsilio of Padua and Pietro da Corvara (the latter of whom had become antipope as Nicholas V on 12 May), in the entourage of Ludwig of Bavaria. The closing months of the Lucchese tyrant's life therefore coincided with the peak of the conflict between the 'Spiritual' wing of the Franciscans and the papacy.

[249] G. Villani, *Cronica*, x. 86.

smooth succession of his dominions to his heirs. His sons, Arrigo, Vallerano and Giovanni, were still young[250] and seem, on the basis of their later lives, to have been completely lacking in their father's political and military talents. Ludwig of Bavaria, by now desperately short of money with which to pay his troops, was in central Italy, ready to exploit any opportunity to restore his fading fortunes.[251] Worst of all was the situation in Pisa over which Castruccio's vicariate had in effect lapsed with his death and where the inhabitants were only too eager to regain their freedom. When Arrigo had seized control of their city, he had met armed resistance. While this had been easily overcome, it escaped neither its citizens nor the emperor when he heard what had happened that, in asserting his authority by force where he had no legal right to rule, the new duke of Lucca had acted unconstitutionally, so risking not only the loss of Pisa but also the forfeiture of his recently inherited title.[252]

Once informed of the latest developments, Ludwig in fact lost no time in going to Pisa. When he arrived on 21 September, Arrigo Castracani added to his error in arbitrarily seizing power there the even greater folly of admitting the emperor.[253] Presumably feeling he could count on the loyalty neither of the mercenary garrison nor the inhabitants of the city, Castruccio's son withdrew to Lucca, leaving Ludwig to take over the reins of government. The latter immediately installed a new vicar, Tarlatino de' Tarlati of Arezzo,[254] and heard from the Pisans of the real and alleged misdeeds of their former Lucchese masters. Reports that Castruccio had, towards the end of his

---

[250] Their ages at this time are not known for certain but their names suggest that they must have been born following the Emperor Henry VII's entry into Italy in 1310.

[251] When news reached him of Castruccio's death Ludwig was besieging Grosseto which he left on 18 September (G. Villani, *Cronica*, x. 100).

[252] According to Villani, it was Castruccio who advised his son Arrigo to make himself lord of Pisa by force of arms (*Cronica*, x. 86). Given the imprudence of such an action, however, one may doubt whether the Lucchese ruler, who had always been very careful to secure legal sanction for his authority, would in fact have counselled it, particularly given Arrigo's need for the emperor's support in the difficult initial stage of his rule.

[253] ASF Missive I Cancelleria no. 3, c. 74ʳ., 77ᵛ., G. Villani, *Cronica*, x. 100. According to Villani, he hurried to Pisa partly because he was afraid that Castruccio's sons might surrender it to the Florentines. The fleet under Peter of Sicily also arrived in Pisa on the twenty-first, thus making any defence against the emperor very difficult. That Ludwig was freely allowed by Arrigo to enter the city is clear from the fact that its keys were handed to him by Nerio Saggina, the guardian of the younger Castracani (BNF MS Palat. 571, c. 26ᵛ.).

[254] Villani, *Cronica*, x. 100, ASP Comune A214, c. 59ᵛ.

life, secretly negotiated with the Florentines particularly set the emperor against that ruler's progeny. To repair the damage done by such accusations, Pina, the widow of the late duke of Lucca, went to Pisa with 10,000 florins worth of money, jewels, and horses in the hope that these gifts would restore her sons to Ludwig's favour. Evidently believing that this had been regained, she then invited him to Lucca where he came on 5 October and was received with great honour. The emperor's presence, however, provided the Lucchese who were chafing at the government of Castruccio's sons with the opportunity to rise against them. Although this revolt which occurred on 7 October was quelled with the help of Ludwig's German mercenaries, it achieved part of its desired effect in that, following it, the emperor entrusted the city to Frederick, the burgrave of Nürnberg, who ruled it as his vicar.[255] When this noble showed himself too sympathetic to the Castracani and, according to Villani, agreed to a marriage alliance with them, he was removed from office on 8 November and replaced by Friedrich von Oettingen. At the same time, Castruccio's sons were deprived of the ducal title they had inherited from their father and, together with their mother, exiled to Pontemoli.[256]

Thus, the principality which had been built up with such effort over the previous twelve years collapsed within a few weeks. The reasons for its rapid disintegration may be found partly in the youth and political inexperience of Castruccio's heirs, partly in the timing of his death, and more fundamentally in the underlying weaknesses of the state which he had constructed. Like the other regional tyrannies of fourteenth-century Italy, the conglomerate of communes which he had attempted to weld into a single unit began to break up into its component parts when he was no longer there to hold it together. In each of the cities he had acquired, dormant republican aspirations were rekindled and, even if they did not result in the re-establishment of communal regimes,[257] served to undermine the existing seigneurial

---

[255] Villani, *Cronica*, x. 104, BNF MS Palat. 571, c. 26ᵛ. The chroniclers refer to the burgrave as 'Porcaro', 'Boltrone', or 'Boldrano', but Davidsohn identified him with Frederick of Nürnberg on the basis of S. Bongi, *Bandi lucchesi* (see *Storia*, iv. 1165). According to Bongi, Frederick was imperial vicar-general in Tuscany from 17 October to 7 November 1328.

[256] Villani, *Cronica*, x. 104, Davidsohn, *Storia*, iv. 1165.

[257] After the departure of Ludwig of Bavaria early in 1329 Lucca fell into the hands of some of his former knights who had deserted him when he failed to pay them and had, since the previous November, made their headquarters on Il Cerruglio above Altopascio. Under the command of Marco Visconti, these mercenaries tried to sell the city to a succession of prospective purchasers and eventually disposed of it to

government. Besides, the state which Castruccio had created had as its capital a small city which could only with difficulty contend with a Florence then at the height of its power and prosperity. In order to match the resources of his enemies, he needed to absorb neighbouring communes; yet in doing so he added to his already considerable problems the further one of reconciling to his rule the state of Pisa which, by virtue of its size and historical tradition, saw itself as the champion of the Ghibelline cause in Tuscany and would thus not easily resign itself to be a mere satellite of a hated Lucca. The problems confronting Castruccio were, in fact, such that all his extraordinary military and diplomatic skills were required for him to overcome them. It was therefore not surprising that, when he was no longer there to compensate for the inherent weaknesses of his position, his dominions should fall apart.

It would, however, be a mistake to conclude from this that what he had attempted to do was, by its very nature, foredoomed to failure. In twelve years he had laid the foundations of a Tusco-Ligurian principality. Probably he would have needed another twelve to consolidate it. Had he lived that time, it is very unlikely that he would have come to dominate Tuscany as his enemies feared, but he could have created a durable state lying between those of Florence and Milan. The mistakes that cost his sons their inheritance were not ones that he would have made. Had he not died when he did, there seems little doubt that he could have preserved his power through the difficult period before the return of Ludwig of Bavaria to Germany and then attempted, through his links with the Gherardesca in Pisa[258] and the Tedici in Pistoia, to strengthen his hold on those two cities. If the reports of his secret negotiations with the Florentines in August 1328 were accurate, it would seem that his aim by this stage was more to

Gherardino Spinola of Genoa for 60,000 florins. It subsequently passed through the hands of several masters before being taken by the Pisans in 1342. Pistoia in May 1329 went over to the Guelph camp, becoming a virtual dependency of Florence, while in Pisa, the following June, Fazio della Gherardesca, Castruccio's son-in-law, expelled the emperor's vicar and officials and established what was virtually a seigneurial regime of his own (G. Villani, *Cronica*, x. 105, 126–8, 131, 'Storie pistoresi', 128–9, Sardo, *Cronaca*, 84, BNF MS Palat. 571, c. 27ʳ. and ᵛ.).

[258] According to N. Toscanelli (*I conti di Donoratico della Gherardesca, signori di Pisa* (Pisa, 1937), 371) the facility with which the Lucchese tyrant managed to exploit the resources of Pisa for his own ends between his return from Rome and his acquisition of his vicariate was due to the support he received from the Gherardesca. (It was also in the premises formerly occupied by Nieri, count of Donoratico, that the duke of Lucca had his office or 'camera' while he was in Pisa (ASL Diplomatico Sbarra, 15/9/1328).)

secure the gains he had made than to seek a further extension of his territories. Given that, with the resources he now had, it was possible for him to hold his own but not completely overcome his main adversary, Florence, this would certainly have been the wisest course for him to follow.

The chroniclers of his lifetime and subsequent historians have both tended to represent him as a man driven by an insatiable lust for conquest. Such an impression of him, however, is largely due to the fact that he died at the relatively early age of 47, after twelve years in power spent in establishing himself as a ruler and then expanding his state to enable it to survive within a region in which the balance of forces naturally favoured his enemies, the Guelphs. If he had had a longer life, he might have been remembered not only for extending the boundaries of his principality but for securing them by accommodation with his neighbours. In that event, he would have taken his place with his contemporaries, Matteo Visconti of Milan and Can Grande della Scala of Verona, not as a mere upstart conqueror, but as the founder of a new type of regional dynastic state. By reason of his early death, Castruccio's tragedy was, as Machiavelli saw, one of accident. Yet underlying this was a deeper drama, that of the conflict between ability and force of circumstance. Singularly favoured in one sense because of his capacity to take advantage of the changes in the nature of government and war which were occurring in the Italy of his day, he was yet limited by the narrowness of his original political base and by the strength of the obstacles with which he had to contend. Confronting a Florence which could replace its armies almost as soon as he had destroyed them and attempting to make of tiny Lucca the capital of a state which could match his enemy's wealth and power, he was vulnerable to the least mischance that could befall him. Up to his death, success had brought him only precarious gains. Later, with his position stronger and more established, it might have been different, but in his final year, the loss of Pistoia, implying in turn the need to control Pisa, had sufficed, by setting Ludwig of Bavaria against his sons, eventually to annul all that he had achieved. His death, too, had at that point the power to undo his whole life's work.

The sharp contrast between his rapid rise and the even quicker loss by his heirs of what he had left them has invested his story with a fatal quality which did not escape his early biographers. To them, Castruccio's career exemplified the workings of fortune as, for the contemporary chronicler Villani, it had illustrated the ways of Providence. To us, seeing him in a longer perspective, the brilliant fragility of his passing achievement seems rather to reflect the experience of a particular historical moment, one in which economic and military pressures were undermining the foundations of the compact political units which had dominated the Middle Ages but when the particularism which these had generated had not yet faded sufficiently to allow for the emergence of cohesive larger states. Castruccio, for all his faults of ambition and brutality, was a hero of that time, swept along by its currents only to have his work swept away by them. As a man, he remains elusive. His flattering portrait by Villani[259] which represents him as tall, thin, fair, pale, attractive, and graceful in face and figure strikes us as mask or effigy-like in its idealized features. It reveals little of his personality which must have been so caught up in action, so absorbed in a single-minded quest for territory and power as to leave in the mind of his contemporaries the impression of a person monumental in quality and presence: the general who never lost a battle, the tyrant who made the Florentines tremble, the native of a small city who raised it briefly to prominence. If his achievements were soon obliterated, the memory of what he had done persisted. Around it, successive generations wove varying legends that paid tribute, even through their distortions, to the force of a character enigmatic in its inner nature but spectacular and meteoric in its outward effects.

[259] For Villani's portrait and estimate of Castruccio see *Cronica*, x. 86.

Bibliography

ARCHIVAL AND OTHER MANUSCRIPT SOURCES

Archivio di Stato in Lucca

Diplomatico. Numerous parchment rolls consulted, dating from period between 1273 and 1328, in following *fondi*: Archivio di Stato, Spedale, Tarpea, Compagnia della Croce, San Nicolao, Serviti, San Romano, Biblioteca F. M. Fiorentini, Biblioteca Sbarra, Corte dei Mercanti, Certosa, Santa Maria Corteorlandini, Fregionaia, Santa Giustina, Archivio dei Notari.

Capitoli nos. 1, 4, 8, 17, 29, 52.
Atti di Castruccio nos. 1–5.
Curia dei Rettori nos. 1 and 2.
Anziani avanti la libertà nos. 7 and 9.
Fortificazioni della città e dello stato no. 1.
Libri di Corredo alle carte della signoria no. 4.
Ufficio sulle differenze dei confini no. 541.
Condotta nos. 1–2.
Proventi nos. 1, 13.
Camarlengo generale no. 2.
Taglia delle 57 mila e della paga dei pedoni no. 1.
Estimo no. 13.
Opera di Santa Croce no. 7.
Podestà di Lucca nos. 1–2.
Curia di San Cristoforo nos. 25–67.
Curia dei Treguani no. 1.
Curia Nuova di Giustizia e dell'Esecutore no. 1.
Curia dei Ribelli e dei Banditi nos. 1 and 4.
Archivio Guinigi nos. 1, 72, 130 bis, 263.
Archivio Arnolfini no. 1.
Manoscritti nos. 10, 15, 38, 49, 54, 69, 124–8.
Manoscritti G. B. Orsucci nos. 36, 40, 43.
Archivio Sardini no. 33.
Raccolte Speciali: Carte di Tommaso Trenta nos. 7 and 10, San Frediano no. 252.
Archivio notarile nos. 14, 15, 17, 19, 22, 23, 27, 29, 30, 31, 32, 40–9, 52–77, 86, 89, 92–6, 98–100.

Archivio capitolare e arcivescovile di Lucca

Registers A + 11, LL 24–7, 30, 31, 32, 33, 36, 49, 52, 53, 54.

Biblioteca statale di Lucca

Manoscritti nos. 64–5, 430–2, 837, 873, 897, 900, 910, 920, 925, 942, 1009, 1093, 1200, 1247, 1556, 1661, 1858–9, 1886, 1889, 2588, 2629, 2941, 3028, 3127, 3138, 3506.

Archivio di Stato in Firenze

Provvisioni nos. 14–25.
Provvisioni Protocolli nos. 5–7.
Liber Fabarum nos. 11–13.
Capitoli Registri no. 16.
Missive Minutari no. 5.
Missive Originali no. 2.
Signori Carteggi: Missive I Cancelleria no. 3.
Archivio Bardi nos. 78, 88.

Biblioteca nazionale di Firenze

Manoscritti Palatino no. 571.
Magliabechiano xxv, 19, 413.

Archivio di Stato in Pisa

Archivio del Comune.
A29 Paces et Protocolli.
A48–50 Consigli, Provvisioni, e Ambasciate.
A82–94 Provvisioni degli Anziani.
A214 Breve Vetus Anthianorum.
Ospedale S. Chiara no. 2079.

Archivio segreto vaticano

Registri Vaticani Giovanni XXII   Registri Comuni 53–94.
                                     Registri Segreti 109–15.
                   Nicolao V (anti-pope) Registri Segreti 118.
Instrumenti Miscellanei no. 951.
Documenti di Castel Sant' Angelo, Armadio C, no. 1064.

Archivio de la Corona de Aragon

Cancelleria Registers 341–2, 408.
CRD Ap 91, 108, Caja 83, 940 Caja 77.

PRINTED DOCUMENTARY SOURCES

Baluze, E. (S. Baluzio), *Vitae Paparum Avenionensium*, 2 vols. (Paris, 1693).

Bevere, R., 'La signoria di Firenze tenuta da Carlo figlio di Re Roberto negli anni 1326 e 1327', *Archivio storico per le provincie napoletane*, xxxiii (1908), 436–65, 639–62; xxxiv (1909), 3–18, 197–221, 403–43, 597–639; xxxv (1910), 3–46, 205–72, 452–8, 607–36; xxxvi (1911), 3–34, 254–85, 407–33.

Boehmer, J. F. *Fontes rerum germanicarum*, 4 vols. (Stuttgart, 1843–68).

—— *Regista imperii inde ab anno MCCCXIII usque ad annum MCCCXLVII (Register Kaiser Ludwigs des Baiern und seiner Zeit 1314—1347)* (Frankfurt-on-Main and Innsbruck, 1839, 1865).

Bonaini, F. ed., 'Ordinamenti di Giustizia del comune e popolo di Firenze compilati nel 1293', *Archivio storico italiano* (Ser. II), i. pt. 1 (1855), 1–93.

Bongars, J., *Gesta Dei per Francos*, 2 vols. (Hanover, 1611).

Bongi S. and L. del Prete, 'Il statuto del comune di Lucca del 1308', (Lucca, 1867), *Memorie e documenti per servire alla storia di Lucca*, vol. iii, pt. 3.

Borgo, F. dal, *Raccolta di scelti diplomi pisani* (Pisa, 1765).

Davidsohn, R., *Forschungen zur Geschichte von Florenz*, 4 vols. (Berlin, 1892–1908).

Doenniges, W., *Acta Henrici VII imperatoris romanorum et monumenta quaedam alia medii aevi*, 2 vols. (Berlin, 1839).

Ficker, J., *Urkunden zur Geschichte des Römerzuges Kaiser Ludwig des Baiern und der italienischen Verhaeltnisse seiner Zeit* (Innsbruck, 1865).

Finke, H., *Acta aragonensia: Quellen zur deutschen, italienischen, französichen, spanischen, zur Kirchen und Kulturgeschichte*, 2 vols. (Berlin and Leipzig, 1908–22).

Hagemann, W., *Documenti sconosciuti dell'Archivio capitolare di Verona per la storia degli Scaligeri (1259—1304)* (Verona, 1973).

Ildefonso di San Luigi, *Delizie degli eruditi toscani*, 25 vols. (Florence 1770–89).

Lazzareschi, E., 'Documenti della signoria di Castruccio Castracani conservati nel R. Archivio di Stato in Lucca', *Atti della R. Accademia Lucchese* (NS), iii (1934), 281–409.

—— ed., *Libro della comunità dei mercanti lucchesi in Bruges* (Milan, 1947).

Mansi, G. D., *Stephani Baluzii tutelensis miscellanea novo ordine digesta et non paucis ineditis monumentis opportunisque animadversionibus aucta*, 4 vols. (Lucca, 1761–4).

Mollat, G., *Lettres communes des papes d'Avignon analysées d'après les registres dits d'Avignon et du Vatican: Jean XXII (1316—1334)* 16 vols. (Paris, 1904–47).

Monumenta Germaniae historica legum, Sectio IV. *Constitutiones*, vol. vi, pt. 1 (Hanover, 1914–27).

Mosiici, L., 'Ricerche sulla cancelleria di Castruccio Castracani', *Annali della scuola speciale per archivisti e bibliotecari dell'università di Roma*, vii (1967), 1–86.

Piattoli, R., 'Documenti per la storia di Castruccio Antelminelli e delle sue imprese', *Bollettino storico lucchese* xv, (1943), 14–21.

Preger, W., 'Die Verträge Ludwigs des Baiern mit Friedrich dem Schönen in den Jahren 1325 und 1326', *Abhandlungen der historische Klasse der königlich bayerischen Akademie der Wissenschaften*, xvii (1883), 103–338.

Riezler, S., *Vatikanische Akten zur deutschen Geschichte in der Zeit Ludwigs des Baiern* (Innsbruck, 1891).

Winkelmann, E. A., *Acta imperii inedita saeculi XIII et XIV*, 2 vols. (Innsbruck, 1880–5).

Zacharia, F. A., *Anecdotum medii aevi* (Turin, 1755).

PRINTED CHRONICLE AND NARRATIVE SOURCES

'Anciennes Chroniques de Flandres', ed. J. N. de Wailly and M. de Lisle, in M. Bouquet, ed., *Recueil des historiens des Gaules et de la France*, xxii (Paris, 1865).

'Annales mediolanenses', *RIS*, xvi, cols. 641–840.

'Annales parmenses maiores', *Monumenta Germaniae historica scriptores* xviii (1863), 664–790.

'Annales senenses', *Monumenta Germaniae historica scriptores*, xix (1866), 223–35.

'Antica cronichetta volgare lucchese già della biblioteca di F-M. Fiorentini', *Atti della R. Accademia Lucchese*, xxvi (1893), 215–54.

Azario, P., 'Chronicon de gestis principum vicecomitum ab anno 1250 ad annum 1362', *RIS*, xvi, cols. 297–440.

Bazano, G. da, 'Chronicon mutinense', *RIS*, xv, cols. 555–634 and (ed. T. Casini), *RIS* (n. edn.), xv, pt. 4.

Calvacanti, G., *Trattato politico-morale*, ed. M. T. Grendler (Geneva, 1973).

Cavitelli, L., *Cremonenses annales* (Cremona, 1588).

'Chronicon estense', *RIS*, xv, cols. 299–548 or (eds. G. Bertoni and E. P. Vicini), *RIS*, (n. edn.), xv, pt. 3.

'Chronicon parmense ab anno 1038 usque ad annum 1338', ed. G. Bonazzi, *RIS* (n. edn.), ix, pt. 9.

'Chronicon pisanum ab urbe condita ad annum 1342', and 'Chronicon sanminiatese usque ad annum 1318', in G-D. Mansi (cited above), i. 448–68.

Comugnori, G. di Lemmo da, 'Diario', *Cronache dei secoli XIII e XIV* (Florence, 1876) in *Documenti di storia italiana pubblicati della R. Deputazione sugli studi di storia patria per le provincie di Toscana, dell'Umbria e delle Marche*, vi (Florence, 1876).

Cornazani, G., *Istoria di Parma 1301–1355, RIS*, xii, cols. 729–50.

Cortusio, G., 'Historia de novitatibus Padue et Lombardiae', *RIS*, xii, cols.

767–954 and entitled 'Chronica de novitatibus Padue et Lombardie', (ed. B. Pagnin) *RIS* (n. edn.), xii, pt. 5.

'Cronaca senese attribuita ad Agnolo di Tura del Grasso, detta *La cronaca maggiore*' and 'Cronaca senese dei fatti riguardanti la città ed il suo territorio', ed. A. Lisini and F. Iacometti, *RIS* (n. edn.), xv, pt. 6, 39–172, 253–564.

'Cronica di Pisa', *RIS*, xv, cols. 973–1086.

'Cronica illorum de la Scala', *Monumenti storici pubblicati della R. Deputazione veneta di storia patria* (Ser. III), *Cronache e diarii*, vol. ii, pt. 1 (Venice, 1890), 497–503.

Dominici, L., 'Cronache', *Rerum pistoriensium scriptores*, i (Pistoia, 1933–7).

Ferreto Vicentino, 'Historia rerum in Italia gestarum ab anno MCCL usque ad annum MCCCXVII', *RIS*, ix, cols. 94–1182 and *Opere*, ed. C. Cipolla, 3 vols., *Fonti per la storia d'Italia* (Rome, 1914).

Flamma, G. de la, 'De rebus gestis ab Azone, Luchino et Johanne Vicecomitibus 1328–1342', *RIS*, xii, cols. 997–1050.

—— 'Manipulus florum sive historia mediolanensis ab origine urbis ad annum 1336', *RIS*, xi, cols. 537–740.

Giustiniani, A., *Annali della repubblica di Genova*, 2 vols. (Genoa, 1854).

Granchi, R., 'De proeliis Tusciae, poema', *RIS*, xi, cols. 291–356 and (ed. C. Meliconi) *RIS* (n. edn.), xi, pt. 2.

Machiavelli, N., 'La vita di Castruccio Castracani', ed. F. Gaeta, *Opere*, vii (Milan, 1962), 9–41.

Manucci, A., *Le azioni di Castruccio Castracani* (Lucca, 1843).

Morigia, B., 'Chronicon modeotinense ab origine usque ad annum 1349', *RIS*, xii, cols. 1061–184.

Muntaner, R., 'Cronica', in *Les Quatre Grans Croniques*, ed. F. Soldevila (Barcelona, 1971), 665–1000.

Mussato, A., 'De gestis Henrici VII Caesaris', *RIS*, x, cols. 27–568.

—— 'De gestis italicorum post mortem Henrici VII Caesaris', *RIS*, x, cols. 573–784.

Mussi, G. de', 'Chronicon placentinum', *RIS*, xvi, cols. 447–560.

Sardo, R., *Cronaca di Pisa*, ed. O. Banti, *Fonti per la storia d'Italia* (Rome, 1963).,

Sercambi, G., *Le croniche*, ed. S. Bongi, 3 vols. *Fonti per la storia d'Italia* (Lucca, 1892).

Stella, G., 'Annales genuenses', *RIS*, xvii, cols. 951–1318.

'Storie pistoresi (1300–1348)', ed. S. A. Barbi, *RIS* (n. edn.), xi, pt. 5.

Tegrimi, N., *Vita Castruccii Antelminelli lucensis ducis* (Lucca, 1742).

Tholomeus von Lucca, *Die Annalen*, ed. B. Schmeidler, *Monumenta Germaniae historica scriptores* (NS), viii (Berlin, 1930).

Villani, G., *Cronica*, ed. F. G. Dragomanni, 4 vols. (Florence, 1844–5).

Villani, M., *Cronica*, ed. F. G. Dragomanni, 2 vols. (Florence, 1846).

Zurita y Castro, J., *Annales de la corona de Aragon*, 6 vols. (Saragossa, 1610).

SECONDARY WORKS

Alferuoli, P., *Historie delle cose più notabili eseguite in Toscana et in altri luoghi et in particolare in Pistoia* (Pistoia, 1628).

Andreolli, B., 'Considerazioni sulle campagne lucchesi nella prima metà del XIV secolo', *Atti del convegno su Castruccio Castracani e il suo tempo* (Lucca, 1986) (henceforth *ACCC*), 277–302.

Ardito, F., *Nobiltà, popolo e signoria del Conte Fazio di Donoratico in Pisa nella prima metà del secolo XIV* (Cuneo, 1920).

Arribas Palau, A., *La conquista de Cerdeña por Jaime II de Aragon* (Barcelona, 1952).

Azzi, G. degli, 'La dimora di Carlo figliuolo di Re Roberto a Firenze (1326–7)', *Archivio storico italiano* (Ser. v) xlii (1908), 45–83, 259–305.

Balaguer, V., *Historia de Cataluña y de la corona de Aragon* (Barcelona, 1862).

Banti, O., 'Castruccio Castracani nelle "Croniche" di Giovanni Sercambi', *Atti del primo convegno di studi castrucciani* (Lucca, 1981), 47–50.

—— 'Nuove osservazioni sulla questione della moneta "lucchese" (sec. XII) e su un accordo monetario fra Pisa e Lucca nel 1319', *Bollettino storico pisano*, xlvii (1978), 157–75.

Baracchini, C., ed., *Il secolo di Castruccio. Fonti e documenti di storia lucchese* (Lucca, 1983).

Barbadoro, B., *Le finanze della repubblica fiorentina* (Florence, 1929).

Barsali, I. B,., *Guida di Lucca*, 2nd edn. (Lucca, 1970).

Barsotti, E., *Sulle origine dell'arte della seta in Lucca* (Lucca, 1905).

Baudry, L., *Guillaume d'Occam: sa vie, ses œuvres, ses idées sociales et politiques* (Paris, 1949).

Beardwood, A., *Alien Merchants in England 1350–1377* (Cambridge, Mass., 1931).

Benassuti, G., *Storia degli Scaligeri, signori di Verona* (Verona, 1826 and Rome, 1936).

Benedetto, G., 'I rapporti tra Castruccio Castracani e la chiesa di Lucca', *Annuario della biblioteca civica di Massa* (1980), 73–97.

Benocci, C., 'La tomba di Guarnerio Castracani degli Antelminelli nella chiesa di S. Francesco a Sarzana: ricerche e contribuiti', *Rivista di archeologia, storia, costume del Istituto Storico Lucchese*, ix (1981), 3, 9–22.

Benvenuti, G., *Storia della repubblica di Pisa* (Pisa, 1968).

Berengo, M., *Nobili e mercanti nella Lucca del Cinquecento* (Turin, 1965).

Bini, T., *I lucchesi a Venezia* (Lucca, 1853–6).

Blomquist, T. W., 'The Castracani Family of Thirteenth Century Lucca', *Speculum*, xlvi (1971), 459–76.

—— 'Commercial Association in Medieval Lucca', *Business History Review*, xlv (1971), 157–78.

—— 'The Dawn of Banking in an Italian Commune: Thirteenth Century Lucca', *The Dawn of Modern Banking*, (New Haven, 1979), 53–75.

— 'La famiglia e gli affari: le compagnie internazionali lucchesi al tempo di Castruccio Castracani', *ACCC*, 145–56.

— 'Lineage, land and business in the thirteenth century: The Guidiccioni Family of Lucca', *Actum Luce*, ix (1980), 7–29, and xi (1982), 7–34.

— 'Trade and Commerce in Thirteenth Century Lucca', (unpublished thesis, University of Minnesota, 1966).

Bonatti, F. ed., *Castruccio Castracani degli Antelminelli in Lunigiana* (Pisa, 1981).

Bongi, S., *Bandi lucchesi del secolo decimoquarto tratti dai regesti del R. Archivio di Stato in Lucca* (Bologna, 1863).

— *Della mercatura dei lucchesi nei secoli XIII e XIV* (Lucca, 1858).

— *Di Paolo Guinigi e delle sue ricchezze* (Lucca, 1871).

— *Inventario del R. Archivio di Stato in Lucca* i–iv (Lucca, 1872–88).

Bowsky, W. M., *Henry VII in Italy* (Lincoln, Nebraska, 1960).

— *A Medieval Italian Commune: Siena under the Nine 1287–1355* (Berkeley, 1981).

Branchi, E., *Storia della Lunigiana feudale*, 3 vols. (Pistoia, 1897–8).

Caforio, L., 'Il sacco di Lucca e il furto di S. Frediano e di S. Romano', *La biblioteca delle scuole italiane*, xvii (1905), 201–3.

Caggese, R., *Roberto d'Angiò e i suoi tempi*, 2 vols. (Florence, 1922–30).

Campetti, P., 'Deodato Orlandi', *Atti della R. Accademia Lucchese* (NS), v (1942), 145–58.

— 'Ritratti di Castruccio Castracani', *Atti della R. Accademia Lucchese* (NS), iii (1934), 261–79.

Canestrini, G., 'Documenti per servire alla storia della milizia italiana dal XIII secolo al XVI raccolti negli archivi della Toscana', *Archivio storico italiano* (Ser. I, xv (1851), pp. xi–clxvii, 1–552.

Carli, A., *Istoria della città di Verona sino all'anno MDXVII*, 7 vols. (Verona, 1796).

Carrara, M., *Gli Scaligeri* (Milan, 1966).

Castelli, P., 'Profezia e astrologia al tempo di Castruccio Castracani', *Rivista di archeologia, storia, costume del Istituto Storico Lucchese*, ix (1981), 3, 23–36.

Cecchini, G., 'La politica di Siena durante la guerra contro Castruccio Castracani', *Atti della R. Accademia Lucchese* (NS), iii (1934), 73–92.

Cianelli, A. N., 'Dissertazioni sopra la storia lucchese', *Memorie e documenti per servire all'istoria del principato lucchese*, i–iii (Lucca, 1813–16).

Cipolla, C., *Can Grande I della Scala* (Verona, 1881).

— *La storia politica di Verona* (with additions by L. Simeoni and O. Pellegrini) (Verona, 1900–54).

Cognasso, F., *La formazione dello stato visconteo* (Turin, 1953).

— 'L'unificazione della Lombardia sotto Milano', *Storia di Milano*, v (Milan, 1954), 65–99.

— *I Visconti* (Milan, 1966).

Contamine, P., *Guerre, état et société à la fin du moyen âge* (Paris and The Hague, 1972).

Corpus nummorum italicorum, x (Milan, 1929).

Coturri, E., 'La chiesa lucchese al tempo di Castruccio', *ACCC*, 113–24.

Cristiani, E., *Nobiltà e popolo nel comune di Pisa dalle origini del podestariato alla signoria dei Donoratico* (Naples, 1962).

—— 'Rileggendo i giudizi del Villani su Castruccio', *ACCC*, 57–66.

Davidsohn, R., *Storia di Firenze*, Italian translation, 8 vols. (Florence, 1956–68). Original German edition, 4 vols. (Berlin, 1896–1927).

Dorini, U., *Un grande feudatorio del Trecento: Spinetta Malaspina* (Florence, 1940).

Edler, F., 'The silk trade of Lucca during the thirteenth and fourteenth centuries' (unpublished dissertation, University of Chicago, 1930).

Ercole, F., *Dal comune al principato* (Florence, 1929).

Ferrer i Mallol, M. T., 'Mercenaris catalans a Ferrara 1307–1317', *Anuario de estudios medievales* (Instituto de historia medieval de Espana) ii (1965), 155–227.

Ferri, C., 'Alcune considerazioni sulla vita civile e amministrativa nel territorio lucchese al tempo di Castruccio Castracani', *ACCC*, 325–51.

Fioravanti, J.-M., *Memorie storiche della città di Pistoia* (Lucca, 1758).

Fiumi, E., *Storia economica e sociale di San Gimignano* (Florence, 1961).

Franceschini, G., 'La vita sociale e politica nel Duecento', *Storia di Milano* (Milan, 1954), iv, 331–92.

Frede, C. de, 'Da Carlo I d'Angiò a Giovanna I 1263–1372', *Storia di Napoli* (Naples, 1969), ii. 5–156.

Fuiano, M., 'Signorie e principati', *Nuove questioni di storia medioevale* (Milan 1964), 325–55.

Galliccioli, G. B., *Delle memorie venete antiche*, 4 vols. (Venice, 1795).

Giannini, G., 'Un contrasto popolare di argomento castrucciano', *Atti della R. Accademia Lucchese* (NS), iii, (1934), 165–200.

Gorrini, G., 'La politica di Lucca dal 1313 al 1345 e le sue relazioni con Giovanni XXII e Benedetto XII', *Miscellanea lucchese di studi storici e letterari in memoria di Salvatore Bongi* (Lucca, 1931), 131–8.

Green, L., 'Il capitolo della cattedrale di Lucca all'epoca di Castruccio Castracani', *ACCC*, 125–41.

—— *Chronicle into History* (Cambridge, 1972).

—— 'Il commercio lucchese ai tempi di Castruccio Castracani', *Atti del primo convegno di studi castrucciani* (Lucca, 1981), 5–19, and 'Lucchese commerce under Castruccio Castracani', *ACCC*, 217–64.

—— 'Lucca under Castruccio Castracani: the social and political foundations of an early fourteenth-century Italian tyranny', *I Tatti Studies* i (Florence, 1985), 137–59.

—— 'Il problema dell'Augusta e della villa di Castruccio Castracani a Massa Pisana', *ACCC*, i. 353–77.

—— 'Society and politics in fourteenth-century Lucca', *Altro polo*, iv. (1982), 29–50.

Hagemann, W., *Die Entstehung der Scaliger Signorie in Verona 1259–1304* (Berlin, 1937).

—— *Forschungen über di Quellen zur Geschichte der Entstehung der Scaliger Signorie in Verona* (Berlin, 1936).

Herlihy, D., *Pisa in the Early Renaissance. A Study of Urban Growth* (New Haven, 1958).

—— *Medieval and Renaissance Pistoia. The social history of an Italian town 1200–1420* (New Haven, 1967).

Jordan, E., *Les Origines de la domination angevine en Italie*, 2 vols. (Paris, 1909).

Kaeuper, R. W., *Bankers to the Crown: The Ricciardi of Lucca and Edward I* (Princeton, 1973).

Laurent, J., 'Feudalismo e signoria', *Archivio storico italiano*, cxxxvii (1971), 155–75.

Lazzareschi, E., *L'arte della seta in Lucca* (Pescia, 1930).

Lera, G., 'Le fortificazioni di Coreglia', *Atti del primo convegno di studi castrucciani* (Lucca, 1981), 21–38.

—— 'Francesco Castracani degli Antelminelli conte di Coreglia', *ACCC*, 405 seq.

Levi, G. , *Bonifacio VIII e le sue relazioni col comune di Firenze* (Rome, 1882).

Livi, G., 'I mercanti di seta lucchesi in Bologna nei secoli XIII e XIV', *Archivio storico italiano* (Ser. IV), vii (1881), 29–55.

Lot, F., *L'art militaire et les armées au moyen âge en Europe et dans le Proche-Orient* (Paris, 1946).

Lucarelli, G., *Castruccio Castracani degli Antelminelli* (Lucca, 1981).

Lucchesini, C., 'Della storia letteraria del ducato lucchese', *Memorie e documenti per servire all'istoria del ducato di Lucca*, ix–x (Lucca, 1825–31).

Luiso, F. P., 'Mercanti lucchesi dell'epoca di Dante II: gli antenati di Castruccio Castracani', *Bollettino storico lucchese*, x (1938), 69–94.

Lungo, I. del, *Dino Compagni e la sua cronica*, 3 vols. (Florence, 1879–87).

—— *I Bianchi e i Neri* (2nd edn., Milan, 1921).

Luzzati, M., 'Castruccio Castracani degli Antelminelli', *Dizionario biografico degli Italiani*, xxii (Rome, 1979), 200–10.

—— 'Castruccio nelle fonti cronachistiche documentarie oltremontane', *ACCC*, 79–97.

—— *Giovanni Villani e la compagnia dei Bonaccorsi* (Rome, 1971).

Maccioni, M., *Difesa del dominio dei conti della Gherardesca sopra la signoria di Donoratico, Bolgheri, Castagneto, etc.*, 2 vols. (Lucca, 1771).

Magnani, C., *Castruccio Castracani degli Antelminelli* (Milan, 1926).

Mancini, A., 'Castruccio in Inghilterra', *Atti della R. Accademia Lucchese* (NS), iii (1934), 147–64.

Manselli, R., 'Castruccio Castracani degli Antelminelli e la politica italiana nei primi decenni del Trecento', *ACCC*, 3–16.

—— 'Lo sinodo lucchese di Enrico del Carretto', *Italia sacra*, xv (1970), 198–246.

Marini, G., *Memorie istoriche degli archivi della Santa Sede e della biblioteca ottoboniana ora riunita alla Vaticana* (Rome, 1825).

Marongiù, A., 'Gli ordinamenti municipali. Momenti e aspetti dell'avvento della Signoria', *ACCC*, 17–34.

Massagli, D., 'Introduzione alla storia della zecca e delle monete lucchesi', *Memorie e documenti per servire alla storia di Lucca*, xi (Lucca, 1870).

Matraia, G., *Lucca nel milleduecento* (Lucca, 1843).

Mazzarosa, A., *Storia di Lucca dalla sua origine fino al 1814*, 2 vols. (Lucca, 1833).

Mazzei, A., 'Il castello di Vallecchia', *La provincia di Lucca* (1966), 63–6.

Mazzini, U., 'L'epigrafe pontremolese di Castruccio', *Giornale storico della Lunigiana*, iii (1911), 149–52.

Meek, C., *The Commune of Lucca under Pisan Rule 1342–69* (Cambridge, Mass., 1980).

—— 'Le finanze e l'amministrazione finanziaria al tempo di Castruccio', *ACCC*, 157–72.

—— *Lucca 1369–1400* (Oxford, 1978).

—— 'The Trade and Industry of Lucca in the Fourteenth Century', *Historical Studies* (Dublin, 1965), 39–58.

Melin, A., *Aragona in Sardegna* (Oristano, 1926).

Miquel Rossel, F., *Regesta de letras pontificias del archivo de la corona de Aragón* (Madrid, 1948).

Mirot, L., *Études lucquoises* (Paris, 1930).

Mommsen, T. E., 'Castruccio Castracani and the Empire', *Medieval and Renaissance Studies*, ed. E. F.,Rice, (Ithaca, New York, 1959), 19–32, originally published as 'Castruccio e l'impero', *Atti della R. Accademia Lucchese* (NS), iii (1934), 33–46.

Najemy, J. M., *Corporatism and Consensus in Florentine Electoral Politics* (Chapel Hill, 1982).

Oerter, H. L., 'Campaldino, 1289', *Speculum*, xliii (1968), 429–50.

Osheim, D., *An Italian Lordship: The Bishopric of Lucca in the Middle Ages* (Berkeley, 1977).

—— 'I sentimenti religiosi dei lucchesi al tempo di Castruccio', *ACCC*, 99–112.

Ottokar, N., *Il comune di Firenze alla fine del Dugento* (Florence, 1926).

Pacchi, D., *Ricerche istoriche sulla provincia della Garfagnana* (Modena, 1785).

Pampaloni, G., 'I magnati a Firenze alla fine del Dugento', *Archivio storico italiano*, cxxix (1971), 387–423.

Paoli, C., 'Le cavallate fiorentine nei secoli XIII e XIV', *Archivio storico italiano* (Ser III), i, pt. 2 (1865), 53–94.

Piattoli, R., 'L'imperatore Carlo IV e una ingloriosa seppur, forse, necessaria azione di Castruccio Castracani degli Antelminelli come signore e vicario imperiale di Pisa', *Studi storici in onore di Ottorino Bertolini* (Pisa, 1972), ii. 599–618.

Plesner, J., *L'Émigration de la campagne à la ville libre de Florence au XIIIe. siècle* (Copenhagen, 1934).

Preger, W., 'Ueber die Anfänge des kirchen-politischen Kampfes unter Ludwig dem Baier', *Abhandlungen der historische Klasse der königlich bayerischen Akademie der Wissenschaften*, xvi, pt. 2 (1882), 114–284.

Prestwich, M., 'Italian Merchants in late thirteenth- and early fourteenth-century England', *The Dawn of Modern Banking* (New Haven, 1979), 77–104.

Raveggi, S., M. Tarassi, D. Medici, P. Parenti, *Ghibellini, guelfi e popolo grasso* (Florence, 1978).

Re, E., 'La compagnia dei Ricciardi in Inghilterra e il suo fallimento alla fine del secolo XIII', *Archivio della società romana di storia patria*, xxxvi (1913), 87–138.

Reyerson, K. L., 'Lucchese in Montpellier in the era of Castruccio Castracani: the mintmasters' penetration of Languedocian commerce and finance', *ACCC*, 203–16.

Rhodes, W. E., 'The Italian Bankers in England and their loans to Edward I and Edward II', T. F. Tout and J. Tait, *Historical Essays* (Manchester, 1907), 137–68,.

Ricotti, E., *Storia delle compagnie di ventura in Italia*, 4 vols. (Turin, 1845–7).

Rinaldi, R., 'Il comune di Lucca, la S. Sede, l'impero i pisani e i garfagnani nel secolo XIII', *Rivista di scienze storiche*, i (1908), 165–8.

Robbert, L. B., 'I lucchesi e i loro affari commerciali al tempo di Castruccio', *ACCC*, 187–202..

Romano, G., *La guerra tra i Visconti e la chiesa* (Pavia, 1903).

Romiti, A., 'Il palazzo signorile ed il palazzo comunale di Lucca nel XIV secolo: problemi strutturali e funzionali', I. B. Barsali ed., *Il palazzo pubblico di Lucca* (Lucca, 1980), 37–47.

Roncioni, R., *Istorie pisane*, 4 vols. (Florence, 1844–5).

Rossi-Sabatini, G., *L'espansione di Pisa nel mediterraneo fino alla Meloria* (Florence, 1935).

—— *Pisa al tempo dei Donoratico 1316–1347* (Florence, 1938).

Rubinstein, N., 'Reprisals and citizenship in a law-suit in Lucca after the death of Castruccio Castracani', *Studi di storia medioevale e moderna per Ernesto Sestan* (Florence, 1980), 203–18.

Salavert y Roca. V., *Cerdeña y la expansión mediterranea de la corona de Aragon 1297–1314* (Madrid, 1956).

Salvemini, G., *Magnati e popolani a Firenze dal 1280 al 1295* (Florence, 1899).

Salvemini, S., *I balestrieri nel comune di Firenze* (Bari, 1905).

Salvi, M. A., *Delle istorie di Pistoia e fazioni d'Italia*, 3 vols. (Rome, Pistoia, Venice, 1656–62).

Salzer, E., *Ueber die Anfänge der Signorie in Oberitalien* (Berlin, 1900).

Sampieri, T., 'Gli inizi di Castruccio Castracani degli Antelminelli fra mercatura e arte militare', *Studi sul medio evo cristiano offerti a Raffaello Morghen* (Rome, 1974), ii. 873–87.

Santoli, Q., 'Pisa e Castruccio', *Atti della R. Accademia Lucchese* (NS), iii (1934), 93–146.

Sapori, A., 'Firenze e Castruccio: tentativi di guerra economica', *Atti della R. Accademia Lucchese* (NS), iii (1934), 59–72.

—— *Studi di storia economica*, 3rd edn., 2 vols. (Florence, 1955).

Schäfer, K. H., *Deutsche Ritter und Edelknechte in Italien*, 3 vols. (Paderborn, 1914).

Seghieri, M., 'I Castracani e l'attività mineraria in lucchesia', *ACCC*, 303–14.

—— 'La degradazione del territorio fra Pozzeveri e Porcari conseguente alla battaglia dell'Altopascio del 23 settembre 1325', *Atti del primo convegno di studi castrucciani* (Lucca, 1981), 39–46.

—— 'Fra Castracani e Antelminelli: note di genealogia e di consortato', *Rivista di archeologia, storia, costume del Istituto Storico Lucchese*, ix (1981), 3, 3–8.

Sestan, E., 'Le origine delle signorie cittadine: un problema esaurito?', *Bollettino dell'istituto storico italiano per il medio evo*, lxxiii (1962), 41–69.

Sforza, G., 'Castruccio Castracani degli Antelminelli e gli altri lucchesi di parte bianca in esilio 1300–1314', *Atti dell'Accademia di Scienze di Torino* (Ser. IIa), xlii, (1891), 47–106.

—— 'Castruccio Castracani degli Antelminelli in Lunigiana', *Atti e memorie delle deputazioni di storia patria per le provincie modenesi e parmensi* (Ser. III), vi, pt. 2 (1891), 302–565.

—— 'Della signoria di Castruccio e de' Pisani sul borgo e forte di Sarzanello in Lunigiana', *Atti e memorie delle deputazioni di storia patria per le provincie modenesi e parmensi* (Ser. I), v (1870), 1–45.

—— 'Le gabelle e le pubbliche imposte a Massa di Lunigiana nella prima metà del secolo XIV', *Giornale storico e letterario della Liguria*, ii (1901).

—— *Memorie e documenti per servire alla storia di Pontremoli*, 3 vols. (Lucca and Florence, 1887–1904).

Simeoni, L., *Un collaboratore di Can Grande: Spinetta Malaspina* (Verona, 1947).

—— 'La formazione della signoria scaligera', *Atti dell'Accademia d'agricoltura, scienze e lettere di Verona*, Ser. V, iii (1926), 117–66.

—— *Le signorie*, 2 vols. (Milan, 1950).

Spangenberg, H., *Can Grande I della Scala*, 2 vols. (Berlin, 1892–5).

Stopani, R., *La via francigena in Toscana* (Florence, 1984).

Stych, F. S., 'Il manoscritto G.B. Orsucci O 36 e "Le azioni di Castruccio Castracani" di Aldo Manucci', *ACCC*, 67–78.

Tirelli, V., 'Sulla crisi istituzionale del comune di Lucca (1308–1312)', *Studi per Enrico Fiumi* (Pisa, 1979), 317–60.

Tommasi, G., *Sommario della storia di Lucca* (originally published in *Archivio storico italiano* (Ser. I), xix (Florence, 1847)).

Toscanelli, N., *I conti di Donoratico delle Gherardesca, signori di Pisa* (Pisa, 1937).

Tronci, P., *Annali pisani* (Lucca, 1829).

Ughelli, F., *Italia sacra; sive de episcopis Italiae* (Rome, 1644).

Vecchio, G. di, 'L'arte militare nelle imprese di Castruccio Castracani degli Antelminelli', *ACCC*, 379–404.

Verci, G. B., *Storia della marca trevigiana e veronese*, 20 vols. (Venice, 1786–91).

Vigo, P., 'La battaglia di Montecatini descritta da Uguccione della Faggiuola', *Rivista storica italiana* vi (1889), 36–9.

—— *Uguccione della Faggiuola* (Livorno, 1879).

Visconti, A., *Storia di Milano* (Milan, 1967).

Vitale, V., *Il dominio della parte guelfa in Bologna (1280–1327)* (Bologna, 1901).

Volpe, G., *Lunigiana medievale* (Florence, 1923).

—— 'Pisa, Firenze, impero al principio del 1300 e gli inizi della signoria civile a Pisa', *Studi storici*, xi (1902), 177–203, 293–337.

—— *Studi sulle istituzioni comunali di Pisa* (Pisa, 1902).

—— *Toscana medievale: Massa Marittima, Volterra, Sarzana* (Florence, 1964).

Volpicella, L., *Repetorio gentilizio per la città e stato di Lucca* (Lucca, 1910).

Waley, D. P., 'The Army of the Florentine Republic from the Twelfth to the Fourteenth Century', N. Rubinstein, *Florentine Studies* (London, 1968), 70–108.

—— '*Condotte* and *Condottieri* in the Thirteenth Century', *Proceedings of the British Academy* lxi (1976), 3–37.

—— 'Le origine della condotta nel Duecento e le compagnie di ventura', *Rivista storica italiana*, lxxxviii (1976), 531–8.

Wenck, K., 'Ueber päpstliche Schatzverzeichnisse des 13. und 14. Jahrhunderts und ein Verzeichnis des päpstlichen Bibliothek vom Jahre 1311', *Mitteilungen des Instituts für oesterreichische Geschichtsforschung*, vi (1885), 270–87.

Whitwell, R. J., 'Italian Bankers and the English Crown', *Transactions of the Royal Historical Society* (NS), xvii (1903), 175–233.

Willemsen, C. A., *Kardinal Napoleon Orsini (1263–1342)* (Berlin, 1927).

Winkler, F., *Castruccio Castracani: Herzog von Lucca* (Berlin, 1897).

Index

Accettanti, branch of Del Fondo family 38n., 86, 90n., 100
Acciaiuoli company of Florence 219, 223n.
Adda, river 148
Addighieri, Addighiero di Polacio degli 197n., 198
Agello, Guglielmo di (of Salerno) 211
Agliana 163, 190, 245
Agna, river 179
Aldobrandini, Tuccio 152
Alfonso, *Infante* of Aragon, son of James II 153, 155–6, 171n., 189
Allucinghi, family 27n., 102n.
  see also Morla
Alluminati:
  Alluminato 116n.
  Done 116n.
Altopascio 13, 166–71, 176, 179, 212
  plain of 165–6, 169–71, 173, 182, 213, 256n.
  battle of 63, 133–4, 136, 173–8, 180, 183, 190, 192, 200–2, 247; preliminaries to 162–71, 182, 190, 201; aftermath of 176–80, 201; troops engaged in 165–8, 171, 173–4; casualties in 175–6; ransoms for prisoners taken in 176
Anchiano, family 20n.
Ancona 25n., 42, 242; March of 196
'Angit nos', papal letter *see* Castracani, Castruccio, excommunication proceedings in 1325
Antelminelli *see* Interminelli
  Alderigo 42, 44–5
Antona 41n.
Apennines 13, 206–7, 214, 247, 251
Appicalcani, family 102n.
Apuan Alps 14
Aquilata 58
Aragon, kingdom of 7, 217
  invasion and conquest of Sardinia 145–6, 151–6, 216
Arborea, 'judge' of 153
Arestano:
  contrada of 110–11

hospital of St Nicholas of 110, 111n.
Arezzo 11, 31, 69, 135, 149, 161, 165, 179, 210, 215, 219n., 255
  bishop of *see* Tarlati, Guido
Armanni, family 92n.
Arnaldi, family 121
Arno, river 13, 163, 169, 178–9, 203, 213, 219, 248
  see also Val d'Arno
Arnolfi:
  Benettuccio 173n., 240
  Guido 240
  Nuccio 240
Arnolfini, Filippo 194n.
Artimino 162, 179, 214, 231n.
Artois 45
Asciano 33, 37, 58
Ascoli 242
Assisi, Matteo da 89n., 195
Augusta, citadel in Lucca 10, 82, 105–11, 183–5, 187
  erection of 105–11
  limits of 107–9
  demolition of 108
Avane 33, 58
Avellano, Ser Martino da 89n.
Avenza 124
Avignon 54, 114, 156, 161, 171n., 195n.
Avvocati, family 27, 38, 86, 88, 100, 117n.
  claims to feudal jurisdiction by 98
  rebellion and condemnation of 93–4, 98, 103–4, 126
  Bernocco degli 93
  Nicolao degli 91n., 93

Bacarella, family 38n.
Bagni di Corsena 186n.
Bambacari, family 102n.
Bandini, family 92n., 101
  Jacopo di Braccio 228–9
  Landuccio 92n.
Baratella, family 102n.
  Nicolao 173n.
Barbadoro, Bernardino 209–10n.
Barbi, S. A. 143n.

Barca, family 38, 100
Benetto 113
Barcelona 153n.
Bardi company of Florence 219, 223n.
Barga 26, 186n.
Bommese da 91n.
Barghini, Jacopo 194n.
Bargiglio 186n.
Baroni, Bernardino 57n.
Barsellotti, family 38n.
Bartolomeo, abbot of San Paolo a Ripa
  d'Arno in Pisa 198n.
Bassignano, battle of 148
Battosi, family 21n.
Baux (Bauce), Bertrand de, count of
  Monte Caveoso and Andria 213
Bazano, Giovanni da 175n.
Beardwood, Alice 43
Beccafava, family 100
Bella Ispera, citadel in Pistoia 187, 230
Bellasta, Ser Ubaldo (Baldo) 90n.
Bellosguardo, citadel at Brandelli 158, 187
Bendinelli, Francesco 109n.
Benedetto, Giuseppe 193, 194n., 200
Benedict XI, pope 55
Benettoni, family 38, 102n.
  Francesco 116n.
Berengo, Marino 122
Bergamo 47
Berlescia, Nuccio 85n.
Bernardini, family 86, 102n.
Bernarducci, family 25, 37, 52, 101, 119,
  121
  Arrigo 24, 28
Bettori, family 21n., 86, 90n., 92n., 100,
  102n., 118n.
  Bonaccorso 115n.
  Coluccio 93n.
  Lando 115n.
Bianchi, family 101
Bientina 37, 51
  marshes 166, 213
Bisceto 89n.
Blomquist, Thomas W. 40, 117
Boccadivacca, branch of Lanfredi family
  86, 89n., 100, 118n.
  Sandeo 76
Boccansocchi, family 86, 90n., 100
  Giovanni 91n.
  Nicolao 91n.
Boccella, family 90n., 118n.
  Giovanni 87
  Ser Nicolao 87, 184

Bologna 18, 19n.,56–7, 63, 127, 152, 167,
  206–7, 212, 243–4
Bona, tributary of Nievole river 66
Bonaccolsi, Passerino, lord of Mantua
  148, 170, 210, 215
Bonanni, family 21n.
  Martinoso 117n.
Bonatti, Guido 69n.
Bonelle 237–8
Bongi, Salvatore 20n., 130n., 185
Boniface VIII, pope 7, 31, 152, 193, 195n.
Bonifazi, Ser Genovese 90n.
Borgnes, French mercenary captain and
  marshal 174
Borgo San Donnino 161n., 170, 214n., 215
Borgognoni, family 101
Bosco, Del, branch of Del Fondo family
  27n., 38, 100
Bottacci, Neruccio 185n.
Bovi, branch of Interminelli family 38, 86,
  89, 90n.
  Nuccio 91n.
  Tommasello di Barca 91n.
Brancasecca, family 27n., 194n.
Brancali (Brancoli), family 113n.
  Filippo di Uguccione 113n.
  Matteo 116n., 173n.
  Ubaldo di Uguccione 113n.
Brancoli, Albizzo da 195, 200
Brandelli 158, 187
Brasco of Aragon, mercenary captain 68
Brescia 9n., 45–6, 48, 215
Brienne, Walter of 203
Broccoli, family 102n.
Brozzi 177
Brunelleschi:
  Francesco 170
  Ottaviano 163
Bugarone, Ser Nicolao 91n.
Buggiano 147
  in Piano 64
  Nicolao da 194n., 195n., 197n.
Buiamonti, family 100
  Francesco 93n.
Bulgarini, Nicolao 198n.
Buonconte, Banduccio 34, 36–7, 220
  Pietro 36–7
  Vanni 220
Buonconvento 9, 30
Buonvisi, Ser Lorenzo di Raniero 91n.
Bure, river 247
  see also Val di Bure
Burlamacchi, family 86, 100, 118n.

Francesco 115n.
Pelloro 115n.
Busdraghi, Nicalao 173n., 240
Buti 33, 37, 51

Caccianimici, family 20n.
Cachiano, Lando da 94, 96n.
Caciaiuolo, Picchio 24, 26, 28
Cagliari 153, 155–6
Cagnoli, family 101
Calci, Ser Jacopo da 218
Calenzano 177
Callianelli, family 100
    brachio or district of 107
Camaiore 72n., 185, 199n.
Camaiore:
    Enrico da 194n.
    Ser Pietro di Bonaccorso da 90n.
Camerino 167, 242
Campaldino, battle of 69–70
Campanari, family 38n.
Campi 177
Camporgiano 89
Canapale 245
Cancellieri, Giovanni 228n.
Cannavecchia, family 102n.
Capalle 177
Capodistria 45–6
Caposelvi in Val d'Ambra 149
Cappella, della, family 118n.
Cappiano 83n., 129, 165–6, 176; Ponte a
    147, 163–5, 175
Capraia 160
Caprona:
    Guido da 104
    Lippo da 104, 105n., 153
Cardellini, family 21n.
Cardona, Ramon de 106n., 148, 150n.,
    161–71, 173–5, 177, 179–80, 190, 211
Careggi 177
Cari, family 121
Carincioni, family 38, 100
Carmignano 135, 157, 163, 176, 179, 202–3,
    206, 214, 231, 237, 239, 246, 251
Carpena 138n.
Carretto, Enrico del, bishop of Lucca 195
Carroccio, Catalan mercenary captain 64,
    68
casastici in Lucca 17, 19–24, 27n., 75, 86,
    91n., 99n., 100–1, 119, 194
Casciani (Cassiani), family 86, 90n., 119n.
    Ser Giovanni 90–1n.

Guelfo 87, 101, 240
    Lemmo 240
Cascina 248
Cassuola, family 27n., 102n.
Castagnacci, family 102n.
Castel Castro 156
Castelfranco 54, 59n., 83n., 147, 160, 163
Castellano, Pietro di 198n.
Castello Cesareo in Lucca 108, 109n.
Castello Ghibellino 186n.
Castelnuovo in Garfagnana 186n.
Castiglione:
    Giovanni da 46, 235, 240–1
    Lemmo da 89n.
Castiglione di Terserio 139, 140n.
Castiglione di Val di Serchio 58, 89
Castracani, family, known as 'of San
    Cristoforo' 40
    Santo 54
Castracani, branch of Interminelli family,
    known as 'of San Martino' 27n., 38–
    42, 86, 89, 184–5, 190–2, 256–7
    Arrigo, Castruccio's eldest son 46n.,
    185, 190–1, 230; Captain-general and
    rector of Lucca 190; betrothal 226;
    accession to and loss of dukedom
    236, 254–6
    Bertecca, Castruccio's daughter and
    wife of Fazio della Gherardesca 191
Castracane di Ruggiero 40–2
Castruccio 1–5, 9n., 10–11, 27, 38; birth
    and boyhood 41–2; exile 42; resi-
    dence in England 42–4, in Pisa 39,
    45; marriage 48–51; life between 1304
    and 1309 46–8; mercenary in
    Flanders and northern Italy 46–8;
    role in sack of Lucca in 1314: 51–5;
    viscount of bishopric of Luni and
    vicar in Luni and Sarzana 60–1, 82n.,
    83, 124, 139, 196; at battle of Monte-
    catini 70–1; wounded at Fucecchio
    71; arrest by Uguccione della
    Faggiuola 72–3; liberation and
    election as captain-general of Lucca
    73–9, 80n., 81; extensions of
    captaincy of Lucca 79, 81, 83–4; lord
    and imperial vicar in Lucca 81–2,
    128, 189–90, 221; duke of Lucca 201,
    221–2, 233; count of Lateran Palace
    and standard-bearer of the Empire
    184, 225–6, 233; rule in Lucca 79, 81–
    4, 88–9, 92–9, 102–3, 112–13, 118–22,
    183, 189–90, 221–2, 251–2; admini-

Castracani, Castruccio (*cont.*)
    stration 88–93; relationship with
    leading families of Lucca 89, 93, 96;
    family and dynastic ambitions 190–2,
    236; policy in Lunigiana and eastern
    Genoese Riviera 123–7, 134–40, 209;
    relations with and rift with Pisa 104–
    5, 123–6, 128–9, 133–5, 145–6, 150–6,
    165, 189, 191, 216–22, 228, 230, 233–6,
    239–41, 247–8, 251–3; imperial vicar
    in Pisa 201, 222, 235–6, 238, 251–2,
    255; early relations with and acquisi-
    tion of Pistoia in 1325: 126, 134, 141–
    7, 156–62, 187; recovery of Pistoia in
    1328: 236–51; hostilities against
    Florence 127–9, 133–6, 140–1, 146–9,
    162–79, 181–3, 189, 201–14, 226–31,
    233–4, 237–9, 241–51; devastation of
    outskirts of Florence 176–80, 201,
    203–4; relations with Aragon 145–6,
    152–6, 189; relations with Ludwig of
    Bavaria 189–90, 192, 198–201, 205,
    208–11, 215–27, 233–6, 239–41, 243,
    252–3; relations with Church 192–3,
    195–201, 241; excommunication pro-
    ceedings against in 1317: 59n., 195,in
    1318: 196, in 1325: 55, 195–6, 200, in
    1328: 199, 254; construction of
    Augusta 105–6, 110–12; palace in
    Lucca 107, 110, 183–4, 187; villa at
    Massa Pisana 184–5, 187–8, 225;
    other building activity 184–7, 189;
    artistic patronage 187–9; property
    holdings 110–11, 184–5; 'triumph' in
    1325: 180–1; will 191n., 192, 254; last
    illness and death 253–5, 258; physical
    appearance 259
Caterina, Castruccio's daughter and
    wife of Giovanni Malaspina 140,
    191–2
Dialta, Castruccio's eldest daughter:
    betrothed to Antonio Cristofani 76–
    7; married to Filippo Tedici 159,
    191–2
Franceschina, wife of Nicolo and
    daughter of Arrigo di Poggio 44n.,
    96n.
Gerio, Castruccio's father 41–2; will
    25n., 42; death 42
Giovanni, Castruccio's son 46n., 191,
    255
Guarnerio, Castruccio's son 46n., 191;
    tomb in Sarzana 188–9

Jacopa, Castruccio's daughter 191
Lutterio 40–1
Marchesana, Castruccio's natural
    daughter 192
Neo 41
Nicolo (Coluccio) 27, 41–2, 44–6, 54,
    79, 84, 96
Ottino, Castruccio's natural son 192
Pina, Castruccio's wife, daughter of
    Jacopo Streghi 49–50, 183–5, 186n.,
    192, 256; property holdings 184–5
Puccia, Castruccio's mother 48n.
Savarigio 40
Vallerano, Castruccio's son 46n., 191,
    230, 255
Verde, Castruccio's daughter 192
'Castruccini', Lucchese coins 180
Catherine of Habsburg, sister of
    Frederick III and wife of Charles of
    Calabria 83, 146
cattani see *proceres*
Cecchi, Baldo 228–9
Ceci, branch of Quartigiani family 100,
    119n.
Celle, Ugolino da 92n.
Cenami, family 100
    Nicolao 93n.
Ceppatello, Ser Tano di 89n.
Cerbaie 173
Cerchi, Bonifacio de' 153
Ceretello 37
Cerreto, Giovanni da 194n., 198
Cerreto Guidi 141
Cerruglio, Il 166, 170, 256n.
Cesena 31
Cesena, Michael of 254n.
Champagne Fairs 21n., 41
Charles IV, of Bohemia, Holy Roman
    Emperor 108, 109n.
Charles, count of Battifolle 68
Charles, duke of Calabria 83, 97, 176n.
    lord of Florence 202–6, 208–10, 223,
        228–9, 231–2, 241–3, 246–8
    war with Castruccio Castracani 206–14,
        226–34, 237–9, 241–51
    relations with Pisa 216–19
    relations with minor Tuscan Guelph
        communes 205, 208–9
    death 10n., 253
Charles of Anjou, king of Naples 7
Charles of Taranto 62, 67
Chiaramonte, count of 228n.
Chiavari, family 54

Ciabatto, Ser 40
Ciampa, family 90n.
Nicolo 85n.
Ciapparoni, family 27-8, 38, 86, 89n., 100,
121
Bacciomeo 25, 27
Ciapparone dei 26
Ser Orlando 39n., 50n., 86n.
Cigoli 59
Cipriani:
Andrea di Lapo 116
Filippo di Lapo 116
Cirindi, Corraduccio di Messer Chello
89n.
Città di Castello 63, 161
Clement V, pope 54, 60
Colle, Coscietto del 105
Colle di Val d'Elsa 66, 167, 209, 244
Colonna:
Sciarra 224-6
Stefano 224
Como 211n.
Compito 34
Comugnori, Giovanni di Lemmo da 32,
52, 62n., 72
Corbolani, family 21n., 49
Pagano 49
Coreglia 84n., 129n.
Coreglia, Latino da 194n.
Corniglia 138
Correggio, Ghiberto da, lord of Parma
138-9, 243
Corsica 152, 156
Corte dei Mercanti 92n.
Corte Paoli 109
Cortevecchia, Francesco 194n.
Cortile del Signore, in Augusta in Lucca
107, 110, 183
Cortusio, Guglielmo 62-3, 65, 68
Corvara (in Liguria) 138
Corvara, Pietro da *see* Nicholas V, anti-
pope
Corvara and Vallecchia, lords of 14, 23,
48-9
Cotone 58
Cremona 9n., 46, 140, 214n., 215, 247
Cristofani, branch of Quartigiani family
27n., 92n., 100, 102
Antonio 76-7
Marco di Lando 91n., 96n.
Pagano 74, 76-9, 97
Ugolino 96n.
Cromwell, Oliver 254

Cul di Pozzo 93
Curia dei Foretani 91n., 96n.
Curia Nuova di Giustizia 91n., 96-7n.
Curia di San Cristoforo 91-2, 93n., 96n.,
101
Curia dei Treguani 91n., 96-7n.

Dardagnini, family 86, 90n., 101, 118n.
Ser Betto 86-7, 101
Dati, Bonturo 24, 28, 33, 35, 37, 52
Davidsohn, Robert 31-2, 47, 142n., 143n.,
147n., 150, 176n., 235n., 256n.
Disfaciati, branch of Bernardini family 86
Diversi, branch of Quartigiani family 86
Coluccio 96n., 100
Dombellinghi, family 102n., 119n.
Donati:
Amerigo dei 132n.
Corso 31, 69
Donoratico, counts of *see* Gherardesca
Doria, Genoese family 127
Bernabò 63n., 105n.
Nicolo 68
Drago, Del, family 117n.

Edward I, king of England 42, 44
Edward II, king of England 43
Elba 241, 251
Elsa, river 163
see also Val d'Elsa
embargoes on trade 242
Empoli 177
Erro, Cecco dell' 24, 28
Este:
Opizo d' 210
Rinaldo, marquis of, lord of Ferrara
148, 210, 215

Faenza 31, 167, 206, 243
Faggiuola:
Francesco della 55n., 59, 66-7, 70-1, 79,
195n.
Nieri della 71-4, 79, 94
Uguccione della: early life 31; imperial
vicar of Genoa 31, 48; captain of Pisa
9n., 11, 14n., 32-7, 39, 51-3, 55, 71,
123, 153, 220; lord of Lucca 58-9, 69,
71-5, 79, 83n., 94, 98, 112; war with
Florence 58-71, 84; expulsion from
Lucca 72-7, 79, 82n., 83, 97, 193; later
life 74, 123, 125

Faitinelli, family 102n., 121, 194n.; houses of 53
  Rosso 199n.
Falabrina, family 100
  Ciomeo 93n.
Falcinello 89n.
Falconi, family 102n.
Farnocchia 49n.
Fermo 196n.
Ferrara 210, 215; war of 48
Ferreto Vicentino 39n., 62, 68, 72n.
Fiandrada, family:
  tower 109–10
  Andreuccio di Cecio de' 92n.
Fibialla 89n.
Fieschi, Cardinal Luca de' 138
Fiesole, bishop of 196
Finke, Heinrich 105n.
Flammi, Bongiorno dei 194n., 199n.
Flanders 43, 48
Florence 3, 11–16, 18–24, 29–31, 53, 56–9, 83–4, 97, 106, 116, 118, 121, 126–9, 131, 193, 257–8
  alliance with Lucca prior to 1314: 14n.
  bishop of 196, 242
  contado 167, 176–80, 206; devastated by Castruccio Castracani 176–9, 201, 203–4
  finances 209, 231–2, 244, 247
  population 133
  relations with Pistoia 142–5, 147n., 157–62
  Signoria (Priors) 18, 231–2, 241–4, 247–9
  under Charles of Calabria 202–9, 223, 228–9, 231–2, 241–3, 246–7
  walls 15n., 178
  war against Castruccio Castracani 127–9, 133–6, 140–1, 147–9, 162–79, 180–3, 201–14, 227–31, 233–4, 237–9, 241–51
  war against Uguccione della Faggiuola 60–71
Foligno 242
Fondo, Del, family 27n., 38, 86, 100
  see also Accettani, Del Bosco, Giordani, Rapa
Fondora, family 102n.
  Armanno da 116n.
  Ceo da 116n.
Forese, Piero 176n.
Forlì 31

Forteguerra, family 20, 102n., 112, 119n., 121; company 114–15
  Ser Orlando 173n.
  Vanni (Giovanni) di Jacopo 115, 119n., 173n.
fortuna (or fortune) 3, 258
Fosciano, Guidotto da 194n.
Fosdinovo 125
  Federigo da 198n.
Francesi, Musciatto 45
Franciscan Schism 254n.
Frederick, burgrave of Nürnberg 235, 236n., 256
Frederick II, King of Sicily 36, 138, 152, 210n.
Frederick III (of Habsburg), duke of Austria and Holy Roman Emperor 61, 82–3, 128, 145, 189
Frediano di Barone 55n.
Frescobaldi, Tommaso 160
Frescobaldi company of Florence 114n.
Fucecchio 13, 53, 59n., 60, 63–4, 71, 83n., 97, 135, 147–8, 160, 163, 177, 212–13
  marshes 177, 251
Fuglingen, Kroff von 69n.
Fulcieri, Fulcerio 40

Galganetti, family 86, 101, 102n., 118n.
  Puccino (Jacopo) 87, 101, 119n., 173, 240
Galleno 213, 214n.
Gallicioni family 20n.
Gallo, Del, family 119n., 194n.
  Arrigo del 194n.
  Fredocchio del 116n.
Gangalandi 178
Garfagnana 14, 84, 123–4, 126, 129n., 251
Gargazzola, battle of 148
Gattaiola 34, 191
Gatello, Alberto de 152, 154n.
Gaulandi, Pisan family 104
Gavinana 206–7
Gay, Ser Tedaldino Lazzari 90
Gelso, Del, family 27n., 102n.
Genoa 8, 13–15, 31, 48, 116, 152, 172n., 216, 217n.
  war between Guelphs and Ghibellines of 126–8, 138, 146, 149
Genoese Riviera *see* Riviera, Genoese
Gentile, family 92n.
Gerona, Cortes of 151
Gherardesca, Pisan family, counts of Donoratico and captains of Pisa 72–3, 83, 152, 257

Fazio (Bonifazio) della, husband of Bertecca Castracani 191, 220, 257n.
Gaddo della 72, 125–6, 128–9, 135, 191, 220
Ginevra della 105n.
Manfredi della 155
Nieri (Ranieri) della 72, 104–6, 151, 160, 220, 257n.
Gherarducci, family 21n., 100
Ghibelline party, rulers and states in Italy 16, 50–1, 83, 123, 151, 165, 205, 208, 216–27 troops of, at battles of Montaperti and Campaldino 64n.; at battle of Montecatini 62, 64–7, 71; in Castruccio's wars 134–6, 145–50, 165–6, 170–9, 215, 238–9, 247
Ghibellines:
of Florence 179; elect Castruccio Castracani their captain 204
of Genoa 126–7, 136–8, 146n., 149, 151, 209
of Lombardy 127–8, 133–5, 140–1, 145, 148, 150, 170, 192, 215–16
of Lucca 24, 52–4, 75–6, 80–1, 100, 119–21, 193
of Pistoia 126, 236; elect Castruccio Castracani their captain 126, 136, 141, 145
see also Whites
Ghiotti (Del Ghiotto), family 38
Ghivizzano 186n.
Gigante, Landino 114
Gigli, family:
palace 109n.
Nicolao 91n.
Giordani, family 38n., 86, 100
Giovanni di Balduccio, Pisan sculptor 188
Giovanni di Lemmo da Comugnori *see* Comugnori, Giovanni di Lemmo da
Giudice, Alberto del, Florentine merchant 114n.
Goghi, Guglielmo de' 197n.
Gonella, branch of Interminelli family 38
gonfaloni: in Florence 18n.; in Lucca 17, 18n.
gonfaloniere of justice, in Lucca 17
Granchi, Raniero 46–7, 77, 78n.
Greve 178
Grosseto 167, 224, 228n., 255n.
Gualdo 89n.
Gualfredi, family 102n.
Guarnieri, Guarniero 113, 115n.

Gracci, Lamberto 194n.
Gubbio 31, 63, 167, 242
Banoso da 139n.
Gucci, Jacopo (da Prato) 194n., 198n.
Guelph party, league and states 8, 12, 16, 24, 30, 83, 123, 127, 133–4, 146, 151, 216, 237, 241–4, 258 troops of, at battles of Montaperti and Campaldino 69; opposed to Henry VII and Pisa 34; in Montecatini campaign 61–8; in Lombardy 127, 140–1, 146, 148, 155, 161; opposed to Castruccio Castracani 135–6, 141, 147–9, 155, 161–3, 166–9, 171, 173–6, 179, 182, 201–3, 206–8, 211–15, 228–31, 237–9, 241–8, 250–1
Guelphs:
of Florence 11, 24, 31
of Genoa 126–7, 147, 149, 151, 204n.
of Lucca 11, 25, 28–9, 52–4, 56, 82, 83n., 120, 124, 193; feud between Blacks and Whites among 41
Black, of Pistoia 142–4, 157–8, 206–8, 236
of Tuscany 30–1, 33, 83, 123, 127, 142, 144n., 205, 208–9, 242
White *see* Whites
Guidi, Florentine family and counts 153, 244
Guidiccioni, family 21n., 102n.
Guinigi, family 20, 86, 89n., 90n., 100, 102n., 112, 118n., 121 trading companies 112–15
Cecio 115n.
Conte di Albertino 113n.
Dino di Lazzaro 115n.
Fassino di Ruberto 113
Filippo di Albertino 113n.
Francesco di Bartolomeo 113, 115n.
Giovanni di Bonifazio 113
Lazzaro di Bartolomeo 113, 115n., 173n., 240
Lazzaruccio di Opizo 113
Nicolao di Filippo 113, 115n.
Nicolozo di Giovanni 113
Paolo, citadel of 109n.
Pero di Filippo 113, 115n.
Puccio di Albertino 113n.
Ruberto di Panfollia 113
terrilogio of 1412: 184

Henry, count of Flanders, marshal of Henry VII 32

Henry VII (of Luxemburg), Holy Roman
    Emperor 7–9, 11–12, 30–1, 46–7, 50,
    55, 60–1, 71, 120, 123, 178, 190, 246,
    255 n.
Hohenstaufen dynasty 7
Homburg, Werner von 46 n., 61, 191

Iglesias 153, 155
Imola 31, 47, 167
Ingramo, archbishop of Capua 45
Innsbruck 210
Interminelli, family 21, 25–8, 38–9, 41, 48,
    52, 71, 76 n., 86, 89, 90–2 nn., 96, 100,
    121, 194 n., 197, 200
  exile of 24, 42
  Bonuccio 25
  Davino 27, 91 n.
  Giovanni 194 n.
  Guglielmo 194 n., 195 n.
  see also Bovi, Castracani, Gonella,
    Mezzolombardi, Mugia, Parghia
    Saggina, Savarigi

Jacobi, family 101
  Ser Alluminato 90 n.
James II, king of Aragon 63 n., 68, 146,
    151–6, 189
John, bishop of Massa 198 n.
John, king of Bohemia 46 n., 98, 191
John XXII, pope 124 n., 148–9 n., 152, 193,
    195, 197 n., 198–200, 237 n., 241–3,
    254 n.

Landa, Vergiù di 246
Lanfranchi, Pisan family 104–5
  conspiracies of; in 1317: 124, 126; in
    1323: 153–4, 156
  Benedetto Maccaioni de' 209
  Betto Malepa de' 153
  Corbino de' 104
Lanfredi, family 86, 92 n., 100
Lecore 167, 176
Leone sbarrato, 'society' of civic infantry in
    Lucca 17 n.
Lerici 204
Levanto 138, 204
Lieto, del (Lieti), family 86
  Dettoro del 173 n., 240
  Jacopo del 240
Liguria 134, 136–8, 145, 204, 209, 251
  see also Riviera, Genoese
Lima, river 186 n.
  see also Val di Lima

Lippaccio of Osimo 196
Lischia, district in Lucca 110
Lommori, Puccinello 85 n.
Löwenberg, Wilhelm von 64
Lucca:
  prior to 1314: 11–29, 33–5, 37–8, 51
    under Uguccione della Faggiuola 58–
    60, 64–5, 123
  under Castruccio Castracani 74–82,
    84–103, 111–12, 118–22, 183, 189–92,
    221–2, 251–2, 256–8
  under Ludwig of Bavaria 256
  anziani 17, 18 n., 59, 78–82, 85–92, 96 n.,
    101, 107 n., 118 n., 121, 190, 196
  bishop of 195, 199
  bishopric of 195, 198 n., 199
  chancellery 90–1
  church in 192–201
  commerce 13 n., 112–22; with England
    44 n., 117; with France 114, 116–17;
    with other parts of Italy 116
  contado 33, 41, 53, 71, 129–31, 133, 194
  Council of the Commune 17
  Council of the People 17, 19
  divisions in 24–6, 37
  economic decline of 56, 58
  exiles expelled in 1314: 56–8, 163
  general council 80, 82, 190
  government and administration under
    Castruccio Castracani 87–93, 100–1,
    130–1, 173
  law courts 89–92
  parlamento 17, 80
  podestà 17, 59, 71, 79–81, 92–3 n., 94 n.,
    124 n., 130, 191
  podestà of subject communes 89–90, 92
  population 20–1, 133
  revenue 129–31, 239–40
  sack in 1314: 52–8, 97
  savi 80, 82, 85–92, 96 n., 101, 118 n., 124,
    190
  silk trade and manufacture, before
    1314: 13; under Castruccio Castra-
    cani 111–18
  flight of silk-workers from 56–8
  territorial expansion, in thirteenth
    century 14, 23; under Castruccio
    Castracani 123–5, 134–40, 146–8,
    159–61, 181–2, 201–4, 209, 222, 234–6,
    248–51
  tax-collection and farming, gabelle and
    proventi 24, 89, 119, 129–31, 240
  vice-vicar in 89, 92

vicar-general in 92n.
walls and moat 15n., 187
see also Castruccio, Castracani, hostilities against Florence; Faggiuola, Ugucciona della, war with Florence; Statute of 1261; Statute of 1308; Statute of 1316
Lucchio 144, 146–7, 149
Ludwig IV, duke of Bavaria and Holy Roman Emperor 4, 49n., 82n., 111, 118, 145–6, 162, 181, 184, 186n., 189, 191n., 192–3, 198–201
ambassadors of, in Italy 148, 171n., 201
entry into Italy 205, 208, 210–11; in Lombardy 214–15
in Tuscany 215–23, 231, 239–41, 242n.
coronation and residence in Rome 84, 224–7, 233–6, 243, 254n.
return to Pisa and Lucca 252–3, 255–6, 258
return to Germany 257
Luni:
bishopric of 60–1, 72, 84n., 124n., 139, 189, 196, 198n.; *see also* Malaspina, Bernardino and Gherardino
province of 89, 92, 130, 221
Lunigiana 13, 14n., 41, 71, 74, 82n., 83–4, 123–7, 128n., 135, 140, 191, 204, 206, 211
Lupocisterna, battle of 156
Luppicini, Bonaccorso 93n.
Lys, river 45

Machiavelli, Niccolo 3, 258
Maestro, Del, family 90n., 118n.
Pietro del 93n., 101, 113
Magnates, in Florence 18–22, 149n.
provisions against, in Florence and in Lucca 21–3
Magra, river 189, 207
mouth of 125
see also Val di Magra
Malagallia, family 117n., 194n.
Malagallia–Manciorini tower 109
Malaspina, family, in Lunigiana 14n., 30, 123–5, 127, 128n.
Azzone 125
Bernardone, bishop of Luni 139–40
Franceschino, marquis of Mulazzo 138
Gherardino, bishop of Luni 60, 124n., 139
Giovanni, husband of Caterina Castracani 140, 191

Giovanni Giacotti 66
Moroello 138
Nicolao (Marchesotto) 139–40
Spinetta, marquis 70, 74, 123–5, 134–5, 139, 145, 206–8
Malia of Grosseto 228n., 238n.
Malisardi, family 21n., 100
Burnetto di Opizo 89n., 197n.
Soffredo di Burnetto 194n., 197n.
Malliveris, Bendino 91n.
Malpigli, family 102n.
Mammiano 206–7
Manarola 138
Mancini, Augusto 43
Manetti, Bavigliano 142n.
Silvestro 243
Manfred, king of Sicily 69
Manfredi, Alberghettino, captain of Faenza 243
Mangialmacchi, family 86, 100, 102n., 118n.
Maniavacca, Lucchino 116
Manni, family 100
Mantua 148, 170, 210, 215
Manucci, Aldo (the younger), biographer of Castruccio Castracani 5n., 48n., 180–4
Maracchi, family 27n., 100
Marcello, Nicolo, doge of Venice 57n.
Marches, the 165
Maremma 219n., 223, 234; coast 204n.
Mariano, Ghibellino 60
Marlia, Ser Federigo del fu Ser Bianchi da 55
Martini, family 21n., 27, 38, 86, 89n., 90n., 100, 119n., 121
Andreuccio 56
Coluccio 56
Vanni 56
Massa in Lunigiana 23, 72, 84n., 124, 185
marquises of 84n.
Massa Macinaia 34
Massa Marittima 217n.
bishop of 198n.
Massa Pisana 34, 184–5
Castracani Villa, adorned by lost fresco, in 184–5, 187–8, 225
Massarosa 89n.
Massa Trabaria 31
Matraia, Giuseppe 108
Mattafelloni:
Nettoro 116n.
Puccino 116n.

Maurini, Vanni 56, 93 n.
Medici, Giovanni di Albizzo de' 176 n.
Meek, Christine 122
Melanesi, family 21 n.
Meliconi, Celestino 105
Meloria, battle of 15
Mercati, family 86, 90 n., 100
mercenary cavalry, foreign 9
    costs of 131–3, 239–40, 244
    at battle of Montecatini 62–4
    at battle of Altopascio 161–2, 165–6,
        167–8
    in Florentine service 62–3, 69 n., 132,
        141, 147, 149, 161–2, 167–8, 173–6,
        201–2, 206, 209, 212, 228–30, 237,
        241–8
    in Lucchese service 84, 131–3, 135, 140,
        147, 149, 165, 173–6, 202–3, 214–15,
        228 n., 230, 233 n., 238, 247, 251 n.
    in Milanese service 135, 170–4, 179
    in Pisan service 32–5, 54, 62, 66–7, 70,
        75, 123, 125, 127, 132, 135, 140, 146–7,
        149, 216, 233 n., 238–40, 251 n., 255
    in Sienese service 69 n., 167, 206, 247
    in Ludwig of Bavaria's service 215, 256
mezzani, in Florence 21
Mezzolombardi, branch of Interminelli
    family 38, 89, 90 n.
Milan 3, 9 n., 26 n., 47, 51, 62, 106 n., 116,
    121, 126–7, 134–6, 146, 148, 150 n.,
    179, 196, 210–11, 214–16, 220, 257
milites in Lucca 16–17
Mingogi, family 86
    Coluccio 87, 101
    Puccinello 101
Mirot, Leon 114
Misericordia, hospital of, in Lucca 109 n.
Moccindenti, family 102 n.
    Coluccio 116 n.
    Francesco 116 n.
    Guiduccio 116 n.
Modena 170
Monsummano 59 n., 64, 69
Montale 163, 207, 211
Montaperti, battle of 69–70
Monte Albano hills 177, 179, 214
Montecalvoli 59, 222
Montecarlo 165
Montecatini 59, 63–5, 69–71
    battle of 66–8; preliminaries to 61–5;
        troops engaged in 62–3; casualties in
        68–9; effects and significance of 69–
        70

Montecuccoli, Pieve a 239
Montefalcone 83 n., 129, 165–6, 168–9,
    176, 211
Montefeltro 31
    Federigo da 106
    Guido da 11
Montefiore, Cardinal Gentile da 54–5, 59
Monteggiori 186
Montelupo 160, 177–8, 212
Montemagno tower 110
Montemassi 217 n., 234
Montemurlo 201–2, 206, 231, 234, 239, 246,
    251
Montepulciano 167, 242
Monterosso 138 n.
Montevettolini 63, 135
Montignoso 84 n.
Monti Pisani 33–4, 73, 166
Montopoli 59 n., 147, 150, 234
Montpellier 116 n.
Montramito 186 n.
Monza 148, 150, 161 n.
Mordecastelli, family 21 n., 25–8, 38, 86,
    89 n., 96, 100, 102 n., 121
Marcovaldo 27 n.
    Nello 27
    Puccio 27 n.
    Ranuccio 25–7
    Totto di Dino 91 n.
Morea, prince of 224
Moriconi, family 21 n., 87, 90 n., 118 n.
    Datone 93 n.
    Lando 115 n.
Morla, branch of Allucinghi family 27 n.,
    102 n.
    tower 109
Mosiici, Luciana 47, 90 n.
Motrone 23, 58
Mugia, branch of Interminelli family 89
    Corradino di Barca 91 n.
Muhldorf, battle of 146, 189
Mulazzo 138
Mussato, Albertino 62–3, 68

Naix, Pierre de 202–3
Naples 62–3, 202–3, 204 n., 223 n., 227, 232,
    253
    kingdom of 3, 12, 30, 61, 83, 133, 152,
        201, 204–5, 216–17, 228, 243, 247
    see also Treaty of Naples
Nerone, count of Frignano 84 n., 129 n.
Nicholas V, anti-pope 199, 254 n.
Nicolai, Ser Perfetto 85 n.

Nievole, river 64, 66
see also Val di Nievole
Notte, family 102n.
Novello, count Guido 157, 209
Nozzano 58, 186n.
Nürnberg:
  Volcoldo (Volkhardt?) of 198
  Frederick of *see* Frederick, burgrave of
    Nürnberg

Obizi, family and faction 21, 24–8, 37, 41,
    52–4, 101, 119, 121, 193
  Lucio degli 68
  Luto degli 83n.
  Obizo degli 25–8
Ockham, William of 254n.
Oettingen, Friedrich von 95, 234n., 256
Ombrone, river near Grosseto 224, 228n.,
    232
Ombrone, river near Pistoia 177, 179, 246
Onesti, family 21n., 38, 52, 75, 86, 89n.,
    100, 102n.
  houses of 53
  Parente di Francesco degli 91n.
Orbicciani, Opizo 93n.
Orcinuovo, parliament of 215
Ordinances of Justice of 1293 in Florence
    19–31, 149n.
  executor of 161
Orlandi, Deodato 188
Orselli, family 102n.
  Giovanni 114
Orsini:
  Cardinal Giovanni 204, 224
  Cardinal Napoleone 47, 154–5, 224
Ortenburg, Meinhardt von 234–5, 236n.,
    240
Orvieto 63, 206
Osimo 196
Ottantauno, Frate Gregorio 159
Overardi, family 102n.

Padua 46
Padua, Marsilio of 254n.
Paganelli, family 21n.
palio:
  outside Milan 179
  outside Pistoia 163
  outside Florence 177, 179
  in Pisa 253
Pancini of Controne, Lucchese physician
    43

Panichi, family 100
Pantassa, family 86, 100, 119n.
  Ciandorino 56
  Franceschino 56
Papacy 3, 12, 30–1, 48, 118, 144, 152, 192,
    197–8, 201, 222, 254 *see also* Boniface
    VIII, Benedict XI, Clement V,
    John XXII
  Papal legate in Lombardy (Bertrand de
    Poujet) 206, 212, 241–5, 250; his
    marshal 247–8
  Papal treasure in San Frediano in
    Lucca 54–6, 59, 192, 195–6; in San
    Romano in Lucca 55, 59, 195n.
Parenti:
  Bartolomeo 115n.
  Jacopo 116n.
Parghia, branch of Interminelli family
    27n., 38
  Coluccio 27n.
  Giovanni di Ubaldo (layman) 27, 52
  Giovanni di Jacopo (priest) 197
Parma 135–6, 138–9, 197n., 208, 243
  contado 215
Paruta, family 92n.
Passamonti, family 87, 101, 119n.
  Ser Nicolao 101
Parello 173n.
Passamonte 101
Passavanti, family 92n.
Passerino 58
Pazzi of Val d'Arno, Florentine family 62
pedites in Lucca 16–17
Peretola 177, 203
Perfettucci, family 101
  Genovese 41
  Guido
Peri, family 27n., 100
Perpoli 186n.
Perugia 55, 63, 167, 206, 242
Peruzzi company of Florence 114n.
  Chiaro di Dino 242n.
  Pietro di Dino 242n.
Pescia 186n.
Peter of Eboli ('Tempesta') 62–3, 66–8
Peter of Sicily 255n.
Petrella, Guido della 135
Pettinati, family 27n.
  Nicolao di Oderigo 113, 115
Philip IV, king of France 7, 45
Philip of Taranto 62–7, 216
Philip of Valois 127, 134
Piacenza 116, 135, 172n., 243–4

284 *Index*

Piazza del Giglio 108–9
Piazza della Magione 108
Piazza Napoleone 108
Piazza Santa Croce, in Florence 212, 245
Piazza XX Settembre 109
Pietracassa 222
Pietrasanta 23, 31, 49 n., 91 n., 96 n., 185, 218
Rocca Arrighina and Porta Ghibellina in 187
Pinelli, family 100
   tower 110
Piombino 251
Pisa 4, 8, 11–16, 23–5, 30–7, 47–8, 50–4, 58–9, 62, 64–8, 72–5, 83, 94 n., 97, 116, 120–1, 172 n., 181, 191, 204, 209, 223–4
   under Uguccione della Faggiuola 31–8, 123–6, 134
   under Gaddo della Gherardesca 83, 123–6, 128–9, 145
   under Nieri della Gherardesca 104–5, 150–6
   under Ludwig of Bavaria and Castruccio Castracani 220–3, 227–8, 230, 233–6, 238–42, 247, 250–8
   under Fazio della Gherardesca 257 n.
   alliance and rift with Lucca 123–9, 133, 135, 145, 150, 153, 165
   defence and loss of Sardinia 145–6, 150–6
   relations with Florence 150–2, 216–18
   anziani 36–7
   contado 33, 219, 221, 222 n., 241 n., 248, 251
   finances 151, 221, 233, 239–41
   podestà 222 n.
   savi 125
   seige of 118, 191 n., 216–20
   walls 15 n.
Pistoia 10, 12, 16, 31, 63, 97, 152, 176–7, 179 n., 187, 203, 206–7, 209, 211, 214
   Castruccio Castracani's designs against and acquisition of 4, 77, 104, 126, 134, 141–5, 146–7, 156–62, 181, 189–91, 200
   truce of 1322 with Lucca 142–5, 158
   under Castruccio Castracani 162–3, 221, 223, 251
   Florentine capture and sack of 226–32, 236–7, 258
   seige of 1302–6: 11 n., 24, 47
   seige of 1328: 10 n., 231, 233–4, 236–51
   developments in after 1328: 254, 257 n.

contado 14 n., 59, 126, 136, 141, 143, 145–7, 158, 162–3, 179, 181, 189–92, 203, 206–8, 212, 221, 234, 237
Pistoia:
   Nicolao di Gualfredotto da 91 n.
   Ser Nicolao di Ser Lapo da 91 n.
Piuvica 141, 163
Plesner, Johan 106 n.
Po, river 214
   valley of 13
Poggio, family 21 n., 27, 38, 44, 52, 75, 86, 88, 89 n., 100, 106, 117 n., 121
   condemnation of 82, 93–6, 98, 103–4
   tower and loggia 94
   Arrigo di 44–5
   Bernarduco di 94
   Colao Porco di 94–5
   Dino di 44 n.
   Lambruccio di Nicolao di 91 n.
   Lemmo di Puccino di Guglielmo di 95–6
   Matteo di Nicolao di 91 n.
   Orlandino di 45, 96 n.
   Stefano di Arrigo di 94–5, 96 n.
   Vanni di 44 n.
Pollani, family 100
   Guido 91 n.
   Vanni 91 n.
Pontadori, family 101
   Ser Chellino 93 n.
Ponte al Serchio 58
Ponte a Moriano 186 n.
Pontedera 248, 251
Ponte San Pietro, near Lucca 13
Pontremoli 13, 14 n., 130, 185, 189, 214–15, 218, 251, 256
   Castruccio Castracani's acquisition of 136–9, 145
   tower at 186
Ponzano 125
popolo grasso, in Lucca 17–19, 23–4
popolo magro, in Lucca 17–19, 23
Popular movement, in Lucca 16–19, 21–4, 26, 28–9, 87, 103, 119, 121–2
Porcari 13, 166, 168–71
Porcari, family 53–4
Porta, family 102 n., 121
Porta Beltrame, lake of 48 n., 49 n.
Porta del Cavallo (or San Romano), gate of Augusta in Lucca 109
Porta San Pietro, in Lucca 34–5, 108 n.
Portico, Dal, family, in Lucca 86, 89 n., 90 n., 92 n., 100, 118 n.

house, acquired by Castruccio Castra-
cani for his palace 107, 110, 183–4,
187
Porto Pisano 216, 219
Portovenere 146n., 151, 204n., 217n.
Potenti in Lucca, see *casastici*
Poujet, Bertrand de *see* Papal legate in
Lombardy
Pozzeveri, abbey of 168–71, 173
Prato 158, 160–1, 163, 190, 207, 209, 229,
239, 243–8, 251
contado 141, 147, 149, 166–7, 179, 223n.
Prato, Ser Lapo di Ciandoro da 91n.
Prato del Marchese, in Lucca 109
Prementario:
Filippo da 116n.
Gabriele da 116n.
Primo Popolo, in Florence 18, 24
proceres et cattani, in Lucca 20n., 27n.
Ptolemy of Lucca 16, 23, 25n., 26, 121n.
Pugliesi, Vita 160

Quarracchi 177
Quarrata 163
Quartigiani, family 21, 27n., 52, 75–7, 86,
88, 92n., 100, 121; conspiracy and
suppression of 93, 95–8, 103–4, 211
Guerruccio 96n., 97n.
see also Ceci, Cristofani, Diversi,
Sesmondi, Simonetti
Quosa 58

Rafagnelli, family 54
Ramondo, Cattanio di, Genoese
merchant 116n.
Ranieri, family 102n.
Raniero, Ser Giovanni di Guido di 90–1n.
Ranolmi mill, near Pistoia 238
Rapa, branch of Del Fondo family 38, 100
Rapondi, family 20, 38, 86, 90n., 100,
102n., 112, 118n., 121
trading company 114–15
Ciucco di Guido 1135
Giovanni (Vanni) di Guido 114–15,
119n., 173n., 240
Ser Spalla 90
Reggio in Emilia 127, 134, 243
Ricchi, Agostino 57n.
Ricciardi, family in Lucca 21
trading company 42, 44–5, 112, 117, 120
Ricciardi, family in Pistoia 143
Bonifazio 143
Rifredi 177, 179n.

Ripafratta 14n., 37, 58, 218
Risichi, Risico 115n.
Riviera, Genoese 13
'di Levante' or eastern 126–8, 130, 134,
136–8, 140, 204
see also Liguria
Robert, king of Naples 11, 31, 33, 36–7, 53,
62, 83, 126–7, 129, 150–2, 156, 193,
201, 206, 213, 216–18, 224, 241n., 232,
241–3
vicar of; in Lucca 53; in Pistoia 142, 157
Rocca, Della, family 20n., 27n., 194n.
Raniero della 194n.
Rocca Arrighina *see* Pietrasanta
Rolenzi, Ser Bonagiunta 85n.
Romagna 31, 63, 165, 247
Rome 13, 30, 54, 210, 221–7, 233–4
Council of Fifty-two in 224–5
Vatican quarter in 224–5
Ronzini, family 43n., 121
Betto 93n.
Ciato 43
Roscimpeli, family 21n.
Rossi, family 100
Rossi, Bendino de', of Florence 163
Rossi, Orlando de', of Parma 243
Rossi, Pietro de', of Parma 130n., 131n.
Rossi-Sabatini, Giuseppe 152
Rossiglioni, family 86
Rosso Monte, Guglielmo da 242
Rotaio 58
Rotina 222
Ruggeroni tower 109

Saggina, branch of Interminelli family 86,
90n.
Ser Lazzaro 139n.
Nerio 255n.
St John of Jerusalem, 'Magione' or
Temple of, in Lucca 107
St Peter's cathedral, in Rome 255–6
Salamoncelli, family 53, 101, 121
Dino 83n.
Nantino 53
Salamoni, family 27n., 100
Salimbeni, Sienese family 205
Salinguerra, Baverio de' (of Gubbio) 222,
233, 235
Sambuca 159, 251
San Baronto 141
San Dalmazio, *contrada*, 108
San Domenico, nunnery of, in Lucca
109n.

San Francesco, church of:
    in Lucca 41 n., 254
    in Sarzana 188
San Frediano:
    borgo in Florence 178
    borgo in Lucca 43 n., 49, 53, 55 n., 56
    church of, in Lucca 53–6, 59, 192, 195
    postern of 53
San Gimignano 167, 209, 242, 244
San Gimignano, Jacopo da 93 n.
Sangineto, Filippo di 211, 223 n., 228–32,
    241, 243–8, 250, 253
San Giorgio, postern of 51
San Giovanni e Reparata, church of, in
    Lucca 198 n.
San Giovanni in Capo di Borgo, *contrada*
    56
San Giovanni in Escheto 184
San Girolamo, convent of, in Lucca 109 n.
San Giuliano 73, 150
San Gregorio, *contrada* 109
San Jacopo del Poggio, church of 51–2
San Leonardo in Treponzio, hospital
    outside Lucca 198 n.
San Lupidio, Gherardo da 53
San Martino, cathedral of, in Lucca 76
    cathedral chapter of 193–5, 197–9
    contrada 109
San Martino alla Palma 178
San Martino in Colle 64, 186 n.
San Mauro 177
San Miniato 147, 167, 209
San Pantaleo 143
San Paolino, tower of 109 n.
San Paolo a Ripa d'Arno, monastery of, in
    Pisa 198 n.
San Pietro a Monticelli 178
San Pietro Gattolino, *borgo* in Florence
    178
San Pietro in Cortina, church of, in Lucca
    108
    contrada 107
San Pietro Scheraggio, church of, in
    Florence 161
San Pietro Somaldi, church of, in Lucca
    198
San Ponziano, monastery of, in Lucca 111
San Romano, Dominican convent of, in
    Lucca 35, 59, 107, 110–11
San Salvatore in Mustiolo, church of, in
    Lucca 110
San Sensio, *contrada* 107
San Sisto, church of, in Pisa 39

San Stefano di Feletria 198 n.
Sant' Alessandro maggiore, *contrada* 107
Santa Chiara, nunnery of, at Gattaiola 191
Santa Croce 54, 59, 83 n., 147, 163
Santa Giulia *contrada* 109
Santa Maria a Monte 54, 59 n., 83 n., 126,
    129, 169, 212–15, 219, 231–2, 245
Santa Maria del Giudice 34
Santa Maria della Rotonda, church of, in
    Lucca 109 n.
Santa Maria Filicorbi *contrada* 107
Santa Maria Forisportam, church of, in
    Lucca 195, 198 n.
Santa Maria in Palazzo, *contrada* 107–8
Santa Maria maggiore, church of, in
    Rome 225
Santa Reparata, *contrada* 108
Santo Remedio, abbey near Pisa 223–4
Sanudo, Marino (the elder) 45, 51
Sapiti, Andrea 194 n., 198 n., 199 n.
Sardinia 145, 150–6, 189, 216–17, 241 n.
Sardo, Raniero 32, 35, 68
Sartori (Sartoy), family 27 n., 86, 90 n., 100,
    118 n., 119 n.
    Guido 115 n.
    Landuccio 91 n.
Sarzana 31, 58, 70, 72, 84 n., 124–5, 150,
    188, 222
    submits to Castruccio Castracani 60–1
Sarzanello 124, 150, 186
Saulli, family 101
Savarigi, branch of Interminelli family 38,
    86, 89
    Ciato 194 n., 187
    Coluccio 39, 45 n.
    Davino di Giovanni 91 n.
Savini, Coluccio 93 n.
Savona 149
Sbarra, family 20, 86, 90 n., 100, 112, 117 n.,
    118 n., 121
    trading company 114–15
    Ser Bartolomeo 90
    Cavalca 91 n.
    Fiore 91 n.
    Giovanni 91 n.
    Jacopo di Puccetto 114, 173 n., 222, 240,
    242 n.
    Puccino 114
Scala (Scaligeri), family, rulers of Verona
    2 n., 10, 48
    Can Grande della 2, 9 n., 10, 46, 62, 65,
    74, 123, 148, 206, 210, 215, 258
    Mastino della 10 n.

Scandaleone, family 102n.
  Nicolao 115
Scatissa, family 117n.
Schiatta, branch of Bernardini family 86,
  89n., 90n., 101, 102n., 119n.
  Lando 115
Schiava, Pietro de' 194n.
Schmeidler, Bernhardt 121n.
Scolari, Ciupo de' 89n.
Scortica:
  Betto 92n., 116n.
  Ghinuccio 92n., 116n.
Scotti, Alberto 45
'Sei miglie', district around Lucca 71
Sercambi, Giovanni 24–5, 52n., 108n.,
  109n.
Serchio, river 13, 186n., 208, 219, 251
  see also Val di Serchio
Serravalle 59n., 126, 142, 157, 177, 231
Serughi, family 90n., 92n.
  Coluccio 101
  Ser Ghirardo 101
Sesmondi, branch of Quartigiani family
  21n., 100
  Dino 116n.
  Gialdello 116n., 173n.
  Mondino 86n.
  Nicolo 97n.
  Upezzino 97n.
Sesto, battle of 127
Sestri Levante 138n., 209
Settimo 178
Sforza, Giovanni 60, 150n.
Sicilian Vespers 7
Sicily 7, 36, 152, 217
Siena 12n., 13, 15, 30–1, 62–3, 66, 69, 116,
  127, 151n., 152, 167, 203n., 205–6, 234,
  242, 244
  contado 149, 212
Signa 177–80, 201–4, 208, 212, 231n., 248
Signorie *see* Tyrannies
Simonetti, branch of Quartigiani family
  27n., 86, 92n., 194n.
  Labro 96n., 100
  Opizo 197
Sismondi, Lemmo 218
Società delle Armi, in Lucca 17–19, 24,
  26
Società di Concordia de' Pedoni, in Lucca
  18–19
Soffredinghi, family 14n.
Sommocolonia 26–7, 124
Soncino 45–6

Sorbano, Giovanni da 199n.
Spada, family 86, 119n.
  Mingo 101, 173n.
  Triumpho 101
Sperone, Lo 142n.
Spezia, La, Gulf of 204, 206
Spiafami, family 102n.
  Filipuccio 115n.
Spinabelli, branch of Del Gelso family
  27n.
Spini, Geri 177
Spinola, Genoese family 127
  Cristiano 63n.
  Gherardino 257n.
Spoletini, family 86, 100
  Ubaldo 194n., 199n.
Spoleto 243
Squarciafico, Michele 116n.
Squarcialupi, family 102n.
  Mottino 56
Statute:
  of 1261, in Lucca 18n., 19, 23
  of 1308, in Lucca 14n., 16–24, 27n., 28,
    52, 59, 75, 80, 86, 186n., 194
  of 1316, in Lucca 80–1, 84
Stazzema 41n.
'Storie pistoresi' 37, 52, 55, 72n., 74, 141–
  2, 157–9, 165n., 174, 219n., 236–7,
  239, 245, 253
Streghi (Dello Strego), family 48–51, 86,
  90n., 183–5
  Bindocco 49, 50n.
  Corbolano 49
  Duccia 49
  Ghirardo (Gadduccio) di Overardo 49
  Ghirardo (Ghirarduccio) di Jacopo
    48n., 49–50, 101, 173n.
  Giovanni 49
  Giuffredo 48n., 50
  Jacopo (the elder, great-grandfather of
    Pina Castracani) 49
  Jacopo (the younger, her father) 49–50,
    51n.
  Overardo 49–50
  Perotto 48n., 49, 101
  see also Castracani, Pina

Tadolini, family 86, 100, 119n.
  Rocchigiano 199n.
Taddicioni, family 102n.
Talgardi, family 21n., 27n., 87, 90n., 101
Talliamelo, family 27n.

288 *Index*

Tarlati:
 Guido, bishop of Arezzo 62, 135, 149,
  151n., 210, 215, 218–19
 Tarlatino de' 255
Tassignano, family 53, 121
Taviani, Pistoian family 143
 Ettolo 143
Tedaldi:
 Bartolomeo di Mapheo 116
 Taldo di Maphco 116
Tedici, Pistoian family 142–3, 257
 Carlino 159
 Filippo 77, 156–60, 176, 191, 237–8
 Ormanno, abbot of Pacciana 142–4,
  156–8
 see also Castracani, Dialta
Tegrimi:
 Nicolao, biographer of Castruccio
  Castracani 5n., 25n., 41n., 42–5, 48,
  49n., 57, 180–1, 186
Tegrimo 91n.
Tegrimo, Bartolomeo 40
Terizendi, family 101
Terzenaia, casa or palazzo of, in Augusta
  107, 110–11
Testa, family 102n.
Thérouanne 45
Tiber, river 225
Tignosini, family 21n.
Tirelli, Vito 77n.
Tivegna 138n.
Tizzana 157, 163–5, 214, 231, 239, 246, 251
Tolomei, Sienese family 149, 205
Toringhelli, family 102n.
 Lippo 56
 Ser Rabbito 76, 112–13, 117n., 118
Tornaquinci, Biagio dei 207
Torre, della, Milanese family 9n., 26n.
Torre, Pietro della (of Orvieto) 142n.
Torrebecchi, castle of 179
Tosa, Giovanni della 170
 Pino della 142n.
 Rodolfo della 68
 Simone della 229–30, 236, 243, 248, 250
Toscanelli, Nello 257n.
Trassilico 124
Tre cappelle, 'society' of civic infantry in
  Lucca 17n.
 tower of 53
Treaty of Naples: of 1314 (repudiated)
  36–8
 of 1317: 83, 123, 126, 213
Trebiano 138n.

Trent 211n., 215, 218
 parliament of 205, 210, 216
Trentacosta, family 118n.
Treustrix, casa or palazzo in Augusta 107,
  110
Treviso 10n.
Tyrannies, in fourteenth-century Italy
  1–3
 regional 3, 9–11, 119–20, 134, 181, 251–
  2, 256–9

Uberti, family 54
Ubertini, Florentine family 62
Upezzini, family 20n., 86
Urlimbach, German mercenary captain
  161, 170
Usciana, river 141, 147, 163–6, 169, 175,
  177, 179, 211–14, 248, 251

Val d'Arno 12, 14, 54, 59, 63, 83n., 97, 120,
  128, 134–5, 141, 145–7, 149, 163, 222,
  243, 248, 251
Val d'Elsa 13, 63, 209, 212
Val di Bure 209
Val di Lima 14n., 146–7, 207–8
Val di Magra 14n.
Val di Marina 179
Val di Nievole 14n., 59, 61–6, 101, 134–8,
  145, 147, 162, 165–6, 179, 211, 213, 251
Val di Pesa 178, 203
Val di Serchio 12, 14n., 120, 251
Val di Taro 140
Vallecchia *see* Corvara
Vaprio, battle of 161n.
Veglio, Del, family 87, 89n.
 tower 52
Veltri, ser Veltrino di Ciandoro 93n.
Venice 8, 15, 46, 47n., 48, 56–7, 116
Vernazza 138n.
Verona 3, 11, 45, 47–8, 62, 74, 116, 123–5,
  210, 215
Verrucola Bosi 125, 206–8
Versilia 12–14, 23–4, 41, 222
Via Aurelia 13
Via Francigena 13
Viareggio 37, 58, 186n.
Via Vittorio Emanuele, in Lucca 108–9
Via Vittorio Veneto, in Lucca 108
Vicenza 45–6, 74n.
Vico, Albizzo da 218
Vicopisano 30, 209
Villa, Simone da 65

Villani:
Giovanni 32, 37, 52, 62–3, 68, 69n., 74,
  76n., 77, 78n., 97, 127–8, 139, 143n.,
  147n., 149–50, 157, 158n., 159–61,
  165–6n., 168–74, 176n., 177–8, 180–1,
  203n., 206, 208n., 213, 214n., 216,
  218–19, 221, 224–6, 228n., 232, 234–6,
  238, 244n., 245, 247–8, 250, 252–3,
  255n., 256, 258–9
Matteo 185
Villanova, family 100
Vinci 79, 84, 141
virtù 3
Visconti, family, rulers of Milan 2–3,
  9–10, 140, 145–6, 148–9, 161, 170, 196,
  215, 218
Azzo 170–5, 179, 210, 214–15, 228, 247
Galeazzo 10n., 51, 106n., 140, 174, 215,
  246, 253
Luchino 215
Marco 148, 210, 256n.

Matteo 2, 9n., 62, 127–8, 258
Viterbo 63, 224
Viterbo, Giovanni di Nuccio da 90n.
Vivinaia 64–5, 71, 165–6, 170, 212
Volterra 59, 167, 221–2, 244
Voltri 149
Vorno 34

Walram, brother of Henry VII 46n., 191
War, costs of 1, 132–3, 239–40, 244
Whites (or White Guelphs):
  in Henry VII's army 48
  of Florence 26
  of Lucca 24–7, 41; exiled in 1301: 25–8,
    87, 193–4; in exile in Pisa 27, 30, 38–9,
    44, 48, 49n., 50–2, 86n., 100–1, re-
    admitted to Lucca in 1314: 56–7,
    59n., 71, 76
  of Pistoia 25n., 26, 50n., 54
William of Holland 211n.